The Measure of Economies

The Measure of Economies
Measuring Productivity in an Age of Technological Change

Edited by **Marshall B. Reinsdorf and Louise Sheiner**

The University of Chicago Press

Chicago and London

The University of Chicago Press, Chicago 60637
The University of Chicago Press, Ltd., London

Published 2024
Printed in the USA

33 32 31 30 29 28 27 26 25 24   1 2 3 4 5

ISBN-13: 978-0-226-83633-1 (cloth)
ISBN-13: 978-0-226-83634-8 (e-book)
DOI: https://doi.org/10.7208/chicago/9780226836348.001.0001

Library of Congress Cataloging-in-Publication Data

Names: Reinsdorf, Marshall B., editor. | Sheiner, Louise, editor.
Title: The measure of economies : measuring productivity in an age of technological change / edited by Marshall B. Reinsdorf and Louise Sheiner.
Other titles: Measuring productivity in an age of technological change
Description: Chicago ; London : The University of Chicago Press, 2024. | Includes bibliographical references and index.
Identifiers: LCCN 2024016782 | ISBN 9780226836331 (cloth) | ISBN 9780226836348 (ebook)
Subjects: LCSH: Industrial productivity—Measurement. | Industrial productivity. | Economic history—21st century.
Classification: LCC HD56.25 .M42 2024 | DDC 338/.06—dc23/eng/20240506
LC record available at https://lccn.loc.gov/2024016782

♾ This paper meets the requirements of ANSI/NISO Z39.48-1992 (Permanence of Paper).

Contents

Editors' Introduction

Marshall B. Reinsdorf and Louise Sheiner

Productivity—the amount of output produced for a given amount of input—is a key determinant of economic growth and, consequently, of changes in standards of living. Measured productivity growth in the United States stepped down in the early 2000s after nearly a decade of strong growth. Output per hour worked in the business sector rose only 1.5 percent per year over the period 2005 to 2019, compared to 3.2 percent from 1995 to 2004. Growth was even slower from 2010 to 2019, at just 1 percent a year. The United States is not alone in facing this problem, as all major advanced economies have seen slow productivity growth.

There is continuing debate about how much of this slowdown is real and how much of it reflects the increasing inadequacy of our official measures. That debate has refocused attention on the shortcomings of productivity measurement in general and the challenges—both conceptual and resource related—that the statistical agencies confront in attempting to capture changes in the quality of goods and services in a rapidly evolving economy.

Why Is Measuring Productivity Accurately Important?

The economy's actual productivity growth is independent from what is measured, but measurement matters in all sorts of ways, many of which may not be obvious. First, mismeasured productivity gives a misleading picture of the performance of the macroeconomy. For example, much research has been devoted to explaining the productivity slowdown, and many have proposed combating the slowdown with policy innovations like increased

Marshall B. Reinsdorf is formerly of the International Monetary Fund.
Louise Sheiner is at the Hutchins Center on Fiscal and Monetary Policy at the Brookings Institution.

government spending on education, research and development (R&D), and infrastructure, as well as reforms to the patent system and increased antitrust enforcement to bolster competition. If it turns out that productivity growth has not been slow, such reforms may be unnecessary and, in some cases, misguided.

Furthermore, our understanding of the sources of productivity growth is itself affected by measurement—if the capital stock is increasingly composed of intangible assets rather than physical assets, and if we are not properly measuring investment in intangible assets, we may misdiagnose the reasons for changes in productivity growth over time, making it more difficult to properly address them.

It is similarly crucial to understand productivity by industry. Is the digital economy boosting productivity in ways that are not being picked up in the official statistics, as many have surmised, or are the gains simply not that big? The answer to that question may affect policy decisions like the degree to which big tech companies should be regulated. Likewise, in evaluating policies aimed at slowing the growth rate of health spending, it is critical to know whether health care is becoming more expensive over time because there is little productivity growth in the sector or because care is becoming increasingly valuable.

The productivity measurement debate is ultimately a debate about the accuracy of key elements of our system of macroeconomic indicators. Productivity is measured as real gross domestic product (GDP) per hour of labor input (or per unit of a composite of labor and other inputs), where real GDP is measured by deflating the components of nominal GDP with price indexes. Some productivity measurement issues are associated with mismeasurement of nominal GDP—including issues related to free online platforms such as Facebook, profit shifting by multinational enterprises that have actual or purported operations in low-tax jurisdictions, and overlooked investment in intangible assets. But much of the concern about productivity mismeasurement centers on the worry that price growth is overstated (and hence real GDP growth is understated) because price indexes do not fully account for improvements in the quality of items we purchase. This not only affects our view of inflation but also has direct implications for government spending and taxes. Better accounting for quality changes could lead to slower growth in official price indexes like the consumer price index (CPI) which would lead to slower growth in spending on Social Security and other indexed transfer programs and faster growth in tax revenues (because tax brackets would not increase as much each year).

Why Have We Put Together This Volume and What Are the Major Takeaways from It?

Properly measuring productivity is an active area of inquiry for researchers but is often inaccessible to economists and others not steeped in the arcana of GDP and price measurement. Our goal is to provide a rigorous yet accessible synthesis of the state of knowledge, providing intuition about the thorny problems facing price measurement and an overview of recent findings. The chapters include recommendations to the statistical agencies about improvements that could be implemented or research that should be pursued. The eight chapters in this volume—described below—address different aspects of productivity measurement, many in great detail. A high-level summary of the conclusions is as follows:

- Even though productivity measurement is not equivalent to economic well-being, it is a reasonable proxy. Focus on productivity as the major determinant of living standards is warranted, as discussed in Dynan and Sheiner (chap. 1).
- Statistical agencies have made numerous changes over time to improve productivity measurement. These include improvements in price deflators, as discussed by Moulton (chap. 2); capitalization of business expenditures on R&D, software, and other investments, as discussed by Corrado (chap. 3); and increased reliance on nonstandard data (including "big data") to improve productivity measurement (Groshen, Horrigan, and Kurz, chap. 8).
- A review of the chapters in this volume—including those on health care, the digital economy, intangible assets, the environment, and new goods—*suggests that productivity growth is likely being underestimated on average*.
- Whether mismeasurement can explain at least part of the *slowdown* in official productivity statistics is less clear: this explanation would require productivity to be underestimated not just on average but to an increasing degree. While it seems likely that most of the slowdown is real, the likelihood of significant mismeasurement of areas of the economy whose importance has grown—the digital economy and health care, for example—leaves open the possibility that at least some of the slowdown reflects mismeasurement.
- Looking forward, many of the improvements statistical agencies have made to productivity measurement in recent years could be expanded on. Corrado (chap. 3) advocates broadening the set of intangible investments that could be capitalized and developing a regular survey of employer-provided training. Byrne (chap. 5) discusses applying techniques like hedonics to more types of digital products, and Groshen, Horrigan, and Kurz (chap. 8) discuss how use of nonstandard data could be expanded.
- Still, as discussed by Coyle (chap. 4), many thorny issues about accounting for new goods in our measures of price change remain, and it is difficult to see how official statistics will ever capture the value of truly new goods and services. In some cases, researchers have proposed novel ways of measuring the value of new goods, but these may be impractical

(e.g., using models to capture the value of increased variety) or too radical (e.g., using online experiments to determine the value of Facebook, or using the value of a statistical life to measure the value of health care and environmental regulation, as discussed in chaps. 6 and 7) to be adopted by statistical agencies. Some have proposed an alternative measure of GDP—dubbed "GDP-B"—which would include these more experimental approaches to measurement.

A more detailed summary of each chapter is as follows.

Chapter 1: "GDP as a Measure of Economic Well-Being," by Karen Dynan and Louise Sheiner

This chapter examines and clarifies the concepts, purpose, and relevance to policy debates of the output measures used to calculate productivity. It attempts to explain often-technical discussions of price indexes and GDP measurement in an intuitive way accessible to all economists and analysts. This endeavor is particularly important given occasional confusion about what current measures do and do not include. The chapter argues that changes in real GDP provide a reasonable measure of changes in aggregate welfare derived from the market-based economy, at least in theory. It discusses areas where measurement issues are most problematic: when quality of goods and services improves, when goods and services are provided for free, when tax-motivated reporting understates the activities of multinationals in the United States, and when new goods and services are introduced. It discusses some theoretically appropriate approaches to accounting for these measurement issues and then points out where current practices differ from those approaches.

Chapter 2: "The Measurement of Output, Prices and Productivity: What's Changed Since the Boskin Commission," by Brent Moulton

The most critical issues in productivity measurement involve the measurement of price change. Price indexes are used to determine how much of the change in sales of a particular good or service is due to price changes and how much is due to changes in real output—that is, the quantity or quality of that good or service. Despite efforts to measure price and quality changes, the view of many economists is that mismeasurement has led to long-term understatement of changes in living standards and productivity. In 1996, the Advisory Commission to Study the Consumer Price Index (known as the Boskin Commission, after its chairman, Michael Boskin of Stanford University) estimated that, relative to a true cost-of-living index, the CPI had an upward bias of 1.1 percentage points per year, with a plausible range of 0.8 to 1.6 percentage points. Without much attention—even from economists—the Bureau of Labor Statistics (BLS) has made substantial improvements to measurement techniques and procedures since then. Examining them all,

Moulton finds the overall bias of the CPI has fallen from about 1.1 percentage points to about 0.85 percentage point today. He makes several recommendations for further improvements.

Chapter 3: "Intangible Investment: What It Is and Why It Matters," by Carol Corrado

Global growth today is largely driven by companies with limited physical assets—think Facebook, Apple, Amazon, Netflix, Google, and their Chinese counterparts Alibaba and Tencent. Less well known are the juggernauts in the emerging synthetic biology space (e.g., Ginkgo Bioworks, Zymergen, and Moderna). These companies make strategic investments in knowledge creation and innovation, collectively referred to as "intangibles." Unlike tangible capital assets, which can only be used in one place, knowledge and innovative ideas can and do diffuse, making intangibles a fundamental source of productivity growth.

Understanding the role of intangible assets, especially non–R&D intangibles, is key to better understanding sources of growth and drivers of innovation. The chapter considers types of intangible investment that are already counted in GDP, which include scientific R&D and software tools and databases, while emphasizing the importance of additional intangibles like industrial design, marketing and branding, organizational and management efficiency, and employer-provided training. It argues that commercially valuable knowledge creation is captured in large part by non–R&D intangibles currently excluded from GDP and suggests their inclusion in macroeconomic analysis and empirical growth accounting alongside R&D. Emerging work suggests that prices of intangible assets have had a deflationary influence and that digitalization has caused intangible marketing and branding asset prices to fall. Finally, the chapter discusses measuring data as an intangible asset, concluding that a substantial part of private investment in data is captured as part of other types of intangible investment, but that full coverage, including of public information assets and scientific data collections, will require extensions to the intangibles currently included in GDP.

Chapter 4: "Productivity Measurement: New Goods, Variety, and Quality Change" by Diane Coyle

Technological innovation is the engine of productivity growth, but progress through innovation is often embodied in new or improved goods and services whose comparative quality is hard to measure. This chapter explains the challenges that new and improved goods and services pose for constructing the price indexes used as deflators in measuring productivity and how statistical agencies confront these challenges. There has been recurring debate about the extent to which inflation measures are upwardly biased because of inadequacies in the treatment of new and improved goods and services—and the extent to which growth rates of real GDP and productivity are consequently understated. This chapter's overview of price measurement issues, set in the context of the current productivity puzzle, also describes some more radical alternative approaches that have recently been proposed for measuring gains from digitalization. It concludes by suggesting that these more radical alternative approaches may be needed to capture long-term changes in real output and productivity.

Chapter 5: "The Digital Economy and Productivity," by David Byrne

Advances in electronics and software have driven down the cost of storing, transforming, and transmitting data. As a result, information technology (IT) permeates nearly every aspect of economic activity, and digitally stored information is growing exponentially. Online platforms and merchants help consumers navigate this sprawling information landscape, matching users or customers to information or products that meet their needs. To avoid the knotty problem of determining the boundary of the digital economy, the chapter uses a growth accounting framework, analyzing the question of how well we measure productivity growth in industries that produce IT capital and industries that use IT capital. The chapter also considers how well we measure households' use of IT capital services and equipment. It argues that the changing quality of IT goods and services is still not well captured in many cases and provides rough estimates of resulting bias in the reported output growth of the US economy and in the reported contributions from IT to economic growth and productivity. The chapter concludes by recommending steps that would yield substantial progress in measurement of the digital economy. These include use of big data and machine learning to perform hedonic adjustments of price indexes, use of benchmark performance scores as quality indicators, regular reestimation of IT depreciation rates, and international harmonization of measurement procedures.

Chapter 6: "Measuring Prices and Productivity in the Health Care Sector," by Louise Sheiner and David M. Cutler

According to official estimates, the health sector is characterized by extremely low productivity growth. But almost no effort has been made to capture improvements in outcomes in official statistics, causing too much of the rise in health spending observed over the past 50 years to be attributed to inflation rather than change in the quality of health care services. With health spending accounting for almost 20 percent of the GDP, up from just 8 percent in 1980, this mismeasurement not only distorts our view of the value of health spending but may have a material effect on our assessment of overall productivity growth trends.

This chapter discusses conceptual issues in measuring health care productivity and assesses the validity of several approaches from the literature. Some outcome-based measures of productivity that seem intuitive—changes in cost per year of life, for example—are shown to understate true productivity growth. The chapter reviews and evaluates the empirical literature on the appropriate magnitude of quality adjustment over time. Next, it delves into how one would integrate properly measured health care spending in the national accounts and productivity measurement, an issue that has received scant attention thus far. In particular, the authors consider how much of health spending could be regarded as purchasing an intermediate good, how much is pure consumption, and how much is investment. The chapter concludes with recommendations for statistical agencies that can be implemented in the near term on treating nonprofit and government health care providers similarly to commercial providers in constructing the national accounts and incorporating cost-based quality adjustments in the health care producer price indexes (PPIs). It also gives recommendations for future research on including outcome-based quality adjustments in a health care satellite account.

Chapter 7: "Productivity and the Environmental Accounts," by Nicholas Z. Muller

GDP does not take environmental externalities into account, so standard GDP and productivity statistics would treat an expensive process that produces cleaner air as a cost with no accompanying benefit. To correct for this omission, this chapter develops a framework for adjusting GDP for environmental damage from pollution and calculating environmentally adjusted productivity (EAP) growth. Incorporating pollution damage estimates from the literature into this framework changes the picture of US output and productivity growth before and after passage of the 1970 Clean Air Act. In the late 1950s and 1960s, EAP was less than 70 percent of measured productivity, meaning that accounting for environmental damage associated with production lowers measured labor productivity by over 30 percent. By 2010, accounting for environmental damage lowers the measure of labor productivity by only 10 percent. The decline in environmental damage reflects a 45 percent fall in damage per hour worked from air pollution that was partially offset by a 127 percent increase in damage per hour worked from greenhouse gas emissions. The growth rate of EAP was substantially lower than the growth rate of the standard measure of productivity in 1957–1970 but substantially higher in 1971–2016. The chapter concludes with a call for statistical agencies to develop measures of output and productivity that adjust for environmental damage from air pollution and greenhouse gases.

Chapter 8: "Modernizing Measurement of Productivity with Nonstandard Data: Opportunities, Challenges and Progress," by Erica L. Groshen, Michael W. Horrigan, and Christopher Kurz

Official US productivity measures are estimated from data on inputs, outputs, and prices obtained from multiple sources and statistical agencies. These measures have improved markedly in timeliness, granularity, and accuracy, and now, increased availability of nonstandard source data has created opportunities for further improvements along with possible cost savings. Today, most official statistics rely heavily on surveys conducted by statistical agencies. These surveys generate data with known statistical properties and answer questions designed precisely to meet measurement objectives, but they are expensive and subject to declining response rates. Increasingly, statistical agencies are seeking ways to tap into burgeoning nonstandard data, including government and private sector administrative data, corporate records, transactional files, web-scraped data, and private sector aggregations. This chapter considers how nonstandard data could improve productivity measures; describes the progress, opportunities, and challenges in using nonstandard data; and identifies particularly promising efforts and opportunities for tapping into these data. It also recommends changes in the organization of the US statistical system and improvements in data sharing within the system that would promote more and better use of nonstandard data while protecting the privacy of survey respondents.

1

GDP as a Measure of Economic Well-Being

Karen Dynan and Louise Sheiner

1.1 Introduction

Recent years have seen a revival of broad interest in how well improvements in standards of living are captured by economic indicators traditionally associated with aggregate economic performance. This interest has been driven in part by disappointment over published figures for growth in productivity and real gross domestic product (GDP) since the early 2000s. Indeed, some of the literature that considers explanations for weak productivity growth explicitly explores measurement issues.[1] More generally, the sense that recent technological advances have yielded considerable benefits for everyday life has spurred widespread concern about whether our statistical systems are capturing these improvements (see, for example, Feldstein 2017).

Concerns about economic measurement are, of course, not at all new to the statistical community and the broader community of economists. For decades, data-producing agencies have worked to improve measurement and ensure that standards are consistent across countries. These efforts have yielded major methodological advances. Moulton (chap. 2, this volume),

Karen Dynan is with Harvard University and the Peterson Institute for International Economics.

Louise Sheiner is with the Hutchins Center on Fiscal and Monetary Policy, the Brookings Institution.

We thank Katharine Abraham, Ana Aizcorbe, Martin Baily, Barry Bosworth, David Byrne, Richard Cooper, Carol Corrado, Diane Coyle, Abe Dunn, Marty Feldstein, Greg Ip, Dale Jorgenson, Greg Mankiw, Dylan Rassier, Marshall Reinsdorf, Matthew Shapiro, Dan Sichel, Jim Stock, Hal Varian, David Wessel, and participants at the Hutchins Center authors' conference for helpful comments and discussion. We are grateful to Sage Belz, Michael Ng, Finn Schuele, Nasiha Salwati, and Lorae Stojanovic for excellent research assistance. All errors are our own.

for example, discusses key improvements to the US national income and product accounts (NIPA) since the late 1990s.

The starting point for research to support statistical agencies should be a basic understanding of how statistics are defined and how they are limited, both in terms of concept and how they are calculated given the concept. While much of this information can be found in writings by the statistical community, this literature is large in volume and often hard to understand for nonexperts, even economists. The goal of this chapter is to supply some basic answers with a focus on real GDP, the most high-profile and closely watched aggregate economic indicator. GDP growth is often used as a measure of growth in the standard of living.

We begin with a discussion of how the established GDP concept relates to welfare, or more specifically to a somewhat narrower concept we term "aggregate economic well-being," which excludes factors outside the scope of GDP such as quality of environment. We explain the advantages of GDP as defined and consider how important its differences with economic well-being actually are. We also discuss alternative and complementary approaches that can help bridge the gap between GDP and economic well-being.

We turn next to how well GDP as conceptualized by the data community is captured in practice. Notwithstanding important advances in measurement, increases in the share of GDP represented by difficult-to-measure sectors (such as health care and the digital economy) mean that published GDP figures may not track the conceptual ideal as well as they did in the past. Moreover, the limited resources of data-producing agencies, which are at risk of cuts in the current political and budget environment, may constrain the ability of these agencies to cope with such challenges.

We consider first whether the nominal (i.e., current dollar) GDP figure adequately captures the size of our economy measured in dollars. It mostly does, but there are two important measurement challenges. One is the treatment of so-called free goods, particularly given the dramatic rise in services provided by the internet for which consumers do not explicitly pay. The other is the tax incentive–driven understatement of the domestic economic activity of multinational enterprises.

Converting current dollar figures to real GDP (that is, GDP expressed in the dollars from a particular base year) presents thornier issues. Hence, the second and much larger part of our discussion concerns challenges related to the deflators used to calculate real GDP. A central issue is how to separate changes in prices that reflect quality improvements (and hence should not be counted as inflation) from those that represent true inflation. Another issue is estimating the value of dollars spent on newly introduced goods and services. The chapter offers a discussion of the ideal way to treat measurement issues and then considers what statistical agencies do in practice.

We draw several conclusions. First, GDP, as currently defined, should retain its stature as a major economic statistic. While it is not a comprehensive measure of welfare or even economic well-being, the GDP concept—along with the pieces of GDP available through the national accounts (as conceptualized)—is useful in and of itself and should provide a great deal of information closely related to welfare. Second, there is scope for materially improving specific parts of the GDP calculation to bring them closer to the conceptual ideal. Doing so should be a goal for the statistical community and the broader community of economists. Third, given the limitations of GDP as a measure of welfare (and the potential for those limitations to increase over time), we support efforts to develop complementary measures or sets of measures, sometimes termed "dashboards," that more completely capture well-being.

1.2 The GDP Concept

The GDP release published by the Bureau of Economic Analysis (BEA) states a clear definition of GDP: "Gross domestic product (GDP) is the value of the goods and services produced by the nation's economy less the value of the goods and services used up in production. GDP is also equal to the sum of personal consumption expenditures, gross private domestic investment, net exports of goods and services, and government consumption expenditures and gross investment."[2] The US Commerce Department began to publish regular estimates of GDP, defined essentially as above, in the early 1940s (Carson 1975). The Commerce Department framework built off the methods that Simon Kuznets had used to estimate US national income for 1929–32 under the auspices of the National Bureau of Economic Research (NBER). Kuznets's work was preceded by two volumes published by the NBER in the early 1920s that provided estimates of national income over the preceding decade. Other organizations and individuals were also engaged in efforts to measure economic activity around this time. For example, the National Industrial Conference Board (which later became just the Conference Board) began publishing a regular estimate of national income in the 1920s. Colin Clark, a British economist and statistician, was doing work measuring the aggregate economy of the United Kingdom that was similar to what Kuznets did for the United States (Coyle 2014).

1.2.1 The Differences between GDP and Welfare

As a long literature has emphasized, GDP as conventionally defined differs in many ways from welfare.[3] The economists who developed the modern concept of GDP were well aware of this distinction. For example, in a 1934 report to Congress, Kuznets stated that "the welfare of a nation . . . can scarcely be inferred from a measurement of national income" (Bureau of Foreign and Domestic Commerce and Kuznets 1934).

Some of the differences between GDP and welfare are outside the scope of this chapter. For example, GDP does not include important societal features such as discrimination and crime. Nor does GDP, an economy-wide concept, provide information about the distribution of income, which bears importantly on the welfare of individuals within an economy.[4] GDP does not capture features of the environment such as climate change and availability of natural resources, although expanded measures of GDP that incorporate environmental considerations have been calculated (see chap. 7 in this volume).

Much of the discussion of GDP and welfare in this chapter focuses on a narrower distinction: the difference between GDP and what we call *aggregate economic well-being*, defined as consumer welfare derived from market-based activities and non-market-based activities that are close substitutes.

The key differences between GDP and aggregate economic well-being are as follows:

1. *GDP includes investment*—by businesses, government, and households (through housing and consumer durables). While this investment may provide future services to households, it does not represent services enjoyed immediately by households.[5]

2. *GDP includes production that makes up for the depreciation of physical assets*. Such production is needed to maintain the current capital stock; it does not increase the future services that can be consumed by households.

3. *GDP excludes most home production and other nonmarket activities such as leisure* even though such activity effectively increases the true consumption of households and thus enhances welfare (more discussion of this below).

4. *GDP represents domestic production, but some of that production is "owned" by foreigners; furthermore, Americans own some foreign production*. The welfare of Americans is more closely correlated with the income they receive from the production they own regardless of where it occurs than simply the production done in this country.

5. *GDP includes some work-related spending*, such as commuting costs, and excludes some personal consumption paid for by employers, such as meals and travel categorized as business expenses.

Despite these well-known differences, GDP is often used—by politicians, reporters, the general public, and even economists—as a proxy for welfare or at least economic well-being. This begs the question of why the economists and statisticians who developed the modern concept of GDP chose the definition they did. Our reading of the literature suggests that several factors contributed to their thinking.

One factor is that the modern market-production-based concept of GDP is better aligned with the Keynesian concept of demand. Although new homes and new cars might yield services for consumers that raise welfare by modest increments over a long period of time, the investment associated with the building of those homes or cars uses a lot of the economy's productive resources over a short period of time. Policymakers trying to use fiscal or monetary tools to stabilize the economy in the face of business-cycle fluctuations need to know how the use of productive resources compares to the economy's supply of such resources.

A second factor might be war-related considerations. Some have argued that it is no coincidence that modern interest in measuring the aggregate economy arose during World War I and that needs related to the war contributed to the production focus of the modern GDP concept. On the practical side, understanding what the economy could produce presumably greatly facilitated planning for war efforts (Landefeld 2000). Coyle (2014) also notes the political advantages of a production focus—production-based measures do not show the economy shrinking during wartime even if what is available for private consumption plummets.

A third factor is feasibility. In particular, the literature suggests that home production and many other activities not captured by market transactions were left out only because they were difficult to measure. Indeed, there was a vigorous debate about whether it made sense, for example, that the services provided by professional housekeepers were included in the GDP concept but that personal housekeeping efforts were not included. It was accepted, though, that the latter was more difficult to measure, and, as Carson (1975) describes, the economists involved in the NBER effort "retreat[ed] . . . to ground more securely buttressed by reliable data" (158). Similarly, trying to put a value on leisure can be quite difficult, particularly given that individuals sometimes freely choose to take leisure but at other times cannot work as many hours as they would like at the prevailing wage—and sometimes may not be able to find work at all.

Regarding this last factor, several additional points are worth noting. First, the precise boundary between market production and nonmarket production for own consumption is not always well defined. In particular, the current methodological framework for GDP is not conceptually consistent regarding the services provided by consumer durable goods (like cars) and those provided by owner-occupied homes. The former are not included in GDP because they are viewed as nonmarket production; the entire cost of a car purchase is treated as consumption in the year of purchase. But the latter *are* included through imputed rentals to oneself (with the rent included on both the product and income sides of the account so that the two sides align). Second, while it may have been extremely difficult to measure nonmarket production at the time national accounts were being developed, new technologies and data sources offer opportunities to capture components of economic well-being that previously were difficult or impossible to measure. Third, there may now be a greater cost to excluding traditionally defined nonmarket services than in the past given that many of the services people enjoy from the internet are arguably a market transaction but not paid for through a traditional market transaction. We return to this issue in our section on free goods below.

1.2.2 Do These Conceptual Differences Matter?

Any assessment of the GDP concept as a measure of aggregate economic well-being needs to recognize that many of the shortcomings noted above can be addressed by looking at measures already available as part of the standard national income accounts. For example, investment (including that making up for depreciation of assets) can be netted out of GDP. To address the issue that some income associated with domestic production belongs to foreigners (and, likewise, that Americans receive some income from production done in other countries), we can look at gross national product (GNP), which captures the production owned by Americans regardless of where in the world it occurs.[6]

Indeed, one might expect consumption—derived from standard national accounts series and broadly defined as spending directly by or on behalf of households (if financed by government, like spending on Medicare and Medicaid services)—to align well with economic well-being. Consumption defined in this way overcomes both shortcomings discussed in the previous paragraph: it excludes investment and is funded by income earned by Americans rather than income related to domestic consumption. The solid black line in figure 1.1 shows cumulative growth in real broadly defined consumption (the sum of personal consumption expenditures plus government consumption expenditures) since 1970.[7] The series has risen by roughly three-and-one-half fold over the 49-year period shown. The figure also shows that cumulative growth in real GDP (depicted by the dashed line) has been about the same over this period—suggesting that GDP, even with

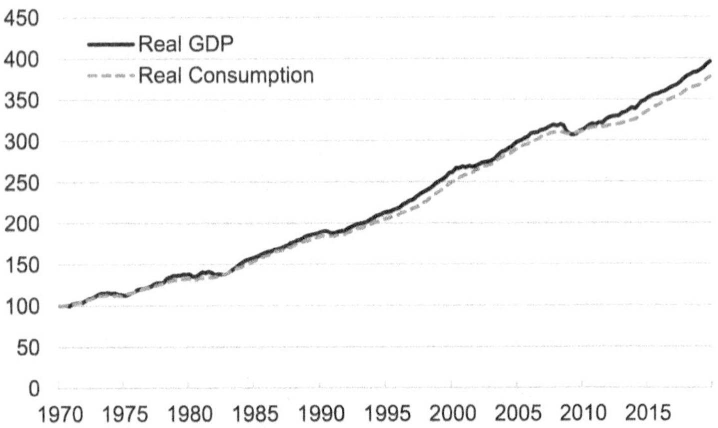

Fig. 1.1 Cumulative growth in consumption and GDP, 1970–2019

Source: Bureau of Economic Analysis via FRED.

Note: Consumption comprises both personal consumption expenditures and government consumption expenditures (combined by applying nominal shares to the growth rates of both categories).

its conceptual differences, is not a bad proxy for broadly defined consumption over long periods of time.

The one important conceptual shortcoming of GDP as a measure of economic well-being that cannot be resolved by looking at series available as part of the standard national income accounts is GDP's exclusion of (most) nonmarket activities that create welfare for households. Trends in the importance of nonmarket activities could lead to gaps between household welfare and GDP such that *changes* in measured GDP may not proxy for *changes* in well-being over the longer run. For example, the surge of women into the labor force in the 1970s, 1980s, and 1990s would have boosted GDP even if newly employed women were previously producing the same amount outside of the marketplace—a case in which the increase in GDP would have overstated the increase in welfare. However, some more recent trends go in the opposite direction. For example, the internet has made it easier for people to arrange for travel directly instead of going through a travel agent; these efforts are not counted in GDP, but the services of a travel agent would be counted, leading GDP growth to understate the increase in welfare. In this case, at least the travel purchased shows up in GDP—in our section on free goods, we discuss the degree to which services consumed more broadly via the internet are showing up in GDP.[8]

The BEA does periodically publish "satellite accounts" with values for some types of nonmarket activities. Recent updates to these accounts (Bridgman et al. 2012 and Bridgman 2016) include estimates for home production (such as cooking, cleaning, and shopping) and services provided to households from durable goods (such as cars and appliances). Building on this work—improving the source data, refining the methods, and releasing the data on a regular basis—would allow users to create measures that perhaps better capture trends in economic well-being than GDP. As satellite accounts, however, these data are inherently of lower priority and thus receive limited scrutiny and are likely to be subject to cuts and resource constraints in the current era of tight statistical agency budgets.

1.2.3 Advantages of the GDP Concept

Figure 1.1 shows that level of GDP is well correlated with broadly defined consumption, suggesting that GDP may not be a bad proxy for at least the market-based portion of economic well-being over long periods of time.[9] On a shorter-term basis, the two measures may deviate materially, as seen in quarter-to-quarter growth rates. Figure 1.2 shows these growth rates. GDP is generally more volatile than consumption and, among other things, tends to fall more during recessions (denoted by the shaded bars in the figure) than consumption.

From the perspective of policymakers trying to stabilize the economy at the business-cycle frequency, such deviations are likely a feature rather than a bug of the GDP concept. The underlying argument echoes the dis-

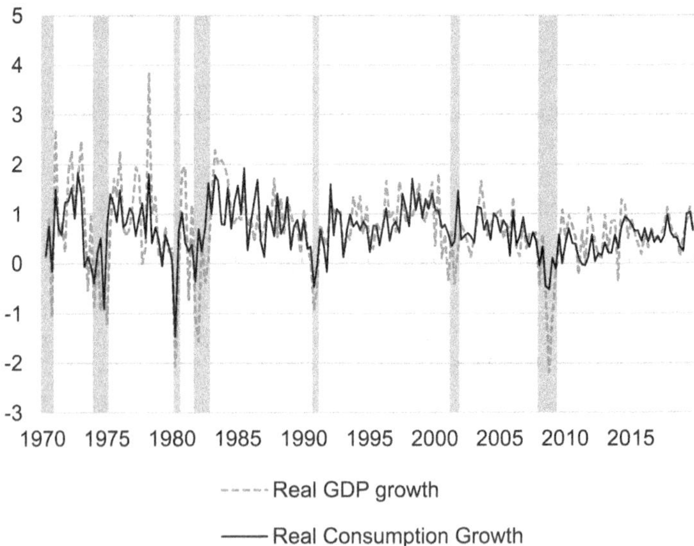

Fig. 1.2 Quarter-to-quarter percent growth in consumption and GDP, 1970–2019
Source: Bureau of Economic Analysis via FRED.
Note: Shaded regions are NBER recessions. Consumption comprises both personal consumption expenditures and government consumption expenditures (combined by applying nominal shares to the growth rates of both categories).

cussion above about the initial designers of GDP preferring a production-based concept in part because it aligned better with the Keynesian notion of aggregate demand. An important indicator of the health of an economy is whether economic resources are being fully utilized. In periods where economic resources are not fully utilized, unemployment is elevated and incomes are lower. It is thus unsurprising that government officials responsible for countercyclical monetary and fiscal policy would want to focus on an aggregate metric that considers all production done domestically—including production related to investment, even if that production does not immediately and directly enhance consumer welfare.

1.2.4 Conceptual Alternatives

Despite recent calls (most prominently Stiglitz, Sen, and Fitoussi 2009) for shifting the emphasis of government statistical indicators from measuring economic production to measuring overall well-being, trying to broadly capture all the factors that enter well-being would be highly ambitious.[10] In addition to the challenge of accurately measuring all of the many factors that bear on households, one needs to grapple with how to weight different factors to produce a single, comprehensive measure. (As Corrado et al. 2017 note, GDP effectively weights the units produced of different goods and services by their prices, which should have a natural correspondence to the values of these items.) Of course, a single measure is not necessary—some proposals, such as the OECD's Better Life Initiative, merely call for a "dashboard" of factors related to welfare. The strength of dashboards is that they allow users to apply their own weights; however, this is also a weakness when it comes to reaching consensus about how different countries compare or how much welfare has increased over time.

Jones and Klenow (2016) and later Bernanke and Olson (2017) took a concrete step toward creating a broader measure of welfare that draws from economic theory to weigh different factors. The authors use a "consumption-equivalent" welfare approach combining data on consumption, leisure, inequality, and mortality into a single summary statistic using an expected utility calculation that applies equal weight to each person. They explore differences over time and across countries between this summary statistic and GDP, finding, for example, that their alternative statistic implies that living standards in Western European countries are much closer to those in the United States than suggested by GDP comparisons because of longer life spans, greater consumption of leisure, and lower inequality.

An entirely different approach to capturing welfare would be to simply ask people how happy they are. Wolfers (2003), Stevenson and Wolfers (2008), and Sack, Stevenson, and Wolfers (2012), for instance, explore measures of so-called subjective well-being. Stevenson and Wolfers (2008) provide a thorough analysis of subjective well-being over time and across countries and conclude that such measures are well-correlated with absolute real income per capita (with some role for relative income). While people exhibit biases when answering questions about their well-being (see Krueger 2008), these measures are potentially important complements to indicators of well-being based on hard data.

1.2.5 Summary

We have highlighted some important conceptual differences between GDP and aggregate economic well-being (which itself is narrower than overall welfare). However, series already included in the standard national income accounts can be used to construct a measure that, on a conceptual basis, should be correlated with many of the goods and services that determine economic well-being. Moreover, we show that such a measure—combined private and public consumption—is well correlated with GDP over long periods of time, suggesting that changes in GDP, at least in principle, could be a good measure of aggregate economic well-being over time.

We believe that one conceptual difference—the exclusion of nonmarket activities that impact economic well-being—merits more attention, particularly given the potential for changes in the importance of such activities over time to alter the degree to which GDP captures economic well-being. However, even if this issue were important, it does not necessarily follow that the definition of GDP should be changed, implying rather that we need to develop good alternative measures to supplement it. Retaining the current definition of GDP has the very significant advantage of keeping GDP comparable across time and countries.

The discussion in this section has concerned GDP *as conceptualized.* The degree to which actual GDP speaks to economic well-being depends heavily on how well the GDP concept is measured, the issue to which we now turn.

1.3 Issues Related to GDP as Expressed in Current Dollars

Given our focus on economic well-being, we are ultimately interested in how well the official statistics measure *real* GDP—that is, GDP that abstracts from the effects of price inflation. The real GDP concept is, for the most part, estimated by collecting data in current dollars to produce the components of nominal GDP and then adjusting these components to remove price inflation, thereby leaving just the "real" activity in the economy. Real GDP measurement problems can thus arise from either errors in the estimation of nominal GDP or errors in the way price adjustment (or "deflation") is done. In this section, we describe two major challenges in measuring nominal GDP.

1.3.1 "Free" Goods

A major recent source of discussion and debate is whether and how GDP should account for the vast amount of information, entertainment, and services that consumers obtain through the internet seemingly for free. The problem of "free" goods is not new—households have been able to consume entertainment and news services via television, for example, for many decades without having to pay for it. But with internet-provided services an ever-growing part of our regular lives, there are increasing questions about the degree to which these services are already accounted for and whether they should be counted in GDP.[11]

Before delving into national accounting issues surrounding free goods, it is useful to think very generally about how these transactions work. The development and maintenance of free internet-provided services are often funded by an interest in selling something, whether it be a traditional good or service (think shoes) or a premium product offered by the internet company supplying the service (think Spotify Premium). In the case of shoes, the shoemaker pays dollars to advertising companies to create ads and pays dollars to internet companies (like Facebook) to place those ads, often targeting the ads using data the internet company has collected from individual users. The internet company uses these dollars to develop content that induces individual users to look at ads and to give over their data. Meanwhile, individual users consume the content, are influenced by the ads, and ultimately use some of their earnings to purchase shoes.

TRADITIONAL APPROACH TO FREE GOODS: Marketing (ads, promotional merchandise, anything used to persuade the consumer to engage with the marketing) is an intermediate input.

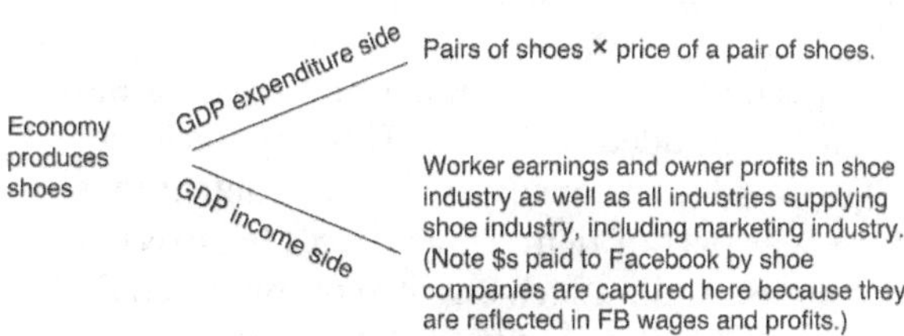

Income and expenditure side match. But system is missing:

(A) Any independent value that the marketing (broadly defined) provides to the consumer.

(B) Anything besides $s that the consumer is giving up to consume the shoes and marketing.

Fig. 1.3

Clearly, much of what is going on is already captured in GDP and related parts of the national accounts. The dollars spent on shoes show up in nominal consumption (the expenditure side of GDP). The wages and salaries of workers at the shoe company, their suppliers, and the internet company all show up in nominal national income (the income side of GDP), as do the profits of these companies. The key question, then, is whether these items are the only parts of the broader transaction described above that should be counted as part of nominal GDP.

The traditional national accounts approach views marketing, broadly defined (including ads, promotional merchandise, and anything else that comes along with ads, such as internet content), as an intermediate input to the production of the final good being promoted. This approach is applied, for example, in the context of free network television supported by advertisements. It means that the marketing does not independently contribute to GDP; it is captured in nominal GDP to the extent that it is reflected in the dollars that consumers spend on the final good.

Figure 1.3 shows how national accounting works for the example above under the traditional approach. The economy is viewed as just producing shoes; the dollars that consumers pay for shoes show up on the expenditure side of nominal GDP, and the dollars that workers earn and owners make show up on the income side of nominal GDP. The dollar amount is the same on both sides of the accounts, so the two sides match (as should be the case with GDP accounting).

However, as noted in the box on the right side of figure 1.3, parts of the transaction are not counted under this approach. In particular, the approach does not count any independent value that the marketing, broadly defined (including internet-provided information, entertainment, and services), provides to the consumer. Such items have become a regular part of many people's lives in a wide range of important ways. They allow people to get home faster, keep up with friends, do their taxes, meet potential romantic partners, manage their finances, cook better, find information at blistering speeds, and consume a rich offering of video and audio entertainment. The approach also does not include anything (besides the dollars spent on shoes) that the consumer is giving up to consume this marketing—more specifically, the time they spend viewing ads and the data they provide that allows for better targeting of ads.

Some commentators have argued that a value should be imputed for the free services of digital platforms and added to GDP.[12] This approach recognizes the independent value provided to consumers by free content that platforms supply to attract users as part of delivering services to advertisers and for data collection purposes. Adding such imputed output to GDP, however, would create conceptual inconsistencies in the GDP measure over time. The proposed guidelines for the 2025 System of National Accounts (SNA) therefore recommend showing this alternative treatment of free platform services in a satellite account.[13] In the alternative treatment, consumers receive imputed payments from the digital platform for consenting to collection of their data (but not for the time they spend viewing ads), and consumers use these imputed payments to purchase free internet content from the platforms. An extended concept of GDP would add in the value of platform services that is not already counted in GDP, and an extended concept of household income would include payments for households giving up their data. Furthermore, both the standard and extended measures of GDP would include the platform's investment in data assets.

Still not counted in nominal GDP under the alternative approach would be internet content created without remuneration, by volunteers—such as Wikipedia—or as someone's hobby. These services are unpaid home production or leisure activities. As a result, it would be appropriate not to include them in a production measure that excludes home production. However, a comprehensive measure of production would include unpaid work in the home and by volunteers.

Translating nominal extended GDP into real extended GDP is also complicated. In the absence of market transactions, the real amount of free platform services could be inferred by finding similar services that do have market prices, recognizing, of course, that the final good in these cases is the content, not the advertising. For example, one could use a deflator for entertainment in the case of videos or software in the case of free applications. This approach would only be possible, of course, in cases where similar services that are traded through traditional markets can be found.

Alternatively, researchers have measured the value to consumers of free services by asking people directly about willingness to pay for free goods and services, as suggested by Corrado et al. (2017). This approach has the potential to get around many of the challenges described. While it is not an approach that has been traditionally used by statistical agencies, Brynjolfsson, Eggers, and Gannamaneni (2018) sample very large numbers of people online about what compensation they would require to forgo use of a digital service like Facebook or email. They find that consumers would require substantial compensation to give up a variety of free digital goods, in particular goods that are essential to many professions—the median willingness to accept to give up a service for a year is $17,530 for search engines, $8,414 for email, and $3,648 for digital maps. This research not only refutes the view that accounting for free goods is simply unfeasible but also underscores the important need for a serious conversation about how to deal with the issue.

1.3.2 Understatement of the Domestic Economic Activity of Multinational Enterprises

As discussed by Varian (2016) and Guvenen et al. (2022), the rise of global supply chains and the legal latitude that companies have in declaring in which countries their economic activity takes place lend material downward bias to estimates of US nominal GDP. In particular, "transfer pricing" and other practices allow multinational enterprises (MNEs) operating in the United States to underprice the sale or lease of intangible assets—such as blueprints, software, or new drug formulas—to affiliates in low-tax jurisdictions so that more of their profits are booked in these countries.

The economic importance of such transactions has been documented in a variety of ways. For instance, in 2012, a Senate subcommittee questioned Microsoft about its agreements to shift some R&D costs and regional royalty rights to affiliates in Singapore and Ireland (United States Committee on Homeland Security and Governmental Affairs 2012). In 2013, the subcommittee found that Apple used favorable transfer pricing agreements to shift billions of dollars of profits from the United States to Ireland (US Committee on Homeland Security and Governmental Affairs 2013). More generally, Hines (2005) and Lipsey (2009) show that US MNEs register more profits in tax havens than can plausibly be accounted for by economic activity. Jenniges et al. (2018) find that US companies that have a cost-sharing agreement with a foreign entity appear less productive than similar companies without such an agreement, and foreign companies that have a cost-sharing agreement with a parent company in the US appear more productive than similar foreign companies. A 2016 OECD brief describes how such transactions drove a 26 percent increase in measured GDP in Ireland in 2015. Tørsløv, Wier, and Zucman (2022) estimate that 36 percent of multinational profits are shifted to low-tax countries each year.

Under current methods, transfer pricing and profit shifting have led to an understatement of both nominal GDP and nominal gross domestic income (GDI) in the United States. Consider the example of a smartphone with software, blueprints, and branding developed in the United States. If the phone is assembled in the United States, then the full value of the phone (at its market price) is included in GDP. If the phone is assembled abroad, then so long as the contract between the company doing the assembly (e.g., Foxconn) is an arm's-length transaction, GDP is still correctly measured, as it includes the value of the phone less the amount paid to the foreign assembler. However, if a foreign affiliate of the US company is introduced in the transaction, GDP can end up understated. Here is one way this can happen: the US company leases the rights to the intangible capital—the software, blueprints, and branding—to an affiliate in a low-tax country (say Ireland) and prices that lease at a value that is much less than its market value. Then the *Irish affiliate* contracts with Foxconn to do the assembly. Phones are exported from Ireland to the United States and from Ireland to the rest of the world. In this case, only the value of the lease from the US company to the Irish company would be included in US GDP, and if this lease is priced at an artificially low level, US GDP would be low as well. Irish GDP would be overstated, and, indeed, actual transactions along these lines have been significant enough in recent years to force Ireland to develop modified gross national income as a way of stripping out the upward distortion to its GDP.[14]

Such transactions also distort the components of GDP and national income. Under current methods, estimates of imports associated with sales of the phone in the United States would be too high because the economic activity associated with the leased assets is unlikely to be attributed to this country.[15] In particular, imports would be too high (because they would overstate the Irish content of the phone imported from Ireland), and exports would be too low (because they would understate the US content of phones exported from Ireland to the rest of the world). The same bias would occur in GDI because of the understatement of the company's US earnings. Note that this transaction works because there is intangible capital that is hard to value and pin down to a location and because the Irish company is an affiliate of the US company, so it does not matter to shareholders whether the Irish affiliate or the US headquarters books the profits.

This problem is of increasing concern both because of the evidence discussed above regarding the importance of profit shifting in today's economy and, more generally, because of the growth in MNE activity in recent decades. MNEs are now a large part of the global economy—according to Guvenen et al. (2022), they accounted for $5.2 trillion of global value added in 2016, an amount about the size of the fourth largest economy in the world at the time.[16] The statistical community recognizes the issue, and the international statistical guidelines most recently adopted by the United Nations Statistical Commission (*System of National Accounts 2008*) call for estimates of the production activity of MNEs to reflect economic ownership of intangible assets rather than legal ownership (Moulton and van de Ven 2018). There are practical challenges associated with doing so, and the BEA has yet to change its official methods to follow this guideline.

Guvenen et al. (2022) explore one way in which the guidelines might be at least partially implemented. The authors use confidential MNE survey data collected by the BEA and reapportion the earnings of US MNE foreign affiliates based on labor compensation and sales to unaffiliated parties. The authors' findings suggest that current practices have materially distorted estimated productivity growth at some points in the past—with an average annual understatement of growth of 0.13 percentage point from 2004 through 2010. This figure represents a lower bound on the distortion, as foreign MNEs are probably also shifting some of their profits out of United States.[17] Using this method, Bruner, Rassier, and Ruhl (2018) find that accounting for profit sharing would increase the level of US measured GDP by 1.5 percent in 2014.

1.4 Translating Nominal GDP into Real GDP

The most complex set of issues relates to how nominal GDP is translated into *real* GDP. Measuring price changes correctly is central to this process. Changes in production processes and the broader economy over time introduce significant challenges. Assessing the best way to proceed requires a clear understanding of the different ways to measure price changes, with a particular focus on how to correct changes in observed prices for quality improvements.

1.4.1 Some Basic Intuition

Nominal GDP (that is, GDP measured at current prices) increases over time because of increases in prices (inflation) and increases in real output (real growth). This subsection offers some intuition on how to split nominal GDP growth into these two components.

It helps to think about what real GDP is. It is an index of the quantity of goods and services produced in a given period, a measure that aggregates the number of tomatoes, haircuts, tractors, and so on. The level of real GDP is difficult to interpret on its own—what does an aggregate of tomatoes and haircuts mean?—but useful for measuring changes in production over time. A key question, then, is how different goods and services are aggregated. This would not matter if the number of every good and service produced increased by the same amount from one year to the next—say, the economy produced 3 percent more of everything in year 2 than in year 1. In that case, growth in real GDP obviously would be 3 percent. But when the production of different goods increases at different rates—for example, when production increases 10 percent for tomatoes and 3 percent for haircuts but falls 2 percent for tractors—the weight put on each category determines what number is reported for real GDP growth.

Real GDP growth can be viewed as growth in nominal GDP less inflation. As noted above, in the United States, real GDP is mainly calculated this way, as most source data capture expenditures in current prices. BEA uses data on spending and producer revenues from a wide variety of sources to calculate nominal GDP and then uses prices collected (mostly) by the Bureau of Labor Statistics (BLS) to deflate nominal spending to calculate underlying quantities and growth rates. The key question from this perspective is how to create an inflation index when prices of different goods increase by different amounts.

Two conceptual frameworks have been used to divide nominal GDP into inflation and real GDP—one based on the perspective of the consumer, where the deflator is called a cost-of-living deflator, and one based on the perspective of the producer, where the deflator is called a producer price index. The cost-of-living index is sometimes called an input price index because it measures the value of inputs into the consumer's utility function, whereas the producer price index is called an output price index because it measures the value to the producer of the output produced.

As noted by Moulton (chap. 2, this volume), BLS's producer price index (PPI) has traditionally used the output price index as its conceptual framework, whereas the consumer price index (CPI) uses a cost-of-living utility-based framework. As we show below, the actual practices used by BEA and BLS (weighting changes in quantities by their nominal shares of GDP) do not correspond exactly to either of these approaches but are pretty good approximations of both.[18]

1.4.2 Two Theory-Based Approaches to Measuring Inflation and Real GDP

The discussion that follows assumes that consumers (who are also producers) do no saving, so that GDP as well as aggregate income equals consumption. We make this assumption to simplify the exposition, not because we think that GDP ought to capture consumption only. Also, because our aim is to provide basic intuition about GDP measurement, in our analysis we present a static model in which there is one representative agent, abstracting from the problems of heterogeneous agents and intertemporal considerations (see Aizcorbe 2014 for a discussion of literature examining these issues).

1.4.2.1 Consumer's Perspective: The Cost-of-Living Index (a Utility-Based Approach)

Under this approach, increases in real GDP are changes in the economy that make the consumer better off. If an increase in nominal GDP does not make the consumer better off, that increase represents inflation rather than an increase in real GDP.

When an increase in nominal GDP does make consumers better off, how do we know how *much* better off they are? Economists do not try to answer that question exactly because we do not have a reliable way of measuring welfare.[19] Instead, we ask, "How much has the real purchasing power of consumers' income increased?" When prices do not change, the answer is simple: purchasing power has increased by exactly the amount that nominal income has increased, and real GDP growth is equal to nominal GDP growth. Similarly, if prices of all goods and services increase by the same amount, then the increase in purchasing power and real GDP is equal to the growth in nominal GDP less the inflation rate.

But when different goods and services have different inflation rates—that is, when relative prices change—the answer is less clear. How much has purchasing power increased when income stays the same but the price of one good falls, for example?

Two approaches have been used within the cost-of-living index framework to determine how much purchasing power changes when relative prices change. The first asks, "How much extra income would the consumer have needed in period 1 (before the price change) to get the same utility as in period 2 (after the price change)?" This amount, which is used to calculate the "equivalent variation," can be bounded from above by the amount of money needed to buy the period 2 bundle at prices of period 1.[20] The second asks, "How much money would the consumer need in period 2 to be just as well off as in period 1?" That is another reasonable, but potentially different, measure of how much better off (in dollar terms) the consumer is in period 2 after a relative price change. This amount, used to calculate the "compensating variation," can be bounded from above by the cost at period 2 prices of the bundle of period 1. In both cases, the idea is to compare income in two periods under a counterfactual where prices have not changed.

Box 1.1 summarizes the technical details. It shows both mathematically and graphically how the cost-of-living index is calculated.

1.4.2.2 Producer's Perspective: The Output Price Index (a Production-Function-Based Approach)

Real GDP can also be viewed from the producer's perspective. Under this approach, real GDP increases when the economy can produce something in period 2 that it could not produce in period 1—for example, when producers of drinks can produce more drinks or producers of food can produce more food. The price index corresponding to this notion of real GDP increases is called an output price index. To measure how much real GDP has increased, the producer perspective asks the question, "Holding prices fixed, how much more revenue could producers earn in year 2 than in year 1?"

Box 1.2 provides the details on how this index is calculated.

1.4.3 How These Two Approaches Compare with What BEA Actually Does

In both the consumer approach and the producer approach, the theoretically appropriate real GDP index uses counterfactual baskets of goods and services that reflect the consumer's or producer's behavioral response to changes in relative prices—what would consumers buy or producers produce if relative prices changed. These counterfactual bundles are unobserved.

Instead of trying to estimate these counterfactuals, the approach used

Box 1.1 Calculating Cost-of-Living Indexes

Figures 1.4a, 1.4b, and 1.4c show how to calculate cost-of-living indexes under the equivalent variation and compensating variation approaches discussed in the main text. They are based on a model of a simple economy of just two goods—drinks (*D*) and food (*F*). We define the price of drinks as always equal to 1 (i.e., drinks are the numeraire). With this definition, we can read the amount of income from the intersection of the budget constraint and the *Y* axis. For example, if the price of *D* is 1 and you can buy 100 units of *D* if you buy no *F*, your income must be $100. In period 1, consumers maximize utility by choosing bundle D_1 and F_1 on indifference curve U_1.

Suppose that an improvement in the technology of producing *F* (say the introduction of an improved seed variety) lowers the price of *F* in period 2 and that income rises from Y_1 to Y_2. The budget constraint shifts out, and consumers buy D_2 units of *D* and F_2 units of *F*.

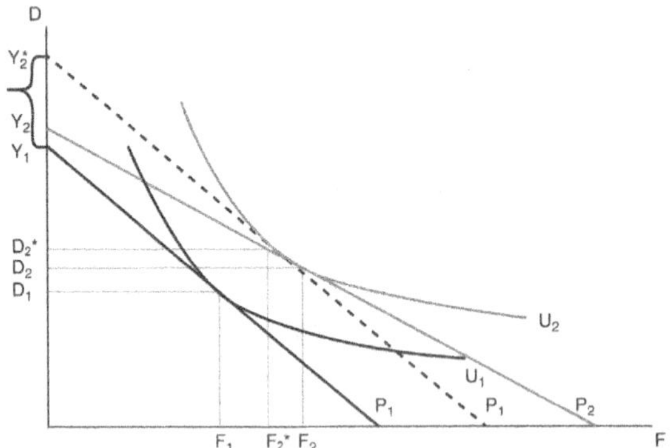

Fig. 1.4a Cost-of-living index under equivalent variation (period 1 prices)

Figure 1.4a shows how to calculate real GDP growth using period 1 prices. It shows that consumers would need to have income equal to Y_2^* in order to get utility U_2 at period 1 prices. With that income and the relative prices given by the slope of the dashed budget line, consumers would choose bundles D_2^* and F_2^*. Holding prices fixed at P_1, consumers would need additional income $(Y_2^* - Y_1)$ to make them as well off as they were in period 2, and thus $(Y_2^* - Y_1)$ is a measure of how much better off they are based on the prices of period 1. In other words, $(Y_2^* - Y_1)$ is the equivalent variation measure of welfare change from the decline in the price of *F*.

An index of real GDP based on the price structure of period 1 would then be the ratio

$$\text{(1)} \qquad \frac{Y_2^*}{Y_1} = \frac{D_2^* + P_1F_2^*}{D_1 + P_1F_1}.$$

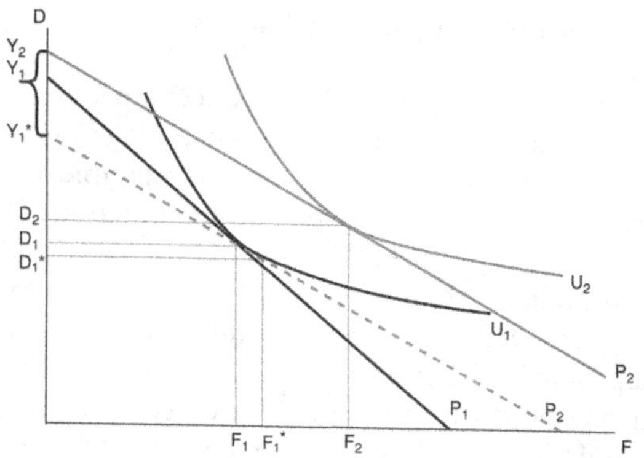

Fig. 1.4b Cost-of-living index under compensating variation (period 2 prices)

Figure 1.4b shows how to calculate real GDP growth using period 2 prices. It shows that consumers would only need income Y_1^* to get period 1 utility at period 2 prices, and thus $Y_2 - Y_1^*$ is how much could be taken away from consumers in period 2 so that they are just as well off as in period 1. $Y_2 - Y_1^*$ is the compensating variation. The index of real income based on the price structure of period 2 is

$$\text{(2)} \qquad \frac{Y_2}{Y_1^*} = \frac{D_2 + P_2F_2}{D_1^* + P_2F_1^*}.$$

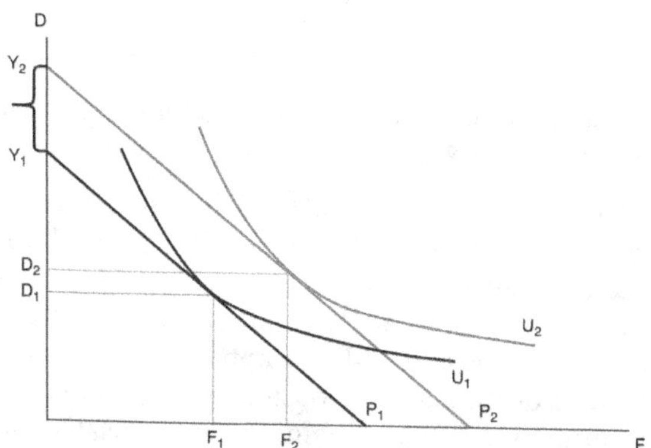

Fig. 1.4c No change in relative prices

In Figure 1.4c, there is no change in prices, but income increases from Y_1 to Y_2. Consumers would need an additional $(Y_2 - Y_1)$ dollars to make them as well off in period 1 as in period 2 and could have $(Y_2 - Y_1)$ dollars taken away in period 2 to leave them as well off as in period 1. In this case, the compensating and equivalent variation are the same, and the index of real income is simply Y_2/Y_1.

Box 1.2 Calculating Output Price Indexes

As discussed in the text, from the producer's perspective, real GDP increases when an economy can produce something in period 2 that it could not produce in period 1. Figure 1.5 shows an example of a production possibilities frontier—the set of all possible combinations of output an economy can produce—again using the example of drinks and food introduced in box 1.1. If an increase in nominal GDP is associated with the economy only moving *along* a production possibilities frontier—that is, if a change in the composition of output leads to an increase in nominal GDP, but the output produced this year could have been produced last year—it is counted as inflation. But if an increase in nominal GDP is associated with the economy being able to produce *more* than it could last year—for example, a change in technology for producing food that lowers the resources needed to produce any given amount of food (meaning that for any given amount of resources devoted to D, more food can be produced and vice

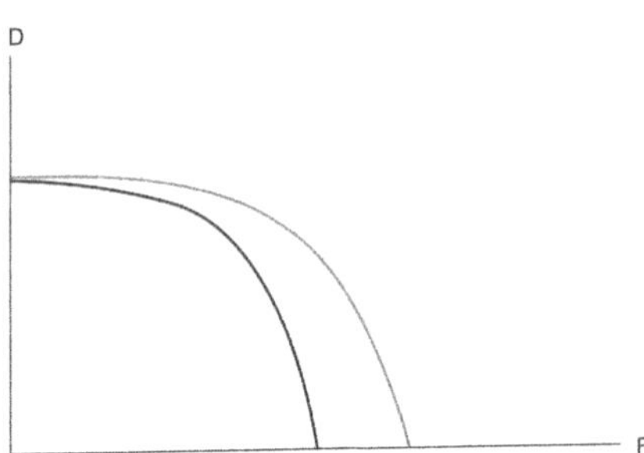

Fig. 1.5 Production possibilities frontier for food and drinks: Technological improvement in production of food

versa)—shown in figure 1.5—then real GDP is viewed as having increased.

To measure how much real GDP has increased, the producer perspective asks the question, Holding prices fixed, how much more revenue could producers earn in year 2 than in year 1? Analytically, the exercise is virtually identical to the one for the cost-of-living approach, but the counterfactual is different. Instead of asking how consumers would adjust the composition of their consumption (the $*$ quantities) when relative prices change, it asks how producers would adjust the composition of their production.

Figure 1.6a walks through the case described above, where a change in technology lowers the resources needed to produce any given amount of food, and we ask how much revenue producers would earn with period 2 technology but period 1 prices. At period 1 prices but period 2 technology, the producer would choose to produce F_2^* and D_2^* and would earn income Y_2^*, which is bounded from below by the value at period 1 prices of the bundle they actually produced. The difference in producer revenues between period 1 technology and period 2 technology, holding prices fixed

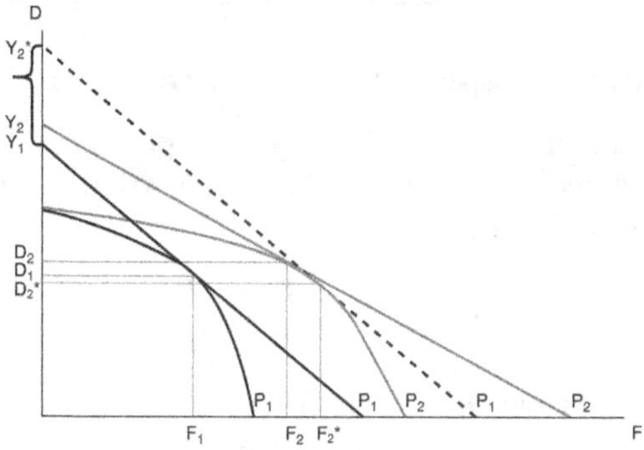

Fig. 1.6a Producer perspective (period 2 technology, period 1 prices)

at period 1 prices, is a measure of the increase in real GDP and is measured by $Y_2^* - Y_1$.

Figure 1.6b shows a similar analysis of producer revenue, this time holding prices fixed at period 2 prices and measuring the change in real GDP by $Y_2 - Y_1^*$. Figure 1.6c shows that when prices are unchanged, change in production is equal to change in nominal GDP.

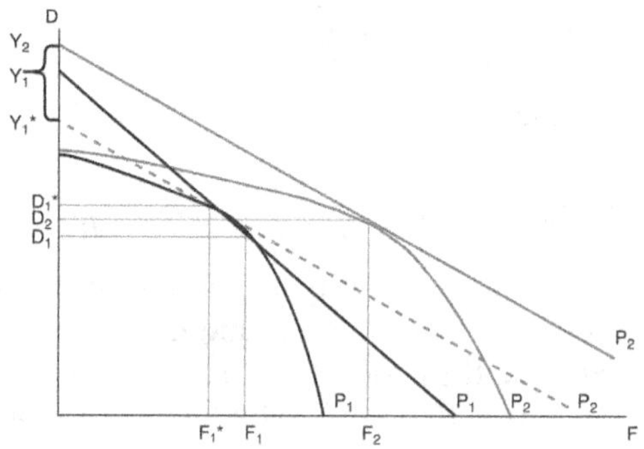

Fig. 1.6b Producer perspective (period 1 technology, period 2 prices)

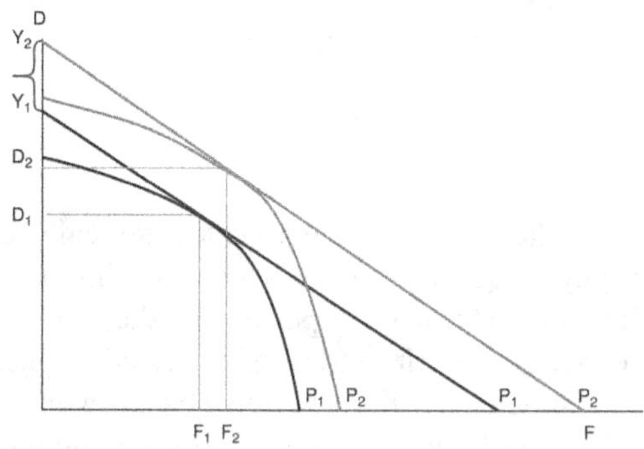

Fig. 1.6c Producer perspective (no change in relative prices)

Box 1.3 Calculating Laspeyres and Paasche Quantity and Price Indexes

The Laspeyres quantity index asks, "Holding prices constant at period 1 prices, how much more is the period 2 basket worth than the period 1 basket?" It is thus calculated as

$$(3) \qquad Q_L = \frac{Y_2^*}{Y_1} = \frac{D_2 + P_1F_2}{D_1 + P_1F_1},$$

which can be rewritten as

$$(4) \quad Q_L = \frac{D_2 + P_1F_2}{D_1 + P_1F_1} = \frac{D_2}{D_1}\left(\frac{D_1}{D_1 + P_1F_1}\right) + \frac{F_2}{F_1}\left(\frac{P_1F_1}{D_1 + P_1F_1}\right) = \frac{D_2}{D_1}S_1^D + \frac{F_2}{F_1}S_1^F,$$

Where S_1^D is the share of D in GDP and S_1^F is the share of F in GDP in period 1. That is, for the Laspeyres quantity index, the growth in real GDP is just the growth in D and F weighted by their period 1 shares in the economy.

The Laspeyres price index asks, "How much more would the period 1 bundle cost in period 2 than it did in period 1?"

$$(5) \qquad P_L = \frac{D_1 + P_2F_1}{D_1 + P_1F_1}$$

This question can likewise be rewritten as

$$(6) \qquad P_L = \frac{D_1}{D_1 + P_1F_1} + \frac{P_2F_1}{D_1 + P_1F_1} = S_1^D + \frac{P_2}{P_1}S_1^F.$$

The Laspeyres price index is a weighted average of the rise in the price of drinks (which is zero in this example) and the rise in the price of food, with the weights equal to the period 1 shares.

The Paasche quantity index asks, "Holding prices constant at period 2 prices, how much more is the period 2 basket worth than the period 1 basket?"

$$(7) \qquad Q_P = \frac{D_2 + P_2F_2}{D_1 + P_2F_1}$$

by BEA simply uses the actual baskets to calculate real GDP growth. For example, the Laspeyres quantity index asks, "Holding prices constant at period 1 prices, how much more is the period 2 basket worth than the period 1 basket?" The Paasche quantity index asks, "Holding prices constant at period 2 prices, how much more is the period 2 basket worth than the period 1 basket?" Box 1.3 shows how these two indexes are calculated.

This equation cannot be rewritten quite as simply, but some algebra shows that Q_p is still essentially a weighted sum using period 2 shares in the economy as weights:

$$Q_P = \left(\frac{D_1}{D_2} S_2^D + \frac{F_1}{F_2} S_2^F\right)^{-1}. \tag{8}$$

The Paasche price index asks, "How much more does the period 2 bundle cost at period 2 prices than it would have cost at period 1 prices?"

$$P_P = \frac{D_2 + P_2 F_2}{D_2 + P_1 F_2} \tag{9}$$

The product of the Paasche quantity index and the Laspeyres price index is an index of nominal GDP (as is the product of the Paasche price index and the Laspeyres quantity index).

In 1996, the BEA began calculating real GDP according to a chain index formula, which uses the geometric average of these two quantity indexes to create a real GDP index known as the Fisher quantity index:

$$Q_{BEA} = \sqrt{Q_L Q_P}. \tag{7}$$

Note from equation (3) and (7) that when changes in GDP are *not* accompanied by relative price changes, the Laspeyres and the Paasche quantity indexes are the same.[1] There is no question about the change in real GDP in that case. If prices all change by the same proportion—so that relative prices do not change—then the change in real GDP is equal to the change in nominal GDP less the rate of price change. It is only when relative prices change that the two measures yield different answers. However, the Fisher quantity index can always be calculated by deflating the change in nominal GDP by the geometric mean of a Laspeyres price index and a Paasche price index.

1. They would also be the same if relative quantities were unchanged, since the weights do not matter if quantity changes by the same proportion.

In 1996, the BEA began calculating real GDP according to a chain index formula, which uses the geometric average of these two quantity indexes to create a real GDP index known as the Fisher quantity index. The Fisher quantity index is generally a very good approximation of the average of the theoretically exact quantity indexes, whether from the consumer's perspective or the producer's perspective (Diewert 1976). The index formula used by

BEA to calculate real GDP is therefore *conceptually* a very good approximation of the change in economic welfare, defined in monetary terms, using either the consumer's or the producer's perspective. That is, abstracting from the important questions of scope discussed above, real GDP growth is a good proxy for the change in real resources available to a society, which is the closest we can get to welfare.[21]

The conclusion that the change in GDP represents the change in (the monetary value of) welfare from the market economy is, in our view, subject to a number of misconceptions. We attempt to provide intuition for it in a number of ways. First, we provide a numerical example with a production function and a utility function to show how changes in real GDP are a good proxy for the changes in welfare one would calculate using the theoretically precise CV and EV. Second, in box 1.4, we provide a graphical analysis to show that the change in real GDP from a price change is essentially equivalent to the change in consumer surplus. As shown by Willig (1976), consumer surplus, the area above the price line under the demand curve, is itself a reasonable approximation of the theoretically ideal CV and EV measures of the welfare changes arising from a price change. We use the graphical analysis to address the oft-heard idea that GDP is a rectangle but consumer surplus is a triangle, so they are not the same. Finally, in box 1.5, we discuss why the paradox of diamonds and water—which explains why the price of a good may not equal its value to the consumer—is not inconsistent with the view that changes in real GDP measure changes in welfare.

1.4.3.1 A Numerical Example

To demonstrate the accuracy of the Fisher index approximation, consider the following example. Assume that the only input to producing D and F is labor, and that the amount of labor is 100. The consumer's utility function is $U = \log(F) + \log(D)$. In year 1, the production function for D is $D = L_D^{1/2}$ and for F, $F = L_F^{1/3}$. Then, there is a technological advance in the production of F so that in period 2, $F = L_F^{2/5}$. With this simple setup, if we assume that the equilibrium is one where consumers and producers are maximizing utility and profits, respectively, we can calculate the BEA's chained price indexes, as well the theoretically accurate cost-of-living index and output price index. We can also calculate BEA's chained quantity index as well the theoretically accurate standard-of-living index and real output index.

These three measures are shown in table 1.1. To calculate inflation and real GDP in the last two columns, we use the geometric average of the Laspeyres and Paasche price indexes and the geometric average of the Laspeyres and Paasche quantity indexes.

As seen in the final two columns, the measures are in practice very similar. Why is that? It is because, in equilibrium in this simple economy, market prices represent both the ratio of marginal production costs of the two goods and the ratio of marginal utilities.

Box 1.4 Change in Real GDP and Change in Consumer Surplus—A Graphical Analysis

One conceptual difficulty with viewing real GDP growth as a measure of change in welfare is that, to the extent economists think of GDP graphically, we think of it as a rectangle (*P* times *Q*), whereas consumer surplus generally involves a triangle.

But, as we show in this simple graphical example, chained GDP, which accounts for substitution effects when prices fall, also gives rise to a triangle. Here we give a simple graphical example to show that change in real GDP is approximately equal to change in consumer surplus.

Assume a simple economy with just two goods, *F* and *D*. The price of *F* falls, and nominal income is unchanged. The change in consumer surplus from that price change can be read off the demand curve for good *F*, as shown below. (Note that this is the entire consumer surplus from the price change, even if the demand for other goods changes as a result of the change in the price of *F*.) We discuss three cases.

Case 1: Only the demand for good *F* changes as a result of the change in the price of *F*.

Income is unchanged, so spending on good *F* is the same in period 1 and period 2, which means that $P_2F_2 = P_1F_1$. Thus, in the diagram below, $H + G = A + G$, or $H = A$. In other words, the savings from the price decline (A) are used to finance increased spending on F (H).

Change in consumer surplus is $A + B$.

Paasche change in GDP (period 2 prices) is $(F_2 - F_1)P_2$, or H.

Laspeyres change in GDP (period 1 prices) is $(F_2 - F_1)P_1$, or $H + B + C$.

Averaging Paasche and Laspeyres (which is approximately what chaining does) gives you change in GDP $= H + B$.

Because $H = A$, change in consumer surplus ($A + B$) = change in real GDP ($H + B$).

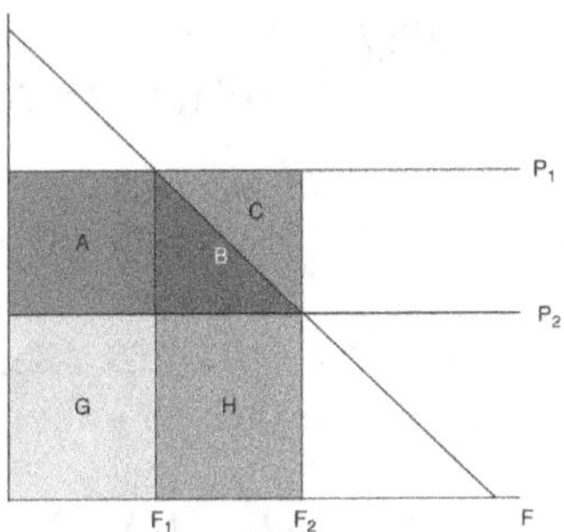

Fig. 1.7 Market for F

(continued)

Box 1.4 (*continued*)

Case 2: Demand for both goods changes as a result of the change in the price of *F*.

F increases from F_1 to F_2, and *D* increases from D_1 to D_2. Because income does not change between the two periods, neither do total expenditures: $P_1F_1 + D_1 = P_2F_2 + D_2$.

Rewriting this yields $P_1F_1 = P_2F_2 + (D_2 - D_1)$. Subtracting P_2F_1 from both sides yields

$$(P_1 - P_2)F_1 = P_2(F_2 - F_1) + (D_2 - D_1).$$

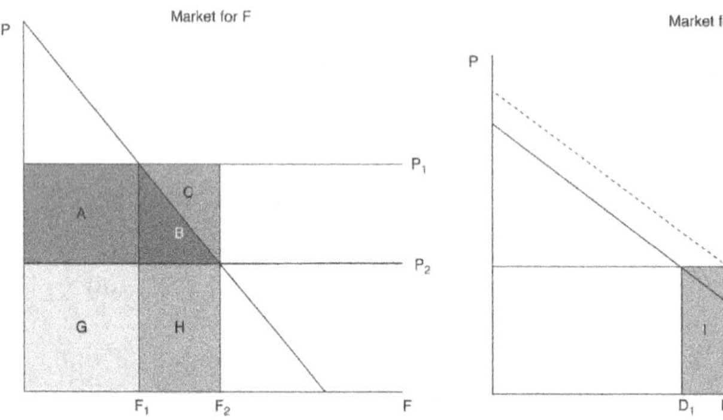

Fig. 1.8a Market for F **Fig. 1.8b Market for D**

Thus, $A = H + I$ (savings on *F* spent on more *F* and more *D*).

Change in consumer surplus: $A + B$

Change in real GDP

Paasche: $H + I$

Laspeyres: $H + B + C + I$

Average change in real GDP: $H + I + B$

Because $A = H + I$, change in real GDP ($H + I + B$) = change in consumer surplus ($A + B$).

Case 3: Only demand for *D* changes as a result of the change in the price of *F*.

F is unchanged, and *D* increases from D_1 to D_2. Because income does not change between the two periods, neither do total expenditures: $P_1F_1 + D_1 = P_2F_1 + D_2$.

Rewriting this yields $(P_1 - P_2)F_1 = (D_2 - D_1)$.

Thus, $A = I$ (savings on *F* spent on more *D*).

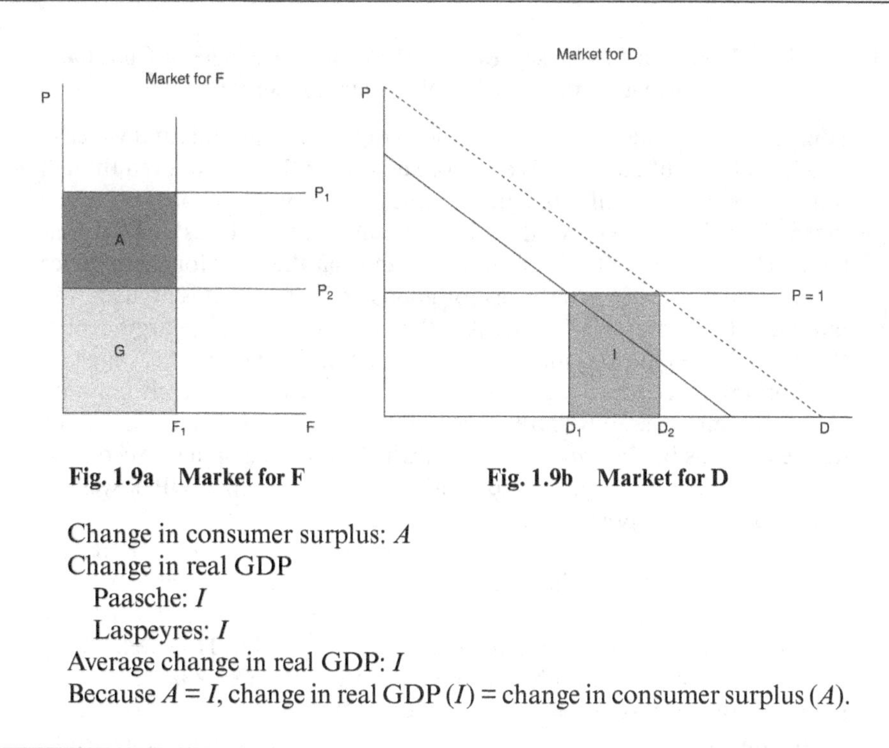

Fig. 1.9a Market for F **Fig. 1.9b Market for D**

Change in consumer surplus: A
Change in real GDP
Paasche: I
Laspeyres: I
Average change in real GDP: I
Because $A = I$, change in real GDP (I) = change in consumer surplus (A).

One conclusion, then, is that the deflators used by BEA yield a measure of real GDP change that is in general a good measure of change in consumer welfare (measured in monetary terms) and change in production. Furthermore, the two concepts are very similar in practice, suggesting that choice of deflator should not matter much to the interpretation of real GDP as a measure of well-being. Below, we explore whether this holds true when it comes to changing quality of goods.

1.4.4 Quality Change and New Goods

The discussion above assumed that the quality of goods and services was fixed; the only way production and welfare could increase was for actual quantities to increase. Of course, the quality of goods and services changes over time, and advances in technology tend to make quality improvements more common than quality deteriorations. Quality improvements also yield improvements in welfare and GDP. That is, instead of having *more* goods and services, real GDP and welfare can improve by having *better* goods and services.

In order to use the formulas described above to compute changes in real

Box 1.5 How Can Changes in Real GDP Measure Changes in Consumer Surplus Given the Paradox of Diamonds and Water?

Some people use the intuition from the paradox of diamonds and water—which explains that diamonds are more expensive than water even though water is essential to life and hence obviously more valuable—to argue that welfare is much bigger than GDP because many goods are, like water, much more valuable to consumers than what they pay for them. Since nominal GDP is what people pay for goods and services, it is argued, welfare must be greater than GDP. Another way of stating the argument is that GDP values the quantities of different goods by their prices, which, in equilibrium, reflect the *marginal* utility people get from their consumption; but to measure overall welfare, one should instead value the quantities of different goods by their *average* utility, which would be higher. According to this argument, you can choose to measure output using GDP or welfare using consumer surplus, but one should not confuse the two.

Although it is true that GDP is not a measure of the level of welfare, it is misleading to imply that the level of welfare could be measured by instead adding up consumer surplus from consumption of each good. The *level* of welfare, or even the *level* of real income, is not measurable. How well off are we? This is a concept that only applies in relative terms: are we better off economically than we were last year, or better off than another country? These are the only types of welfare questions we can answer. Real (as opposed to nominal) GDP is only defined as a relative concept—that is, we choose a year to set real GDP equal to nominal GDP and then use the change in the quantity index for GDP from that year to other periods to calculate real GDP for those periods. Prices, which are used for the weights of the quantity index, provide a suitable measure of value for measuring changes in welfare, so real GDP growth is an indicator of relative welfare. But it does not make sense to say that the *level* of welfare is higher than the *level* of real GDP.

There is no alternative to GDP that would measure the absolute level of welfare based on consumer surplus: the sum of consumer surpluses good

GDP when the quality of goods and services improves, two unobserved prices are needed: the price of year-1-quality items in year 2 (to compute how much the year 1 basket would have cost with year 2 prices) and the price of year-2-quality items in year 1 (to compute how much the year 2 basket would have cost in year 1). With these prices, everything flows through as above.

Although these prices are unobserved, it is possible to impute them in some cases. The standard approach—the hedonic method—first advocated by Griliches (1961) and Rosen (1974) and explored in depth by Triplett by good is *not* a measure of overall welfare. Consumer surplus (defined as the triangle under a demand function) is an approximation of the **amount of money** one would have to give a consumer if the price of *one* good got so high that they chose not to buy it at all—or, equivalently, if the good did not exist. By definition, it holds everything else constant and answers a well-specified and answerable question: if the good under analysis were priced so high that you would not buy any of it, how much income would you need to be able to buy enough of other goods to be as well off as before? For example, how much money would you need in a world without iPhones to be as well off as you are with your current income and the ability to buy an iPhone for $700? The increment to income to make you as well off as you are now is the consumer surplus you get from the ability to buy an iPhone for $700.

One cannot add consumer surpluses together good by good to get welfare. How much money would we have to give you if you could not buy anything? This is not a meaningful question.

What, then, are the true lessons of the diamonds and water example? One is that scarcity or abundance is a key driver of product prices. When a good is abundant, its consumption may expand to a point where marginal utility is low.

The example is also a reminder that price is only a good measure of value for measuring the welfare impact of changes in consumption at the margin. Finally, the discussion of consumer surplus shows the need to identify the type of measurement questions for which this concept can provide valid answers. If some good is left out of GDP because it is free, an estimate of its consumer surplus may be used to adjust the cumulative growth of real GDP since the time of its appearance to capture the welfare impact of the availability of the new free good. However, simultaneously adjusting for multiple free goods by adding consumer surplus estimates that are conditional on other goods included in the adjustment still being free could yield misleading results.

(1982) is to view goods as combinations of their underlying characteristics. People purchase goods and services because people value their underlying characteristics. Under this approach, when a good's quality improves, that good must now embody more of a desirable characteristic. If the characteristic can be measured and priced, then the price of the good can be adjusted for the effect of the quality change. For example, if you know in a particular year that each additional 100 square feet in a house raises the selling price by 5 percent, then it is possible to impute prices of houses with various square

Table 1.1 Comparing the BEA deflator, the cost-of-living index, and the output price index

	Prices		Quantities			
	Laspeyres Index	Paasche Index	Laspeyres Index	Paasche Index	Inflation	Real GDP Growth
BEA deflator	0.89	0.87	1.15	1.12	–11.7%	13.3%
Consumer perspective	0.88	0.88	1.13	1.13	–11.7%	13.3%
Producer perspective	0.90	0.86	1.16	1.11	–11.8%	13.4%

Note: The indexes calculated here assume that the economy is in equilibrium, with producers maximizing profits and consumers maximizing utility. D is drinks, F is food, and L is labor. The year 1 production functions are $D = L_D^{1/2}$, $F = L_F^{1/3}$. The year 2 production functions are $D = L_D^{1/2}$, $F = L_F^{2/5}$. The utility function is $U = \log(D) + \log(F)$, and $L = 100$ in both years.

footages. If, in year 2, the average square footage of houses has increased, it is possible to know what those houses would have sold for last year; similarly, it is possible to know what smaller houses (year 1 houses) would sell for this year.

In a simple world where *the set of embodied characteristics is fixed,* there would be no issue of changes in quality if characteristics were priced instead of goods. This caveat about a fixed set of characteristics is important. It means that better goods and services are just combinations of existing goods and services. For example, an increase in the size of a cereal box might mean the cereal box is better, but one could have purchased as much cereal before by buying two (smaller) boxes. Similarly, an increase in computer "MIPS"—millions of instructions per second—means that you need fewer computers to accomplish a particular task, but that task was doable the year before as well. When all characteristics exist in two consecutive years, the necessary adjustment for quality change is theoretically straightforward and intuitive, as we show in case 1 below.

When a product improvement creates something that is truly novel—a medical treatment that increases survival, a cell phone app that allows users to figure out where their kids are, a printer that can print in 3-D—then market data alone are not sufficient to impute the missing prices necessary to calculate the indexes described above because the class of item did not exist previously. In that case, the item embodying the quality improvement must be treated as a new good. In this section, we provide an overview of how to account for quality change when the characteristics approach applies and when a good needs to be treated as new.

1.4.4.1 Case 1: Quality Improvements That Embody More of Existing Characteristics

Table 1.2 presents a very simple example to demonstrate this approach. Imagine that instead of buying "food," the consumer buys "boxes of cereal."

Table 1.2 **Quality adjustment: Example 1**

Cereal box becomes larger; no change in underlying technologies

	Drinks (price = 1)	Cereal Boxes	Box Price	Nominal GDP	Cereal per Box	Cups of Cereal Purchased	Price per Cup
Year 1	8	8	2	24	1 cup	8	2
Year 2	8	4	4	24	2 cups	8	2
Percent change	0%	–50%	100%	0%	100%	0%	0%

Price and Quantity Changes

	No Quality Adjustment			Correct Quality Adjusted		
	Laspeyres	Paasche	Fischer	Laspeyres	Paasche	Fischer
Inflation:	67%	50%	58%	0%	0%	0%
Real GDP growth	–40%	–33%	–37%	0%	0%	0%

What goes into consumers' utility function is not the box of cereal, of course, but the cereal itself. Imagine that there is no change in the underlying production technology for the economy—both a unit of cereal and a unit of drinks need the same amount of labor to produce in period 1 as in period 2—but for some reason, producers have decided to sell cereal in larger boxes, let us say doubling the cereal content, and the price of the box of cereal goes up accordingly.

Table 1.2 shows how this increase in quality can distort measured prices and quantities using Fisher (geometric average of Laspeyres and Paasche) quantity and price indexes for both. The price of a box of cereal doubles because it contains double the cereal. Nominal GDP—which is equal to total nominal spending (the number of drinks plus the number of cereal boxes times the box price)—is unchanged. Without making an adjustment for this improved quality, though, it looks like prices increased 58.1 percent and real GDP decreased 36.8 percent. But it is obvious that real GDP and prices would be unchanged with appropriate quality adjustments to the price of cereal boxes.[22]

In this example, there is only one defining characteristic—the quantity of cereal—and it is directly observable. It is intuitively obvious that one would adjust the price of the cereal box for the change in quantity. But the same issues arise when the underlying characteristic is not so easily measured and when products improve on multiple dimensions.

For cases in which the proper quality adjustment is not obvious, two approaches have been advocated. One is based on cost, which is generally linked to the producer's perspective and the output price index. The other is based on utility, viewed as the appropriate method for the consumer's cost-of-living index perspective. We compare these two methods in this simple case.

Cost-based method. This method of adjusting for quality involves asking the producer how much the change in quality cost and adding that change—marked up to a selling price—to the box price in year 1. The box in year 2 contains an additional cup of cereal compared with the box in year 1. At a price of $2 per cup (the producer's cost plus any markup), this change is worth $2. To quality adjust the price, add $2 to the year 1 box price to get a quality-adjusted price of $4, the same as in period 2.

Note that, in this case, one gets the same answer using the period 1 basket instead. How much would the period 1 box have cost the producer in period 2? $2 less. Subtract that from the cost of the period 2 box to get a quality-adjusted period 1 price of $2, the same as in period 1. In both cases, the price index shows no change in the quality-adjusted price of cereal boxes.[23]

Utility-based method. A second method of adjusting for quality change is to add to the price of the period 1 product the consumer surplus received as a result of the productivity improvement. Since the marginal value of a cup of cereal is worth $2 to the consumer, that extra cup of cereal in the larger cereal box is worth $2. Add that from the price, and the quality-adjusted period 1 price is $4.

The cost-plus-markup method is a way of directly estimating the prices that period 1 and period 2 boxes would have sold for in the market had they been sold. A common approach to gathering those prices is to use hedonic functions—regressions that relate selling prices to the characteristics of goods and services sold in a given period.

The basic idea of hedonic regressions is that, if there are enough different models of similar goods with varying amounts of underlying characteristics, a regression analysis using cross-sectional variation within a given year can uncover how much having more of certain characteristics contributes to price. With this regression, any given combination of characteristics can be priced.[24]

The utility-based method does not try to directly measure the prices that goods would be sold at but rather the difference in value to the consumer of different quality items. The utility-based method yields the same answer because, in equilibrium for most goods, people purchase goods and services until their marginal value equals their price.

The equivalence between a cost-plus-markup quality adjustment and a utility-based adjustment breaks down when a quality improvement introduces a characteristic that was not available previously. We now go through that case and argue that the utility-based approach is appropriate when the two approaches differ.

1.4.4.2 *Case 2: Quality Improvements That Introduce Something New*

When a quality improvement introduces a characteristic that was not available previously, the good can be viewed as a new good. New goods might be, for example, treatments that increase survival time for cancer, the smartphone, the laptop. The value to society of a new good is the difference between the value people place on the new characteristic embedded in the new model and its cost.

Standard methods that attempt to impute the prices of new goods in the previous year (hedonics or the cost method) are likely to be unsuccessful, since comparable goods did not previously exist. For example, when a camera is first added to a phone, there are simply no observations with cell phone cameras in the previous year's data, so there is no way to infer what such a product would have sold for.

As Hicks first showed (Triplett 2004), the theoretically correct price to use for the previous year's price is the consumer's reservation price[25]—the lowest price at which consumers would not purchase the good.[26] As shown in figure 1.10, the decline in price from the reservation price to the introduction price captures the consumer surplus that consumers derive from the introduction of the good.

It is not always clear when a good is new versus when it simply represents a repackaging of existing characteristics. Pakes (2003) notes, for example, that "when the laptop computer was introduced, its closest competitors were desktop machines. The desktops had more speed, storage capability and reliability than laptops and significantly lower prices. However, the significant reduction in size and weight in a laptop was highly valued by consumers. None of the indexes discussed here [referring to hedonic measures] could ever pick up the increase in utility that the laptop generated. To capture these effects, we need a more complete model of household utility." We need to know the consumer's reservation price for laptops, which was apparently

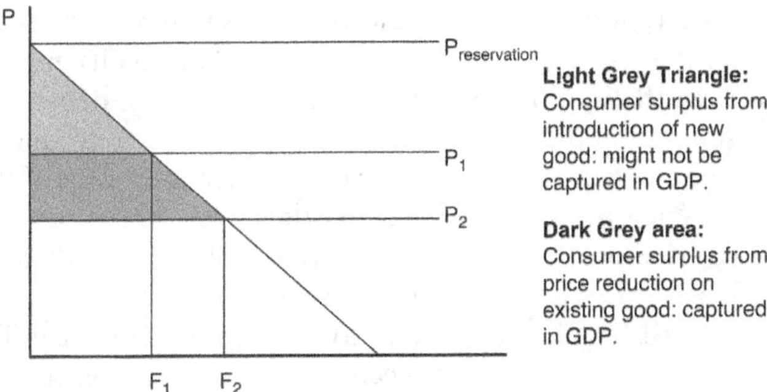

Fig. 1.10 Consumer surplus from new goods

higher than the price that would have been paid for a desktop with the same computing power.

In these cases, the hedonic method will appear feasible—because the characteristics might not appear new—but something about the improvement is introducing a characteristic that was not available before, and, as Triplett (2004) notes, "the arrival of a new characteristic cannot be evaluated satisfactorily with hedonic methods." One important case where this situation arises is when a technological limit prevents people from getting as much of a characteristic as they like, holding all else equal. This could be the case for computer chips that increase computing power without increasing the size of the chip, allowing for the production of laptops, smartphones, and smart watches, and many other areas where innovation is pushing the technological frontier. One important area is in medical advances, which are discussed in chapter 6 of this volume.

To sum up: The use of chained indexes means that, for goods and services with constant quality, it does not matter much whether you use an output price or an input, and, in any case, the current methodology is a very good approximation of both. When the set of characteristics of goods is fixed but goods and services improve over time because they contain more of certain characteristics, there is similarly no difference in the quality-adjusted price using either the cost method or the utility method. But when a new characteristic is introduced, either as a quality adjustment to an existing good or as an entirely new good, prevailing prices in the year before introduction will not yield the correct result for GDP, making a utility-based approach necessary.

1.5 How Does BLS Actually Adjust for Quality Changes?

The data required to adjust prices for every significant quality change are substantial and unlikely to be available to BLS, particularly in real time. BLS does not really tackle the issue of novel types of goods, such as the invention of the smartphone, or quality improvements that represent new types of characteristics. Instead, BLS tries to ensure that quality increases are not counted as inflation. In the cereal example above, say, BLS would want to make sure that the price increase stemming from the introduction of a larger cereal box is stripped out from the observed market price of the larger cereal box. If a new model replaces an existing model, BLS may adjust for the estimated price impact of the changes in characteristics if all the changes are quantifiable and compare the quality-adjusted prices.

Even though BLS makes no attempt to directly measure the utility value from new goods and newly introduced characteristics, the main method it uses to control for exit and entry of items in the pricing sample *does* sometimes capture consumer surplus from these innovations indirectly—

for example, when the introduction of a new product leads to declines in prices of incumbent products. Still, these implicit quality adjustments are, in many cases, insufficient. If the quality of most types of goods and services tends to improve over time—as seems likely with continued technological innovation—undermeasured quality change will be a common source of price index overestimation.[27] For details on current quality adjustment practices, see Coyle (chap. 4), and for a review of improvements in BLS practices over time, see Moulton (chap. 2).

1.6 Summary and Conclusion

Our goal in this chapter is to explore the basic economics surrounding the measurement of GDP. We have focused on whether GDP should be viewed as a measure of aggregate economic well-being. Our goal, of course, is to understand the extent to which productivity growth captures changes in living standards, but we have limited ourselves to discussing GDP, the numerator in productivity, not the denominator, which reflects hours of work and other inputs.

Our preliminary conclusions are as follows. First, from a theoretical perspective, one should not use GDP per se as a comprehensive measure of economic well-being. There are some important conceptual differences between GDP and aggregate economic well-being. Most notably, as a production-based measure, GDP captures investment (spending that does not immediately translate into higher welfare) in addition to consumption. However, it is not difficult to use data available in the national accounts to construct combined private and public consumption, which not only conceptually aligns better with economic well-being but is also well correlated with GDP over long periods of time, suggesting that changes in GDP, at least in principle, could be a fairly good measure of aggregate economic well-being over long periods of time. At higher frequencies, the growth rate of GDP is more volatile than that of our consumption measure, but that feature of GDP is useful to government officials responsible for stabilizing the economy in the face of business-cycle fluctuations, as they are focused on the degree to which the economy is using all of its productive resources.

That said, we believe that one conceptual difference—the exclusion of nonmarket activities that bear on economic well-being—merits more attention, particularly given the potential for changes in the importance of such activities over time to alter the degree to which GDP captures well-being.

We also flag a number of issues that warrant more attention when it comes to translating the conceptual ideal into GDP as measured. To start, the national accounts may mismeasure nominal GDP arising from the digital economy and the operation of multinationals corporations.

In addition, the deflators used to separate GDP into nominal and real may produce a biased measure of inflation. Our analysis of the theory behind deflators shows us that, by definition, a cost-of-living deflator is an index that measures changes in consumer surplus. Furthermore, except in some specific cases, there is little difference in practice between cost-of-living deflators and output price indexes. For goods and services that do not change in quality over time, current deflator methods already capture the change in consumer surplus from a price change. But for e-goods and services that change in quality and for new goods and services, current methods may not capture consumer surplus well. We believe that efforts to improve price measures so that they better capture consumer surplus would be useful.

Notes

1. Many of these papers conclude that measurement is at best a small part of the explanation for slower trend productivity growth (Byrne, Fernald, and Reinsdorf 2016, Syverson 2017, and Fernald et al. 2017), but a few argue that measurement has played a larger role (Varian 2016 and Hatzius 2017).

2. See www.bea.gov/newsreleases/national/gdp/gdpnewsrelease.htm.

3. Coyle (2014) has an excellent summary of the historical debate over this issue. Jorgenson (2018) also provides an extensive discussion of the difference between GDP and welfare. See Constanza et al. (2009), Wesselink et al. (2007), Kassenboehmer and Schmidt (2011), and Boyd (2007) for more on this topic and alternative measures of economic progress.

4. Piketty, Saez, and Zucman (2018) create distributional national accounts for the United States that shed light on how standards of living have evolved at different points in the income distribution. The Bureau of Economic Analysis (BEA) began publishing data on the distribution of personal income in 2020.

5. Corrado et al. (2017) argue that because well-being depends on both current and future consumption, including investment potentially makes GDP a better measure of well-being.

6. The BEA treated GNP (called gross national income in the System of National Accounts) as the primary measure of US economic activity for many decades but switched its focus in 1991 to conform with practices of statistical agencies in other countries.

7. For this exercise, we ignore the fact that consumption expenditure includes some durable goods, which yield consumption services (i.e., provide utility to the household) over time. Looking at only nondurables and services would not materially change our conclusion.

8. Importantly, while these types of trends might distort measured GDP growth, they will *not* generally distort measured growth in productivity (output per hour) because hours are undercounted or overcounted in the same way as GDP.

9. We end the graphs in this chapter in 2019 because of the huge swings in economic data during the pandemic.

10. See Coyle and Mitra-Kahn 2017, Nordhaus and Tobin 1972, and United Nations Human Development Program n.d. (https://hdr.undp.org/data-center/human-development-index#/indicies/HDI) for discussions of alternatives to GDP that might better capture welfare.

11. The statistical community is engaging in significant discussion of this particular issue and other implications of the "digitalization" of the economy. For example, the OECD has published numerous studies on recording and valuing data as an asset (e.g., Corrado et al. 2022, Lange et al. 2022, and Mitchell, Lesher, and Barberis 2022). The Advisory Expert Group for the System of National Accounts has proposed showing cost-based values of investment in data assets in the core national accounts and cost-based values of free services of digital platforms in satellite accounts.

12. See, for example, Nakamura, Samuels, and Soloveichik (2017).

13. See "Recording and Valuing 'Free' Products in an SNA Satellite Account" at https://unstats.un.org/unsd/nationalaccount/RAdocs/DZ4_Free_Digital_Products_Satellite_ENDORSED.pdf.

14. See https://www.cso.ie/en/interactivezone/statisticsexplained/nationalaccountsexplained/modifiedgni/.

15. Imports are estimated using customs data, not tax data, so it would be possible for a company to report numbers that are inconsistent with tax data (but a better representation of where the economic activity occurred). However, it seems unlikely that a company would do so.

16. The growth in MNE activity has coincided with growth in the United States of "factoryless goods producers" (FGPs), which develop the intellectual property, manage the production process, and market but contract out the physical production to manufacturers in other countries. Discussions of the MNE problem often cite the rise of FGPs as related. Although FGPs are often associated with the high-tech industry, Varian (2016) emphasizes that production is offshored in many sectors (for example, a US company may develop the pattern for a sweater or the design for a toy in this country and send it to a foreign affiliate to produce). Prior to 2013, a wide range of intangible capital, particularly intellectual capital, was excluded from most measures of GDP because spending on R&D was counted as an intermediate expense. Corrado, Hulten, and Sichel (2009) find that as much as $800 billion of intangible capital was excluded from US published data between 2003 and 2009. As a result, more than $3 trillion of business intangible capital stock was excluded, with significant consequences for measured economic growth and productivity. In 2013, the BEA began treating R&D as a fixed asset (part of investment) to address this issue (Moris et al. 2015). Chen et al. (2017) suggest using global value chains to decompose the value of a product into the value added at each stage of production to measure returns on intangible assets.

17. The Guvenen et al. methods would also miss the contribution of items developed domestically that are used in production but do not generate profits because they are not proprietary, such as open-source software.

18. In any case, the BEA uses a mix of PPIs and CPIs when deflating GDP. The differences between PPIs and CPIs mostly relate to what they are used to deflate, with PPIs used to deflate the revenues producers receive and CPIs used to deflate consumer spending. PPIs do not include sales taxes, for example, because producers do not receive them, but CPIs do, because consumers pay them. BEA uses CPIs to deflate most consumption, but not all. For example, spending on Medicare and Medicaid is included in personal consumption expenditures (PCE) but because it is not paid directly by consumers, it is not captured in the CPI. Medical expenditures in PCE are measured by the revenues received by medical providers and deflated by medical PPIs. For a detailed description of the particular deflators used to calculate real PCE, see https://www.bea.gov/national/xls/pce_deflators_faq_new_stub.xls.

19. That is, we think welfare depends on real purchasing power but typically do not quantify the relationship between real purchasing power and welfare.

20. That is, if people had enough income to purchase the period 2 bundle in period 1, they would be at least as well off as in period 2. With differences in prices, however, they might alter their consumption basket to be actually somewhat better off at this income. Thus, this measure is the maximum increase in income that would be needed to be as well off in period 2 as in period 1.

21. To be more technically precise, consider the indirect utility function $V(Y, P_a, P_b, \ldots)$ and let utility change from $V(Y_1, P_{a1}, P_{b1}, \ldots)$ in period 1 to $V(Y_2, P_{a2}, P_{b2}, \ldots)$ in period 2. The two possible cost-of-living indexes P_L and P_P adjust either initial or final income by enough to offset the effects of price changes, so they are, respectively, such that $V(Y_1 P_L, P_{a2}, P_{b2}, \ldots) = V(Y_1, P_{a1}, P_{b1}, \ldots)$ or $V[(Y_2/P_P), P_{a1}, P_{b1}, \ldots] = V(V_2, P_{a2}, P_{b2}, \ldots)$. Deflating the income change by a cost-of-living index gives a standard-of-living index, interpreted in this example as the change in real GDP. One theoretically correct standard-of-living index uses final prices to measure the welfare change and is $S_P = (Y_2/Y_1)/P_L$. The other uses initial prices and is $S_L = (Y_2/Y_1)/P_P$. The change in income at constant prices of the initial period that would yield the same utility change as the one that actually occurred is S_L, so $V(Y_1 S_L, P_{a1}, P_{b1}, \ldots) = V(Y_2, P_{a2}, P_{b2}, \ldots)$. The change in income at constant prices of the final period that would yield the actual utility change is S_P, so $V[(Y_2/S_P), P_{a2}, P_{b2}, \ldots] = V(Y_1, P_{a1}, P_{b1}, \ldots)$. In the special case where the standard-of-living index is independent of prices, the single measure of welfare change is directly proportional to real GDP.

22. Triplett (2004) argues that this package size adjustment is too simple because the relationship between volume and price is generally not linear—that is, bigger boxes usually sell at a lower price per unit. We ignore this issue for the purpose of creating a simple example that gives the basic intuition of quality adjustments.

23. This symmetry will not always occur. In particular, when goods have multiple characteristics instead of just one, the effect on price of a reduction in price and increase in quantity of just one characteristic may depend on the set of characteristics (i.e., the particular basket) being priced.

24. Of course, this is putting a functional form on the relationship between characteristics and prices. Plugging in characteristics that are very different in magnitude from the ones actually observed will likely be quite problematic. For example, a regression of house prices on square footage might not do a very good job predicting the cost of a 100 square foot house, or a 50,000 square foot house, if the houses actually observed in the data range from 1,000 to 7,000 square feet.

25. This is obviously the correct price from the consumer's perspective. From the producer's perspective, the correct price might be price at which they would have produced this new product last year, but that price might be infinity if the technology simply did not exist.

26. When a new good that is a combination of existing characteristics is introduced, the reservation price is equal to the price of the characteristics in the previous year, so this method works for any good.

27. Quality improvements enabled by technological progress are not the only factors affecting the accuracy of the main method used to handle sample exits and entrances. The method uses the subsample containing just continuing items to calculate the price index, but some sellers hold prices steady for continuing models and time price changes to coincide with new model introductions. When sellers are taking advantage of new model introductions to raise prices, the method understates inflation.

References

Aizcorbe, Ana. 2014. *A Practical Guide to Price Index and Hedonic Techniques*. Oxford University Press, Oxford Scholarship Online. http://www.oxfordscholarship.com/view/10.1093/acprof:oso/9780198702429.001.0001/acprof-9780198702429.

Bernanke, Ben S., and Peter Olson. 2017. "Are Americans Better Off Than They Were a Decade or Two Ago?" In *Brookings Big Ideas for America*, edited by Michael E. O'Hanlon. Washington, DC: Brookings Institution.

Boyd, James. 2007. "Nonmarket Benefits of Nature: What Should Be Counted in Green GDP?" *Ecological Economics* 61 (4): 716–23.

Bridgman, Benjamin. 2016. "Accounting for Household Production in the National Accounts: An Update, 1965–2014." *Survey of Current Business* (February).

Bridgman, Benjamin, Andrew Dugan, Mikhael Lal, Matthew Osborne, and Shaunda Villones. 2012. "Accounting for Household Production in the National Accounts, 1965–2010." *Survey of Current Business* (May).

Bruner, Jennifer, Dylan G. Rassier, and Kim J. Ruhl. 2018. "Multinational Profit Shifting and Measures throughout Economic Accounts." Conference on Research in Income and Wealth.

Brynjolfsson, Erik, Felix Eggers, and Avinash Gannamaneni. 2018. "Using Massive Online Choice Experiments to Measure Changes in Well-Being." *Proceedings of the National Academy of Sciences* 116 (15): 7250–5. https://doi.org/10.1073/pnas.1815663116.

Bureau of Foreign and Domestic Commerce, and Simon Kuznets. 1934. *National Income, 1929–1932*. Washington, DC: US Government Printing Office.

Bureau of Labor Statistics. 2011. "Producer Prices." In *BLS Handbook of Methods*, chap. 14. https://www.bls.gov/opub/hom/pdf/ppi-20111028.pdf.

Bureau of Labor Statistics. 2018. "The Consumer Price Index." In *BLS Handbook of Methods*, chap. 17. https://www.bls.gov/opub/hom/pdf/cpi-20180214.pdf.

Byrne, David M., John G. Fernald, and Marshall B. Reinsdorf. 2016. "Does the United States Have a Productivity Slowdown or a Measurement Problem?" *Brookings Papers on Economic Activity* (Spring).

Carson, Carol S. 1975. "The History of the United States National Income and Product Accounts: The Development of an Analytical Tool." *Review of Income and Wealth* (June): 153–81. http://www.roiw.org/1975/153.pdf.

Chen, Wen, Reitze Gouma, Bart Los, and Marcel P. Timmer. 2017. "Measuring the Returns to Intangibles: A Global Value Change Approach." World Intellectual Property Organization Economic Research Working Paper No. 36.

Constanza, Robert, Maureen Hart, Stephen Posner, and John Talberth. 2009. "Beyond GDP: The Need for New Measures of Progress." Pardee Papers, No. 4.

Corrado, Carol, Kevin Fox, Peter Goodridge, Jonathan Haskel, Cecilia Jona-Lasinio, Dan Sichel, and Stian Westlake. 2017. "Improving GDP: Demolishing, Repointing, or Extending?" Indigo Prize Winning Entry.

Corrado, Carol, Jonathan Haskel, Massimiliano Iommi, and Cecilia Jona-Lasinio. 2022. "Measuring Data as an Asset: Framework, Methods and Preliminary Estimates." OECD Economics Department Working Paper No. 1731, OECD Publishing, Paris. https://doi.org/10.1787/b840fb01-en.

Corrado, Carol, Charles Hulten, and Daniel Sichel. 2009. "Intangible Capital and U.S. Economic Growth." *Review of Income and Wealth* 55 (3).

Coyle, Diane. 2014. *GDP: A Brief but Affectionate History*. Princeton, NJ: Princeton University Press.

Coyle, Diane, and Benjamin Mitra-Kahn. 2017. "Making the Future Count." Indigo Prize Winning Entry.

Diewert, W. Erwin. 1976. "Exact and Superlative Index Numbers." *Journal of Econometrics, Elsevier* 4, no. 2 (May): 115–45.

Feldstein, Martin. 2017. "Underestimating the Real Growth of GDP, Personal Income, and Productivity." *Journal of Economic Perspectives* 31 (Spring): 145–64.

Fernald, John, Robert Hall, James Stock, and Mark Watson. 2017. "The Disappointing Recovery of Output after 2009" *Brookings Papers on Economic Activity* (Spring).

Griliches, Zvi. 1961. "Hedonic Price Indexes for Automobiles: An Econometric Analysis of Quality Change." In *The Price Statistics of the Federal Government*, report to the Office of Statistical Standard of the Price Statistics Review Committee of the National Bureau of Economic Research, 173–96. New York: National Bureau of Economic Research.

Guvenen, Fatih, Raymond J. Mataloni Jr., Dylan G. Rassier, and Kim J. Ruhl. 2022. "Offshore Profit Shifting and Aggregate Measurement: Balance of Payments, Foreign Investment, Productivity, and the Labor Share." *American Economic Review* 112 (6): 1848–84.

Hatzius, Jan. 2017. "Update on Productivity Measurement." *Goldman Sachs U.S. Daily*, August 15.

Hines Jr., James R. 2005. "Do Tax Havens Flourish?" In *Tax Policy and the Economy*, edited by James M. Poterba, 19:65–99. Cambridge, MA: MIT Press.

Jenniges, Derrick, Raymond J. Mataloni Jr., Sarah Strutzman, and Yiran Xin. 2018. "Strategic Movement of Intellectual Property within U.S. Multinational Enterprise." Conference on Research in Income and Wealth.

Jones, Charles I., and Peter J. Klenow. 2016. "Beyond GDP? Welfare across Countries and Time." *American Economic Review* 106 (9): 2426–57.

Jorgenson, Dale. 2018. "Production and Welfare: Progress in Economic Measurement." *Journal of Economic Literature* 56(3): 867–919.

Kassenboehmer, Sonja C., and Christoph M. Schmidt. 2011. "Beyond GDP and Back: What Is the Value-Added by Additional Components of Welfare Measurement?" IZA Institute of Labor Economics Discussion Paper, No. 5453.

Krueger, Alan. 2008. "Comment on 'Economic Growth and Well-Being: Reassessing the Easterlin Paradox' by Stevenson and Wolfers." *Brookings Papers on Economic Activity* (Spring).

Landefeld, Steven J. 2000. "GDP: One of the Great Inventions of the 20th Century." *Survey of Current Business* (January).

Lange, Simon, John Mitchell, Vincenzo Spiezia, and Jorrit Zwijnenburg. 2022. "Measuring the Value of Data and Data Flows." OECD Digital Economy Papers No. 345, OECD Publishing, Paris. https://doi.org/10.1787/923230a6-en.

Lipsey, Robert E. 2009. "Measuring International Trade in Services." In *International Trade in Services and Intangibles in the Era of Globalization*, NBER chapters, 27–70. National Bureau of Economic Research.

Mitchell, John, Molly Lesher, and Marion Barberis. 2022. "Going Digital Toolkit Note: Measuring the Economic Value of Data." https://one.oecd.org/document/DSTI/CDEP/GD(2021)2/FINAL/en/pdf.

Moris, Francisco, John Jankowski, Mark Boroush, Marissa Crawford, and Jennifer Lee. 2015. "R&D Recognized as Investment in U.S. GDP Statistics: GDP Increase Slightly Lowers R&D-to-GDP Ratio." InfoBrief NCSES, March 30, 2015, NSF 15–315. https://www.nsf.gov/statistics/2015/nsf15315/.

Moulton, Brent. 2017. "The Measurement of Output, Prices, and Productivity: What's Changed Since the Boskin Commission." Manuscript (November).

Moulton, Brent, and van de Ven, Peter. 2018. "Addressing Changes of Globalization in National Accounts." Conference on Research in Income and Wealth.

Nakamura, Leonard, Jon Samuels, and Rachel Soloveichik. 2017. "Measuring the 'Free' Digital Economy with the GDP and Productivity Accounts." Federal Reserve Bank of Philadelphia Working Paper No. 17–37.

Nordhaus, W. D., and Tobin, J. 1972. "Is Economic Growth Obsolete." Economic Growth, Fiftieth Anniversary Colloquium, V, National Bureau of Economic Research, New York.

Pakes, Ariel. 2003. "A Reconsideration of Hedonic Price Indexes with an Application to PC's." *American Economic Review* 93 (5): 1578–96.

Piketty, Thomas, Emmanuel Saez, and Gabriel Zucman. 2018. "Distributional National Accounts: Methods and Estimates for the United States." *Quarterly Journal of Economics* 133, no. 2 (May): 553–609. https://doi.org/10.1093/qje/qjx043.

Rosen, Sherwin. 1974. "Hedonic Prices and Implicit Markets: Product Differentiation in Pure Competition." *Journal of Political Economy* 82, no. 1 (January-February): 34–55.

Sack, Daniel W., Betsey Stevenson, and Justin Wolfers. 2012. "The New Stylized Facts about Income and Subjective Well-Being." *Emotion* 12 (6): 1181–7. http://users.nber.org/~jwolfers/papers/NewStylizedFacts(Emotion).pdf.

Stevenson, Betsey, and Justin Wolfers. 2008. "Economic Growth and Subjective Well-Being: Reassessing the Easterlin Paradox." *Brookings Papers on Economic Activity* (Spring).

Stiglitz, Joseph E., Amartya Sen, and Jean-Paul Fitoussi. 2009. *Report of the Commission on the Measurement of Economic Performance and Social Progress*.

Syverson, Chad. 2017. "Challenges to Mismeasurement Explanations for the U.S. Productivity Slowdown." *Journal of Economic Perspectives* 31 (2): 165–86. 10.1257/jep.31.2.165. https://www.aeaweb.org/articles?.

Tørsløv, Thomas, Ludvig S. Wier, and Gabriel Zucman. 2022. "The Missing Profits of Nations." *Review of Economic Studies*, rdac049. https://doi.org/10.1093/restud/rdac049.

Triplett, Jack E. 1982. "Concepts of Quality in Input and Output Price Measures: A Resolution of the User-Value Resource-Cost Debate." In *The U.S. National Income and Product Accounts: Selected Topics*, edited by Murray F. Foss. Chicago: University of Chicago Press.

Triplett, Jack E. 2004. "Handbook on Hedonic Indexes and Quality Adjustments in Price Indexes: Special Application to Information Technology Products." Organization for Economic Co-operation and Development, STI Working Paper 2004/9.

United Nations Statistical Commission. 2009. *System of National Accounts 2008*. https://unstats.un.org/unsd/nationalaccount/docs/SNA2008.pdf.

United States Committee on Homeland Security and Government Affairs. 2012. Offshore Profit Shifting and the U.S. Tax Code—Part 1 (Microsoft and Hewlett Packard, Hearings, September 20, 2012. 112th Congress, 2nd session. Washington: US Government Publishing Office. https://www.gpo.gov/fdsys/pkg/CHRG-112shrg76071/pdf/CHRG-112shrg76071.pdf.

United States Committee on Homeland Security and Government Affairs. 2013. Offshore Profit Shifting and the U.S. Tax Code—Part 2 (Apple). Hearings, May 21, 2013. 113th Congress, 1st session. Washington: US Government Publishing Office. https://www.gpo.gov/fdsys/pkg/CHRG-113shrg81657/pdf/CHRG-113shrg81657.pdf.

Varian, Hal. 2016. "A Microeconomist Looks at Productivity: A View from the Valley." Slides prepared for the Brookings Hutchins Center Conference on Slow Growth in Productivity: Causes, Consequences, and Policies, September.

Wesselink, Bart, Jan Bakkes, Aaron Best, Friedrich Hinterberger, and Patrick ten Brink. 2007. "Measurement Beyond GDP: Measuring Progress, True Wealth, and the Well-Being of Nations." International Conference, November 19–20, Brussels.

Willig, Robert. 1976. "Consumer Surplus Without Apology." *American Economic Review* 66 (4).

Wolfers, Justin. 2003. "Is Business Cycle Volatility Costly? Evidence From Surveys of Subjective Wellbeing." *International Finance* 6 (1): 1–26. http://users.nber.org/~jwolfers/papers/Happiness.pdf.

2 The Measurement of Output, Prices, and Productivity
What's Changed Since the Boskin Commission

Brent R. Moulton

2.1 Introduction

In a dynamic economy, the national statistical system faces a perennial challenge in accounting for the effects of innovation on new products and quality changes. Despite efforts by US statistical agencies to stay abreast of these changes, many economists believe that mismeasurement has led to long-term understatement of changes in living standards and productivity. For example, Feldstein (2017) writes that official gross domestic product (GDP) statistics provide "at best a lower bound on the true real growth rate with no indication of the size of the underestimation." Furthermore, since 2004, and especially since 2010, official statistics indicate that productivity growth has substantially slowed, raising concerns about prospects for long-run growth in living standards (Baily and Montalbano 2016). This productivity slowdown has brought renewed attention to bias in the statistics that feed into the productivity calculations. While Syverson (2017) and Byrne, Fernald, and Reinsdorf (2016) conclude that mismeasurement explains little of the prepandemic slowdown, users of economic data continue to be troubled by persistent biases and the challenges of accurately measuring changes in productivity and living standards.

This chapter endeavors to shed some light on these issues by focusing on efforts made by US statistical agencies—especially the Bureau of Labor Statistics (BLS) and the Bureau of Economic Analysis (BEA)—to improve

Brent R. Moulton is formerly of the Bureau of Economic Analysis.

The author appreciates the helpful comments received from Karen Dynan, Louise Sheiner, David Wessel, Katharine Abraham, David Byrne, Abe Dunn, Matt Russell, David Friedman, Bill Thompson, Jeffrey Hill, Claudia Sahm, Greg Ip, Matthew Shapiro, Marshall Reinsdorf, Carol Corrado, Vivien Lee, Susan Kellam, and other participants at the authors' conference hosted by the Brookings Institution's Hutchins Center on Fiscal and Monetary Policy.

the price and volume statistics used in calculating real GDP and productivity measures. I use as my starting point the *Final Report of the Advisory Commission to Study the Consumer Price Index*, commonly known as the Boskin Commission (Boskin et al. 1996), which kicked off major efforts to improve core economic statistics. I document how official measurement methods have changed and improved since 1996. I conclude that the overall bias of the consumer price index (CPI) has fallen from about 1.1 percent in 1996 to about 0.8 percent today. Because the CPI and other price indexes are used as deflators in the estimation of productivity, improvements in the CPI and the producer price index (PPI) have fed directly into reducing bias in productivity statistics. Despite the continuing challenges in economic measurement, I see no evidence that overall bias has worsened since 1996. I catalog changes in methodology that have affected real output or prices since January 1997. I also offer three recommendations on ways to renew progress on reducing or eliminating bias in total factor productivity (TFP), GDP growth, and related price indexes.

US statistical agencies made many important changes following the Boskin Commission recommendations, some of which were in the works before the commission report. In particular, the BLS overhauled the CPI, adopting a better method for estimating lower-level price indexes and improving sampling procedures while expanding the use of hedonic methods for quality adjustment. The PPI greatly expanded its coverage of services, allowing for improved analyses of industries and full coverage of major industries for TFP analysis. GDP statistics were upgraded with new coverage of investment in intangible intellectual property and improved measurement of hard-to-measure categories such as financial services.

The most critical issues in productivity measurement relate to measurement of price change. Real output—the numerator in the productivity calculation—is generally not observed directly. Instead, price indexes are used to determine how much of the change in the sales of a particular good or service is due to price change and how much is due to change in real output—that is, the quantity or quality of that good or service. For this method to work, the price index needs to hold quality constant, which can be very difficult to do. How much of the increase in spending on health care, for instance, reflects better quality as opposed to higher prices for the same services? Unmeasured improvements in quality can have significant impacts on long-term trends in measured productivity.

This chapter begins with background on the Boskin Commission. Section 2.3 provides an overview of the methodologies used in calculating TFP. Section 2.4 discusses changes in CPI methods, and section 2.5 covers other major price programs—the PPI, export price index, and import price index. Section 2.6 discusses changes made to the scope of output covered by the private nonfarm business sector.[1] It also discusses the expansion of GDP accounts to include intellectual property products such as computer software, research and development, and entertainment, literary, and artistic originals. Section 2.7 discusses changes in economic environment, such as the relative growth of services and diminution of goods production, and the role of offshoring and globalization. Section 2.8 concludes and offers recommendations for further progress in economic measurement.

2.2 Background: The Boskin Commission

The US Senate appointed the Boskin Commission (chaired by Michael Boskin of Stanford University) in 1995 to study possible bias in computation of the CPI. Its final report, released in December 1996, estimated that relative to a true cost-of-living index,[2] the CPI had an upward bias of 1.1 percentage points per year, with a plausible range of 0.8 to 1.6 percentage points (see table 2.1).

The Boskin Commission focused specifically on the CPI and the effects on the federal budget of its programmatic uses, such as for cost-of-living adjustments for Social Security and other benefit programs and for escalation of income tax brackets. But other national statistics, such as GDP and productivity, use CPI component indexes for deflation, and many types of CPI bias carry over to statistics deflated with other price indexes. Because similar methodologies are used in the estimation of other price statistics, such as the BLS producer, export, and import price indexes, some of the same biases affect those indexes as well.

The commission considered four underlying sources of CPI bias: upper-level substitution bias (the bias from using a fixed-weight Laspeyres formula[3] that does not allow for substitution); lower-level substitution bias (bias in the formula used to aggregate the price changes of items within an expenditure category); new products/quality change bias (bias due to inadequate quality adjustment for improved products or the tardy introduction of new

Table 2.1 **Boskin Commission (1996) estimates of CPI biases**
Percentage points per year

Sources of Bias	Estimate
Upper-level substitution	0.15
Lower-level substitution	0.25
New products/quality change	0.60
New outlets	0.10
Total	**1.10**
Plausible range	(0.80–1.60)

Source: Boskin et al. (1996), 44.

products); and new outlet bias (failure to capture lower prices consumers receive when new, lower-cost retail outlets enter a market).

The BLS immediately took important steps to ameliorate several of these biases (Abraham, Greenlees, and Moulton 1998), including adopting in January 1999 the geometric mean formula for aggregating individual prices to form elementary-level price indexes. This step largely eliminated lower-level substitution bias (Dalton, Greenless, and Stewart 1998). Section 2.4 describes the other steps.

In 1999, the US General Accounting Office (2000) asked four of the five members of the Boskin Commission to provide updated estimates of the remaining CPI bias. The estimates ranged from 0.73 to 0.90 percentage point per year.[4]

The National Research Council (2002) presented a report by a multidisciplinary panel of 13 experts, chaired by Charles L. Schultze, which considered the conceptual framework and measurement basis for the CPI. The panel did not attempt to provide an estimate of bias but rather focused on providing consensus recommendations for the BLS to utilize in subsequent work to improve the CPI. In comparison with the Boskin Commission, the Schultze Panel took a more nuanced and rigorous approach to basic issues, such as whether the basis for the CPI should be a cost-of-living index. A true cost-of-living index would measure change in the cost of obtaining a fixed level of economic well-being, or utility.

The panel concluded that the CPI should not be based on an unconditional cost-of-living index but rather on a conditional cost-of-living index restricted to private goods and services and holding environmental background factors constant. The Schultze Panel also presented detailed recommendations for an experimental medical care price index based on the cost of treating various diagnoses.

Lebow and Rudd (2003) provided an extensive review of the research underlying CPI bias and offered new analysis that suggested that upper-level substitution bias had increased since the Boskin Commission. They added an analysis of systematic biases in weights for the CPI, which are derived from the consumer expenditure survey, concluding that weighting bias contributed another 0.1 percentage point to an upward CPI bias. Lebow and Rudd's estimate of CPI bias was about 0.9 percentage point per year.

2.3 Overview of the Measurement Methods Used for Output, Prices, and Productivity

Productivity measures the efficiency of economic production—how units of input, such as labor and capital, are converted into units of output. Over prolonged periods, growth in productivity is the main source of improvement in a population's standard of living, as represented by growth in real GDP or real consumption per capita.

2.3.1 Labor and Total Factor Productivity Concepts and Methods

The BLS has conducted studies of labor productivity—output per hour worked—in individual industries since 1898 and has regularly published labor productivity for major sectors since 1959 (see Bureau of Labor Statistics 2008, Bureau of Labor Statistics n.d.). The rate of growth in labor productivity is equal to the rate of growth in output minus the rate of growth in labor hours.

Labor productivity contrasts with total factor productivity (TFP), which BLS has published on a regular basis since 1983 (see Dean and Harper 2001).[5] Rather than the denominator accounting for a single input (labor), it accounts for a *bundle* of inputs—typically both labor and capital. Capital-labor TFP in year t is calculated as the ratio of a quantity index of output to a quantity index of combined labor and capital input.

Both labor productivity and TFP growth accelerated from 1995 through 2004 and decelerated from 2004 to 2019, though the acceleration and deceleration were more pronounced for labor productivity than for TFP (table 2.2).[6]

This chapter focuses on BLS's featured measure of TFP for the private nonfarm business sector.[7] The BLS major sector TFP measure is produced annually and compares growth in sector output to combined effects of growth in labor and capital inputs. The sector output—the numerator of the TFP calculation—is the same as BEA's value added of the nonfarm business sector, except that the output of government enterprises (public-sector enterprises primarily engaged in producing output for sale) is omitted because of difficulties in measuring the impact of subsidies for those enterprises. The denominator is an index of *primary* inputs—that is, labor and capital services.[8]

Indexes of real (inflation-adjusted) outputs and inputs are constructed by deflating revenues or expenditures by a price index. Thus, the methodologies used for constructing price indexes play a critical role in measuring real output and productivity. I next turn to the methodologies of major BLS price index programs that provide most of the GDP deflators.

Table 2.2 **Labor productivity and total factor productivity, US private nonfarm business**

Average annual rates of change over selected periods

Productivity Measure	1995–2004	2004–2019
Labor productivity	3.1%	1.4%
Total factor productivity	1.5%	0.5%

Source: Bureau of Labor Statistics (https://www.bls.gov/). Labor productivity data released December 7, 2022; total factor productivity data released November 18, 2022.

2.3.2 Consumer Price Index Methods

The Bureau of Labor Statistics (2018) describes the methods used to estimate the CPI; additional information on how quality change and new goods are treated is provided by Groshen et al. (2017) and Coyle (chap. 4 of this book). This section briefly describes CPI sample selection, estimation and weighting methods, and quality adjustment procedures.

The CPI produces price indexes for consumer spending by two target populations: all urban consumers (the "CPI-U" population) and urban wage earners and clerical workers (the "CPI-W" population). The CPI-U population covers about 93 percent of the US population—all civilian, noninstitutional population living in US urban core-based statistical areas (Paben, Johnson, and Schilp 2016). The CPI-W population represents only about 28 percent of the total US population and is, importantly, used for annual cost-of-living adjustments to benefits for Social Security and Supplemental Security Income. The CPI-U components are used for the deflation of components of real GDP, so it is the index that matters for measurement of TFP.

CPI samples are culled from samples of urban areas, retail or services outlets, and items sold at outlets. The samples of outlets are based on the consumer expenditure survey, which provides frame data on the retail outlets from which households purchase goods and services. Based on responses to this survey, a sample of outlets is selected, with about 27,000 outlets visited each month and with prices collected for about 83,000 individual goods and services. Additionally, a housing survey collects rents and rental equivalence for a sample of 43,000 units.

The observations in these samples are organized into about 8,018 *elementary* cells, each representing one of 211 item categories times 38 areas, and an *elementary index* is calculated for each cell to serve as the first step in CPI aggregation. Samples of nonhousing outlets and items in each elementary cell are refreshed over a four-year cycle in a continuous rotation scheme, a process also known as *sample rotation*.[9] Housing samples are rotated at six-year intervals. When samples are rotated, the component index estimated from the new sample of items and outlets is linked to the index based on the previous sample. The selection of outlets and items within each elementary cell is based on probability proportional to expenditure to ensure a representative sample.

Once the sample has been selected, a computer-assisted data collection system provides electronic checklists of item specifications to ensure that the data collector can identify the same item on each subsequent data collection from the outlet. Prices are collected either monthly or bimonthly depending on the commodity category and the urban area size. Each month, data collection is scheduled for one of three pricing periods that together cover the entire month. New goods can enter the sample either during regular four-year sample updates or when an item in an existing sample is no longer available and needs to be replaced. That is, with rare exceptions, BLS sampling methods do not actively search out new goods as they are introduced to the market, though BLS occasionally initiates an outlet sample in less than four years to get new products into the sample more quickly.

According to Groshen et al. (2017), during the 12 months ending November 2014, CPI data collectors could reprice specified commodities and services sample items 73 percent of the time. Of the remaining 27 percent of items scheduled for repricing, 22 percent reflected temporarily unavailable items, such those only available in certain seasons. The other 5 percent were items that permanently disappeared, triggering the selection of a replacement and quality adjustment procedure.

When a sample item becomes permanently unavailable, the CPI data collector tries to find a similar item at the same outlet to take its place. If the characteristics of the replacement item are very similar to those of the disappearing item, the two are deemed directly comparable, and the price of the replacement item is simply used in the price change estimation as if it were the original item; in 2014, these cases represented three-fifths of CPI item replacements. The remaining two-fifths of replacements were handled using either direct quality adjustment or imputation. Direct quality adjustments come from hedonic regressions, which allow BLS commodity analysts to include an estimate of the value for difference in quality (as summarized by the coefficients of commodity characteristics from a regression of price on characteristics), or from manufacturers' data on the cost of producing the higher quality item. When information is not available for direct quality adjustment, one of two imputation methods is used to estimate the change in relative price of the item that has disappeared from the sample.[10] The following month, the price change of the new item is linked into the index sample.

Although economists may assume that the quality bias of traditional price indexes is always upward, biases can be upward or downward; their direction and magnitude must be established empirically. For the imputation method of implicit quality adjustment, OECD (2006, 27) describes the effects of imputation as "one of the most misunderstood aspects of price index numbers." Imputation assumes that quality-adjusted price change can be inferred from related items whose quality did not change and imputes quality-adjusted price change from the price changes of those related items. But sellers often time price changes (either increases or decreases) to coincide with quality changes. This suggests that imputed price changes—which are based on items not experiencing any quality change—may be smaller in absolute magnitude than price changes of items whose quality is changing. If the prices for that category are generally decreasing (as in the case of computers and electronic goods), the imputed price change is likely to understate the appropriate quality-adjusted price decline. Conversely, if prices in the category are generally increasing (as for some services), the imputed price change is likely to understate the appropriate quality-adjusted price increase.

In other words, the imputation method of adjusting for quality change is biased in the direction of showing little or no change in prices, which can be either upward or downward depending on the direction of price change for the item category.

In contrast, quality adjustments based on production cost, which are more commonly used for the PPI than for the CPI, are based on manufacturers' estimates of how much it costs to change production conditions to build the item with its new characteristics. Because manufacturers may find it easier to report all cost changes rather than just those associated with the quality change, adjustments using this method may overstate the value of quality changes and thus understate the pure price change (OECD 2006, 35).

It should be emphasized that, with rare exceptions, direct quality adjustments are only applied when an item disappears from the sample and is replaced. While this timing allows BLS to make many quality adjustments in routine model replacements, such as the replacement of an old car or television model by a newer model, introductions of entirely new products often do not immediately lead to the disappearance of older items. Consequently, new products frequently enter the CPI as part of sample rotations. For example, when smartphones were first introduced to the market, basic cell phones remained available for several years (and, indeed, are still available, albeit with a quite small market share). Thus, smartphones probably entered the CPI sample primarily through sample rotation rather than item replacement, since a disappearing basic cell phone would have initially been replaced in the sample by a similar basic cell phone rather than by a smartphone. Similarly, the introduction of ride-sharing services such as Uber and Lyft did not cause traditional taxi services to disappear; these services probably entered the CPI sample through sample rotation rather than item replacement.

Likewise, new outlets are only introduced through sample rotation. As such, if new outlets provide, on average, lower prices than old outlets for the same goods, these lower prices are never reflected in the CPI and are instead treated as entirely due to quality differences. This is the source of the outlet bias studied by Reinsdorf (1993) and included in the Boskin Commission's CPI bias estimates. Hausman and Leibtag (2009), using scanner data on household purchases of food, found that supercenters, mass merchandisers, and club stores—a category of outlet that grew rapidly during the 1980s and 1990s and reached 25 percent of food expenditures by 2003—charged prices that were about 27 percent lower than traditional supermarkets. They found that a CPI for food that captures the effects of outlet substitution rose 0.32 percentage point per year more slowly—a similar estimate to Reinsdorf's. BLS researchers Greenlees and McClelland (2011), however, found evidence suggesting that much of the price difference between new and old outlets was attributable to quality differences.

In the CPI, estimation and aggregation of individual prices into an overall index take place at two levels. At the first, or lower, level, prices for categories of items and urban areas ("strata") are aggregated without availability of household expenditure data for weighting. From 1978 through 1998, BLS attempted to estimate a modified Laspeyres formula for these elementary aggregates, but because the weighting information assumed by the estimator was not available in practice, resulting estimates were shown to have systematic upward bias—see research by Reinsdorf (1998), Moulton (1993), and Reinsdorf and Moulton (1996).[11] Since 1999, BLS has instead primarily used the geometric mean formula, which, as discussed below, avoids this bias. Subsequently, the geometric mean formula was recommended by the international CPI manual (ILO et al. 2004) and is now used by statistical agencies throughout the world.

For the upper level of aggregation—that is, combining the elementary indexes for item-area strata to calculate higher-level aggregates up to the all-items CPI-U and CPI-W—BLS continues to use a fixed-weight Laspeyres (or modified Laspeyres) formula. The upper-level substitution bias tends to be larger when the weights are older. Beginning in 2002, BLS was able to reduce this bias by updating the weights at two-year intervals, in contrast to the ten-year intervals it previously used. And in 2023, BLS began to update weights annually.[12]

BLS also produces the Chained CPI for All Urban Consumers (C-CPI-U), which uses chain weighting and the superlative Törnqvist formula.[13] With the enactment of the Tax Cuts and Jobs Act of 2017, the chained CPI is now used to adjust income tax brackets for inflation. From December 2000 through December 2019, the average annual growth rate of the chained CPI was 0.26 percentage point lower than that of the featured CPI-U, suggesting that upper-level substitution bias was about a quarter percentage point per year. Because TFP statistics are based on GDP data that BEA constructs using chained indexes and the Fisher formula, these statistics are generally not affected by the headline CPI's upper-level substitution bias.

To summarize, CPIs' lower-level substitution bias, which would have caused deflators used in constructing TFP estimates to be too high, has been largely eliminated. But to the extent that BLS methods do not fully adjust for quality changes, new goods, or new outlets, those CPI biases are reflected in GDP and TFP statistics. Finally, although the chained CPI is not used to deflate GDP, it provides a measure of consumer inflation that avoids upper-level substitution bias.

2.3.4 Producer, Export, and Import Price Index Methods

Bureau of Labor Statistics (2015) describes the methods used to estimate the PPIs, a family of indexes that measure changes over time in prices received by domestic producers of goods and services. The PPI measures prices from the perspective of the producer, which means it excludes sales and excise taxes and distribution costs that may be included in the CPI. The

PPI also typically captures goods at an earlier stage in the process of production and distribution than the CPI; for example, the PPI measures prices received by manufacturers of a good rather than prices paid by consumers at a retail store.[14] The PPI includes intermediate goods and services used as inputs in production, which are not included in the CPI, and excludes imported goods and services.

PPIs are available for nearly all goods-producing sectors of the US economy and cover about 72 percent of the service sector's output. Expansion in coverage of the service sector has been one of the PPI program's major accomplishments over the last 30 years. Prior to the mid-1990s, the PPI was not close to covering most service industries.[15] While the coverage of services follows the same general strategy for price measurement as that for goods—that is, representative samples of services were selected, described in detail, and are repriced each month—at times, special methods have had to be employed. For example, in some cases, respondents are asked to report a price for a standardized service that may or may not have been provided during the reporting period. With each new services industry, BLS has conducted research to identify and define the industry's output and to identify quality characteristics that can be used to derive a constant-quality price index.[16]

The PPI collects about 88,000 price quotations each month for products from about 21,000 establishments. BLS emphasizes that businesses need to report transaction prices rather than list prices and include all discounts, premiums, rebates, and allowances. Less than 20 percent of collected prices are based on list prices, according to BLS estimates.

Because the same product is priced each month, adjustments are needed when a product is replaced by an updated version or when a product's characteristics change. For goods that undergo periodic model changes, BLS applies an explicit quality adjustment usually based on the costs that companies report they incur relating to the quality change. If, however, the respondent is unable to provide this information, BLS assumes that the difference in price between the old item and the new one is entirely due to differences in quality. For a few high-tech industries, the PPI uses quality adjustments based on hedonic regressions, which BLS has been actively trying to expand where possible.[17]

PPI indexes are calculated with a modified Laspeyres formula and use net output values of shipments for goods and revenue data for services as weights. Weights are based on data from the five-year economic censuses and are typically incorporated with a lag of four to five years after the census year.

Bureau of Labor Statistics (1997b) describes the methods used to estimate export and import price indexes. Import and export prices cover nearly all merchandise trade categories and selected categories of international services. Import and export price indexes are aggregated using the Laspeyres formula with weights based on trade value figures from the Census Bureau. The sample of US exporters is derived from shippers' export declarations, and the sample of importers is derived from entry documents. Respondents are asked to provide prices for actual transactions, though estimated or list prices may be accepted when transaction prices are not available. The index includes prices associated with intracompany transfers regardless of whether the prices are market based.

Import and export price indexes are matched-model indexes; the same items are repriced each month. If there is a substantive change in an item, the quality difference is generally handled either by direct quality adjustment using information from respondents (or, in the case of computers, from the PPI hedonic model) or by linking, which essentially assumes that the difference in price between the old item and the new one reflects quality differences. The international price program now uses some quality adjustments based on hedonic methods, but information about characteristics is frequently unavailable, making the hedonic approach infeasible. Kim and Reinsdorf (2015) studied the feasibility of expanded use of hedonic regressions for quality adjustment of import prices.

2.4 Improvements to the Consumer Price Index

This section discusses some of the major changes made to the CPI since publication of the 1996 *Final Report* of the Boskin Commission. Table B2.1 in appendix 2B, which is available online,[18] provides a comprehensive list of major changes in methodology that could affect the growth of the CPI or its components (and thus, indirectly, may affect real GDP and measured TFP). Not all methodological improvements are cataloged in the table. For example, it does not include methodologies that affect the timing of measured price change but not the long-term trend, such as seasonal adjustment. It also does not catalog methodological changes that focus on topics such as geographic sampling (because this chapter's focus is on the national CPI) or data processing efficiencies.

Leading up to and immediately after release of the Boskin Commission report, BLS greatly expanded its work on CPI bias.[19] By January 1995, BLS had implemented steps to reduce the most significant biases associated with the lower-level substitution problem. But it had not yet decided whether to drop the old estimator, which was based on a modified Laspeyres concept, and move to the geometric formula suggested by Dalén (1992) and Moulton (1993). By the time of the release of the Boskin Commission's *Final Report*, BLS had conducted additional research on the issue (e.g., Reinsdorf and Moulton 1996; Reinsdorf 1998) and Diewert (1995) had recommended the geometric index formula, based on index number theory. Nevertheless, BLS senior management remained concerned that making such a fundamental change to the framework for the CPI would need a stronger basis of theoretical and empirical support.

In the follow-up to the Boskin Commission's clear recommendation that "BLS should move to geometric means at the elementary aggregates level," BLS was under pressure to reach a decision. In April 1998, Commissioner Katharine Abraham announced that for most items, the CPI would adopt, effective January 1999, the geometric mean formula for the first stage of aggregating prices—the lowest, or elementary, level of aggregation. Dalton, Greenlees, and Stewart (1998) provided an explanation of BLS's decision and a description of how it would be implemented. Evidence that consumers regularly substitute or shift their spending within elementary categories—for example, increasing spending on a particular brand of ice cream when it goes on sale—led to the adoption. As prices change, quantities may move in a way that keeps expenditure shares constant if items in the index are close substitutes. This kind of substitution behavior makes the theoretical cost-of-living index equal to a (weighted) geometric mean index. In contrast, when items in the index basket are not substitutable at all, the theoretical cost-of-living index is a Laspeyres or fixed-basket index. As items in the same elementary category are close substitutes in most cases, the geometric mean index more accurately reflects consumer spending.[20] However, a few item categories were excluded from the switch to the geometric mean index because of limited opportunities for item substitution within those categories.

The adoption of the geometric mean on the all-items CPI reduced its growth by about 0.2 percentage point per year; I estimate that the effect on private nonfarm business output was to increase growth by about 0.15 percentage point per year. (table B2.1, online, provides a comprehensive list of improvements made to the CPI since 1997.)

An important associated aspect of this change is that BLS began producing a CPI research series that backcasts the various methodological improvements and corrections, providing a time series dating back to 1978 that accounts for methodological changes (Stewart and Reed 1999). Using this series, now known as the CPI Retroactive Series (R-CPI-U-RS), BEA carried changes back to 1978 in GDP statistics, thereby reducing bias over an extended period.[21]

BLS undertook additional actions to address quality adjustment and other biases identified by the Boskin Commission. One of the first changes was to use a hedonic regression model to quality adjust personal computers purchased by households. Since the BLS PPI program had already developed hedonic regressions for quality adjusting the PPI for computers, the CPI was initially able to use the coefficients from those regressions to adjust computer prices for quality change. The estimated effect of adopting this method was large—lowering price changes for the CPI for computers by about 6.5 percentage points per year. Additional research was soon underway on hedonic quality adjustments for other components.

Hedonic quality adjustments for televisions were adopted in 1999, and adjustments for video and audio equipment; major appliances such as refrigerators, washing machines, and dryers; and college textbooks soon followed. Interestingly, after the initial substantial impact of hedonic quality adjustment on computers, the measured impact on most other items was relatively small and sometimes actually led to higher measured rates of inflation.

As the Boskin Commission carried out its mandate, the CPI undertook its once-a-decade major revision, which had been planned before CPI bias became the center of attention. Consequently, major elements of the CPI revision were statistical improvements outside the scope of the Boskin Commission's recommendations, such as revisions to item classification structure, the survey and process used for selecting outlets, and housing sample. Some of these improvements clearly helped address the biases discussed by the Boskin Commission—for example, the revamped item structure helped BLS data collectors identify and classify newer goods and services like personal computers and cellular telephone services. But it was not possible to quantify the impact of most of these statistical improvements on overall CPI bias.

Improvements to CPI methods appear to have slowed during the decade from about 2005 to 2015. In recent years, improvements have picked up, with several notable improvements in the last few years. For example, from 2017 to 2019, hedonic quality adjustments were introduced in the price indexes for telecommunications services and smartphone equipment. Improvements were also made to the weighting used for the physicians' services and health insurance indexes. The BLS recently introduced innovative uses of alternative big data sources to greatly improve the accuracy of components such as gasoline and new motor vehicles (see Bieler et al. 2019 and Williams and Sager 2019), and National Academies of Sciences, Engineering, and Medicine (2022) recommends further uses of alternative data.[22] These methods are aimed more at improving representativeness and accuracy through use of larger sample sizes. They avoid outlet substitution bias by pooling data across outlets within a geographical area. The motor vehicle index also adjusts for regular patterns of price change between model years (the regular pattern of a model entering at a higher price, which then declines until it is replaced by the next model year). It uses a Törnqvist index, allowing it to better capture substitution among vehicle types.

2.5 Changes to Other Major Price Indexes

This section discusses some of the major changes made to the PPI program and to export and import price indexes since 1997. Table B2.2 of appendix 2B, which is available online,[23] provides a comprehensive list of major changes in methodology that might affect the growth of these indexes.

Most of the methodological improvements in the PPI program over this period involve the service sector. Price indexes were added for many service-sector categories that carry substantial weight in the deflation of GDP and the measurement of private nonfarm business-sector output. For example, within personal consumption expenditures (PCE) for health care services, PPIs are used for the deflation of physicians' offices, hospitals, proprietary and government nursing homes, home health care services, medical care laboratories, and diagnostic imaging centers. New service-sector PPIs are also used for the deflation of various financial services within PCE. BEA began using a new price index for prepackaged software (Hill 1998) when it expanded the coverage of fixed investment in GDP to include computer software, starting in October 1999.

Not all new service-sector PPIs can be used in the deflation of expenditure-based GDP. For example, some types of services in the PPI are used as intermediate inputs and thus not included in final expenditures. For distributive industries such as wholesale and retail trade, expenditure-based GDP estimates rely on CPIs that measure price paid by the consumer rather than separately valuing retail and wholesale margins as measured by the PPIs. However, nearly all the new PPIs are used by BEA's industry accounts or in BLS industry productivity estimates and are important for measuring the contributions of industries to GDP or productivity growth.

New price indexes for nonresidential construction were another PPI initiative introduced in the mid- 2000s. Lack of price deflators for investment in nonresidential structures had been a long-standing gap in GDP source data, which BEA had previously attempted to fill with several ad hoc price measures from various sources. A PPI initiative allowed the development of new price indexes for several types of nonresidential construction, which BEA now uses to deflate roughly two-thirds of expenditures on investment in nonresidential structures (nearly 4 percent of private nonfarm business-sector value added).

Finally, the PPI program introduced augmented sampling of pharmaceutical prices and improved the way it handled generic drugs. The program introduced quality adjustments for the hospital PPI, using data collected by the Department of Health and Human Services (HHS) in its Hospital Compare database. These data capture changes in care indicative of changes in service quality, according to the panel of experts responsible for designing the database. HHS recently stopped measuring some of the conditions used by the PPI, and the quality adjustment is no longer implemented.[24]

Compared with the CPI and PPI programs, there have been fewer methodological changes to the BLS international price program. The most notable improvement was the move in 2004 to annual reweighting, which is important because the commodity mix of exports and imports can change significantly from year to year. There were also some expansions to the coverage of imports and exports of services, but unfortunately these expansions were reversed by budget cuts in 2008 that eliminated many of the international services price indexes.

2.6 Improvements to the Measurement of Real GDP and TFP

Over the last 25 years, BEA has made many improvements to the measurement of real GDP. To keep the analysis manageable, I focus on a subset: primarily factors that influence longer-term trends in TFP. Consequently, I do not attempt, for example, to catalog BEA's efforts to improve the accuracy of early GDP estimates, even though the accuracy of the early estimates is one of the main ways the public judges the reliability of GDP estimates. Indeed, many or most improvements to nominal GDP affect quarterly or annual estimates, yet it is the five-year benchmark estimates that primarily determine long-term trends in nominal GDP growth. Thus, I focus on improvements to deflators, which tend to have the largest impact on long-term trends in real GDP and productivity. Also, I look at BEA's periodic conceptual changes to the scope of transactions covered by GDP. Many of these changes reflect periodic updates in international standards for national accounts; the latest version is *System of National Accounts 2008*.[25] These changes in standards are motivated by real changes to a modern, increasingly globalized economy.

Table B2.3 of appendix 2B, which is available online,[26] lists the conceptual and statistical changes to GDP that I have identified as potentially affecting long-term trends in private nonfarm business TFP.

As mentioned, one of the main ways that changes to GDP affect TFP, other than through changes to deflators, is through periodic changes to the scope and coverage of GDP. The first major conceptual change, described by Moulton, Parker, and Seskin (1999), was BEA's recognition of spending on computer software as fixed investment. Previously, purchased software had been counted as intermediate consumption, and software developed by a business's own employees (own-account software) had simply been treated as part of the cost of producing the business's other output. Recognition that software has the characteristics of an investment good—it lasts more than a year and is used in the production of other goods and services—led to the change, paving the way toward subsequent recognition of other intangible assets, such as research and development (R&D), in later revisions (see Corrado, chap. 3 in this book, for an extensive discussion of intangible investments). Considering software as investment had a large effect on measured GDP growth because the production of software had grown rapidly, especially during the 1980s and 1990s, to a level of 2.4 percent of nominal GDP by 1999. Thus, recognition of software as investment led to notable upward revisions to GDP growth.

During that same period, BEA was actively working to push the frontier on quality-adjusted price indexes. During the 1980s, BEA worked with IBM to develop early quality-adjusted computer price indexes for GDP; during the 1990s, that work moved forward and expanded to other topics like semiconductors, telephone-switching equipment, and, more recently, electro-medical equipment. BEA does not see itself supplanting BLS as a producer of price indexes. Rather, it hopes to help BLS move forward in producing quality-adjusted PPIs and CPIs that BEA could use as deflators. As BLS has developed its own quality-adjusted indexes, BEA has dropped its work on hedonic quality adjustments for those components.

Measurement of financial services and insurance became another area of considerable attention for BEA. Over the years, BEA implemented several improvements to concepts and methods for measuring nominal and real financial services for banking, insurance, and other financial services. In 1999, the BEA changed its volume measure for financial services provided without payment (that is, services that banks provide to customers from the margin between interest received for loans and interest paid to depositors), switching to a BLS productivity measure that directly counts various bank activities such as checks cleared, ATM transactions, and electronic funds transfers. The new measure raised the measured real growth of these services by 2.8 percentage points per year, boosting the growth of real output of the private nonfarm business sector by 0.1 percentage point per year.

In 2003, BEA began using a reference rate methodology to allocate implicit banking services between borrowers and depositors; previously, the entire implicit service had been assigned to depositors. This change had a negligible effect on price index and real growth rates, but because most borrower services are classified as intermediates, the change reduced the weight of banking services in GDP final expenditures. Furthermore, because the long-term growth rate of real implicit banking services was close to the growth rate of real output of the private nonfarm business sector, the lower weight had little effect on productivity growth. In the same revision, BEA's treatment of property and casualty insurance services also changed significantly. However, while the changes reduced the volatility of measured services, the effect on long-term growth rates was small.

In 2013, the BEA further expanded the asset boundary for GDP by recognizing expenditures for R&D and for entertainment, literary, and artistic originals as fixed investment (BEA 2013). These changes affected the entire time series of nominal GDP, going back to BEA's earliest GDP estimates from 1929.

We can gauge the importance of these newly recognized types of investment by calculating their contribution to GDP expenditures (that is, how much of the annual growth in total expenditures is attributable to these types of investments). For the three major new types of intellectual property products capitalized in GDP—computer software (beginning in 1999), scientific R&D (beginning in 2013), and entertainment, literary, and artistic originals (beginning in 2013)—I have calculated contributions to percent change in real GDP. The impact through 2019 is shown in table 2.3. (Again, I have omitted 2020 and 2021 due to the large effects of the COVID-19 pandemic and associated recession.)

Investment in computer software had a substantial impact, contributing

Table 2.3 **Contributions of investment in intellectual property products to real GDP expenditure growth, United States**

Impact on average annual growth rate (percentage points), selected periods

Intellectual Property Product	1987–1995	1995–2004	2004–2019	1987–2019
Computer software	0.14%	0.16%	0.14%	0.14%
Research and development	0.03%	0.11%	0.09%	0.08%
Entertainment, literary, and artistic originals	0.02%	0.02%	0.01%	0.02%

Source: Calculations by author based on BEA NIPA data.

Table 2.4 **Contributions of capital services of intellectual property products to aggregate value-added growth, US, all industries**

Contribution to average annual growth rate (percentage points), selected periods

Intellectual Property Product	1987–1995	1995–2004	2004–2019	1987–2019
Computer software	0.16%	0.20%	0.18%	0.18%
Research and development	0.12%	0.12%	0.11%	0.12%
Entertainment, literary, and artistic originals	0.02%	0.03%	0.02%	0.02%

Source: BEA/BLS integrated industry-level production account (KLEMS), contribution tables, 1987–2020, https://www.bea.gov/data/special-topics/integrated-industry-level-production-account-klems.

about 0.14 percentage point to the measured annual growth of GDP from 1987 to 2019. This impact reflects the relative importance of software as a type of investment and long-term growth in that investment. The impact of investment in R&D has also been sizable, though somewhat smaller and more modest, at 0.08 percentage point. The contribution of R&D was lower from 1987 to 1995 and has been higher since. Entertainment, literary, and artistic originals have had smaller relative importance; their contribution to GDP has averaged about 0.02 percentage point per year.

Table 2.3 shows the contribution of investment in intellectual property products on GDP, which is similar to the numerator of the productivity statistics (except that it applies to all sectors rather than just the private nonfarm business sector). Using the new BEA/BLS industry production accounts, we are also able to measure the contributions of the capital services of intellectual property products that appear in the denominator of TFP calculations. These are shown in table 2.4.[27] The effect of capitalization of intellectual property on TFP is roughly equal to the contributions in table 2.3 (which affect the numerator) less the contributions in table 2.4 (which affect the denominator.)

The contributions to growth shown in table 2.4 are larger than those in table 2.3, reflecting differences in scope, timing, and concept between the two tables. The larger effect on capital services than on output simply illustrates a long-standing principle in productivity research—that expanding the number of intangible factors covered in TFP measurement can reduce measured TFP (Corrado, Hulten, and Sichel 2009). Overall, the capitalization of intellectual property products had only a modest impact on labor productivity and appears to have had a small impact on TFP. As such, increased capitalization of intellectual property is not a major factor in explaining the slowdown in measured TFP.

2.7 Changes to the Economic Environment

The US economy continues its long-term movement toward services production and away from goods production. From 1987 to 2019, the share of GDP produced by private services-producing industries increased from 64.2 to 70.3 percent, whereas the share produced by private goods-producing industries declined from 22.5 to 17.5 percent. Within goods production, manufacturing declined from 16.1 to 11.1 percent of GDP, with about two-thirds of the decline occurring in the 10 years prior to the Great Recession (1997–2007). Within services production, from 1997 to 2016 the share of professional and business services in GDP increased from 9.8 to 12.7 percent, and the share of health care and social assistance increased from 6.0 to 7.5 percent. On the other hand, retail trade's share declined from 6.8 to 5.5 percent.

Most economic measurement techniques were first developed for measuring goods production and consumption. Some services are fundamentally heterogeneous, making it difficult for BLS to specify units of consistently defined products that can be repriced each month and requiring BLS to collect prices for a standardized service rather than a service actually sold during the period. Thus, the growth of services presents challenges in defining and measuring price change and real output and exposes gaps in the statistical system. The long-term growth of services would have been particularly problematic for economic measurement if statistical agencies had not taken steps to expand and improve their coverage of services, especially by expanding coverage of services' prices. While there continue to be gaps in measurement of the prices and real output of services, the coverage and quality of the data for this sector have substantially improved since the release of the Boskin Commission report.

The growth of globalization is another factor affecting economic measurement. Trade agreements and legislation that reduced impediments to trade, including the adoption of permanent normal trade relations with China in 2000, spurred innovation in global production arrangements.

Globalization raises many concerns about economic measurement. The offshoring bias in measuring real GDP examined by Houseman et al. (2011) results from failure of import price indexes to capture the price declines that domestic producers enjoy when switching from higher-priced domestic suppliers to lower-priced foreign suppliers. They estimate that average annual growth in real value added in manufacturing was overestimated by 0.2 to 0.5 percentage point per year from 1997 to 2007 and that TFP growth in manufacturing was overstated by 0.1 to 0.2 percentage point per year. Reinsdorf and Yuskavage (2014) show that the problem is exacerbated by the failure of import price indexes to capture price declines resulting from switching from higher-priced to lower-priced international suppliers when sources of supply switch from one country to another—they name this broader concept, which encompasses offshoring bias, sourcing substitution bias. Their study also examines sourcing substitution in imports of consumer goods. For 1997 to 2007, they estimate the overall impact on TFP to be an overstatement of about 0.1 percentage point per year.

I have also mentioned the omission of imported intermediate goods and services in major sector−level TFP calculations used by BLS, as described by Eldridge and Harper (2010). The traditional major sector productivity decomposition includes two inputs—labor services and capital services—and omits imported intermediate inputs from the accounting (in contrast with the industry-level TFP calculation, which accounts for intermediate inputs). From 1997 to 2006, adding imported intermediate inputs to the calculation reduced average TFP growth by about 0.1 percentage point per year.[28] Both the offshoring/sourcing substitution bias and the sectoral TFP bias were particularly pronounced during the decade of rapid growth in globalization prior to the Great Recession, which contributed to the measured TFP slowdown since the Great Recession.

A third way that globalization has affected the measurement of GDP and TFP is through offshore profit shifting. As described by Guvenen et al. (2017), profit shifting occurs when multinational enterprises shift profits earned from intangible assets (typically royalties or rentals) to affiliates in tax havens—countries with very low tax rates.[29] They found that adjusting for tax shifting boosts aggregate productivity growth rates by 0.1 percent per year for 1994 to 2004, 0.25 percent per year for 2004 to 2008, and has little effect after 2008. Note that these effects go in the *opposite* direction of the previous two—that is, the effect of tax shifting was to understate US productivity growth during the decade prior to the Great Recession, whereas sourcing substitution and sectoral TFP biases tended to overstate productivity growth during that period.

Another major change in the economic environment over the last two decades has been the growing use of the Internet in enabling low-cost provision of services. One aspect has been the so-called sharing economy—the provision of services such as transportation (Uber and Lyft) or lodging (Airbnb) through independent contractors sharing self-owned assets. From a measurement perspective, the main challenge of these services is that, while CPIs eventually included these services in their samples, they probably failed to capture the reduced cost and greater availability of those services. Under the matched-model approach used by CPI,[30] the prices of these newer services were likely never compared directly to the prices of older services.

As previously noted, Nakamura, Samuels, and Soloveichik (2016) studied the availability of "free" Internet services (that is, services paid for by advertising revenue). They found that adding these services to GDP would produce a slightly higher growth rate, though much of the effect is offset by a decline in consumption of advertising-supported print media. As with other new services, their results are sensitive to how price changes for these services are measured.

2.8 How Much Progress Has Been Made? What Are the Next Steps?

Compared with the statistics and methodologies that US statistical agencies were using in 1996, clear progress has been made. The lower-level or elementary substitution bias that affected the CPI has essentially been eliminated. Several new hedonic regression models have been introduced for quality adjustment of durable goods, though the impact of hedonic methodology turned out quite a bit smaller than anticipated by the Boskin Commission. CPI weights and samples are now updated much more frequently, enabling new goods and services to enter the sample more rapidly, and some steps have been taken toward collecting data through new big data collections. The CPI housing survey now has a process that keeps its sample continuously updated. The PPI program has been transformed by a major expansion of its coverage of services, providing deflators for most services produced by US businesses. Gaps in price deflators for investment in nonresidential structures have largely been filled with newly available PPIs. GDP statistics have moved from covering investment only in tangible equipment and structures to including several major types of intellectual property: computer software; entertainment, literary, and artistic originals; and R&D. Substantial progress has also been made on the measurement of financial services and health care.

2.8.1 Updated Estimates of Bias

To summarize the progress, I revisit the Boskin estimates of CPI bias to see where bias now stands. Most of my analysis comes from two sources that have reviewed the available literature—Lebow and Rudd (2003), who studied the numerous BLS CPI methodology improvements in the years after the Boskin Commission report, and Byrne, Fernald, and Reinsdorf (2016), who also analyze biases in investment and import prices. I have supplemented these with a few other sources, as well as my own judgmental estimates for components that have not been studied but affect GDP and TFP.

Table 2.5 **Updated estimates of CPI and PCE biases**
Percentage points per year

	Consumer Price Index			PCE	
Sources of Bias	Boskin Commission (1996)	Lebow and Rudd (2003)	This chapter (2022)	This chapter, based on Boskin (1996)	This chapter (2022)
Upper-level substitution	0.15	0.30	0.25	–	–
Lower-level substitution	0.25	0.05	0.05	0.25	0.05
New products/quality change	0.60	0.37	0.33	0.60	0.30
New outlets	0.10	0.05	0.07	0.10	0.07
Weighting	–	0.10	0.10	–	–
Total	**1.10**	**0.87**	**0.80**	**0.95**	**0.42**
Plausible range	(0.80–1.60)	(0.30–1.40)	(0.25–1.30)		

Sources: Boskin et al. (1996), 44; Lebow and Rudd (2003), 161; this author's estimates.

The second and third columns of table 2.5 show the estimates of CPI bias from the Boskin Commission (1996), as well as from Lebow and Rudd (2003).[31] The fourth column presents my own update of Lebow and Rudd's estimates to reflect current CPI bias. I have modified two of the estimates. The Lebow and Rudd estimate of upper-level substitution bias is 0.3, double the Boskin Commission's estimate of 0.15 percentage point. Their estimate, however, was heavily influenced by substantial differences between the chained CPI and fixed-weight official CPI in 1999 and 2000. From December 2000 to December 2019, the difference has been, on average, smaller (0.26 percentage point per year), so I have lowered the estimate of upper-level substitution bias to 0.25. It is possible that unusual circumstances during 1999 and 2000 (such as the dot-com boom and bust or BLS's switch to geometric means at the lower level) contributed to the unusual differences for those years, but the unusual circumstances have not persisted.

I have also slightly boosted Lebow and Rudd's estimate of outlet substitution bias based on larger estimates obtained by Hausman and Leibtag (2009) and on the continuing growth of online retail. I note, however, that new CPIs for gasoline and motor vehicles are able to avoid outlet substitution bias. For the weighting bias, I have looked at the "weight effect" shown in BEA's Table 9.1U (Reconciliation of percent change in the CPI with percent change in the PCE price index), which suggests that the impact of CPI weight mismeasurement continues to be about 0.1 percentage point per year.

For quality and new goods bias, I note that BLS has made several recent CPI methodological changes addressing these issues, such as hedonics for smartphones and communications services, leading me to adjust downward the Lebow-Rudd estimate. Reinsdorf and Schreyer (2017) take another look at quality and new goods bias. Their estimates are not directly comparable with those of Lebow and Rudd; they look at the average for all OECD countries and analyze the case of free products, which are not considered by Lebow and Rudd. Nevertheless, their estimated quality/new goods bias for 2015 of 0.43 percentage point is close to the Lebow-Rudd estimate of 0.37 percentage point.

In the last two columns of table 2.5, I have translated the estimates of CPI bias into the context of the PCE price index. This is the first step in deriving estimates of bias for value added of the private nonfarm business sector, which are used as the numerator of major-sector productivity statistics. For 1996, the biases estimated by the Boskin Commission mostly passed through directly to PCE, except for upper-level substitution bias. In early 1996, BEA adopted chain indexes using the superlative Fisher formula, thereby removing upper-level substitution bias. The PCE index is not subject to the systematic weight mismeasurements that arise from use of the consumer expenditure survey for CPI weights. PCE weights are mostly based on business surveys and administrative data reconciled in a supply-use framework, avoiding the reporting biases that arise in the consumer expenditure survey.

For 2021, I estimate that the PCE index's quality/new goods bias is slightly smaller than the CPI's, mostly because the PCE index uses PPIs rather than CPIs for several components of health care. The PPIs for physicians' services, home health care, hospitals, and nursing homes all have consistently estimated inflation rates that are significantly lower than the equivalent CPIs.[32] Dunn, Grosse, and Zuvekas (2018) found that the difference is largely attributable to the broader coverage of the PPIs and PCE index—the CPI covers only consumer out-of-pocket expenditures and thus does not cover Medicare or Medicaid. But even after removing Medicare and Medicaid, the PPI inflation rates are lower. Either way, quality changes that lead to improvements in health outcomes are probably still largely being missed by both the CPIs and PPIs.

I next estimate the bias for the nonfarm business sector output, which is the productivity numerator. Because output is usually based on deflation, *biases in measured real output generally have the opposite sign as the equivalent biases in price indexes*. Thus, the biases shown in the next table are mostly negative (the measured output *understates* actual growth in real output). As explained earlier, this series is estimated from GDP data excluding government, nonprofit, farm, and owner-occupied housing value added. Thus, I build up estimates by adding the PCE bias estimates from table 2.5 to estimates for private investment, exports (less imports), and government goods and services purchased from private businesses. These estimates are comparable to those derived by Byrne, Fernald, and Reinsdorf (2016), though their estimates are largely based on an industry approach to aggregation, whereas my estimates are based on the expenditure approach.

Table 2.6 **Estimates of bias for private nonfarm business output**

Percentage points per year

	1996		2021	
Major Component	Component Bias	Contribution to Total	Component Bias	Contribution to Total
PCE	–0.95	–0.72	–0.42	–0.32
Private investment				
Information-processing equipment	–7.3	–0.26	–7.0	–0.15
Other equipment	–0.3	–0.02	–0.35	–0.02
Structures	–1.0	–0.09	–0.8	–0.08
Intellectual property products	—[a]	—[a]	–0.2	–0.01
Exports	–0.2	–0.03	–0.2	–0.03
Imports	–0.5	0.09	–0.5	0.10
Government purchases from business	–0.7	–0.05	–0.25	–0.02
Total	—	–1.08	—	–0.53

Source: Author's estimates.

[a] In 1996, intellectual property products components were not included in the output measure.

Table 2.6 splits the private nonfarm business sector into major components—PCE; private investment in information-processing equipment, other equipment, structures, and intellectual property products; exports; imports; and government purchases of goods and services from businesses. To understand how measurement has changed since the Boskin Commission, estimates of biases are given for 1996 and for the most recent (2021) measures.

The component bias for PCE is taken directly from table 2.5, and its contribution to the total is based on the share of PCE (excluding households and institutions) within private nonfarm business, which was about 75 percent both years. (Again, note that implied biases for the output measure are negative, in contrast with the positive biases for the CPI and PCE price index.)

The estimates of bias for information-processing equipment are based on the work of Byrne, Fernald, and Reinsdorf (2016). They found that mismeasurement of this category has increased, in part because more computer and communications equipment is imported and the quality adjustments for import price indexes are especially suspect. I find that improvements to the measurement of electro-medical equipment have an offsetting effect. The bias of this component of the overall index has fallen from 0.26 percentage point in 1996 to 0.15 percentage point in 2021 as the share of IP investment has shrunk.

I have little evidence for other equipment investment. I estimate the bias at 0.3 percent for 1996 and assume that it increased to 0.35 percent in 2021, reflecting the growing share of imported equipment. Deflators for investment in structures have been a long-standing data gap in federal statistics, and the inadequacies of proxy deflators previously used by BEA undoubtedly contributed to estimates of negative TFP growth in the construction sector. By 2021, BEA was able to use several newly available PPIs for construction. But improvements from the new PPIs have been partly offset by poor measurement of growth in mining structures due to failure to capture dramatic improvements in fracking, as described by Byrne, Fernald, and Reinsdorf (2016).

In 1996, intellectual property products were not yet part of GDP or productivity measures. Software, R&D, and entertainment originals are now part of GDP investment, and in 2018, BEA revised the software indexes to substantially reduce remaining biases in price indexes. While developing R&D estimates, BEA experimented with many approaches to price measurement before ultimately adopting a conservative approach. Taking account of recent changes to software deflators, I assume a bias for these products of 0.2 percent per year, though I recognize that it could be higher.

For imports, I draw on estimates from Reinsdorf and Yuskavage (2014), which show substantial sourcing bias for durable goods and apparel, as well as quality adjustment bias for information-processing equipment. For exports, I use a conservative estimate of bias based on a presumption that sourcing and quality adjustment biases are less pronounced for exports. Finally, for government purchases of goods and services from business, the deflation uses a mixture of CPIs and PPIs. The measurement of this component has benefited from both overall improvements to the CPI and expansion of the PPI services prices.

I estimate that the overall bias of the private nonfarm business output measure has fallen from about 1.1 percent in 1996 to about 0.53 percent today. In comparison, Aghion et al. (2017), using an entirely different method, estimate a recent bias of 0.6 percent for private nonfarm business sector output. Despite continuing challenges in economic measurement, I do not see any evidence that overall bias has worsened since 1996. The post–Boskin Commission reduction in bias has mostly been associated with CPI and PPI improvements, which were especially concentrated in the first few years after the publication of the Boskin Commission report—especially 1996 through 2003. However, biases for certain components, such as investment in information processing equipment, have probably worsened over time.

2.8.2 Challenges and Recommendations

Despite much progress, statistical agencies continue to face significant challenges. Some progress has been offset by changes in the economy, such as increased globalization and transactions facilitated by the Internet, which have placed hurdles in the way of accurate measurement. While the BLS has made progress in implementing some of the recommendations of the Boskin and Schultze reviews, other problems, such as outlet substitution bias, have not yet been fully addressed. And finally, as I have noted, the statistical agencies' progress in attacking measurement biases appears to have decelerated as budgets tighten and other issues need attention.

The National Academies of Sciences, Engineering, and Medicine (2022) have made several recommendations for improving the CPI estimates. I conclude this chapter by giving three additional recommendations for the statistical agencies on ways to renew progress on reducing or eliminating bias in TFP, GDP growth, and related price indexes.

First, BLS and BEA should expand and reconstitute work on the digital economy, focusing particularly on improving the measurement of quality-adjusted prices for information and communications technology (ICT) equipment and associated digital services. In recent years, David Byrne and a few of his colleagues at the Federal Reserve Board have done excellent research on ICT equipment prices, but it would be better if more of that work took place at BLS and BEA, the agencies responsible for producing price indexes and real GDP. I am encouraged by recent BLS research and improvements to the quality adjustment of microprocessors in the PPI (Sawyer and So 2018) and smartphones in both the CPI and PPI (Brown, Sawyer, and Bathgate 2020). Work is also moving forward on new digital services, such as cloud data services. It is important that this work include strong coordination among the statistical agencies.

My second recommendation is that the BLS reconsider its practice of dealing with product substitution or change by limiting quality adjustments to when an item has disappeared from its sample. As Groshen et al. (2017) explain, "when a match permanently ends in the Consumer Price Index and the same good cannot be tracked from one period to the next, then . . . the Bureau of Labor Statistics initiates a *quality adjustment procedure* after a replacement good has been established." In other words, quality adjustments are generally made only when an item disappears from the sample.[33] If a new good appears that does not displace its predecessor, it will generally only enter the index when the sample is rotated—and sample rotations are always linked to the old sample without adjustment for changes in quality.

The BLS practice of limiting quality adjustment to product disappearance was probably motivated by the ideal of repricing a fixed basket of goods and services. Although the fixed basket ideal may have been BLS's goal long ago, BLS has acknowledged the cost-of-living index as its conceptual framework and overarching objective since the Boskin Commission (Abraham, Greenlees, and Moulton 1998). In some cases, the arrival of a new version of a product to replace an older one may be a reasonable way to think about quality change; for example, it may describe the refreshing of car models each year or the periodic release of new versions of computer software. More generally, however, this practice substantially constrains BLS's ability to adjust for quality, new goods, and new outlets.

In a study of hedonic quality adjustment of televisions, Moulton, LaFleur, and Moses (1998) found that a hedonic index covering all items in the

CPI sample decreased 5.7 percent per year from 1993 to 1997. In contrast, an index only adjusting for items that dropped out of the sample, as with the CPI, decreased just 3.6 percent per year. I hypothesize that the most important quality improvements for televisions occurring during that period were introductions of new models with larger screens and better resolution. They were not simply upgrades to older models. These higher-quality televisions did eventually enter the sample, but probably mostly through sample rotation (without quality adjustment) rather than item replacement and quality adjustment.

The long-standing problem of outlet substitution bias could also be addressed by allowing quality-adjusted price comparisons to accompany sample replenishment. For example, the rapidly growing share of electronic shopping often provides lower prices as well as convenience to shoppers. Because CPI samples are drawn from specific outlets, and item substitutions are made within the same outlets, new or growing outlets only enter the sample via rotation. This means that prices from new outlets, which generally grow due to lower quality-adjusted prices, are never directly compared with prices at old outlets; the Boskin Commission estimated that this practice resulted in a bias of about 0.1 percentage point per year over the period it considered. A sample replenishment process in which portions of the sample are periodically replaced with comparable items from new outlets and prices in the new outlets are directly compared with prices of comparable items in the old outlets would allow BLS to address and eliminate this bias.

This type of sample replenishment process could even help address new goods bias, at least in cases where the new good is sufficiently like the old good, to allow for a quality-adjusted price comparison. For example, Uber and Lyft are similar in many respects to traditional taxi services. Suppose that the BLS sample includes the price of taking a taxi from a certain location to the airport on a Saturday afternoon. The CPI sample could then be replenished with prices for Uber or Lyft, allowing for direct comparisons of price difference. For other services, such as a late-night ride home from a bar, Uber or Lyft may provide superior service to a taxi in terms of waiting time or reliability of service, but a quality adjustment might be able to account for those differences. Aizcorbe and Chen (2022) tested different approaches for calculating a price index for ride-sharing and taxis in New York City in 2015–2017 and found that treating ride-sharing and taxis as directly comparable during nonsurge pricing periods reduced the annual growth rate of the price index by 0.5 percentage points. Directly comparing the prices of new services to traditional items would surely improve the CPI's measurement compared with current practice, which in most cases involves simply linking in samples with new services, albeit without quality adjustment, at the time of sample rotation.

My third recommendation is that BLS and BEA make a concerted, systematic effort to account for the effects of globalization in the measurement of GDP, value added by industry, and productivity.

This project would include the production of input price indexes for industries; Alterman (2015) provides an outline of what such an index would entail. This index would require collecting price data from the perspective of the industry buyer, taking account of substitutions to various domestic and offshore sources of supply. In addition, aspects of globalization such as imported intermediate inputs bias in major sector TFP and offshore profit shifting bias should be studied further and addressed.

Asking for this type of research and development in a time of tight statistical agency budgets is difficult, but as the Boskin Commission made clear, the cost of improved statistics is modest compared to the costs of policies conducted with deficient statistics. Accurate statistics are critical for effective implementation of a wide range of economic policy—everything from monetary and fiscal policy for countercyclical macroeconomic policy to providing cost-of-living adjustments for social security recipients to providing accurate data for economic research. For economic statistics to achieve the best potential quality, the effort must involve not only the work of statistical agencies but also the cooperative engagement of the economics profession. For economic theory and policy to continue to advance, the profession needs to engage in the work of improving official economic statistics.

Appendix 2A

Conceptual Frameworks for the CPI, PPI, and GDP

In response to a recommendation by the Boskin Commission that the BLS adopt the cost-of-living index as its measurement objective, BLS basically agreed to use the framework as its guide for operational decisions about the CPI (Abraham, Greenlees, and Moulton 1998). But less attention has been given to the questions of whether the PPI and GDP have the same conceptual frameworks or different ones.

The PPI has traditionally used the output price index developed by Fisher and Shell (1972) and Archibald (1977) as its conceptual framework. This framework is based on the model of a firm engaged in production that maximizes revenue conditional on its technology and inputs.

The framework for price and quantity indexes in GDP and the national accounts is a bit more complicated. Most of the conceptual framework for the national accounts, such as the *System of National Accounts 2008*, is developed in nominal measures or current prices. The accounting framework is based on a general equilibrium model in which every transaction reflects two sides: a supplier and a user. Thus, GDP can be thought of as integrating the output of firms with the final expenditures of consumers and investors. The System of National Accounts (SNA) chapter on calculation of price and volume indexes is mostly pragmatic and does not dwell on conceptual issues, but the overall framework suggests that SNA could incorporate either the cost-of-living or the output price framework.

Thinking about the two measurement frameworks and the differences in how they interpret markets where consumers and firms transact leads to some index number puzzles, however. Let me first introduce some notation to describe these conceptual indexes.

The cost-of-living index is derived from cost functions, which represent the solution to a consumer's cost or expenditure minimization problem.[34] The function $c(p, u)$ represents the minimum cost the consumer can pay to reach utility level u given a vector p of prices of consumer goods. Given price vectors for two periods, p^0 and p^1, a cost-of-living index is the ratio of the two cost functions:

(A2.1) $$P_K(p^0, p^1, u) = \frac{c(p^1, u)}{c(p^0, u)}.$$

The Konüs cost-of-living index can be contrasted with the Laspeyres price index PL and the Paasche price index PP, which hold quantities, q, fixed at the consumption patterns for period 0 (in the case of the Laspeyres index) and for period 1 (in the case of the Paasche index).

(A2.2) $$P_L = \frac{\sum p^1 q^0}{\sum p^0 q^0}$$

(A2.3) $$P_P = \frac{\sum p^1 q^1}{\sum p^0 q^1}$$

If $u = f(q)$, then the following the cost-of-living index satisfies the following bounds:

(A2.4) $$P_K(p^0, p^1, u^0) \leq P_L, \text{ and}$$

(A2.5) $$P_K(p^0, p^1, u^1) \geq P_P.$$

That is, the cost-of-living index that conditions on period 0 consumption patterns and utility is bounded from above by the Laspeyres price index, while the cost-of-living index that conditions on period 1 consumption patterns and utility is bounded from below by the Paasche price index. The Fisher index, which is a geometric average of the Laspeyres and Paasche price index, provides a good (second-order) approximation of the true cost-of-living index.

The Fisher-Shell output price index is the solution to the producing firm's revenue maximization problem.[35] Let p be the vector of output prices for the goods and services produced by the firm, and let v be the vector of inputs used in production. $R(p, v)$ is the solution to the revenue maximization problem given output prices p and inputs v. Conditional on technology available in period t, the output price index is

(A2.6) $$P^t(p^0, p^1, v) = \frac{R(p^1, v)}{R(p^0, v)}.$$

Interestingly, the conceptual output price index satisfies different boundary conditions from the cost-of-living index. In particular,

(A2.7) $$P^0(p^0, p^1, v^0) \geq P_L, \text{ and}$$

(A2.8) $$P^1(p^0, p^1, v^1) \leq P_P.$$

The cost-of-living index is conditional on preferences, while the output price index is conditional on technology and inputs. In practice, statistical agencies calculate unconditional indexes, so it is probably a mistake to identify them too closely with underlying conceptual indexes. Empirically, the Laspeyres index usually tends to be larger than the Paasche index, which suggests that the bounds of the cost-of-living index theory are more often satisfied than those of the output price index theory. This situation might arise if consumer preferences are mostly stable and change very slowly while firm technology and inputs change more rapidly.

The aggregation of households and firms adds additional complexities to the economic theory of these indexes. For example, while an aggregate CPI may be a reasonable approximation of the cost-of-living index for a household near the middle of the income distribution, it may be quite different from the cost-of-living index of a very high-income or low-income household. While the economic theory of price indexes gives guidance for how to handle problems like substitution bias, one should be cautious in assuming that official indexes closely approximate the cost-of-living index for any actual household.

Notes

1. The *private nonfarm business sector* is the sector of the economy that consists of private nonfarm businesses and excludes government, nonprofit institutions, and household and domestic employees.

2. A *cost-of-living index* is a theoretical price index that measures change in the cost of obtaining a fixed level of economic well-being, or utility. Although it is not possible to directly measure a cost-of-living index, it can be closely approximated using a superlative index.

3. A *Laspeyres price index* measures relative change in the cost of a fixed basket of goods and services that reflects the expenditure patterns of an earlier period. It does not take account of a buyer's ability to substitute between items when relative prices change. *Upper-level substitution bias* arises from use of a fixed-weight or

Laspeyres price index to combine elementary price indexes for individual products into the all-items CPI. The more flexible weights of superlative price indexes, such as the Törnqvist index, capture the effects of consumers' ability to substitute items with falling relative prices for items with rising relative prices while keeping utility constant. The substitution bias of a Laspeyres index can therefore be estimated by comparing it to a superlative price index. See Appendix 2A.

4. Zvi Griliches, the fifth member of the Boskin Commission, was unable to respond due to illness.

5. *Total factor productivity* (TFP) measures output per unit of combined inputs, including labor and capital services. In 2021, the BLS changed the name of this productivity measure from *multifactor productivity* to *total factor productivity*.

6. In table 2.2, I have omitted the years 2020 and 2021. The productivity changes in those years were large because of the COVID-19 recession; it is too soon to tell if they represent a temporary blip or a change in trend.

7. Productivity measurement for the government, nonprofit, and household sectors raises many interesting issues that are important for international comparisons but are beyond the scope of this chapter.

8. For TFP, the measure of labor input is adjusted for changes in labor composition and hours worked. The measure of labor input thus adjusts for improvements in education and changes in age and sex distribution of the workforce based on an assumption that differences in wages among types of workers reflect differences in productivity (Bureau of Labor Statistics 2016). When calculating TFP of individual industries, BLS uses the industry's total output rather than its value added for the numerator and an index of capital, labor, energy, nonenergy materials, and purchased business services inputs as the denominator (Bureau of Labor Statistics 1997a).

9. *Sample rotation* is the periodic replacement or updating of a sample of items or outlets in a price index. When a sample is rotated, the index from the new sample is "linked" to the index from the old sample.

10. The two imputation methods are the cell-relative method and the class-mean method. Both impute the price change using a mean price change of observations that did not experience substitution. The former uses all such observations in the cell; the latter uses only the comparable replacement and quality-adjusted replacement observations, which is appropriate for goods that experience periodic introduction of new lines or models. See Bureau of Labor Statistics (2018).

11. Reinsdorf first identified this issue for the US CPI in a presentation at the Allied Social Sciences Associations meeting in January 1993. Dalén (1992) had reported similar findings for Swedish CPI estimates. Because weighting information is not available, the bias is better described as statistical bias rather than as a type of substitution bias.

12. Bureau of Labor Statistics (2023).

13. The Fisher and Törnqvist formulas are both superlative indexes that can, under certain assumption, provide close approximations to a cost-of-living index—see appendix 2A. In practice, the two formulas tend to produce similar estimates of price change.

14. For retail and wholesale trade, PPIs measure changes in margins, which are the relevant producer price for these industries.

15. Prior to the availability of services-sector PPIs, BEA had to rely on indirect indicators such as wages or employment to measure prices and quantities of services for which CPIs were not available.

16. See Swick, Bathgate, and Horrigan (2006).

17. For more information on quality adjustment, see Bureau of Labor Statistics (2014), "Quality Adjustment in the Producer Price Index."

18. Appendix 2B is available online at https://www.brookings.edu/wp-content/uploads/2018/07/Moulton-report-v2.pdf.

19. BLS summarized its research on CPI biases in the December 1993 *Monthly Labor Review* in articles by Fixler (1993), Aizcorbe and Jackman (1993), Kokoski (1993), and Moulton (1993), which presented early work on the new issue of lower-level substitution bias identified by BLS's Marshall Reinsdorf (Reinsdorf 1993; Reinsdorf 1994).

20. Reinsdorf and Triplett (2009, 56–58) offer an alternative rationale for the geometric mean index. If the (unknown) expenditure shares are equally likely to be identical to one another in the initial period as in the final period, the expected value of the exact cost-of-living index will approximately equal the geometric mean index even if the items in the index are not substitutes.

21. Because the BLS started using the modified Laspeyres formula at the elementary level in 1978, that year was the natural breaking point; the empirical research on bias is not applicable to the pre-1978 period.

22. Goolsbee and Klenow (2018) used data on online transactions for millions of products to construct a digital price index that shows lower inflation than the CPI. Konny, Williams, and Friedman (2022) described several alternative data sources that BLS has studied for possible incorporation in the CPI and provided a discussion of the practical issues with using nontraditional data.

23. https://www.brookings.edu/wp-content/uploads/2018/07/Moulton-report-v2.pdf.

24. See Bureau of Labor Statistics Health Quality Valuation Team (2008).

25. The United Nations and other international organizations are preparing an updated version of the System of National Accounts, which is scheduled for adoption in 2025.

26. https://www.brookings.edu/wp-content/uploads/2018/07/Moulton-report-v2.pdf.

27. I thank Matt Russell for pointing me to these data.

28. There may, however, be an interaction between the Eldridge-Harper sectoral TFP bias and sourcing substitution bias, suggesting that it might not be appropriate to simply add together those two estimates.

29. Aggressive use of transfer pricing may also allow profits from intra-enterprise trade in goods to be shifted to low tax countries.

30. A *matched-model index* is a price index in which the sample of models being repriced is held fixed.

31. Groshen et al. (2017) provide estimates of bias for PCE and for private fixed investment in equipment and software that are similar to the estimates I provide in this section. I have expanded on their work by providing judgmental estimates for other GDP components; for PCE and equipment investment, my estimates are based on most of the same sources they used, though there are minor differences in interpretation.

32. For example, from 2002 to 2015, the CPI for hospitals increased at a 6.1 percent annual rate, whereas the PPI for hospitals increased at a 3.1 percent rate. The PPI for private health plans, which excludes government payers such as Medicare and Medicaid, increased at a 4.4 percent rate (Dunn, Grosse, and Zuvekas 2018). Part of the difference between the PPI for private health plans and the CPI may be attributable to self-payers (that is, uninsured patients) covered in the CPI, and part may be due to differences in quality adjustment. The effect of using PPI instead of CPI would be larger if BEA used the PPIs for deflating the output of nonprofit

hospitals and nursing homes; instead, BEA uses cost-based estimates for nonprofit institutions. Thus, I applied the PPI-CPI differences for hospitals and nursing homes only to the weights for proprietary (for-profit) institutions.

33. An exception is that both the CPI and PPI programs, on relatively rare occasions, introduce directed substitutions, in which replacement items are identified and selected prior to the previous item disappearing from the marketplace with quality adjustments applied to the price comparisons. This method has been used, for example, for computers and game software publishing, and in 2018 BLS began using this approach for smartphones, as described by Brown, Sawyer, and Bathgate (2020).

34. Chapter 17 of the international *Consumer Price Index Manual* provides a nice explication of the theory of the cost-of-living index; see ILO et al. (2004).

35. Chapter 17 of the international *Producer Price Index Manual* explains the theory of the Fisher-Shell output price index; see IMF (2004).

References

Abraham, Katharine G., John S. Greenlees, and Brent R. Moulton. 1998. "Working to Improve the Consumer Price Index." *Journal of Economic Perspectives* 12, no. 1 (Winter): 27–36.

Aghion, Philippe, Antonin Bergeaud, Timo Boppart, Peter J. Klenow, and Huiyu Li. 2017. "Missing Growth from Creative Destruction." Federal Reserve Bank of San Francisco Working Paper 2017–04, November. http://www.frbsf.org/economic-research/publications/working-papers/2017/04/.

Aizcorbe, Ana, and Jeff Chen. 2022. "Outlet Substitution Bias Estimates for Ride Sharing and Taxi Rides in New York City." BEA Working Paper WP2022–1. https://www.bea.gov/system/files/papers/BEA-WP2022-1.pdf.

Aizcorbe, Ana M., and Patrick C. Jackman. 1993. "The Commodity Substitution Effect in CPI Data, 1982–91." *Monthly Labor Review* 116 (December): 25–33.

Alterman, William. 2015. "Producing an Input Price Index." In *Measuring Globalization: Better Trade Statistics for Better Policy*, edited by Susan Houseman and Michael Mandel, 1:331–57. Kalamazoo, MI: W. E. Upjohn Institute for Employment Research.

Archibald, Robert B. 1977. "On the Theory of Industrial Price Measurement Output Price Indexes." *Annals of Economic and Social Measurement* 6 (1): 57–72.

Baily, Martin Neil. 2006. "Policy Implications of the Boskin Commission Report." *International Productivity Monitor* 12 (Spring): 74–83.

Baily, Martin Neil, and Nicholas Montalbano. 2016. "Why Is US Productivity Growth so Slow? Possible Explanations and Policy Responses." Brookings Institution, Hutchins Center Working Paper No. 22. https://www.brookings.edu/wp-content/uploads/2016/09/wp22_baily-montalbano1.pdf.

Berndt, Ernst R. 2006. "The Boskin Commission Report after a Decade: After-Life or Requiem?" *International Productivity Monitor* 12 (Spring): 61–73.

Bieler, John, David Popko, Sarah Niedergall, and Ilmo Sung. 2019. "A Nontraditional Data Approach to the CPI Gasoline Index: CPI Crowd-Sourced Motor Fuels Data Analysis Project." Bureau of Labor Statistics conference paper. https://www.aeaweb.org/conference/2020/preliminary/paper/n8b4hBsT.

Bils, Mark. 2009. "Do Higher Prices for New Goods Reflect Quality Growth or Inflation." *Quarterly Journal of Economics* 124, no. 2 (May): 637–75.

Blair, Caitlin. 2015. "Constructing a PCE-Weighted Consumer Price Index." In *Improving the Measurement of Consumer Expenditures*. Studies in Income and Wealth, edited by Christopher D. Carroll, Thomas F. Crossley, and John Sabelhaus, 74:53–74. Chicago: University of Chicago Press.

Boskin, Michael J., Ellen R. Dulberger, Robert J. Gordon, Zvi Griliches, and Dale Jorgenson. 1996. *Final Report of the Advisory Commission to Study the Consumer Price Index*. Committee on Finance, US Senate, William V. Roth Jr., Chairman. 104th Congress, 2nd Session, S. Prt. 104–72. Washington, DC: Government Printing Office, December. https://www.finance.senate.gov/imo/media/doc/Prt104-72.pdf.

Bradley, Ralph, Jaspreet Hunjan, and Lyubov Rozental. 2015. "Experimental Disease Based Indexes." Bureau of Labor Statistics. https://www.bls.gov/pir/journal/rb03.pdf.

Broda, Christian, and David E. Weinstein. 2010. "Product Creation and Destruction: Evidence and Price Implications." *American Economic Review* 100, no. 3 (June): 691–723.

Brown, Craig, Steven Sawyer, and Deanna Bathgate. 2020. *A Review of Hedonic Price Adjustment Techniques for Products Experiencing Rapid and Complex Quality Change*. Washington DC: Bureau of Labor Statistics.

Brynjolfsson, Erik, and JooHee Oh. 2012. "The Attention Economy: Measuring the Value of Free Digital Services on the Internet." Proceedings of the International Conference on Information Systems, Orlando, FL, December.

Bureau of Economic Analysis. 2013. "Preview of the 2013 Comprehensive Revision of the National Income and Product Accounts: Changes in Definitions and Presentations." *Survey of Current Business* 93, no. 3 (March): 13–39.

Bureau of Economic Analysis. 2016. "Concepts and Methods of the US National Income and Product Accounts." https://www.bea.gov/national/pdf/all-chapters.pdf.

Bureau of Economic Analysis. 2017. "Updated Summary of NIPA Methodologies." *Survey of Current Business* 97 (November). https://www.bea.gov/scb/pdf/2017/11-November/1117-updated-summary-of-nipa-methodologies.pdf.

Bureau of Economic Analysis. 2022. "Preview of the 2022 Annual Update of the National Economic Accounts." *Survey of Current Business* 102 (May). https://apps.bea.gov/scb/2022/05-may/0522-gdp-economy.htm.

Bureau of Labor Statistics. 1997a. "Productivity Measures: Business Sector and Major Subsectors." *BLS Handbook of Methods* (April). https://www.bls.gov/opub/hom/pdf/homch10.pdf.

Bureau of Labor Statistics. 1997b. "International Price Indexes." *BLS Handbook of Methods* (April). https://www.bls.gov/opub/hom/pdf/homch15.pdf.

Bureau of Labor Statistics. 2000. "Extending the Use of Hedonic Models to Adjust Prices for Changes in Quality." *CPI Detailed Report: Data for January 2000*, 4.

Bureau of Labor Statistics. 2006. "Overview of Capital Inputs for the BLS Multifactor Productivity Measures." https://www.bls.gov/mfp/mprcaptl.pdf.

Bureau of Labor Statistics. 2007. "Technical Information about the BLS Multifactor Productivity Measures." https://www.bls.gov/mfp/mprtech.pdf.

Bureau of Labor Statistics. 2008. "Technical Information about the BLS Major Sector Productivity and Costs Measures." https://www.bls.gov/lpc/lpcmethods.pdf.

Bureau of Labor Statistics. 2014. "Quality Adjustment in the Producer Price Index." https://www.bls.gov/ppi/qualityadjustment.pdf.

Bureau of Labor Statistics. 2015. "Producer Prices." *BLS Handbook of Methods* (June). https://www.bls.gov/opub/hom/pdf/homch14.pdf.

Bureau of Labor Statistics. 2016. "Changes in the Composition of Labor for BLS

Multifactor Productivity Measures, 2014." https://www.bls.gov/mfp/mprlabor.pdf.

Bureau of Labor Statistics. 2018. "The Consumer Price Index." *BLS Handbook of Methods* (February 14). https://www.bls.gov/opub/hom/pdf/homch17.pdf.

Bureau of Labor Statistics. 2023. "Weight (Wait) Up! Increasing the Relevance of Consumer Price Index Weights." *Commissioner's Corner* (blog), January 10. https://www.bls.gov/blog/2023/weight-wait-up-increasing-the-relevance-of-consumer-price-index-weights.htm.

Bureau of Labor Statistics. n.d. "Industry Productivity Measures." *BLS Handbook of Methods.* https://www.bls.gov/opub/hom/pdf/homch11.pdf.

Bureau of Labor Statistics Health Quality Valuation Team. 2008. "Proposal for Adjusting the General Hospital Producer Price Index for Quality Change." http://conference.nber.org/confer/2008/si2008/PRCR/murphy2.pdf.

Byrne, David M., John G. Fernald, and Marshall B. Reinsdorf. 2016. "Does the United States Have a Productivity Slowdown or a Measurement Problem?" *Brookings Papers on Economic Activity* 1: 109–57.

Cage, Robert, John Greenlees, and Patrick Jackman. 2003. "Introducing the Chained Consumer Price Index." Paper presented at the seventh meeting of the International Working Group on Price Indices, Paris, France, May. https://www.bls.gov/cpi/additional-resources/chained-cpi-introduction.pdf.

Commission of the European Communities, International Monetary Fund, Organization for Economic Co-operation and Development, United Nations, and the World Bank. 2009. *System of National Accounts 2008.* New York. https://unstats.un.org/unsd/nationalaccount/docs/SNA2008.pdf.

Corrado, Carol, Charles Hulten, and Daniel Sichel. 2009. "Intangible Capital and US Economic Growth." *Review of Income and Wealth* 55, no. 3 (September): 661–85.

Dalén, Jörgen. 1992. "Computing Elementary Aggregates in the Swedish Consumer Price Index." *Journal of Official Statistics* 8: 129–47.

Dalton, Kenneth V., John S. Greenlees, and Kenneth J. Stewart. 1998. "Incorporating a Geometric Mean Formula into the CPI." *Monthly Labor Review* 121 (October): 3–7.

Dean, Edwin R., and Michael J. Harper. 2001. "The BLS Productivity Measurement Program." In *New Developments in Productivity Analysis.* Studies in Income and Wealth, edited by Charles R. Hulten, Edwin R. Dean, and Michael J. Harper, 63:55–84. Chicago: University of Chicago Press.

Diewert, W. E. 1995. "Axiomatic and Economic Approaches to Elementary Price Indexes." Discussion Paper no. 95-01, Department of Economics, University of British Columbia, Vancouver. http://econ.sites.olt.ubc.ca/files/2013/06/pdf_paper_erwin-diewert-95-01-axiomatic-economic-approaches.pdf.

Dunn, Abe, Scott D. Grosse, and Samuel H. Zuvekas. 2018. "Adjusting Health Expenditures for Inflation: A Review of Measures for Health Services Research in the United States." *Health Services Research* 53, no. 1 (February): 175–196.

Dunn, Abe, Lindsey Rittmueller, and Bryn Whitmire. 2015. "Introducing the New BEA Health Care Satellite Account." *Survey of Current Business* 95, no. 1 (January). https://www.bea.gov/scb/pdf/2015/01%20January/0115_bea_health_care_satellite_account.pdf.

Eldridge, Lucy P., and Michael J. Harper. 2010. "Effects of Imported Intermediate Inputs on Productivity." *Monthly Labor Review* 133, no. 6 (June): 3–15.

Feldstein, Martin. 2017. "Underestimating the Real Growth of GDP, Personal Income, and Productivity." *Journal of Economic Perspectives* 31, no. 2 (Spring): 145–64.

Fisher, Franklin M., and Karl Shell. 1972. *The Economic Theory of Price Indices:*

Two Essays on the Effects of Taste, Quality, and Technological Change. New York: Academic Press.

Fixler, Dennis. 1993. "The Consumer Price Index: Underlying Concepts and Caveats." *Monthly Labor Review* 116 (December): 3–12.

Fleck, Susan, Steven Rosenthal, Matthew Russell, Erich H. Strassner, and Lisa Usher. 2014. "A Prototype BEA/BLS Industry-Level Production Account for the United States." In *Measuring Economic Sustainability and Progress*. Studies in Income and Wealth, edited by Dale W. Jorgenson, J. Steven Landefeld, and Paul Schreyer, 72:323–72. Chicago: University of Chicago Press.

Goolsbee, Austan D., and Peter J. Klenow. 2018. "Internet Rising, Prices Falling: Measuring Inflation in a World of E-Commerce." *AEA Papers and Proceedings* 108: 488–92.

Gordon, Robert J. 2006. "The Boskin Commission Report: A Retrospective One Decade Later." *International Productivity Monitor* 12 (Spring): 7–22.

Greenlees, John S. 2006. "The BLS Response to the Boskin Commission Report." *International Productivity Monitor* 12 (Spring): 23–41.

Greenlees, John S., and Robert McClelland. 2011. "New Evidence on Outlet Substitution Effects in Consumer Price Index Data." *Review of Economics and Statistics* 93, no. 2 (May): 632–46.

Groshen, Erica L., Brian C. Moyer, Ana M. Aizcorbe, Ralph Bradley, and David M. Friedman. 2017. "How Government Statistics Adjust for Potential Biases from Quality Change and New Goods in an Age of Digital Technologies: A View from the Trenches." *Journal of Economic Perspectives* 31, no. 2 (Spring): 187–210.

Guvenen, Fatih, Raymond J. Mataloni, Jr., Dylan G. Rassier, and Kim J. Ruhl. 2017. "Offshore Profit Shifting and Domestic Productivity Measurement." BEA Working Paper WP2017-2, March.

Hausman, Jerry, and Ephraim Leibtag. 2009. "CPI Bias from Supercenters: Does BLS Know That Wal-Mart Exists?" In *Price Index Concepts and Measurement*. Studies in Income and Wealth, edited by W. Erwin Diewert, John S. Greenlees, and Charles R. Hulten, 70:203–31. Chicago: University of Chicago Press.

Hill, Brent. 1998. "New Producer Price Index for Prepackaged Software–SIC 7372." US Department of Labor, Bureau of Labor Statistics, *PPI Detailed Report*, January 1998, 6.

Houseman, Susan, Christopher Kurz, Paul Lengermann, and Benjamin Mandel. 2011. "Offshoring Bias in US Manufacturing." *Journal of Economic Perspectives* 25, no. 2 (Spring): 111–32.

Houseman, Susan, and Michael Mandel, eds. 2015. *Measuring Globalization: Better Trade Statistics for Better Policy*. Vol. 1. Kalamazoo, MI: W. E. Upjohn Institute for Employment Research.

Howells, Thomas, and Dave Wasshausen. 2016. "Source Data Acceleration & Impacts on GDP." Presentation at BEA Advisory Committee Meeting, Washington, DC, November 18. https://www.bea.gov/about/pdf/acm/2016/source-data-acceleration.pdf.

ILO, IMF, OECD, UNECE, Eurostat, and World Bank. 2004. *Consumer Price Index Manual: Theory and Practice*. Geneva: International Labour Office.

IMF. 2004. *Producer Price Index Manual: Theory and Practice*. Washington, DC: International Monetary Fund.

Kim, Mina, and Marshall B. Reinsdorf. 2015. "The Impact of Globalization on Prices: A Test of Hedonic Price Indexes for Imports." In *Measuring Globalization: Better Trade Statistics for Better Policy*, edited by Susan Houseman and Michael Mandel, 1:293–329. Kalamazoo, MI: W. E. Upjohn Institute for Employment Research.

Kokoski, Mary F. 1993. "Quality Adjustment of Price Indexes." *Monthly Labor Review* 116 (December): 34–46.

Konny, Crystal G., Brendan K. Williams, and David M. Friedman. 2022. "Big Data in the US Consumer Price Index: Experiences and Plans." In *Big Data for Twenty-First-Century Economic Statistics*. Studies in Income and Wealth, edited by Katharine G. Abraham, Ron S. Jarmin, Brian C. Moyer, and Matthew D. Shapiro, 79:69–98. Chicago: University of Chicago Press.

Lawson, Ann M., Brian C. Moyer, Sumiye Okubo, and Mark A. Planting. 2006. "Integrating Industry and National Economic Accounts: First Steps and Future Improvements." In *A New Architecture for the US National Accounts*. Studies in Income and Wealth, edited by Dale W. Jorgenson, J. Steven Landefeld, and William D. Nordhaus, 66:215–61. Chicago: University of Chicago Press.

Lebow, David E., and Jeremy B. Rudd. 2003. "Measurement Error in the Consumer Price Index: Where Do We Stand?" *Journal of Economic Literature* 41, no. 1 (March): 159–201.

McCully, Clinton P., Brian C. Moyer, and Kenneth J. Stewart. 2007. "Comparing the Consumer Price Index and the Personal Consumption Expenditures Price Index." *Survey of Current Business* 87, no. 11 (November): 26–33.

Moulton, Brent R. 1993. "Basic Components of the CPI: Estimation of Price Changes." *Monthly Labor Review* 116 (December): 13–24.

Moulton, Brent R., Timothy J. LaFleur, and Karin E. Moses. 1998. "Research on Improved Quality Adjustment in the CPI: The Case of Televisions." Bureau of Labor Statistics (September).

Moulton, Brent R., Robert P. Parker, and Eugene P. Seskin. 1999. "A Preview of the 1999 Comprehensive Revision of the National Income and Product Accounts: Definitional and Classificational Changes." *Survey of Current Business* 79, no. 8 (August): 7–20.

Moyer, Brian C., Mark A. Planting, Mahnaz Fahim-Nader, and Sherlene K. S. Lum. 2004. "Preview of the Comprehensive Revision of the Annual Industry Accounts: Integrating the Annual Input-Output Accounts and Gross-Domestic-Product-by-Industry Accounts." *Survey of Current Business* 84, no. 3 (March): 38–51.

Nakamura, Emi, and Jón Steinsson. 2012. "Lost in Transit: Product Replacement Bias and Pricing to Market." *American Economic Review* 102, no. 7 (December): 3277–316.

Nakamura, Leonard, Jon Samuels, and Rachel Soloveichik. 2016. "Valuing 'Free' Media in GDP: An Experimental Approach." BEA Working Paper WP2016–3, June.

National Academies of Sciences, Engineering, and Medicine. 2022. *Modernizing the Consumer Price Index for the 21st Century*. Washington, DC: National Academies Press. https://doi.org/10.17226/26485.

National Research Council. 2002. *At What Price? Conceptualizing and Measuring Cost-of-Living and Price Indexes*. Panel on Conceptual, Measurement, and Other Statistical Issues in Developing Cost-of-Living Indexes, edited by Charles L. Schultze and Christopher Mackie. Committee on National Statistics, Division of Behavioral and Social Sciences and Education. Washington, DC: National Academy Press.

Organization for Economic Co-operation and Development. 2001. *Measuring Productivity: Measurement of Aggregate and Industry-Level Productivity Growth*. OECD Manual. http://www.oecd.org/std/productivity-stats/2352458.pdf.

Organization for Economic Co-operation and Development. 2006. *Handbook on Hedonic Indexes and Quality Adjustments in Price Indexes: Special Application to Information Technology Products*. Paris: OECD.

Paben, Steven P., William H. Johnson, and John F. Schilp. 2016. "The 2018 Revision of the Consumer Price Index Geographic Sample." *Monthly Labor Review* (October). https://www.bls.gov/opub/mlr/2016/article/the-2018-revision-of-the-cpi-geographic-sample.htm.

Pakes, Ariel. 2003. "A Reconsideration of Hedonic Price Indices with an Application to PC's." *American Economic Review* 93, no. 5 (December): 1578–96.

Pakes, Ariel. 2005. "Hedonics and the Consumer Price Index." *Annales d'Economie et de Statistique* 79–80: 729–49.

Passero, William, Thesia I. Garner, and Clinton McCully. 2015. "Understanding the Relationship: CE Survey and PCE." In *Improving the Measurement of Consumer Expenditures*. Studies in Income and Wealth, edited by Christopher D. Carroll, Thomas F. Crossley, and John Sabelhaus, 74:181–203. Chicago: University of Chicago Press.

Redding, Stephen J., and David E. Weinstein. 2016. "A Unified Approach to Estimating Demand and Welfare." NBER Working Paper No. 22479, National Bureau of Economic Research.

Reinsdorf, Marshall. 1993. "The Effect of Outlet Price Differentials in the U.S. Consumer Price Index." In *Price Measurements and their Uses*. Studies in Income and Wealth, edited by Murray F. Foss, Marilyn E. Manser, Allan H. Young, 57:227–54. Chicago: University of Chicago Press.

Reinsdorf, Marshall. 1994. "Price Dispersion, Seller Substitution, and the U.S. CPI." Bureau of Labor Statistics Working Paper No. 252, Washington, DC.

Reinsdorf, Marshall. 1998. "Formula Bias and Within-Stratum Substitution Bias in the US CPI." *Review of Economics and Statistics* 80 (2): 175–87.

Reinsdorf, Marshall B., and Brent R. Moulton. 1996. "The Construction of Basic Components of Cost-of-Living Indexes." In *The Economics of New Goods*. Studies in Income and Wealth, edited by Timothy F. Bresnahan and Robert J. Gordon, 58:397–423. Chicago: University of Chicago Press.

Reinsdorf, Marshall, and Paul Schreyer. 2017. "Measuring Consumer Inflation in a Digital Economy." Paper presented at fifth IMF Statistical Forum, Washington DC, November 16–17. http://www.imf.org/~/media/Files/Conferences/2017-stats-forum/session-1-schreyer-and-reinsdorf.ashx?la=en.

Reinsdorf, Marshall, and Jack Triplett. 2009. "Ninety Years of Professional Thinking about the Consumer Price Index." In *Price Index Concepts and Measurement*, edited by W. E. Diewert, J. S. Greenlees, and C. R. Hulten, 17–84. Chicago: University of Chicago Press.

Reinsdorf, Marshall, and Robert Yuskavage. 2014. "Offshoring, Sourcing Substitution Bias and the Measurement of US Import Prices, GDP and Productivity." BEA Working Paper WP2014–6, April.

Sawyer, Steven, and Alvin So. 2018. "A New Approach for Quality Adjusting PPI Microprocessors." *Monthly Labor Review* (December). https://doi.org/10.21916/mlr.2018.29.

Stewart, Kenneth J., and Stephen B. Reed. 1999. "Consumer Price Index Research Series Using Current Methods, 1978–98." *Monthly Labor Review* 122, no. 6 (June): 29–38.

Swick, Roslyn, Deanna Bathgate, and Michael Horrigan. 2006. "Services Producer Price Indices: Past, Present, and Future." Paper presented to the Federal Economic Statistics Advisory Committee (FESAC), June 9. Bureau of Labor Statistics. https://www.bls.gov/advisory/fesacp1060906.pdf.

Syverson, Chad. 2017. "Challenges to Mismeasurement Explanations for the US Productivity Slowdown." *Journal of Economic Perspectives* 31, no. 2 (Spring): 165–86. https://pubs.aeaweb.org/doi/pdfplus/10.1257/jep.31.2.165.

Triplett, Jack E. 2006. "The Boskin Commission Report after a Decade." *International Productivity Monitor* 12 (Spring): 42–60.
Triplett, Jack E., and Barry P. Bosworth. 2004. *Productivity in the US Services Sector: New Sources of Economic Growth.* Washington, DC: Brookings Institution Press.
United States General Accounting Office. 2000. *Consumer Price Index: Update of Boskin Commission's Estimate of Bias.* Report to the Ranking Minority Member, Committee on Finance, US Senate, GAO/GGD-00–50, February.
Williams, Brendan, and Erick Sager. 2019. "A New Vehicles Transaction Price Index: Offsetting the Effects of Price Discrimination and Product Cycle Bias with a Year-Over-Year Index." BLS Working Paper. https://www.bls.gov/osmr/research-papers/2019/pdf/ec190040.pdf.

3

Intangible Investment
What It Is and Why It Matters

Carol Corrado

"We will be more likely to promote innovative activity if we are able to measure it more effectively and document its role in economic growth."
Federal Reserve Board Chairman Ben S. Bernanke, May 16, 2011.

3.1 Introduction

Investment in innovation and commercial knowledge creation—commonly known as investment in intangibles—was largely ignored in macroeconomic analysis until very recently. But as global growth has become increasingly driven by companies with relatively limited physical assets, the study of intangible assets and their role in production has burgeoned.

What is intangible investment, and why does it matter? Is it not just research and development (R&D)? Though R&D has long been seen as essential for sustaining growth-promoting advances in science and technology, it alone cannot explain the success of many of today's top performing firms. Instead, their success appears driven by business models built by intangible investments, i.e., investment in in digital platforms, services innovation, efficient delivery systems, and supply chain structures.

This chapter discusses how intangible investment affects the measurement and analysis of investment and productivity. The initial sections of the chapter (sections 3.2.1 and 3.2.2) set out definitions and the status of work measuring intangible capital for productivity analysis. According to widely used statistics, the review finds that only about 40 percent of intangible investment is included in official macroeconomic data for the United States and that including the full range of intangibles in productivity accounting significantly alters the contribution of capital as a source of growth. Section 3.3 explains how including intangible investment in national accounts affects GDP, growth accounting, and the interpretation of innovation. Sec-

Carol Corrado is with the Center for Business and Public Policy, McDonough School of Business, Georgetown University

I thank Marshall Reinsdorf and Louise Sheiner for helpful comments and discussion.

tion 3.4 discusses how productivity estimates are distorted when intangibles are ignored and concludes with remarks on the relevance of the intangibles framework for interpreting recent developments in productivity. The next section of the chapter (3.5) reviews how national accounts methods are applied to the measurement of intangibles, followed by three sections (sections 3.6, 3.7, and 3.8) that explore specific issues in intangibles measurement: Is brand really a productive asset? What are "public" intangibles? Are firm investments in AI and data reflected in intangibles? Section 3.9 sums up and suggests next steps.

3.2 Intangibles: Definitions and Major Findings

The terms *knowledge economy* or *knowledge capital* have been used for many years. Fritz Machlup set out a definition of "the knowledge industry" in 1962, stating that "total knowledge production in 1958 was almost 29 percent of adjusted [US] GNP" (362). Machlup defined his knowledge industry generously. It included R&D and education, which accounted for about half of his total. He further included communications media, information services (which he believed to be undercounted), and the production and distribution of stationery, typewriters, and equipment in the then-new industry, electronic computers—all of which suggested that the US industrial economy *circa 1958* was run using a massive information-processing apparatus. The systems driving this apparatus (standardization, interchangeable parts, printed forms, recordkeeping, purchasing and delivery regularity, advertising, and management) arguably were the unseen drivers of the economic growth of the time.

Today, the notion that information-processing systems are productive assets of firms is well established in economics, management, and corporate finance literature. That the assets of an organization also encompass marketing strategies, management practices, and firm-specific capital built from employer-provided training (the full intangibles approach) sits a bit harder among some economists and economic statisticians; the reasons why are discussed below.

3.2.1 What Is Intangible Investment?

The intangibles approach to understanding productivity builds on the standard insight that production reflects a transformation of capital and labor services but expands the range of expenditures considered as capital spending. The approach defines investment as a use of resources that reduces current consumption to increase future consumption, which implies a simple economic criterion may be used to determine investment: namely, that capital is built from outlays expected to yield returns in future periods. This intertemporal view of investment is common sense yet firmly grounded in economics via optimal growth theory (e.g., Weitzman 1976; Hulten 1979).

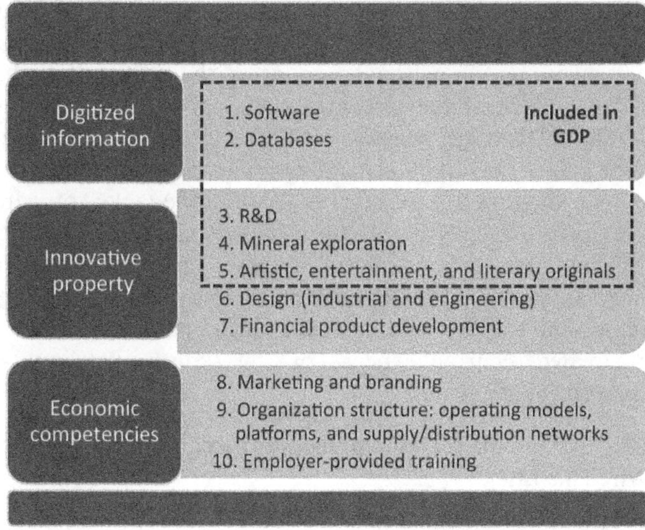

Fig. 3.1 Intangible Investment: Broad groups and individual asset types
Source: Author's adaptation of Corrado, Hulten, and Sichel (2005, 2009).

This definition is straightforward to apply to durable goods spending—for example, spending on machinery represents investment—but it also applies to expenditures on product R&D, market development, and organizational and management efficiency. All told, the intangibles approach captures how long-lived spending on new business models, technologies, and marketing strategies drive economic growth. This expanded view of investment also suggests that the economic literature's focus on patented R&D alone as a source of innovation is too narrow.

The notion that there might be more to business investment than is captured by spending on physical assets like plant and equipment was pursued by Corrado, Hulten, and Sichel (2005, 2009). Building on prior works (e.g., Young 1998 and Nakamura 1999, 2001), they formalized expanding the coverage of fixed investment in national accounts to include spending on long-lived intangible assets.

The framework for intangible investment set out by Corrado, Hulten, and Sichel is summarized in figure 3.1. As seen on the left, intangible investments are grouped into three broad categories—digitized information, innovative property, and economic competencies. Each category includes two or more specific investment asset types (shown on the right). The assets shown in figure 3.1 play a crucial role in the success of companies built around software, data, design, operations networks, and customer loyalty (brand), as many top-performing companies are these days.

The definition of investment in national accounts has, in fact, been expanded in recent decades to begin to account for the role of intangibles. R&D and artistic, entertainment, and literary originals (E&AO) were included in investment in national accounts in the United States in a revision issued in 2013; computer software (combined with databases produced for firms' internal use) was added in 1999. But as seen by the box superimposed over figure 3.1, at least for the time being, official GDP only includes investments in the first five asset types listed in the table: software, databases developed internally by organizations, R&D, mineral exploration, and E&AO. Investments in purchased databases, industrial and engineering design, financial product development, marketing and branding, organization structure, and employer-provided training remain uncapitalized—that is, they are treated as current expenses of firms (intermediate inputs) rather than investment (final output).[1]

3.2.2 Why Expand the National Accounts Definition of Investment (and Why This List)?

The development of the taxonomy in figure 3.1 was prompted, at least in part, by analysis of the widening gap between equity market and accounting valuations of firms that emerged during the 1990s. A prominent analysis of this gap (Lev 2001) suggested that intangible assets such as brand, new products, and software-enabled systems for business processes (e.g., for procurement and customer management) were drivers of the financial outcomes of many of the nation's then most innovative companies but were not included as assets in accounting valuations. Lev and Radhakrishnan (2005) further recommended that company reports include spending information on new products/services development, customer relations, human resources, and organizational capital as assets. While these categories are slightly different from those listed in figure 3.1, the Lev and Radhakrishnan framework defines investment as business spending that creates long-lived revenue-generating capacity, just as in the macro-oriented framework used to create figure 3.1.

A large microdata literature supports the productivity-enhancing character of assets not currently included in national accounts investment. Influential studies have established the long-lasting performance impacts of management and human resource practices (Bloom and Van Reenan 2007; Ichniowski and Shaw 1999), employer-provided training and apprenticeships (Black and Lynch 2001, 2005; Frazis and Spletzer 2005; Zwick 2007), and brand and advertising (Nelson 1974; Kwoka 1984, Rauch 2013), among others. All told, evidence-based support for the capitalization of spending streams associated with the organizational practices and business functions corresponding to lines 6–10 of figure 3.1 is strong.

A substantial research effort has enabled expansion of the number of countries for which estimates of the full complement of intangible assets as set out in figure 3.1 are available.[2] The Organization for Economic Co-operation and Development (OECD) (2013) adopted the taxonomy in figure 3.1 for the macroeconomic analysis of productivity, described as "knowledge-based capital," and the European Union commissioned its latest update of the industry-level EU KLEMS productivity accounts to include, to the extent possible, the figure 3.1 list of intangible assets in production accounts for all member countries for its economic policy analysis.[3]

3.2.3 Intangible Investment: Five Facts

The expanded investment framework is widely used to study productivity change. Five findings, or "facts," of intangible investment have emerged from this body of work and are set out below.

3.2.3.1 Fact 1

Investment in intangible capital often exceeds investment in nonresidential tangible capital in modern innovative economies.

Figure 3.2a shows rates (percentages of GDP) from 1985 on of nonresidential tangible and intangible investment for the United States according

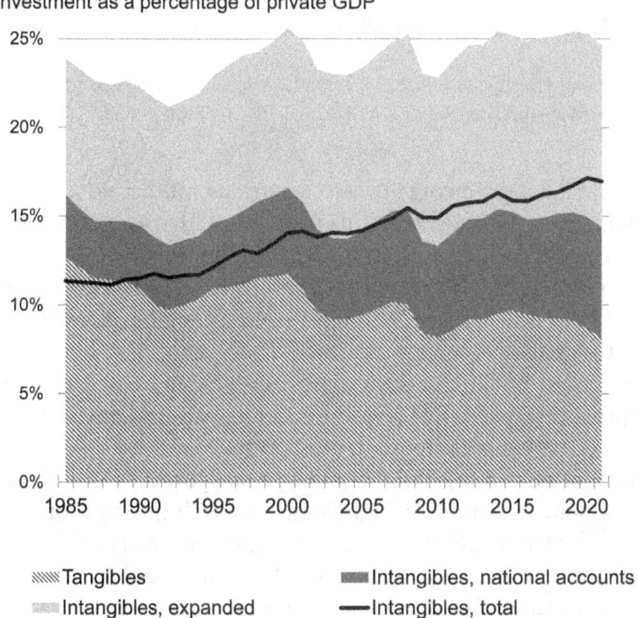

Fig. 3.2a Private nonresidential investment in the United States, tangible and intangible, 1985–2021

Note: Private GDP is adjusted to include all intangibles.

Source: Author's elaboration of data from the US national accounts augmented with estimates of intangible investment expanded to include all assets listed in figure 3.1. Corrado et al. (2022b) provide the data and document data sources.

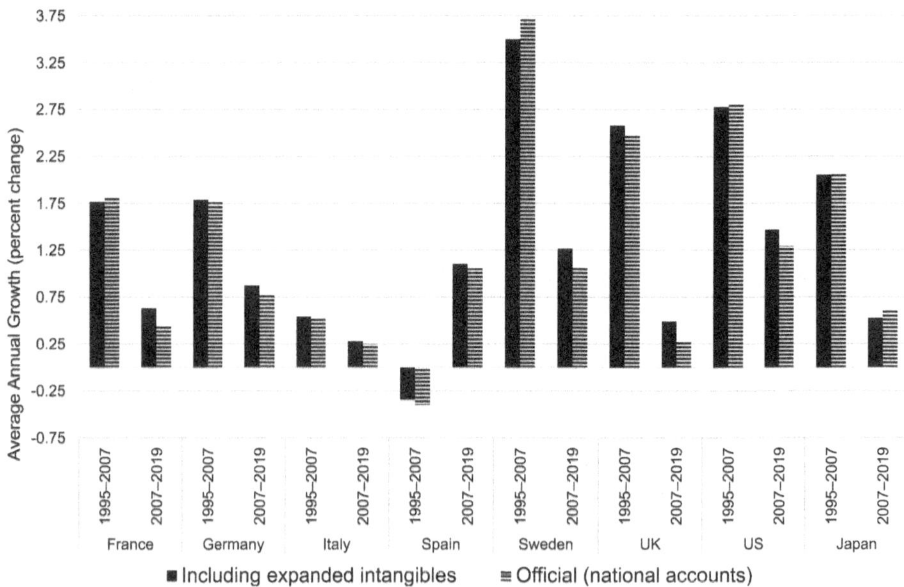

Fig. 3.2b Labor productivity growth, selected countries, 1995–2007 and 2007–2019

Note: Market sector industries. Excludes agriculture in all countries except Japan.
Source: Author's elaboration of EU KLEMS and INTANProd estimates (LLEE 2023).

to the figure 3.1 framework; it also separates intangible investment currently included in national accounts from intangible investment included in the expanded definition of intangibles. The rate for nonresidential tangible investment (the dark shaded area at the bottom) fell 4 percentage points over the period shown, whereas the rate for total intangible investment (plotted as a line) rose nearly 6 percentage points.

In the United States, total intangible investment now stands at 17 percent of private sector GDP (GDP excluding government services), about 40 percent of which is currently treated as investment in national accounts (the solid light blue area). Thus, a message of figure 3.2a is that the value of total investment in intangibles significantly exceeds the value of components currently included in US official statistics; the same can be said for many of the major economies of Europe (Bontadini et al. 2024).

If investment and GDP are higher when *all* intangibles are capitalized, so too is output per hour, or labor productivity. Figure 3.2b shows the degree to which labor productivity *growth* is affected in selected European countries, Japan, and the United States by the inclusion of all intangibles. As seen, the impacts have been stronger for most countries since 2007.[4]

Practitioners analyzing macroeconomic trends who have been taught that R&D development is a sufficient proxy for innovation effort in modern economies should be aware of the relative magnitudes displayed in figures 3.2a and 3.2b. As pointed out in Corrado et al. (2022a, 8–9), in cross-country data covering selected countries in Europe and the United States from 1995 to 2018 (LLEE 2023), the correlation between growth in market sector R&D capital and total intangible capital excluding R&D is small—just 0.32. The correlation between official components of intangible capital and expanded components is only 0.28. These correlations suggest that much is missing in official macroeconomic data on private investment.

3.2.3.2 Fact 2

Once intangible capital is accounted for in analysis of factors affecting economic growth, capital deepening—the degree to which workers are equipped with capital in an economy—becomes the most important source of growth in labor productivity in modern economies.

Figure 3.3 shows sources-of-growth calculations for the United States—the decomposition of labor productivity growth into contributions from labor composition, capital deepening, and total factor productivity (TFP)[5] with the same breakpoint between early and recent periods used in figure 3.2b. The statistics shown in figure 3.3 are akin to those issued by the Bureau of Labor Statistics (BLS), but here the analysis is augmented to include all intangible assets. A striking takeaway from this figure, though perhaps unsurprising considering figure 3.2a, is the sheer size of the contribution of

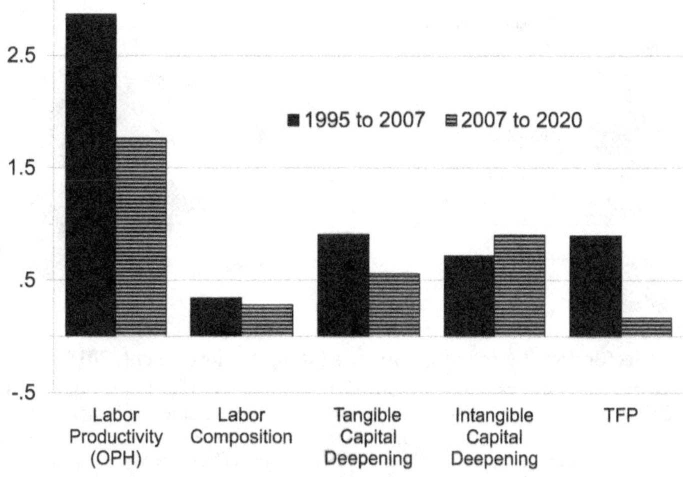

Fig. 3.3 Decompositions of growth in US labor productivity

Note: Based on industry-level estimates for market sector industries, excluding agriculture. Figures are contributions in percentage points.

Source: Author's elaboration of EU KLEMS & INTANProd estimates (LLEE 2023). Bontadini et al. (2023) provide details on industry coverage and estimation methods.

intangible capital deepening—in the first period, it is nearly as large as that of tangible capital, and in the second, it is nearly double.

Furthermore, intangible capital is a key determinant of TFP in endogenous growth theory (Romer 1990, Jones 1995) because diffusion of innovations creates productivity spillovers. The connection between growth of intangible capital and TFP caused by knowledge spillovers has been studied in the empirical productivity literature.[6] All told, when considering factors that influence pace of labor productivity growth in modern economies, the contribution of intangible investment cannot be ignored—it shows through in the direct contribution of knowledge-based capital as well as in knowledge spillovers, which are included in TFP. We elaborate further on this high-level finding in sections 3.3 and 3.4 below.

3.2.3.3 Fact 3

Innovation investments are widely distributed across industry sectors.

Figure 3.4 shows the distribution of total private intangible investment across major industry sectors in the United States in 2019.[7] As shown on the left, major sector shares of total intangible investment range from 20 to nearly 30 percent. The sectoral breadth of innovation investments is driven by investments in non−R&D intangibles. The conduct of R&D occurs largely in the industrial sector, which accounts for about 60 percent of total

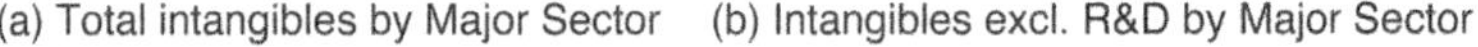

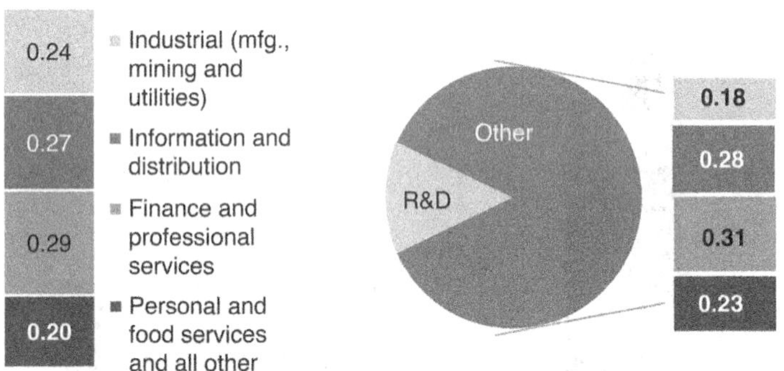

Fig. 3.4 Sector distribution of US private intangible investment, 2019

Note: Sectors are defined as follows: Industrial is mining (NAICS 21), manufacturing (NAICS 31–33) and utilities (NAICS 22); information and distribution is information (NAICS 51); trade (NAICS 42, 44–45) and transportation and warehousing (NAICS 48–49, excl 491); financial and professional services is finance and insurance (NAICS 52) and professional and business services (NAICS 54–56); personal and other services is education, health, social assistance, arts, and recreation (NAICS 61, 62, and 71), accommodation and food (NAICS 72); all other is other services (NAICS 81), agriculture (NAICS 11), construction (NAICS 23), and real estate and rental and leasing (NAICS 53).

Source: Author's elaboration of data from the US national accounts augmented with estimates of intangibles expanded to include all assets reported in figure 3.1.

R&D. But as shown in the "pie" in the middle of the figure, total R&D accounts for only about one-sixth of total intangible investment. When R&D is excluded, investment in other intangibles is seen to be distributed rather broadly across services-producing sectors of the US economy (the panel on the right).

The financial and professional services sector currently accounts for the largest fraction of intangible investment in the United States. The sector's share was much lower in 1995 (22 percent) and below the share posted by the industrial sector in that year (32 percent); swings in R&D and other intangibles account for this dramatic switch. Other sector shares of intangible investment, in total and by broad type, have been essentially stable since 1995, though the information sector's share did edge up by 1.5 percentage points, due mainly to an increase in its share of R&D.

The variation across industries in intangible intensity summarized in figure 3.4 has implications for understanding how digital technologies are diffusing throughout the economy. Research finds that the intangible investment intensity of industries is correlated with independent indicators of their digitization, a link not driven by R&D and that occurs largely in industries outside manufacturing (Corrado, Criscuolo et al. 2021).[8] Intangible investment also is found to be correlated with output and productivity growth at the sector level (Hazan et al. 2021). These linkages suggest that intangible investment captures firms' efforts to innovate using digital technologies to enhance (or change) business models and provide value-producing opportunities in wide range of industries. Figure 3.4 could then be said to underscore the notion that to see how digital technologies diffuse throughout the economy, we can look at investment expanded to include the full complement of intangibles. We examine this insight further in section 3.8, discussing how investments in AI and data are reflected in intangibles.

3.2.3.4 Fact 4

The realized after-tax rate of return to capital investments is much lower and more stable when investment is expanded to cover intangibles.

Using the investment data on tangible and intangible investment underlying the earlier figure 3.2a, figure 3.5 shows that the measured after-tax rate of return implied by *macroeconomic data* is dramatically different when investment is expanded to cover intangibles. Instead of rising over time, the rate of return becomes trendless once intangibles are included. (The figure also appears in Corrado et al. 2022a).

This finding casts doubt on the commonly expressed view that the market power of corporations has increased in recent years. To examine this topic, researchers analyze microdata for evidence of monopoly power and find what appears to be a worrisome rise in price markups and profitability, especially in US-based publicly traded corporations (see the chapter on corporate market power in the IMF's April 2019 *World Economic Outlook*).

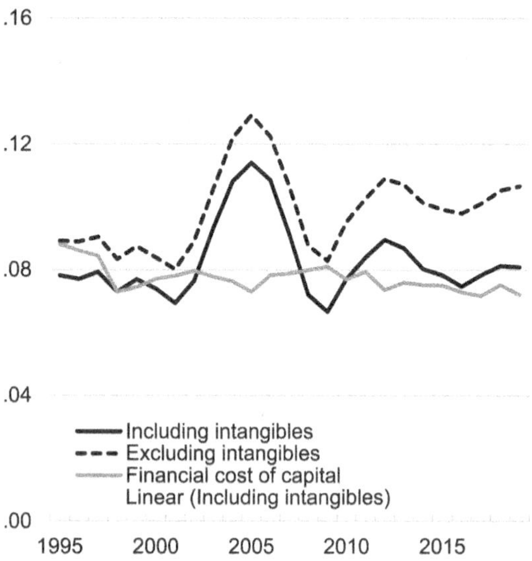

Fig. 3.5 After-tax rates of return, US private industries, 1995–2019

Note: Real estate and private households are excluded from private industry in these calculations. Private capital includes fixed assets, inventories, and nonresidential land. Intangibles covers all assets listed in figure 3.1.

Source: Corrado et al. (2022b).

Yet the microdata these findings rely on are derived from company reports or official surveys, which do not account for intangibles appropriately (or at all).

If investments in intangible capital are not included in analyses of profitability, firms and economies may appear to have abnormally high profits relative to the (mismeasured) capital employed—and the higher the uncounted intangible investment, the greater the misperception. This is precisely what figure 3.5 shows. There is no trend in the overall profitability of US private industry measured by its realized after-tax rate of return when intangibles are included in the analysis (the dark line) whereas the exclusion of intangibles results in estimates of returns that increase, on balance, over time (the dashed line).

The figure further shows that there is no material gap between the financial cost of capital, calculated as a weighted average of the expected return on stocks and after-tax cost of debt (the gray line), and the realized (actual) rate including intangibles. The message suggested by the (erroneous) large gap based on the rate of return when intangibles are excluded is akin to the message obtained when price markups are estimated using microdata sources that exclude intangibles.[9] Figure 3.5 reinforces the analysis of Basu (2019) that the evidence to date that markups are rising and hampering competition is not dispositive and that improved microdata on intangibles are needed to calibrate accurate market power indicators for competition policy analysis.

3.2.3.5 Fact 5

Uncounted intangible capital can explain the observed increase in within-industry productivity dispersion.

Andrews, Criscuolo, and Gal (2016) show that the gap between the measured TFP of leader companies and of laggards in similar industry sectors has widened since 2000. However, their estimates of TFP did not take the contribution of intangibles into account because they relied on company financial data in which companies did not report intangibles consistently. Indirect evidence that intangibles may be driving the dispersion in productivity via financial outperformance comes from Corrado, Martin, and Wu (2020), who found that 100 firms selected from the 1000 companies in Morgan Stanley's all country world index (ACWI) of stock prices based on their ability to generate value from intangible assets significantly outperform the ACWI benchmark.

Figure 3.6 shows that the increase in within-industry productivity dispersion mostly occurs in intangible-intensive industries (Corrado, Criscuolo, et al. 2021). The study from which this figure is drawn finds that productivity dispersion is driven by financial barriers to accumulation of intangible assets—which affect some firms more than others—and by the previously mentioned complementarity of intangibles with expenditures on digitization.

3.3 Calculating GDP and Productivity with Investment in Intangibles Included

The previously described facts about intangible capital in modern economies are based on GDP and productivity figures adjusted to include the intangible assets listed in figure 3.1. To consider just how intangibles fit into GDP and productivity statistics, consider first a simplified model of an economy.[10]

3.3.1 Upstream/Downstream Model of an Economy

A simplified model of an economy with intangibles divides production into two broad sectors: (1) an "upstream" sector that *produces new knowledge* that can be commercialized, like a new or improved product design (or product formula) or a software program adapted to the needs of an organization; and (2) a "downstream" sector that *uses the knowledge* generated by the upstream sector to produce final output. For simplicity, the model assumes that there are no exports or imports of intangible assets and no intermediate purchases of other goods and services.

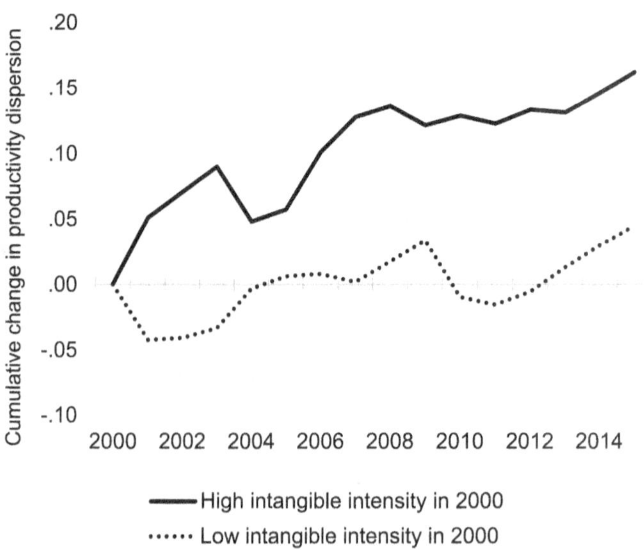

Fig. 3.6 Evolution of productivity dispersion by intangibles intensity, 2000–2015

Note: The graph plots the evolution of establishment-level productivity dispersion over time within manufacturing and market services industries. Unweighted averages across two-digit industries are shown, normalized to 0 in the starting year. Productivity dispersion is measured as the 90–10 difference in total factor productivity following Woolridge (2009), i.e., the difference in productivity between firms at the ninetieth percentile of the productivity distribution in a country industry and firms at the tenth percentile. The vertical axes represent log-point differences from the starting year: for instance, productivity dispersion in market services has increased by about 0.11 in the final year, which corresponds to approximately 11 percent higher productivity dispersion in 2015 compared to 2000.

Source: Corrado, Criscuolo et al. (2021). Estimation based on the OECD MultiProd database in combination with INTANInvest. Countries included are AUT, BEL, DEU, DNK, FIN, FRA, IRL, ITA, NLD, PRT.

Box 3.1 sets out the upstream/downstream model in detail. In the model, the upstream sector produces intangible capital ("knowledge"); in other words, its output corresponds to the time series depicted by the dark line in figure 3.2a. The stock of intangible capital reflects the accumulation of upstream output less losses due to economic depreciation (e.g., aging). The downstream production sector uses the stock of knowledge to produce final goods and remands the upstream sector a portion of income earned from the sale of final goods in return. Because producers that purchase new, commercially valuable knowledge must earn returns on this investment, the value of knowledge stocks must be included in calculations of the return to capital; the consequences of not doing so are seen in figure 3.5.

What about the advances in basic science that we have been taught are the ultimate drivers of productivity and living standards? Basic knowl-

Box 3.1 A Model of an Economy with Intangibles

In a simplified model of an economy with intangibles, production is divided into two broad sectors: (1) an "upstream" sector that produces new knowledge that can be commercialized; and (2) a "downstream" sector that uses the knowledge generated by the upstream sector to produce final output.

Sectoral activity is described and denoted as follows:

- Upstream output reflects the production of new commercial knowledge. This is also intangible investment, which in volume terms is N and in nominal terms is $P^N N$, where P^N is the price of intangible assets.
- Downstream output reflects the production of (tangible) investment and consumer goods, $P^Y Y$, or $P^I I + P^C C$, in nominal terms, where P^Y, P^I, and P^C are the prices of downstream output, investment goods, and consumer goods, respectively. (For simplicity, intermediate inputs are ignored, an assumption that is easily relaxed.)
- The outstanding stock of intangible capital, denoted R, reflects the accumulated upstream sector output of new commercial knowledge N after deducting economic depreciation (i.e., aging).
- Freely available basic knowledge (e.g., open-source software) is represented by R^{Basic}. It is an input to upstream production and is assumed to be produced outside the model. (Another assumption that is easily relaxed with no major change in model implications.)
- The value of intangible capital (at replacement cost) is given by $P^N R$.
- Payments made to the owners of R are denoted by $P^R R$, where P^R is the per period rental price equivalent of using intangible capital in production.
- The stock of tangible assets is denoted by K, its value by $P^I K$, and payments to owners by $P^K K$. Labor inputs and their price are L and P^L, respectively.
- Productivity in the production of upstream and downstream output is determined by A^N and A^Y.

Regarding monopoly power,

- R is inherently nonrival and thus only partially appropriable. Appropriability lasts for the length of time the producer-innovator can sell the knowledge to the downstream sector at a monopoly price.

(*continued*)

Box 3.1 (*continued*)

- The downstream sector is assumed to be a price taker for knowledge (i.e., monopoly power resides in the upstream sector). Final output prices for consumption and tangible investment are assumed to be competitive, as are factor input prices for labor and tangible capital.
- The upstream sector sells newly produced knowledge assets to the downstream sector at a price that allows it to enjoy rents (monopoly profits) from, denoted π^N, from its innovations. This implies that the price of commercial knowledge P^N *embeds these rents.*

The sectoral production and income flows in this economy can be written as follows:

$$N = A^N F^N(L^N, K^N, R^{\text{Basic}}); P^N N = P^L L^N + P^K K^N + \pi^N$$

$$Y = A^Y F^Y(L^Y, K^Y, R); P^Y Y = P^L L^Y + P^K K^Y + P^R R$$

where the asset price of commercial knowledge P^N and the price of its services for a year P^R are linked via the Jorgenson (1963) user cost expression $P^R = (r + \delta - \dot{p})P^N$, where $r - \dot{p}$ is the real interest rate and δ is the depreciation rate. The user cost of tangible capital is similarly linked to its asset price. The costs of depreciation and interest (or return on investment) are assumed to be included in P^Y. The model is closed via arbitrage of competitive returns (r) across sectors—returns to investments in innovation (that build intangible capital R) with returns to alternative long-term investments (that build tangible capital K).

The existence of "abnormal" innovator profits may persist for periods of time in this model, but in long-run equilibrium intertemporal arbitrage operates to constrain existing innovators' profits to zero (i.e., $\pi^N = 0$). With continuous entry of new innovators and waves of technological change, however, the model is consistent with a degree of market power continuously embedded in time series for intangible asset prices.

edge (scientific, technical, or collaborative) certainly is one factor driving applied investment in innovation/intangibles. There also is a well-known gap between breakthrough invention and commercial application that can only be bridged with spending—consisting, at least in part, of intangible investment. For example, firm-level studies demonstrate that branding and marketing, organization structure, and employer-provided training are complements with R&D (especially pharma R&D; see Vinod and Rao 2000). Therefore, in the model set out in box 3.1, basic scientific knowledge is assumed to be a free input to upstream production. This "free" knowledge is generated, say, by publicly funded research in universities and national laboratories, by technical standards developed by industry consortia, or acquired via open-source software and data hosted on collaborative platforms like GitHub.

Commercially valuable knowledge is accessed by downstream producers in two fundamentally different ways. It may be purchased, leased, rented—in other words, paid for. Or, because knowledge is fundamentally nonrival and only partially appropriable, it may be copied and used in downstream production essentially for free. Once "leakage" to free availability is complete, the knowledge stops generating earnings for its owner, and the value of the intangible asset falls to zero. But as this knowledge becomes freely available, it becomes the main driver of growth in TFP in modern economies.

The model's two-sector depiction of production captures important aspects of business innovation in modern economies. The upstream sector covers firms that are almost fully reliant on the production of innovation in the form of intangible capital (e.g., biotech startups using massive data experiments to produce new formulas for drugs), with the downstream sector comprising producers that acquire innovations via outright purchase or licensure agreements with annual payments. Firms may also have their own "innovation labs" and "business strategy teams" to produce and commercialize new ideas used in their downstream production. These innovation labs and strategy teams—factories within factories—are upstream knowledge producers residing within larger organizations whose total revenue reflects a contribution that covers (or exceeds, at least for a time) the opportunity cost of resources devoted to these labs and teams. For example, many banks have software writers developing software such as mobile banking apps. The bank's investment in software assets is measured by the writers' compensation plus costs such as computing charges and office space.

In the model, innovators/intangible capital owners hold temporary market power that provides them with monopoly rents; these rents motivate the entrepreneurial investments that lead to innovation. The temporary nature of market power is due to the inherent nonrival character of knowledge-based assets: as commercial knowledge diffuses (is copied), innovator profits are competed away.

We are now in a position to make some explicit points about how the recognition of intangibles affects (a) GDP and gross domestic income and (b) the ability to "see" innovation in productivity data.

3.3.2 Intangibles, GDP Measurement, and Decomposing the Sources of Growth

The treatment of intangibles affects the measurement of GDP and the decomposition of sources of GDP growth in several ways. When spending on intangibles is not recognized as investment, the production of intangibles (upstream output in the upstream/downstream model) is treated as intermediate consumption. Final output produced using the intermediate inputs of intangibles still reflects their contribution to production, but GDP consists of downstream output only. Given that spending on innovation (or intangibles) really represents investment, when these expenditures are capitalized—that is, treated as investment in intangible assets rather than as intermediate consumption—upstream output is included in GDP, as shown in equation (1) in box 3.2. This makes GDP larger, increasing the level of output per hour, a measure of labor productivity.

The effect on GDP *growth* of capitalizing intangibles can be positive or negative depending on how fast investment in intangibles is growing compared to the rest of GDP. As is evident from equation (2) in box 3.2, if upstream sector output is rising more quickly than downstream output, GDP growth is boosted by the capitalization of intangibles. If it is rising more slowly, GDP growth is reduced. Labor productivity *growth* (the growth of GDP relative to aggregate hours worked) could similarly be higher or lower with the capitalization of intangibles.

Solow's model of sources of growth relates output growth to growth of inputs of labor and capital plus a TFP residual. Inputs are weighted by income shares, and when intangibles are capitalized in GDP, part of the total return to capital is allocated to intangible capital inputs, as shown in equation (3) in box 3.2—lowering the measured return to capital. Capitalizing intangibles also results in a larger measure of gross capital income from production because the cost of acquiring capital assets is treated as investment rather than current expense. Thus, the move boosts measured economic profits if the new investment in intangibles exceeds their gross return (i.e., the return including economic depreciation) and vice versa.

The Solow sources-of-growth model with intangible capital is shown in equation (4) of box 3.2. What is different in the model with intangibles is that the contribution of paid-for, commercially valuable knowledge has become a source of growth, as previously indicated in the discussion of figure 3.3. That is, the stock of intangibles becomes one of the inputs used to explain the growth of output while investment in new intangibles becomes one of the outputs.

The intangible capital framework helps explain the origins of TFP growth. The knowledge embedded in intangible assets is nonrival and only partially appropriable. To explain these terms, consider first the properties of a rival asset—a car, say. Its use is controlled by its owner, and its "work" cannot be duplicated without duplicating the number of cars employed in production. By contrast, nonrival assets—blueprints or software codes, say—may be copied and used repeatedly at low cost. Because intangible assets can be copied and used in production by owners and nonowners alike, owners of intangible assets typically do not capture the full returns to their investment. These unappropriated returns are a source of growth in measured TFP. The

Box 3.2 The Effect of Capitalizing Intangibles on GDP and on Growth Accounting

Without the capitalization of intangibles, the downstream sector's spending on intangibles $P^N N$ (from box 3.1) cis treated as a purchase of intermediate inputs. GDP then equals the output of the downstream sector output $P^Y Y$ regardless of whether it is measured by final expenditures or by summing the sectors' value added.

When the definition of investment is expanded to include spending on intangibles, intangible investment become a final expenditure along with consumption and tangible investment. GDP then becomes $P^Y Y + P^N N$, the sum of upstream and downstream sector value added, or $P^Q Q$, *which now also equals final expenditure.*

$$P^Q Q = P^Y Y + P^N N = P^C C + P^I I + P^N N. \tag{1}$$

Here, the P terms are prices, C is consumption, and I is investment in tangible capital K. When investments in innovation, N, are capitalized, both GDP and level of output per hour become larger.

In contrast, the impact on GDP *growth* could be positive or negative. With intangibles capitalized, the growth rate of GDP, denoted by dq, equals a weighted average of the growth rates of downstream and upstream production. Denoting as the growth rates (defined as log-changes) of downstream and upstream production by dy and dn respectively, and letting s_Q^N be the share of nominal GDP accounted for by investment in intangibles in equation (1a), this weighted average is

$$dq = s_Q^N dn + (1 - s_Q^N) dy. \tag{2}$$

The impact on GDP growth, $(dq - dy)$, which from (2) equals $s_Q^N(dn - dy)$, depends on the relative growth rate of intangible investment.

Capitalization of intangibles also implies that part of the income from production represents returns to intangible investment. From box 3.1, with L as labor input, K and R physical and intangible capital services, respectively, and the P terms factor prices, gross income from production equals

$$P^Q Q \equiv P^L L + P^K K + P^R R. \tag{3}$$

The rental price of intangibles, P^R, may contain monopolistic returns to innovation via P^N as discussed in box 3.1. Factor payments to the inputs to production are assumed to exhaust total income. When intangibles are capitalized, the gross income attributed to capital—physical and

(*continued*)

Box 3.2 (*continued*)

intangible—increases by $P^N N$ because acquiring intangible assets is no longer expensed.

Finally, the Solow model decomposes sources of GDP growth into contributions from changes in inputs and from TFP, where TFP is residual growth not explained by input changes. Let σ_Q^X be the combined factor income share for the conventional inputs L and K, dx be the combined growth of these two inputs, σ_Q^R be the factor income share attributed to intangible capital, and dr be the growth of inputs of intangible capital. The Solow sources-of-growth decomposition is

$$dq = \sigma_Q^X dx + \sigma_Q^R dr + da. \tag{4}$$

This decomposition says that output growth consists of a contribution from conventional inputs $\sigma_Q^X dx$, a contribution from paid-for, commercially held knowledge $\sigma_Q^R dr$, and TFP growth da. The contribution of freely available knowledge, whether basic knowledge or commercial innovations able to be replicated at low cost, is included in da.

costless diffusion (or spread) of innovators' knowledge from one organization to another—a phenomenon termed "knowledge spillovers" by Griliches (1992, 1994) in the context of R&D—drives the increasing returns on investment in knowledge that plays a central role in modern growth theory.

3.3.3 Intangibles and Innovation

When considering innovation, economists typically look to TFP as a measure of underlying technical progress. TFP is, however, calculated as a residual by subtracting growth of share-weighted paid-for inputs from output growth, and it is rather hard to talk meaningfully about a residual with practitioners interested in innovation. Innovation analysts typically focus on how individual firms innovate, e.g., develop a new business model or launch a new product or improve employee work arrangements. Innovation analysts view business decision makers as needing to weigh resource costs involved in bringing about change through innovation against current profits. The intangible capital approach aims to capture the outcome of these actions in macrodata.

3.3.3.1 Interpretation of Innovation

Dale Jorgenson explains growth by stressing the role of innovation versus duplication (Schramm et al. 2008). Consider their distinct roles by asking (as in Corrado et al. 2023a), How might the firm Peloton make more sales? One way would be to employ more capital and labor to produce more bikes and treadmills, generating growth via *duplication*. The other path would be to get more sales from existing capital and labor: mixing new exercise music, developing new software, or reengineering the supply process. Jorgenson calls this growth via *innovation*.

The intangible capital framework gives Jorgenson's "growth via duplication vs. innovation" distinction a natural interpretation: innovation is output change less the contribution of duplication (Goodridge, Haskel, and Wallis 2012). This suggests that the contribution of innovation to economic growth is measured by increases in TFP *plus* the contribution of intangible capital.[11] Moreover, because the stock of intangibles is an indirect determinant of TFP via knowledge spillovers due to its inherent nonrival character, the intangible capital framework further suggests that one should look to intangibles as *the* proximate source of innovation in a market economy.

Let us return to the questions asked at the beginning of this chapter: How can this be? Have we not been taught that new commercial knowledge is created by R&D and that we should look to R&D to learn about innovation? We now have some answers. First, the concept of innovation is not confined to R&D−driven inventions, as has been confirmed by research on the broader set of intangibles identified in figure 3.1. Second, R&D investment is included in intangible investment, so the R&D view is not contradicted, only expanded. And third, just as knowledge created via basic and applied R&D in national laboratories and universities contributes to technological advancement via its transfer to actors in the commercial arena, the spillover of commercially created knowledge across market-based organizations also contributes to TFP in the intangible capital framework.

3.3.3.2 *Innovation and Output Growth Due to Quality Change*

The benefits of innovation frequently come through new products or new product attributes that improve product quality. Product quality change stems from producers' actions that create new demand or stimulate existing demand, e.g., the conduct of market research, product design, and marketing—actions that fulfill unmet needs by introducing new products or improved varieties of existing products (product differentiation) and captured by the long-lived product development components of intangible capital.

The capitalization of intangibles underscores the importance of adjusting real final demand for quality change. Research on measurement of quality change frequently finds that official price deflators under adjust for product quality changes. When comparing productivity growth in different periods, such as those displayed in figure 3.3, a first-order concern then is whether product quality bias has changed and affected the interpretation of developments in TFP and, hence, knowledge spillovers.

Measurement of quality improvements from innovation is not a topic of this chapter.[12] The measurement of intangible asset prices, however, is central and is discussed in section 3.5, 3.8 and Appendix A of this chapter.

3.4 Missing Intangibles and Productivity Mismeasurement[13]

"Investmentless growth" surfaced as a factor possibly restraining US economic growth in the aftermath of the 2008–2009 global financial recession. In unraveling the puzzle of low investment that prevailed, many studies found that a shift in the composition of investment away from traditional forms of capital spending toward uncounted intangibles played an important role (e.g., Gutiérrez and Philippon 2017). Suppose, then, that we do not include intangible capital in the empirical frameworks used to estimate TFP. How would the missing investment affect the measurement and interpretation of TFP statistics?

3.4.1 Missing Intangibles and TFP

There is a running theme in the productivity literature that errors of measurement contaminate TFP in various ways because TFP is measured as a residual. Here, we focus on the possibility that intangibles are mismeasured in a first-order manner: namely, they are ignored.[14] Intangible assets are sometimes purchased and sometimes generated internally within firms. In the former case, ignoring investment in intangibles means treating such purchases as transactions in services used as intermediate inputs. In the latter case, the production of intangibles for own-account (internal) purposes is not counted at all.

Accounting for investment in intangibles can either raise or lower measured TFP growth. Capitalizing intangibles affects measurement of both output growth and input growth. As discussed in section 3.3.2 and set out in box 3.3, the effect on output growth depends on the growth of investment in intangible capital relative to the growth of downstream output. The main effect on the input side is captured by returns to intangible capital which depends on both the level and growth of the stock of intangibles. Though the net impact of capitalizing intangibles on TFP growth is difficult to generalize, the impact is *likely* to be positive if investment in intangibles is accelerating and negative if it is slowing.

3.4.2 Intangibles and the Slowdown in (Mis)measured TFP Growth

The slowdown in productivity growth in advanced economies that began shortly after the turn of the millennium has been a topic of much discussion. The intangible capital framework suggests three reasons why mismeasured TFP (that is, measure of TFP when intangibles are ignored) can slow.

First, actual, properly measured TFP might slow for reasons such as a slowdown in technological progress, which in the upstream/downstream model is commercial knowledge spillovers and new basic knowledge flowing into the commercial arena. In an important book, Robert Gordon (2016) argues that technical progress consists of, essentially, one big wave around industrialization, electrification, transportation, and information technol-

Box 3.3 The Effect of Capitalizing Intangibles on Measurement of TFP

How does the measure of TFP, da, in equation (4) of box 3.2, compare to a measure with intangibles ignored? From before, measured aggregate economic activity is given by $P^Y Y$ when intangibles are omitted. Now let da' be mismeasured TFP when using $P^Y Y$, and let dx' be the contribution of conventional inputs (K and L) to the growth in dy.[1]

The Solow decomposition when intangibles are missing is then

$$(4') \qquad dy = dx' + da'.$$

Combining equations (2) and (4) from box 3.2 with (4′), TFP with missing intangibles may be expressed as follows:[2]

$$\begin{aligned}(5) \qquad da' = {} & da && \{\text{Knowledge spillovers}\} \\ & - s_Q^N(dn - dy) && \{\text{Missing output } N\} \\ & + \sigma_Q^R dr && \{\text{Missing input } R\} \\ & - (dx' - \sigma_Q^X dx) && \{K \text{ and } L \text{ share mismeasurement}\}.\end{aligned}$$

Equation (5) suggests that when intangibles are left out of investment data, total factor productivity growth da' is mismeasured (i.e., differs from knowledge spillovers da) for three reasons: First, the missing investment affects TFP because it affects GDP growth (understating TFP if intangibles are growing faster than other output and overstating it if they are growing slower). Second, failure to recognize intangible capital as an input overstates measured TFP growth if growth of intangible capital inputs is positive because it improperly ascribes to TFP the contribution of intangible capital. Third, and working in the opposite direction to the impact of ignoring intangible capital as an input, share weights on the K and L inputs are too large and so overstate their contribution to dq.

1. The combined measure of conventional inputs dx' differs from dx in (4) because profits earned by intangibles are inappropriately ascribed to tangible capital when intangibles are omitted, which causes tangible capital to be overweighted in dx' relative to dx.

2. Rearranging terms from equation (2) in box 3.2, we can write: $dq - dy = s_Q^N(dn - dy)$. From equations (4) and (4′), we can write $dq - dy = (\sigma_Q^X dx + \sigma_Q^R dr + da) - (dx' + da')$. Combining these two equations and rearranging terms gives the decomposition of equation (5).

ogy (IT) that has run its course. Such an argument has some support in that the slowdown in productivity growth has been common across countries (Cette, Fernald, and Mojon 2016).

Second, an apparent slowdown can be caused by omitted investment in intangibles. Consider, for example, the "J-curve" effect due to mismeasured investment in artificial intelligence (AI) analyzed by Brynjolfsson, Rock, and Syverson (2021): In the early stages of AI, firms make substantial investments in databases, software, and data analytic applications that go unmeasured. During this period, unmeasured real intangible investment grows faster than measured real output. This causes measured TFP growth to understate true productivity growth because real GDP growth is understated. As that initial growth burst of investment falls off, the effect diminishes, but intangible stocks and their payments start to grow—this causes (mis)measured TFP to rise, because the contributions of intangible stocks are attributed to TFP. The Brynjolfsson et al. (2021) study finds that returns to investment in AI may come many years after the initial investment, creating a "J" pattern in (mis)measured productivity. In contrast, Corrado, Haskel, and Jona-Lasinio (2021) use data on intangibles to examine the impact of missing AI investment on productivity and find that the positive "swoosh" of the "J" appears rather quickly and is not all that strong. The intuition behind their result is that the mismeasured capital payments effect comes in quite quickly, perhaps because intangibles depreciate rapidly. Recent research on the lag between AI adoption and firm productivity suggests that large firms reap benefits from the adoption of AI after three years (Bäck et al. 2022)—quick relative to the assumptions used in Brynjolfsson et al. (2021) but suggestive of somewhat slower rates of depreciation for investments in AI than assumed for the components of intangibles expected to be most affected by AI and AI use (software, databases, marketing and organization structures) in Corrado et al. (2021).

Third, the divergence in TFP between leader companies and laggards in similar industry sectors referenced in fact 5 (section 3.2.3.5) has been found to contribute to recent slow productivity growth through its effect on sectors' average TFP. The TFP measures used in these studies do not include intangibles, suggesting that the (mis)measured productivity dispersion between leaders and laggards could owe to the returns enjoyed by leaders using unmeasured intangible capital. Can the productivity slowdown seen in figure 3.3 be attributed to the failure of innovations developed by leaders to diffuse to laggards? Akcigit and Ates (2021) find that there has been a breakdown in R&D−based knowledge diffusion in the past decade. They also suggests that the increased use of proprietary data in modern production processes might be a factor staunching knowledge diffusion.

Corrado et al. (2024) directly examine how increased use of proprietary data may have altered the production of intangibles in the US and European economies. They argue that many intangibles—especially marketing and organizational assets—are increasingly based on intelligence developed from data and that such knowledge is not easily replicated by competing firms in the absence of policy interventions or voluntary industry data sharing. Bontadini et al. (2024) in fact find a trend toward weakened productivity spillovers from intangibles in the post-global financial crisis period, underscoring that weakened knowledge diffusion—likely due to increased use of proprietary data—is an important part of the recent productivity story. The possibility that public open data (discussed in section 3.7 below) could mitigate this development deserves additional investigation.

3.5 Measurement of Intangibles: Challenges and Methods

We have seen how omission of intangibles affects measurement and interpretation of productivity growth. But even when productivity is adjusted for intangibles, it is possible that measurement errors in intangibles contaminate the picture. This is not a first-order concern—using a noisy estimate of intangibles is undoubtedly better than ignoring them. That said, measuring intangibles with the approach used to measure investment in national accounts (using investment flows and depreciation rates to derive asset stocks, asset values, and asset incomes) is challenging. When questioned about the existing asset boundary for intangibles in national accounts, then director of the US BEA Steven Landefeld answered, "No one disagrees with [the capitalization of intangibles such as R&D] conceptually. The problem is in the empirical measurement" (Mandel 2006, 66).

Measuring intangible investment begins with the empirical identification of long-lived spending flows, a task that is problematic when intangibles are coproduced along with other products. Furthermore, absent arm's-length transactions in markets with prices, it is difficult to identify a price deflator to express past investment in real terms. And given that intangible assets have no physical substance, how should we think about addressing adjusting asset values for economic depreciation?

These three measurement issues—estimation of investment flows, asset price deflators, and depreciation rates—are reviewed from a conceptual perspective in Corrado et al. (2022a). Here, these issues are discussed in the context of methods and data used to estimate the intangibles data for the United States used in this chapter, focusing mainly on investment streams not currently included in GDP: design originals, new financial products, brand and market research, organizational structures, and formal employer-provided training (firm-specific human capital).

3.5.1 Estimating Nominal Investment in Intangible Assets

Intangible assets may in some cases be acquired via market transactions, like purchasing a customer relationship management software system or

Box 3.4 Organizational Capital: What Is It and How Is It Estimated?

Organizational capital is a firm-specific asset produced jointly with output and embodied in the organization itself (Atkeson and Kehoe 2005, Corrado, Hulten, and Sichel 2005). The asset is distinct from other intangibles yet complementary with them and other factor inputs, as illustrated by the well-documented complementarity of investments in IT equipment and workplace organization (Bresnahan, Brynjolfsson, and Hitt 2002).

As figure 3.1, line 9, indicates, organizational capital reflects strategic investments in a company's structure and business processes. Anecdotal examples of organizational capital abound: Walmart's supply chain, Amazon's customer recommendation system, Apple's inventory management system. While Apple is famous for its innovation and design, its inventory supply management has been equally crucial to the company's success (Cuthbertson, Furseth, and Ezell 2015).

Approach

Imagine there is a "strategy factory" within a larger organization charged with creating new, productivity-enhancing processes/practices. Spending on the strategy factory is investment in organizational capital. This spending includes payments to employees assigned to the factory (in-house production) and payments to outside suppliers (management consultants).

Estimation Procedures

Investment in purchased organizational capital and in-house production of organizational capital are estimated separately. Purchased organizational capital is captured by expenditures on *management consulting* and *computer design* services (NAICS 54611,9 and 54152), where only the strategic consulting portion of computer design services is included. Benchmark values of these expenditures come from BEA's quinquennial input-output tables starting with the 1987 table, with data on NAICS 5461 and NAICS

strategic management consulting advice. But, as previously indicated, intangibles are often produced for own use within firms. As a result, to measure intangible investment, statisticians must estimate two components: purchased investment and own-account investment. Estimation of the two components is illustrated in box 3.4 using the example of organizational capital; the same approach is used to estimate other types of intangible investment, including the software component in national accounts.

Industry-level purchases of intangibles not currently treated as invest-

54152 from BEA's annual use tables used to interpolate between the benchmark years. The in-house component is captured by the value of *professional managers' time on strategic development* of new business practices estimated as a proportion of managers' compensation (20 percent). The time series is developed from BLS survey data (Current Population Survey and Occupational and Employment Wage Statistics) on professional managers' employment and wages for major Standard Occupational Classification (SOC) group 11–0000 (management occupations). Estimates of subcomponents for marketing versus other business functions are also developed (i.e., four components are estimated). Price deflators for nonmarketing components are based on corresponding gross output price indexes; marketing subcomponents use the brand and marketing price index described in section 3.5.2 and appendix..

Evaluation

How reliable are these estimates? The evidence for the assumptions underlying these estimates at the aggregate level is strong. The proportionate rate applied to managerial compensation to estimate the in-house component is aligned with estimates of managers' marginal revenue product derived from a study using linked employer-employee data (Piekkola 2016) and a recent assessment of manager time-use studies (Martin 2019). The results also are generally consistent with approaches that estimate organizational capital based on selling, general, and administrative (SG&A) expenses and market capitalizations in corporate financial reports (e.g., Lev and Radhakrishnan 2005). On the other hand, studies that have developed a task-based approach to quantifying "key" employees who contribute to organizational capital suggest that a broader group of occupations are involved in developing organizational capital (Squicciarini and Le Mouel 2012) and that the involved occupations vary substantially across organizations by size and ownership type (Le Mouel and Squicciarini 2015).

ments in national accounts are derived from supply-use tables (SUT), which reflect a reconciliation of comprehensive data from economic censuses, annual surveys, administrative sources, and international transactions. Industrial design, market research and advertising, and management consulting services are not separate products in BEA's annual SUTs, however, but are rather lumped together along with other products in a "miscellaneous professional, scientific, and technical services" commodity group (5412OP). Factors derived from quinquennial benchmark SUTs and annual gross output data, both of which are available at more detailed levels, are used to create annual estimates for the purchased components of intangibles included in BEA's 5412OP commodity group.

Own-account investment components are estimated using a *sum-of-costs* approach. As indicated in box 3.4, the idea is to imagine a firm as having a "software factory" or "training factory" inside of it and to estimate the gross output of this hypothetical factory based on the payments made to factors (labor, capital, intermediates) used inside it. The lynchpin of this approach is identifying the workers in the internal factory and estimating the allocation of their work time and their compensation. From these elements, statisticians can estimate a figure for total payments to all factors used in in-house production.[15] The investment series for industrial design, brand, organizational capital, and employer-provided training included all contain own-account components estimated with the sum-of-costs approach. The series for new financial products consists solely of own-account production and is estimated using the sum-of-costs approach. Details on the method and source data used to estimate these assets are found in the appendix to Corrado et al. (2022a).[16]

The methods used to estimate intangibles surely could be improved, but the results shown in part 3.2 of this chapter suggest that current methods produce estimates of substantial relevance. Regarding organizational capital, the brief evaluation in box 3.4 suggests that, though existing methods are not without critique, they are generally robust. An obvious improvement to existing purchased components would be for BEA to provide commodity-level estimates for industrial design, market research and advertising, and management consulting in its annual supply-use tables.

Could own-account intangible investment be determined more accurately via a survey instrument, for example, as in surveys of R&D? Collecting information via surveys is a proven approach for R&D activity primarily because those surveys capture a well-defined business function within organizations. The same cannot be necessarily said of software or other types of own-account investment in intangibles. Surveys of capital expenditure have been used to collect information on software investment in several OECD countries, including the United States, but results tend to yield implausibly small figures for own-account production.

The intangible component most in need of firmer empirics for the United States is employer-provided training. European countries gather biannual information on firms' expenditures on formal training, internal and external, including the opportunity cost of workers' time. At the request of Congress, the BLS investigated the cost and design of a new survey of employer-provided training in the United States and concluded against such a survey, apparently due to budget constraints and other priorities.[17] Lack of official statistics on private sector job training is a serious gap in knowledge of business processes and organizational changes in the aftermath of massive job displacement due to COVID-19, a gap hampering US policymaking as well as productivity analysis.

3.5.2 Estimating Price Deflators for Intangible Assets

A price deflator is needed to express investment in an asset in real terms. Because most types of investment in intangibles have a purchased product component, a common approach is to use price deflators of these products to deflate intangible investment. Price indexes for purchased products are, in fact, the principal source for deflators of the expanded intangible assets in figure 3.1 to derive the growth accounting estimates discussed in this chapter. For example, the price deflator for architectural and engineering services (NAICS 5413) is used for industrial design, price deflators for management and technical consulting services and for computer system design services (NAICS 54161,9 and NAICS 54152) are used for organizational capital (excluding marketing), and the price deflator for other educational services (NAICS 6114–7) is used for employer-provided training.

Another approach to determining a deflator for intangibles is to estimate upstream factor input costs and apply a productivity adjustment based on related market activity.[18] After conducting studies and examining alternatives (including examining available deflators for the R&D services industry), BEA selected a productivity-adjusted input cost approach for deflating private R&D investment in the US national accounts (Robbins et al. 2012). The productivity adjustment for R&D is derived from BLS major business sector TFP.

Special care is needed in constructing the deflator for the marketing and branding intangible investment component of intangibles because the available deflator for the advertising and public relations industry (NAICS 5418) mainly captures the charges for producing advertising and public relations content. It does not reflect media delivery costs, which are borne by customers whose goods and services are being marketed.

Digital media and data-driven customer targeting have dramatically lowered the costs of marketing and advertising. These developments and the associated competitive effects are illustrated in figure 3.7, which shows a plunge in the cost of advertising in digital media and a cessation of cost increases for advertising in traditional media since 2009. A brand and marketing investment deflator reflecting these developments has been constructed (see Appendix 3A) and incorporated in the intangible asset price deflator used to obtain the estimates of real intangible investment and capital reported in this chapter. The brand and marketing investment price deflator, as well as slower price change for investments in organizational capital, produces an overall price deflator for intangible investment that turns sharply disinflationary beginning in 2009 (fig. 3.8 and table 3.1). The relevance of this trend change is discussed in the concluding remarks on data, AI, and intangibles in section 3.8.

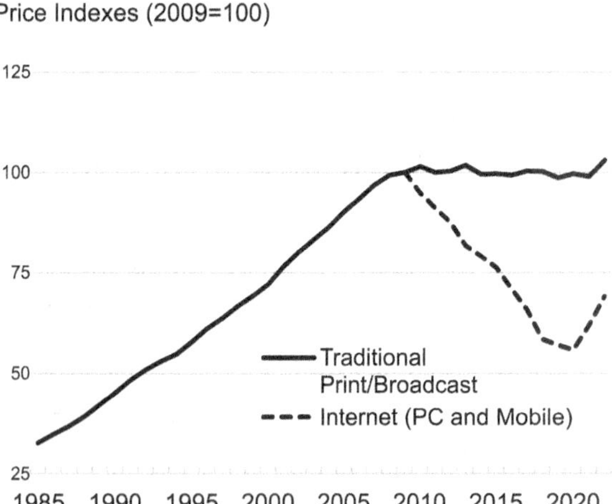

Fig. 3.7 Advertising media costs, 1985–2022

Source: Author's calculations based on input cost producer price indexes from the BLS; see appendix for further details.

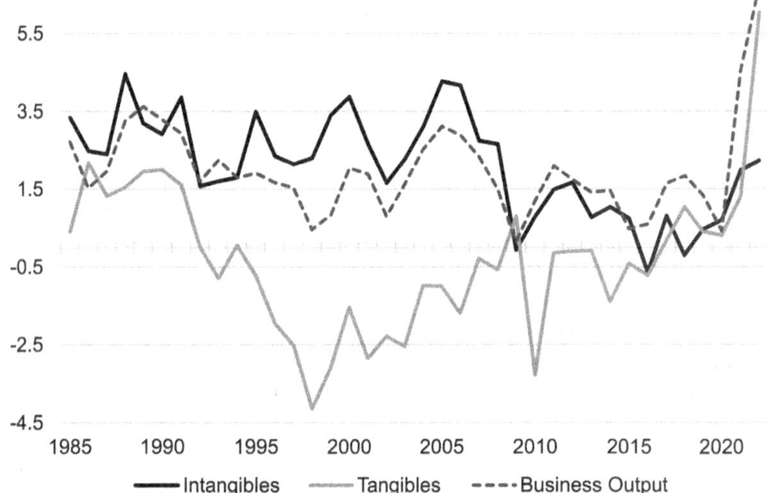

Fig. 3.8 Intangible and tangible asset price change, United States, 1985–2022

Note: Business output price is adjusted to include all figure 3.1 intangibles. Tangibles refer to nonresidential assets only.

Source: Author's calculations using national accounts investment price indexes (tangibles and national accounts intangibles) and intangible asset prices for components in the expanded measures as described in section 3.5.2.

Table 3.1 **Intangible and tangible asset price change (selected periods), 1995 to 2022, selected periods (percent per year)**

Asset group	1995 to 2009 (1)	2009 to 2019 (2)	2019 to 2022 (3)
1. Intangibles	2.7	0.7	1.6
2. Tangibles	–1.7	–0.4	2.5
Memo:			
3. Business output	1.6	1.5	4.1

Source: Time series displayed in figure 3.8.

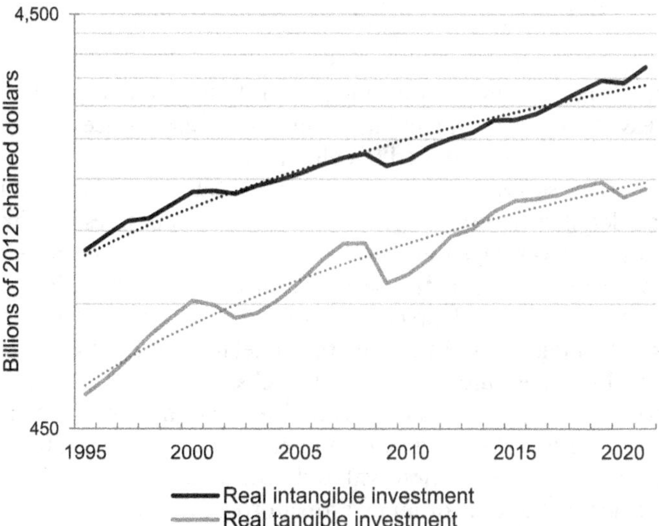

Fig. 3.9 Real intangible and tangible investment, United States, 1995–2021
Note: Dotted lines plot estimated trendlines for each series.
Source: Developed from nominal investment series shown in figure 3.2a deflated by price indexes built from the annual percent changes displayed in figure 3.8.

3.5.3 Real Investment and Capital: Intangible and Tangible

Intangible and tangible private nonresidential investment aggregates for the United States expressed in millions of chained 2012 dollars are shown in figure 3.9. Their growth rates over selected periods are reported in table 3.2. Real intangible investment and real tangible investment grow at strikingly similar rates over much of the period shown. Cyclical variability is evident in both series but is more damped for investment in intangibles. And the pace of real intangible investment has apparently stepped up of late, with estimated growth averaging 4.8 percent per year from 2015 to 2021. The

Table 3.2 **Real intangible and tangible investment, United States, 1995 to 2021 (selected periods, percent per year)**

Asset group	1995–2007 (1)	2007–2015 (2)	2015–2021 (3)
1. Intangibles	4.3	3.0	4.8
2. Tangibles	7.0	3.4	1.1
Memo:			
3. Business output	3.7	1.8	2.4

Source: Time series displayed in figure 3.9 and National Income and Product Accounts Table 1.3.6.

recent strength reflects, in roughly equal measure, robust nominal spending (primarily on R&D and software) and lower intangible asset price change (table 3.1, line 1, column (3) compared to column (2)).

The real investment series shown in figure 3.9 and table 3.2, along with their underlying detail, were used to generate the capital measures used in the growth accounting displayed in figure 3.2b. Capital stocks are developed from investment flows using the perpetual inventory method (PIM), a calculation that assumes that depreciation of each asset is geometric and constant across all vintages of the asset and that asset investment flows may be cumulated to obtain measures of real asset stocks.[19]

The conceptual basis of economic depreciation for intangible assets is much discussed in the literature (e.g., Corrado et al. 2022a; Martin 2019). In short, because intangibles are nonrival and returns to investments are not fully appropriable, the value of an investment to a firm or innovator is limited to the returns the owner/investor can capture. Partial appropriability of intangibles implies that the value of commercial knowledge declines rather rapidly, in stark contrast to the notion that depreciation of intangible assets must be slow because ideas last a very long time. This pattern is documented in empirical studies (reviewed in De Rassenfosse and Jaffe 2017; see also Pakes and Schankerman 1984) and supported by survey evidence that asks firms to report the average useful life of their intangible assets (Awano et al. 2010).

The rates of depreciation for market sector intangibles used in this chapter are summarized in Corrado et al. (2020, 366, table 16.1). They do not differ materially from the assumptions used in the earliest studies, where most innovative property assets were assumed to have eight-to-ten-year service lives, computerized (or digitized) information five-year service lives, and economic competencies three-to-four-year service lives. Additional details are available in the Bontadini et al. (2023) documentation of EU KLEMS & INTANProd.

3.6 Brand: A Productive Asset?

Brand is an intangible asset whose value depends on an association made by consumers that influences their willingness to pay for a product. Yet national accountants tend to hit the pause button when it comes to treating brand as a productive asset in macrodata. Brand equity and brand strategy are business concepts born in the 1980s, notwithstanding that the history of branding activity (e.g., by merchant traders and pottery makers) goes back at least 4000 years (Corrado and Hao 2014). The concepts gained swift acceptance in management and marketing literature, and the notion that brand equity represents an intangible asset of firms and that building brand equity is a strategy for firms to differentiate their products and services from competitors was well established by the early 1990s.

3.6.1 The Issue(s)

Firms undertake investments in marketing and brand development to gain competitive advantage. Whether these spending streams (in part or in whole) should be viewed as additions to capital turns on two issues: First, does the spending stream have the longevity we typically expect of a capital investment? Second, if competing firms engage in marketing and brand management strategies, do these efforts tend to cancel each other out rather than the spending of each firm adding to capital?

The classic statement of the zero-sum critique was by Solow (1967, 1968), who argued that the main impact of advertising is on the market shares within a particular industry or between product classes that are close substitutes. He expressed serious doubts about whether advertising affects the distribution of demand across broad product classes and whether the level of aggregate consumption can be influenced by promotion expenditures. And no less than Alfred Marshall pondered whether advertising increased or decreased equilibrium consumer prices in his 1919 book, *Industry and Trade*.

A conceptual basis for treating spending on marketing and brand promotion as investment is supplied by a relatively recent literature on signaling theory (Milgrom and Roberts 1986). The view also is consistent with findings that product differentiation can be welfare enhancing (Dixit and Stiglitz 1977) and that spending on marketing and promotion does not necessarily result in higher product prices. Furthermore, the developers of the planned 2025 System of National Accounts (SNA) have argued that the business importance of marketing assets makes investment in these assets conceptually appropriate to count as production (Globalization Task Team 2022).

Brand equity is defined as *an intangible asset that reflects a valuation of the revenue stream that accrues to a firm from its brand name*. It is derived from information about a firm and/or its products and services and includes customers' knowledge of a product's existence and its quality, its sourcing, and after-sales service quality. The information accumulates as a stock of knowledge appropriable by the firm. Brand investments exhibit *scope* economies because the value of brand increases when within-firm product and ancillary services variety increases. The basic idea is that brand is built by strategic marketing and promotion expenditures complemented by a range of firm competencies that together determine a company's success.

3.6.2 The Evidence

A rich structural modeling literature has identified brand and brand effects in financial market valuation. Studies that have looked at how *brand investment* (in the form of advertising and promotion expenditures) builds brand value have found significant effects of investments *after* controlling for product quality, R&D, and other firm characteristics (e.g., Erdem and Keane 1996, Erdem, Keane, and Sun 2008).[20]

In addition, while the original context of much work on intangibles was technological innovation via R&D investments, the analysis of intangibles also has roots in industrial organization literature that focused on the supporting role of marketing in innovation (Hulten 2011). The complementarity between R&D and promotion, both theoretical and empirical, is an established characteristic of globally innovative pharmaceutical firms (Clarkson 1977; Vinod and Rao 2000), as well as other manufacturers (e.g., Clarkson 1996). Among services producers, Hulten (2011) found an important role for marketing in the growth of Microsoft; Crouzet and Eberly (2018) argued that the growing value of brand equity supported the more efficient practices that spurred the expansion of large retailers in the United States.

Theory of course does not preclude the possibility that some product promotion is purely persuasive (or carried to wasteful excess) and leads to higher consumer prices and lower demand. But the balance of empirical evidence suggests that product advertising does *not* lead to higher consumer prices. Individual industry/product studies have found that advertising stimulates competition and lowers prices, e.g., for optometric services (Kwoka 1984); Steiner (1973) demonstrated similar findings for the toy industry. More broadly, a recent study took advantage of a national policy change and found product advertising to be informative—or brand building—at a national level (Rauch 2013). Though results varied by industry, the study concluded that product advertising leads to a *decrease* in overall consumer prices.[21]

Macroeconomic practitioners continue to differ in opinion over the need to include marketing and brand building in intangible investment for purposes of measuring GDP. Nevertheless, the argument against counting intangible investment in marketing and branding because brand management and similar activities are a zero-sum battle breaks down in the presence of innovation and the realities of how modern companies create competitive advantage and differentiate their products. Furthermore, for marketing assets to have no net impact on aggregate economic activity via the consumption-wealth channel, investments in them must have zero impact on aggregate market capitalization, yet a large body of theory and evidence shows that branding does raise market valuations of firms.

3.7 Public Intangibles

Intangible assets are also purchased and generated by the nonmarket sector. The nonmarket sector in GDP consists of governments, national laboratories, universities, and other nonprofits serving households. Treating the intangible assets that these sectors produce as investments would improve the measurement of productivity but the change presents conceptual and measurement challenges.

3.7.1 Conceptual Issues

According to a recent analysis (Corrado, Haskel, and Jona-Lasinio 2017b), public services are intangible investments to the extent that (a) they are long-lived and (b) their services are directly provided, or *proximate* in nature. Condition (a) is straightforward. The proximate distinction of condition (b) is explained below.

Public investment is typically regarded as consisting of spending on physical infrastructure (roads, bridges, dams, etc.), where returns to society accrue for many years. This accords with the classic economic notion of public infrastructure as a capital-intensive natural monopoly. But over the past decade or two, a broader notion of public infrastructure has gained recognition—namely, that governments provide long-lasting "soft" infrastructure via the nature of services they provide. This notion is based on evidence demonstrating that the economic benefits of providing "social infrastructure" outweigh the costs and result in a positive net return on investment. This view is consistent with the intangible investment framework in which the relevant economic criterion for defining public investment is whether the publicly provided good or service produces long-lived proximate returns.

The proximate distinction is important because, while many social services and public institutions are critical to the smooth functioning of society, spending on them does not yield an identifiable flow of capital services. Consider, for example, public spending on institutions that help build and maintain the rule of law. The rule of law may be an *ultimate* determinant of national investment in that it prevents the appropriation of private capital—shown to be critical for economic development (De Soto 2000)—but spending on institutions that support the rule of law does not yield a flow of knowledge services for use in production in future periods as do, say, education services or services that provide information/data assets to the public.

A framework comparable to figure 3.1 can be developed for public intangibles. Public intangibles may be categorized as (a) assets for which correspondence to items in figure 3.1 is very close and where similar measurement methods are appropriate (e.g., R&D); (b) assets corresponding to items in figure 3.1 but for which modifications to scope and/or new alternative measured approaches are required (e.g., information assets, discussed below); and (c) intangible social infrastructure (e.g., education services, also discussed below), for which there is no correspondence to items in figure 3.1.[22]

3.7.2 Information Assets

Government-generated information assets—climate data, economic and social data, genomic data, innovation data (patents), and national security intelligence, among others—loom large as public intangibles (MEPSIR 2006). The Open Data Institute (ODI), located in the UK, commissioned work to assess the value of "core" public data assets—data such as addresses, maps, weather, land, and property ownership—at different points in the data access spectrum: paid access, public access with a restricted license, and open data. Exploiting information across this spectrum, the ODI-sponsored work concluded that core public open data provides an additional 0.5 percent of UK GDP in economic value every year (ODI 2016).

Beyond the market-equivalent value of open data, public information assets are important because they generate productivity spillovers. The US Census Bureau's Topologically Integrated Geographic Encoding and Referencing (TIGER) dataset is a case in point—its release in 1991 is commonly thought to have bootstrapped companies whose apps and services are based on the nation's geospatial data. Similarly, the public release of data from NASA's Landsat satellite mapping program had a documented positive impact on the productivity of gold exploration projects (Nagaraj 2022). All told, the case for capitalizing scientific data curation and scientific libraries as well as economic statistics (business, demographic, and geographic) is strong.

The US bioeconomy—economic activity in biotechnology, bioengineering, and biobased manufacturing—is an example of large social returns to open scientific data (National Academies of Sciences, Engineering, and Medicine 2020, hereafter NAS 2020). R&D investments that create biological data collections (e.g., genome sequences) and fund their use (and reuse) to formulate new industrial products and health treatments are currently capitalized in national accounts. But the stores of open data created by that R&D are not recognized as explicit assets, and expenditures to provide and update them in open-access digitized libraries are not included in investment.

Consider the case of the GenBank sequence database reported in NAS (2020). GenBank is an open-access, annotated collection of all publicly available nucleotide sequences and their protein translations. This database and the software to access it are produced and maintained by the National Center for Biotechnology Information (NCBI), a division of the National Library of Medicine. As shown in figure 3.10, since GenBank's inception at

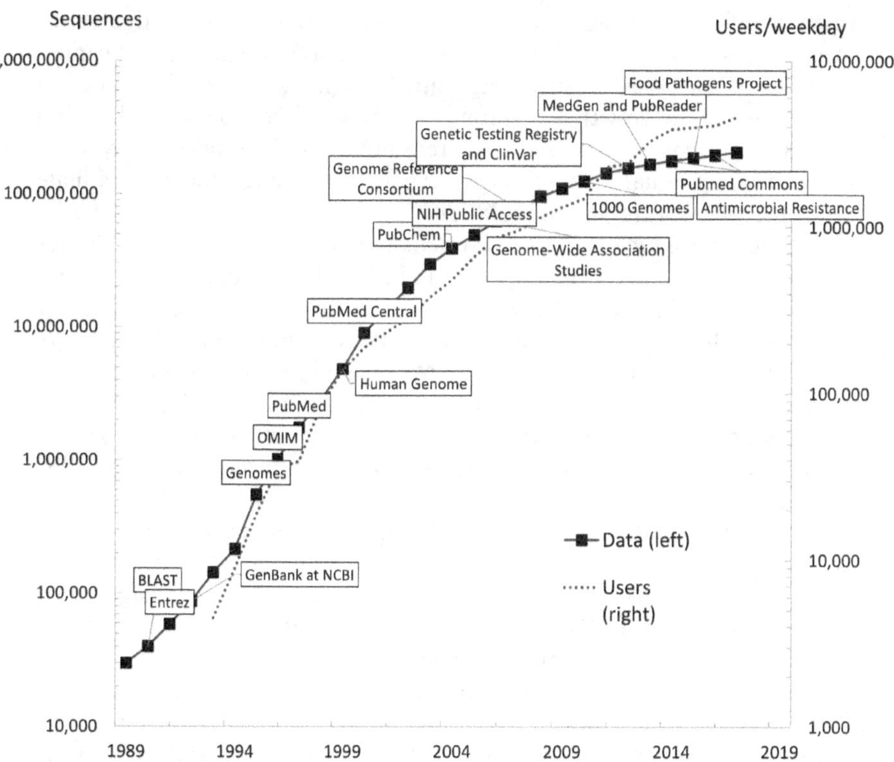

Fig. 3.10 Information assets at NCBI: Data and users

Note: NCBI = National Center for Biotechnology Information. Data refer to the number of sequences.

Source: National Academies of Sciences, Engineering, and Medicine (2020), based on statistics reported at https://www.nlm.nih.gov/about/2019CJ.html#Budget_graphs.

NCBI in 1992, use of the database and the number of sequences (i.e., data) in it have grown exponentially. It is tempting to suggest that the relationship of biological data stores to total R&D stocks is proportional, acknowledging that it is challenging to specify a value for these stores but user value is related to utilization, not stocks, and figure 3.10 suggests that the number of NCBI users (the dotted line) has been growing faster than the accumulation of sequences in recent years. The economic value of spillovers to modern scientific biodata repositories such as NCBI has not been investigated specifically, though benefits to human health from public sequence information (e.g., in vaccine development) are widely acknowledged to be significant.

3.7.3 Education as Intangible Social Infrastructure

Education services are investment in the social infrastructure approach to public intangibles as set out above. In this approach, education investment is defined as the acquisition of schooling-produced knowledge assets, assets expected to provide a return to society in a future period; the capital services of the stock of schooling knowledge are a factor of production in total economy growth accounting. Newly acquired stocks of education assets are, of course, not used in current production—it takes many years to produce a graduate—but rather held in inventory until students graduate and enter the working-age population.

To measure education as investment in social infrastructure requires consideration of earnings impact outcomes; the standard sum-of-costs approach used in national accounts to measure education services is not adequate.[23] In an application of the social infrastructure approach, Corrado, O'Mahony, and Samek (2021) model investment in schooling as the lifetime income generated by an additional year of schooling, following Jorgenson and Fraumeni (1989, 1992a, 1992b). The study looks at school systems in the United Kingdom and the United States.[24] The addition to GDP (i.e., the difference between the net growth in the value of schooling knowledge stocks and value of educational services in existing measures of GDP based on the sum of costs) averages about 10 percent of existing UK GDP from 2015 to 2018 and slightly less than that in the United States. These are significant boosts to the level of GDP. However, in both countries, the boost to GDP in recent years is about 3 percentage points lower than 20 years earlier. The treatment of education as intangible social infrastructure therefore exerts a small drag on economic growth: the now larger estimate of education output has relatively slow growth in both countries. This mainly reflects the dwindling growth in school-age populations.

The productivity measurement impacts of the social infrastructure approach to measuring education output are sensitive to certain assumptions, including the extent to which earnings outcomes can be attributed to formal education versus knowledge acquisition via job training. All told, after deflating the output and investment estimates following procedures suggested in Gu and Wong (2010), productivity in the education sector in the UK and the US is found to grow faster than when measured by existing estimates. But because the rates of change in the sector's productivity remain slow relative to the rest of the economy, the increase in the size of the sector exerts a downward influence on the measured productivity change of the total economy.

3.8 Data as an Asset: Pinpointing the Challenges

Business commentary views data as an unmeasured input to production and frequently opines that economic statistics are seriously flawed with the growing use of data. The case for including data assets as intangible capital seems clear: business-held data are plentiful, long lived, and, along with public open data, share the characteristic of nonrivalry and the potential for economies of scale and scope with other intangibles.

But just what constitutes a data asset? Examples in recent business commentary include the following:

- creation of a robust master data management program for efficient supply chains
- data-driven improvements in the speed of clinical trials
- merging of data from various sources using AI and machine learning applications
- data analytics used to improve projections and customer relations management

These examples would seem to be, in part or in whole, investments in software tools, R&D, marketing, and organizational capital—items already counted in the intangible investment measures reported in this chapter.

This pinpoints a key challenge for assessments of productivity and its mismeasurement: a need for rigorous analysis of the coverage of data assets and AI (which utilizes data for decision-making) in existing estimates of intangibles both in national accounts *and* in expanded measures.

3.8.1 Measurement of Data Assets

To consider how data fits into the intangible framework, we first identify specific data-related activities and the likely asset types produced. The literature considers a range of activities and asset types, summarized in table 3.3.[25]

Table 3.3 delineates three asset types, beginning with raw data collected as a by-product of economic activity (e.g., sales, medical records, clickstreams) or generated intentionally (via experiments or surveys). The second type consists of transformed raw data, or data that have been cleaned, formatted, and structured for further analysis or visualization (e.g., a query-ready database, an active customer list). The third type is data intelligence, which reflects further integration of data with advanced analytic tools (e.g., machine learning

Table 3.3 **Data as an asset: Investment activities and assets produced**

Investment Activity	Asset Type	Comments
1 Generation/collection	Data stores ("raw" data)	Experiments and platforms that create and/or collect data
2 Aggregation	Databases (query-ready)	Processes and platforms for combining and curating data from multiple sources
3 Analysis/analytics	Data intelligence (actionable)	Gleaning of insights from data that can be acted on

training algorithms). Data intelligence is a set of quantitative inputs that provide actionable guidance for decision-making or solutions to problems.

Business observers (e.g., Mayer-Schönberger and Cukier 2013) view the categories in table 3.3 as a value chain, where data start off as raw materials and then undergo multiple layers of "value added" processing before becoming actionable intelligence. Corrado et al. (2024) show that the data value chain corresponds to the "data stack" approach of technologists (e.g., Varian 2019), and data forms can be arranged in terms of layers of value corresponding to an asset type amenable to measurement and analysis.

Economic statisticians have used schemata akin to table 3.3 to measure data assets using a sum-of-costs approach (e.g., Statistics Canada 2019a, 2019b), the same approach used to estimate own-account production of intangibles described earlier (section 3.5.1). Statistics Canada implemented the approach by selecting the relevant employees working on each of the three stages of data asset production based on detailed statistics on employment by occupation for each industry in the economy to estimate domestic production of data assets.[26] The selection criteria was essentially judgmental, based on text descriptions of the activities of occupations as currently classified.

A more comprehensive analysis of how data is used in production based on detailed employment by occupation type is needed to better measure data capital. Alternatives for classifying workers include a skills- or task-based approach, as in Acemoglu and Restrepo (2018). Detailed task-level information on occupations from O*NET were used by Squicciarini and Le Mouel (2012) to measure investment in organizational capital, and data on employee IT skills from LinkedIn were used by Rock (2022) to capture AI investment. The US BEA has begun to apply a skills-based approach in conjunction with online job postings to measure investments in data (Santiago-Calderón and Rassier 2022).

3.8.2 Investments in Data and AI: Are They Really Missing?

Following work by Statistics Canada (2019a, 2019b) and using the schema set out in table 3.3, Corrado et al. (2024) developed experimental estimates of industry-level investments in data and found them to be significantly correlated with intangible investment as defined in figure 3.1 in cross-country data for nine European countries. So it is natural to ask, Does intangible investment as defined in figure 3.1 "miss" investments in data and AI?

Consider first intangible investment included in national accounts. The first two asset types in table 3.3, data stores and databases, would appear to be included in the broad category of digitized information in the intangible framework. When this category is represented by national accounts measures (as done in this chapter), only internally developed databases are included. This implies that purchases of databases and production of data stores are excluded unless they are embedded and sold as software products.

Yet before concluding that these investments in data are entirely missed, the overlaps between investment in data and other types of national accounts intangible investment are important to consider. For example, acquisitions of data stores or databases for the conduct of R&D or mineral exploration may be included in these components of national accounts investment.

Consider now data intelligence—arguably the most valuable, final stage of the data value chain set out in table 3.3. The intangibles framework of figure 3.1 captures much, if not all, of the activity that creates data intelligence via the data value chain of table 3.3, namely:

(a) The occupations used to estimate own-account software production likely include many of the data scientists who assemble databases and training datasets for AI applications.

(b) Custom-designed AI application software likely are included in the custom applications subcomponent of purchased software investment.[27]

(c) The development of novel machine learning and AI training algorithms and computer designs for processing these AI algorithms should be captured in R&D.

(d) Purchases of data analytic services are included in the computer design intangible component or the IT consulting services component of organization capital (see box 3.4).

(e) Database development in the financial sector is included in the financial product development category of intangibles.[28]

(f) Data-driven engineering design intelligence is covered in the industrial design category of intangibles.

(g) Data-driven marketing and supply-chain intelligence is covered in the own-account component of brand investment, market research, and the marketing subcomponent of organizational capital.

Items (a), (b), and (c) are already included in national accounts investment. The remaining items are mostly excluded from national accounts intangibles but are included in the espanded measures used in this chapter. All told then, the inclusion of investments in business operations, industrial design, financial products, and general marketing intelligence in the expanded measures means that the intangible capital framework of figure 3.1 will pick up the degree to which these components are data-driven.

Other approaches, including those that conceptualize data assets as a value chain, tend to miss certain data intelligence assets. For example, the Statistics Canada (2019a, 2019b) estimates of data assets include financial and marketing forms of data-derived intelligence but do not appear to include data-derived intelligence related to engineering design and business operations. See Corrado et al. (2024) for further elaboration.

The new national accounts guidelines of the planned 2025 SNA may include investment in data and marketing assets in GDP, which includes business big data and training data used in AI. The many overlaps between data and marketing assets and the extended set of intangibles of figure 3.1 mean that including investment in data assets in GDP will likely capture some types of intangible investment not directly included in GDP. At the same time, the overlaps imply a risk of double counting some part of the intangible investment already explicitly included in GDP.

Moreover, the AI literature is replete with examples of how modern data use fosters faster, more efficient experimentation and feedback in business and marketing processes. Existing SNA guidance does not address how the relative efficiency of the new assets is to be captured in price statistics. This is a major omission. As discussed in some depth in Corrado et al. (2024) and illustrated by the 2009 to 2019 trend in intangible asset prices shown in figure 3.7, the relative efficiency of data-driven intangibles reduces their relative price and, all else equal, the expansion of national accounts to include data and marketing assets *should* boost the path of real GDP and productivity in the aftermath of the global financial recession.

3.9 Measuring Intangible Capital: Concluding Remarks and Next Steps

The changing nature of the global economy has put a spotlight on intangible capital as a source of economic growth and driver of innovation. This chapter reviews the measurement of intangible capital using an expanded investment approach. The primary virtue of this approach is its alignment with the macroeconomic growth accounting data used in productivity analysis, which is grounded in statistics from national accounts. Cutting-edge research in the field is likely to further exploit linked employee-employer databases with employees classified by occupation and/or tasks and skills to generate new insights about the production and use of intangibles at the firm level.

The chapter sets out elements needed to measure intangible assets—a list of intangible assets to be measured, magnitudes for nominal investment flows (purchased and own production), deflators that separate investment flows into price and quantity elements, and service lives to enable the compilation of net stocks. These are the same elements needed to measure fixed tangible assets, though as emphasized in the chapter, intangibles are less likely than tangibles to be transacted at arm's length. Research has greatly improved the measurement of these elements for many types of intangible assets since the observations of Machlup, Griliches, Lev, and others that investments in knowledge and innovation are unseen in economic and financial statistics.

Looking ahead, requisite investments to address post-COVID-19 restructuring of private organizations will likely involve a mix of technological, organizational, and reputational changes that will heighten the relevance of intangibles, especially given their scope economies with digital tools and digital infrastructure. Not all intangibles are currently recorded in national accounts, however, and this chapter sets out the case for acceptance of a broader coverage of intangible capital in macroeconomic statistics. The chapter stresses that extending the empirical growth accounting paradigm to include capital accumulation resulting from intangible investment results in a more general notion of the supply-side of the economy, one that arguably brings together widely used theories of endogenous growth and innovation with the macroeconomic data used to measure productivity.

The chapter suggests certain priorities for new data development and further microdata development. A periodic survey of employer-provided training is imperative for multiple reasons; the last such survey conducted by the BLS was in 1995. Resurrecting a survey of employer-provided training would generate important new data and buttress the accuracy of existing estimates of intangible capital, as would adding commodity detail on professional services to BEA's annual supply-use tables. Adding questions to existing Census Bureau survey vehicles (e.g., the Annual Capital Expenditure Survey) is an equally important initiative given the lack of comprehensive microdata on intangibles other than R&D. Finally, the continued development of price indexes for professional services, including terms for licensing patents and other intellectual property products, is necessary to advance the measurement of real intangible investment and capital, as well as industry-level output and TFP.

Appendix 3A

The Brand and Marketing Intangible Investment Price Deflator

The intangible investment price index introduced in this chapter is based on price indexes for each component of intangibles. This includes a newly developed price deflator for brand and marketing investment.

Investments in brand and marketing reflect strategic planning, production/content creation, and media costs. Sometimes a firm hires media consultants to conduct this work, and sometimes the work is developed by the using firm (or a combination of the two). The brand and marketing deflator is developed from market prices for the "purchased" component of these activities and applied to total investments in brand and marketing, whether produced on own account or purchased. The cost of strategic planning and production/content creation is measured by BEA's gross output price index for the advertising and public relations services industry (NAICS 5418). Media costs are based in BLS input price indexes for advertising sales.

The conceptual basis for the BLS indexes that track price change for advertising media sales is an average unit rate. For TV advertising, it is calculated by dividing the total revenue earned from advertising sales for a specific period by the number of spots that aired during the period; other forms of traditional media use similar average unit rate constructs. For internet advertising, the average price calculation is the total revenue earned from all sales of a specific type of online advertisement made within a specified period divided by the total number of clicks (or appearances on a website) that occurred. (For further information, see the "About" page on the PPI page of the BLS website.) Five BLS advertising media price indexes, four of which cover traditional media (periodicals, newspapers, television, and radio) and one covering internet advertising, are used. Periodicals and newspapers include print and digital subscription versions. TV covers advertising on broadcast channels, cable networks, and local cable. Internet advertising covers ads on PCs and mobile devices. The individual input price index BLS retrieval codes for these series are WPU361101, WPU361102, WPU362, WPU363, WPU365, respectively, from series start to 2022.

BLS price indexes are annualized and aggregated using weights based on private industry advertising sales by media type from WARC (World Advertising Media Center) from 1981 to 2011 as reported in Corrado and Hao (2014) and extended to 2021 using information from eMarketer, Statistica, and other industry sources. Internet advertising sales are from statistics issued by the Internet Advertising Bureau/PwC. Advertising sales in the five media differs from total spending on advertising and promotion in the private economy by (a) miscellaneous media spending, mainly direct mail and outdoor advertising, and (b) production and content creation costs. The miscellaneous components are not covered in the price index.

For analytical purposes, a subindex aggregating the four traditional media types is formed; this index is aggregated with price indexes for internet advertising and production/content creation to form the overall brand and marketing investment price index. The traditional media and internet input cost price indexes are shown in figure 3.7.

Notes

1. This chapter describes the current state of play in national accounts, but the international guidelines for compiling GDP given by the 2008 *System of National Accounts* (SNA, European Commission et al. 2009) will be soon superseded by the planned 2025 SNA. This new SNA is expected to expand the types of intangible investment in GDP or in extended measures of economic activity. Purchased databases will likely be included in investment as part of the incorporation in GDP of investment in data assets. Marketing assets may also be included in investment if measuring them is determined to be feasible. Finally, employer-provided training may be included in investment in human capital in extended accounts covering aspects beyond GDP.

2. Initial work focused on a comparative analysis of countries in Europe, led by estimates for the UK (Marrano, Haskel, and Wallis 2009), followed by proj-

ects funded by the European Commission (e.g., COINVEST, INNODRIVE, and SPINTAN) and two efforts funded by the European Investment Bank (van Ark et al. 2009; Corrado et al. 2016a). In conjunction with these projects, Corrado et al. (2012, 2013, 2016b) developed and intermittently updated harmonized, industry-level estimates for European economies and the United States based on the figure 3.1 framework (the INTANInvest database). Estimates of intangible investment based on figure 3.1 also are for Japan (Fukao et al. 2009)—the first study to examine intangible assets for major industry sectors—Canada (Baldwin, Gu, and MacDonald 2012), China (Hulten and Hao 2012), and Korea (Chun and Nadiri 2016).

3. The results of this project, EU KLEMS & INTANProd, reflect a merging of the EU KLEMS and INTANInvest databases and are available at https://euklems-intanprod-llee.luiss.it/ (LLEE 2023). Documentation and analysis of this database are provided in Bontadini et al. (2023, 2024).

4. Intangible investment needs to be expressed in inflation-adjusted, or real, terms to arrive at its impacts on output per hour. The deflation of intangible investment is described in section 3.3.1.2 and appendix to this chapter.

5. Total factor productivity (TFP) is the growth in output not explained by growth in labor and other inputs, which includes intangible capital if intangibles are capitalized. TFP is a residual, measured as the difference between actual output growth and the share-weighted change in inputs.

6. See Griliches (1992, 1994) for firm-level estimates of productivity spillovers to R&D investments in manufacturing and Corrado, Haskel, and Jona-Lasinio (2017a) for cross-country evidence of productivity spillovers to non−R&D intangibles.

7. The sectors shown in figure 3.4 account for about 85 percent of total private intangible investment.

8. The indicators used in Corrado, Criscuolo et al. (2021) include ICT equipment, purchases of IT services, and employment of workers in "tech" occupations.

9. See also the discussion of competition and competition policy in Haskel and Westlake (2018, 2022).

10. The model is based on Corrado, Hulten, and Sichel (2009) as adapted in Corrado, Goodridge, and Haskel (2011).

11. Looking at equation (4) in box 3.2, output change is the (single) term on the left-hand side (LHS), and duplication is the first term on the RHS, so output change less duplication is the sum of the remaining two terms on the RHS: the contribution of intangible capital and TFP. Note that this result is akin to considering both private *and* social returns to R&D as the full contribution of R&D as discussed in the R&D literature.

12. This topic is discussed in Dynan and Sheiner (chap. 1), Moulton (chap. 2), Coyle (chap. 4), Byrne (chap. 5), and Sheiner and Cutler (chap. 6).

13. This section draws on Corrado, Haskel, and Jona-Lasinio (2021).

14. Alternatively, we can assume that only some of them are omitted, in which case the included portion can be thought of as being in measures of tangible capital.

15. Workers are typically identified by occupation, and an important assumption in determining value for own-account production concerns the allocation of work time of identified workers; BEA's estimate of own-account software, for example, assumes software developers (occupation used to identify workers producing software for a firm's own use) spend half of their work time creating *new* software. Martin (2019) summarizes studies that report worker time devoted to creating new marketing and manager-produced assets; see also box 3.4.

16. Regarding the identification of relevant employees for own-account components, the occupation codes used for the own-account component of brand are found in Corrado and Hao (2014, 85), for new financial products in Corrado et al.

(2012, 29–31), and for organizational capital in box 3.4. Note that the employment-based approach to estimating coproduction requires separating firms that produce the intangible asset as a line of business from those with hypothetical factories that produce for own use; the output of firms that sell software products or training services for final sale would not be included in the estimates of software or training services produced on own account. BEA's detailed benchmark input-output tables are used to determine this exclusion.

17. BLS last conducted a survey of employer-provided training in 1995. The figures for employer-provided training reported in this chapter are benchmarked to this survey and extended using annual surveys reported in *Training* magazine combined with information from annual supply-use tables and estimates of the annual payroll of workers assigned to the training function within private organizations.

18. The change in output prices should equal the change in share-weighted input prices *less* the change in TFP.

19. More specifically, PIM measures the real stock R of individual asset a for a given industry at time t as $R_{a,t} = N_{a,t} + (1 - \delta_a^R)\, R_{a,t-1}$, where $N_{a,t}$ is the real investment flow for asset a in the industry. Once each $R_{a,t}$ for an industry is obtained, the usual procedures for aggregating over assets and industries are applied.

20. Hayakawa, Imai, and Nakata (2018) provide a review of this empirical literature.

21. The country studied was Austria, the only country in the OECD that charges a tax on advertising. Each of Austria's 10 regions had its own tax rate until 2000, after which rates were harmonized across regions at 5 percent. With the cost of advertising increasing in some parts of the country and decreasing in others, it was viewed as a natural experiment to examine the question pondered by Marshall a century ago.

22. See Corrado et al. (2017b, s367, table 2) for an illustrative framework. Besides information assets, the scope of other assets is modified for relevance in the nonmarket sector. For example, the public counterpart to artistic and entertainment originals is renamed cultural assets and expanded to include curation of long-lived museum collections; and organization capital for hospitals includes the contribution of professional medical doctors who serve in managerial roles without the "manager" moniker.

23. In GDP, free education supplied by the government is valued by the cost of producing these services. Many analysts use the human capital framework to conceptualize and measure investment in education (and training) and suggest that national accounts regularly produce a human capital account as a supplement, or satellite, account. This approach expands the sectoral boundary of GDP to include household production because the opportunity cost of time spent in school by households is included in investment in human capital; see Abraham (2010) for a discussion. The social infrastructure approach does *not* expand the sectoral boundary of GDP, though as with intangibles produced by the market sector, the asset boundary of existing GDP is expanded by the nonmarket sector's current production of schooling knowledge.

24. The study also considers the effects of the net immigration of school-age residents, as well as inward and outward flows of nonresident foreign students.

25. This literature includes McKinsey Global Institute 2016, Goodridge and Haskel 2016, Statistics Canada 2019a and 2019b, and Nguyen and Paczos 2020.

26. Separate information on data asset purchases is not used mainly because statistical systems do not record such purchases (and perhaps also because they are assumed to be rather small).

27. Purchased software investment includes two subcomponents: purchases of

"prepackaged" software applications and purchases of custom, "made-to-order" applications.

28. Note that the component is constructed to avoid an overlap with software and reported R&D, as detailed in table 3 of Corrado et al. (2012, 30).

References

Abraham, Katharine. 2010. "Accounting for Investments in Formal Education." *Survey of Current Business* 90 (6): 42–53.

Acemoglu, Daron, and Pascual Restrepo. 2018. "The Race between Man and Machine: Implications of Technology for Growth, Factor Shares, and Employment." *American Economic Review* 108 (6): 1488–542.

Andrews, Dan, Chiara Criscuolo, and Peter N. Gal. 2016. "The Best versus the Rest: The Global Productivity Slowdown, Divergence across Firms and the Role of Public Policy." OECD Productivity Working Paper No. 5, November, OECD Publishing, Paris. https://doi.org/10.1787/63629cc9-en.

Akcigit, Ufuk, and Sina T. Ates. 2021. "Ten Facts on Declining Business Dynamism and Lessons from Endogenous Growth Theory." *American Economic Journal: Macroeconomics* 13 (1): 257–98.

Atkeson, Andrew, and Patrick J. Kehoe. 2005. "Modeling and Measuring Organization Capital." *Journal of Political Economy* 113 (5): 1026–53.

Awano, Gaganan, Mark Franklin, Jonathan Haskel, and Zafeira Kastrinaki. 2010. *Investing in Innovation: Findings from the UK Investment in Intangible Assets Survey*. NESTA Index Report (July). https://media.nesta.org.uk/documents/investing_in_innovation.pdf.

Bäck, Asta, Arash Hajikhani, Angela Jäger, Torben Schubert, and Arho Suominen. 2022. "Return of the Solow-Paradox in AI? AI-Adoption and Firm Productivity." Papers in Innovation Studies No. 2022/01, Centre for Innovation Research, Lund University.

Baldwin, John R., Wulong Gu, and Ryan MacDonald. 2012. "Intangible Capital and Productivity Growth in Canada." Canadian Productivity Review Research Paper No. 29.

Basu, Susanto. 2019. "Are Price-Cost Markups Rising in the United States? A Discussion of the Evidence." *Journal of Economic Perspectives* 33, no. 3 (Summer): 3–22.

Black, Sandra, and Lisa Lynch. 2001. "How to Compete: The Impact of Workplace Practices and Information Technology on Productivity." *Review of Economics and Statistics* 83 (3): 434–45.

Black, Sandra, and Lisa M. Lynch. 2005. "Measuring Organizational Capital in the New Economy." In Corrado, Haltiwanger, and Sichel 2005, 65:205–34.

Bloom, Nicholas, and John Van Reenan. 2007. "Measuring and Explaining Management Practices across Firms and Nations." *Quarterly Journal of Economics* 122 (4): 1351–408.

Bontadini, Filippo, Carol A. Corrado, Jonathan E. Haskel, Massimiliano Iommi, and Cecilia Jona-Lasinio. 2023. "EUKLEMS & INTANProd: Industry Productivity Accounts with Intangibles." LUISS Lab of European Economics. https://euklems-intanprod-llee.luiss.it/wp-content/uploads/2023/02/EUKLEMS_INTANProd_D2.3.1.pdf.

Bontadini, Filippo, Carol A. Corrado, Jonathan E. Haskel, Massimiliano Iommi, and Cecilia Jona-Lasinio. 2024. "Productivity and Intangible Capital: New Evidence from the EUKLEMS & INTANProd Dataset." Paper delivered to the Directorate General for Economic and Financial Affairs (DG-ECFIN) of the European Commission; presented at the ESCoE Conference on Economic Measurement, Manchester, UK (May).

Bresnahan, Timothy F., Erik Brynjolfsson, and Lorin M. Hitt. 2002. "Information Technology, Workplace Organization, and the Demand for Skilled Labor: Firm-Level Evidence." *Quarterly Journal of Economics* 117 (1): 339–96.

Brynjolfsson, Erik, Daniel Rock, and Chad Syverson. 2021. "The Productivity J-Curve: How Intangibles Complement General Purpose Technologies." *American Economic Journal: Macroeconomics* 13 (1): 333–72.

Cette, G., John Fernald, and B. Mojon. 2016. "The Pre-Great Recession Slowdown in Productivity." *European Economic Review* 88:3–28.

Chun, Hyunbae, and M. Ishaq Nadiri. 2016. "Intangible Investment and Changing Sources of Growth in Korea." *Japanese Economic Review* 67 (1): 50–76.

Clarkson, Kenneth W. 1977. *Intangible Capital and Rates of Return, Effects of Research and Promotion on Profitability*. American Enterprise Institute Studies in Economic Policy, 138. Washington, DC: American Enterprise Institute for Public Policy Research.

Clarkson, Kenneth W. 1996. "The Effects of Research and Promotion on Rates of Return." In *Competitive Strategies in the Pharmaceutical Industry*, edited by Robert B. Helms, 238–68. Washington, DC: American Enterprise Institute for Public Policy Research.

Corrado, Carol, Chiara Criscuolo, Jonathan Haskel, Alexander Himbert, and Cecilia Jona-Lasinio. 2021. "New Evidence on Intangibles, Diffusion and Productivity." OECD STI Working Paper 2021/10, July. https://doi.org/10.1787/de0378f3-en.

Corrado, Carol A., Goodridge, Peter, and Haskel, Jonathan E. 2011. "Constructing a Price Deflator for R&D: Calculating the Price of Knowledge Investments as a Residual." Available at SSRN: http://dx.doi.org/10.2139/ssrn.2117802.

Corrado, Carol, and Janet X. Hao. 2014. "Brands as Productive Assets: Concepts, Measurement, and Global Trends." World Intellectual Property Organization Economic Research Working Paper 14, January.

Corrado, Carol, Jonathan Haskel, Massimiliano Iommi, and Cecilia Jona-Lasinio. 2016a. "Growth, Tangible and Intangible Investment in the EU and US before and since the Great Recession." In *Investment and Investment Finance in Europe 2016*, 73–101 (chap. 2). Luxembourg: Economics Department, European Investment Bank.

Corrado, Carol, Jonathan Haskel, Massimiliano Iommi, and Cecilia Jona-Lasinio. 2020. "Intangible Capital, Innovation and Productivity à la Jorgenson: Evidence from Europe and the United States." In *Measuring Economic Growth and Productivity*, edited by Barbara Fraumeni, 363–85. Cambridge, MA: Academic Press/Elsevier.

Corrado, Carol, Jonathan Haskel, Massimiliano Iommi, Cecilia Jona-Lasinio, and Filippo Bontadini. 2024 (forthcoming). "Data, Intangible Capital, and Productivity." In *Technology, Productivity, and Economic Growth*, NBER Studies in Income and Wealth, edited by Susanto Basu, Lucy Eldridge, John Haltiwanger, and Erich Strassner. Chicago: University of Chicago Press.

Corrado, Carol, Jonathan Haskel, and Cecilia Jona-Lasinio. 2016b. "Intangibles, ICT and Industry Productivity Growth: Evidence from the EU." In *The World Economy: Growth or Stagnation?*, edited by Dale W. Jorgenson, Kyoji Fukao, and Marcel P. Timmer, 319–46. Cambridge: Cambridge University Press.

Corrado, Carol, Jonathan Haskel, and Cecilia Jona-Lasinio. 2017a. "Knowledge

Spillovers, ICT, and Productivity Growth." *Oxford Bulletin of Economics and Statistics* 79, no. 4 (August): 592–618.
Corrado, Carol, Jonathan Haskel, and Cecilia Jona-Lasinio. 2017b. "Public Intangibles: The Public Sector and Economic Growth in the SNA." *Review of Income and Wealth* 63, supplement 2 (December): S355–S380.
Corrado, Carol, Jonathan Haskel, and Cecilia Jona-Lasinio. 2021. "Artificial Intelligence and Productivity: An Intangible Assets Approach." *Oxford Review of Economic Policy* 37 (3): 435–58.
Corrado, Carol, Jonathan Haskel, Cecilia Jona-Lasinio, and Massimiliano Iommi. 2012. "Intangible Capital and Growth in Advanced Economies: Measurement Methods and Comparative Results." IZA Discussion Paper No. 6733, July.
Corrado, Carol, Jonathan Haskel, Cecilia Jona-Lasinio, and Massimiliano Iommi. 2013. "Innovation and Intangible Investment in Europe, Japan, and the United States." *Oxford Review of Economic Policy* 29, no. 2 (Summer): 261–86.
Corrado, Carol, Jonathan Haskel, Cecilia Jona-Lasinio, and Massimiliano Iommi. 2022a. "Intangible Capital and Modern Economies." *Journal of Economic Perspectives* 36 (3): 3–28.
Corrado, Carol, Jonathan Haskel, Cecilia Jona-Lasinio, and Massimiliano Iommi. 2022b. Data and Code for: Intangible Capital and Modern Economies. American Economic Association (publisher), Ann Arbor, MI: Inter-university Consortium for Political and Social Research (distributor), 2022–08–09. https://doi.org/10.3886/E171101V1.
Corrado, Carol, Charles R. Hulten, and Daniel Sichel. 2005. "Measuring Capital and Technology: An Expanded Framework." In *Measuring Capital in the New Economy*, NBER Studies in Income and Wealth, edited by Carol Corrado, John Haltiwanger, and Dan Sichel, 11–46. Chicago: University of Chicago Press.
Corrado, Carol, Charles R. Hulten, and Daniel Sichel. 2009. "Intangible Capital and U.S. Economic Growth." *Review of Income and Wealth* 55 (3): 661–85.
Corrado, Carol, David Martin, and Qianfan Wu. 2020. "Innovation α: What Do IP-intensive Stock Price Indexes Tell Us About Innovation?" *AEA Papers and Proceedings* 110: 31–35.
Corrado, Carol, Mary O'Mahony, and Lea Samek. 2021. "How Does Education Contribute to Productivity? An Intangible Infrastructure Approach Applied to the UK and the US." Paper prepared for the 36th IARIW Conference, August. https://iariw.org/wp-content/uploads/2021/08/Education_productivity_paper.pdf.
Crouzet, Nicolas, and Janice C. Eberly. 2018. "Investment, Intangibles, and Efficiency." *AEA Papers and Proceedings* 108: 426–31.
Cuthbertson, Richard, Peder Inge Furseth, and Stephen J. Ezell. 2015. "Apple and Nokia: The Transformation from Products to Services." In *Innovating in a Service-Driven Economy: Insights, Application, and Practice*, chapter 9. London: Palgrave Macmillan.
De Rassenfosse, Gaétan, and Adam B. Jaffe. 2017. "Econometric Evidence on the R&D Depreciation Rate." NBER Working Paper No. w23072 (January). Cambridge MA: National Bureau of Economic Research.
De Soto, Hernando. 2000. *The Mystery of Capital.* New York: Basic Books.
Dixit, Avinash K., and Joseph E. Stiglitz. 1977. "Monopolistic Competition and Optimum Product Diversity." *American Economic Review* 67 (3): 297–308.
Erdem, T., and M. P. Keane. 1996. "Decision-Making Under Uncertainty: Capturing Dynamic Brand Choice Process in Turbulent Consumer Goods Markets." *Marketing Science* 15 (1): 1–20.
Erdem, T., M. P. Keane, and B. Sun. 2008. "A Dynamic Model of Brand Choice

When Price and Advertising Signal Product Quality." *Marketing Science* 27 (6): 1111–25.

European Commission, International Monetary Fund, Organization for Economic Cooperation and Development, United Nations, and World Bank. 2009. *System of National Accounts 2008.* New York: United Nations.

Frazis, Harley J., and James Spletzer. 2005. "Worker Training: What We Have Learned from the NLSY79." *Monthly Labor Review* (February): 48–58.

Fukao, Kyoji, Tsutomu Miyagawa, Kentaro Mukai, Yukio Shinoda, and Konomi Tonogi. 2009. "Intangible Investment in Japan: Measurement and Contribution to Growth." *Review of Income and Wealth* 55 (3): 717–36.

Globalization Task Team. 2022. "Payments for Nonproduced Knowledge-Based Capital (Marketing Assets)." Globalization Guidance Note G.9. New York: United Nations Intersectariat Working Group on National Accounts. https://unstats.un.org/unsd/nationalaccount/aeg/2022/M18/M18_10_G9.pdf.

Goodridge, Peter, Jonathan Haskel, and Gavin Wallis. 2012. "UK Innovation Index: Productivity and Growth in UK Industries." NESTA Working Paper 12/09. London: National Endowment for Science, Technology, and the Arts.

Goodridge, Peter, and Jonathan Haskel. 2016. "Big Data in UK Industries: An Intangible Investment Approach." Imperial College Business School Discussion Paper 2016/01. London: Imperial College Business School.

Gordon, Robert J. 2016. *The Rise and Fall of American Growth: The U.S. Standard of Living Since the Civil War*. Princeton, NJ: Princeton University Press.

Griliches, Zvi. 1992. "The Search for R&D Spillovers." *Scandinavian Journal of Economics* 94 (Supplement): S29–47.

Griliches, Zvi. 1994. "Productivity, R&D, and the Data Constraint." *American Economic Review* 84 (1): 1–23.

Gu, Wulong, and Ambrose Wong. 2010. "Estimates of Human Capital in Canada: The Lifetime Income Approach." Economic Analysis Research Paper Series No. 062, June, Statistics Canada.

Gutiérrez, Germán, and Thomas Philippon. 2017. "Investmentless Growth: An Empirical Investigation." *Brookings Papers on Economic Activity*, no. 2,: 89–169.

Haskel, Jonathan, and Stian Westlake. 2018. *Capitalism without Capital: The Rise of the Intangible Economy.* Princeton, NJ: Princeton University Press.

Haskel, Jonathan, and Stian Westlake. 2022. *Restarting the Future: How to Fix the Intangible Economy*. Princeton, NJ: Princeton University Press.

Hayakawa, Hitoshi, Susumu Imai, and Kazuko Nakata. 2018. "The Empirical Analysis of Brand: A Survey." *Japanese Economic Review* 69 (3): 324–39.

Hazan, Eric, Sven Smit, Jonathan Woetzel, Biljana Cvetanovski, Mekala Krishnan, Brian Gregg, Jesko Perrey, and Klemens Hjartar. 2021. "Getting Tangible about Intangibles: The Future of Growth and Productivity?" McKinsey Global Institute Discussion Paper, June.

Hulten, Charles R. 1979. "On the 'Importance' of Productivity Change." *American Economic Review* 69 (1): 126–36.

Hulten, Charles R. 2011. "How Did Microsoft Become 'Microsoft'? Intangible Capital and the Endogenous Growth of the Firm." Mimeo, Conference Board Economics Program, May, revised February 2013.

Hulten, Charles R., and Janet X. Hao. 2012. "The Role of Intangible Capital in the Transformation and Growth of the Chinese Economy." NBER Working Paper 18405 (September). Cambridge MA: National Bureau of Economic Research.

International Monetary Fund. 2019. "The Rise of Corporate Market Power and Its Macroeconomic Effects." In *World Economic Outlook: Growth Slowdown, Precarious Recovery*, chapter 2. Washington DC: International Monetary Fund.

Ichniowski, Casey, and Kathryn Shaw. 1999. "The Effects of Human Resource Systems on Productivity: An International Comparison of U.S. and Japanese Plants." *Management Science* 45 (5): 704–21.

Jones, Charles I. 1995. "R&D-Based Models of Economic Growth." *Journal of Political Economy* 103 (4): 759–84.

Jorgenson, Dale W. 1963. "Capital Theory and Investment Behavior." *American Economic Review* 53 (2): 247–59.

Jorgenson, Dale W., and Barbara M. Fraumeni. 1989. "The Accumulation of Human and Nonhuman Capital, 1948–84." In *The Measurement of Saving, Investment, and Wealth*. NBER Studies in Income and Wealth, edited by Richard Lipsey and Helen Tice, 52:227–82. Chicago: University of Chicago Press.

Jorgenson, D. W., and B. M. Fraumeni. 1992a. "Investment in Education U.S. Economic Growth." *Scandinavian Journal of Economics* 94 (supplement): 51–70.

Jorgenson, D. W., and B. M. Fraumeni. 1992b. "The Output of the Education Sector." In *Output Measurement in the Service Sectors.* NBER Studies in Income and Wealth, edited by Z. Griliches, 56:303–41. Chicago: University of Chicago Press.

Kwoka, J. 1984. "Advertising and the Price and Quality of Optometric Services." *American Economic Review* 74 (1): 211–6.

Le Mouel, Marie and Mariagrazia Squicciarini. 2015. "Cross-Country Estimates of Employment and Investment in Organizational Capital: A Task-Based Methodology Using the PIACC Database." DIW Discussion paper 1522. Berlin: German Institute for Economic Research.

Lev, Baruch. 2001. *Intangibles: Management, Measurement, and Reporting.* Washington, DC: Brookings Institution Press.

Lev, Baruch, and Suresh R. Radhakrishnan. 2005. "The Valuation of Organizational Capital." In *Measuring Capital in the New Economy*, edited by Carol Corrado, John Haltiwanger, and Dan Sichel 2005, 73–110. Chicago: University of Chicago Press.

LUISS Lab of European Economics (LLEE). 2022. "EU KLEMS & INTANProd Database." LUISS University. https://euklems-intanprod-llee.luiss.it/.

Machlup, Fritz. 1962. *The Production and Distribution of Knowledge in the United States.* Princeton, NJ: Princeton University Press.

Mandel, Michael. 2006. "Unmasking the Economy." *Business Week,* February 13.

Mandel, Michael. 2019. "Building the New Manufacturing Stack." *Forbes Magazine*, August 20.

Marrano, Mauro Giorgio, Jonathan Haskel, and Gavin Wallis. 2009. "What Happened to the Knowledge Economy? ICT, Intangible Investment, and Britain's Productivity Record Revisited." *Review of Income and Wealth* 55 (3): 686–716.

Marshall, A. 1919. *Industry and Trade*. London: Macmillan.

Martin, Josh. 2019. "Measuring the Other Half: New Measures of Intangible Investment from the ONS." *National Institute Economic Review* 249 (August), R17–R29.

Mayer-Schönberger, V., and K. Cukier. 2013. *Big Data: A Revolution That Will Transform How We Live, Work, and Think*. New York: Houghton Mifflin Harcourt.

McKinsey Global Institute. 2016. *The Age of Analytics: Competing in a Data-Driven World.* MGI Research Report (December). https://www.mckinsey.com/capabilities/quantumblack/our-insights/the-age-of-analytics-competing-in-a-data-driven-world.

MEPSIR. 2006. "Final Report of Study on Exploitation of Public Sector Information—Benchmarking EU Framework Conditions." https://www.researchgate.net/profile/Marc-Jacquinet/publication/297032292_Measuring_European_Public_Sector

_Information_Resources/links/56dcb56b08aebe4638c0355e/Measuring-European-Public-Sector-Information-Resources.pdf.

Milgrom, Paul, and John Roberts. 1986. "Price and Advertising Signals of Product Quality." *Journal of Political Economy* 94 (4): 796–821.

Nagaraj, Abhishek. 2022. "The Private Impact of Public Data: Landsat Satellite Maps Increased Gold Discoveries and Encouraged Entry." *Management Science* 68 (1): 564–82.

Nakamura, Leonard. 1999. "Intangibles: What Put the New in the New Economy?" *Federal Reserve Bank of Philadelphia Business Review* (July/August): 3–16.

Nakamura, Leonard. 2001. "What Is the U.S. Gross Investment in Intangibles? (At Least) One Trillion Dollars a Year!" Federal Reserve Bank of Philadelphia Working Paper, No. 01–15.

National Academies of Sciences, Engineering, and Medicine (NAS). 2020. *Safeguarding the Bioeconomy.* Washington, DC: The National Academies Press. https://doi.org/10.17226/25525.

Nelson, Phillip. 1974. "Advertising as Information." *Journal of Political Economy* 82 (4): 729–54.

Nguyen, David, and Marta Paczos. 2020. "Measuring the Economic Value of Data and Cross-Border Data Flows: A Business Perspective." OECD Digital Economy Papers No. 297, OECD Publishing, Paris.

Open Data Institute (ODI). 2016. "The Economic Value of Open versus Paid Data" (April). London: Open Data Institute. https://theodi.org/insights/reports/research-the-economic-value-of-open-versus-paid-data/.

OECD. 2013. *Supporting Investment in Knowledge Capital, Growth and Innovation.* Paris: OECD Publishing.

Pakes, Ariel, and Mark Schankerman. 1984. "The Rate of Obsolescence of Patents, Research Gestation Lags, and the Private Rate of Return to Research Resources." In *R&D, Patents, and Productivity*, edited by Zvi Griliches, 73–88. Chicago: University of Chicago Press.

Piekkola, Hannu. 2016. "Intangible Investment and Market Valuation." *Review of Income and Wealth* 62, no. 1 (March): 28–51.

Rauch, Ferdinand. 2013. "Advertising Expenditure and Consumer Prices." *International Journal of Industrial Organization* 31 (4): 331–41.

Robbins, Carol, Olympia Belay, Matthew Donahoe, and Jennifer Lee. 2012. "Industry-Level Output Price Indexes for R&D: An Input-Cost Approach with R&D Productivity Adjustment." BEA research paper. https://www.bea.gov/system/files/papers/WP2013-2.pdf.

Rock, Daniel. 2022. "Engineering Value: The Returns to Technological Talent and Investments in Artificial Intelligence." Center on Regulation and Markets at Brookings Working Paper, June. https://www.brookings.edu/wp-content/uploads/2022/05/Engineering-value.pdf.

Romer, Paul M. 1990. "Endogenous Technological Change." *Journal of Political Economy* 98 (5 Part 2): S71–S102.

Santiago-Calderón, José B., and Dylan Rassier. 2022. "Valuing the US Data Economy Using Machine Learning and Online Job Postings." Paper prepared for the NBER/CRIW Conference on Technology, Productivity, and Economic Growth, March 17–18.

Schramm, C. J., A. Arora, R. K. Chandy, K. Cooper, D. W. Jorgenson, D. S. Siegel, D. L. Bernd, S. Ballmer, J. Blanchard, G. Buckley, A. Collins, M. L. Eskew, L. Hodges, S. J. Palmisano, and J. Menzer. 2008. *Innovation Measurement: Tracking the State of Innovation in the American Economy.* Technical report, US Department of Commerce.

Solow, Robert M. 1967. "The New Industrial State: Son of Affluence." *Public Interest* 9 (Fall): 100–108, 118–9.

Solow, Robert M. 1968. "The Truth Further Refined: A Comment on Marris." *Public Interest* 11 (Spring): 47–52.

Squicciarini, Mariagrazia, and Marie Le Mouel. 2012. "Defining and Measuring Investment in Organisational Capital: Using US Microdata to Develop a Task-Based Approach." OECD Science, Technology and Industry Working Paper 2012/5, OECD Publishing, Paris.

Statistics Canada. 2019a. "Measuring Investment in Data, Databases and Data Science: Conceptual Framework." June.

Statistics Canada. 2019b. "The Value of Data in Canada: Experimental Estimates." July.

Steiner, Robert L. 1973. "Does Advertising Lower Consumer Prices?" *Journal of Marketing* 37 (October): 19–26.

van Ark, Bart, Janet X. Hao, Carol Corrado, and Charles Hulten. 2009. "Measuring Intangible Capital and Its Contribution to Economic Growth in Europe." *EIB papers* 14, no. 1: 62–93.

Varian, Hal. 2019. "Artificial Intelligence, Economics, and Industrial Organization." In *The Economics of Artificial Intelligence: An Agenda*, edited by Ajay Agrawal, Joshua Gans, and Avi Goldfarb, 399–419. Chicago: University of Chicago Press.

Vinod, H. D., and P. M. Rao. 2000. "R&D and Promotion in Pharmaceuticals: A Conceptual Framework and Empirical Exploration." *Journal of Marketing Theory and Practice* 8 (4): 10–20.

Weitzman, Martin L. 1976. "On the Welfare Significance of National Product in a Dynamic Economy." *Quarterly Journal of Economics* 90 (1): 156–62.

Wooldridge, Jeffrey M. 2009. "On Estimating Firm-Level Production Functions Using Proxy Variables to Control for Unobservables." *Economics Letters* 104 (3): 112–4.

Young, Alison. 1998. "Towards an Interim Statistical Framework: Selecting the Core Components of Intangible Investment." OECD Secretariat. https://web-archive.oecd.org/2012-06-15/166655-1943301.pdf.

Zwick, Thomas. 2007. "Apprenticeship Training in Germany—Investment or Productivity Driven?" ZEW Zeitschrift für ArbeitsmarktForschung—Journal for Labour Market Research, Institut für Arbeitsmarkt- und Berufsforschung (IAB), Nürnberg

4 Productivity Measurement
New Goods, Variety, and Quality Change

Diane Coyle

4.1 Introduction

Technological innovation is the engine of productivity, and hence the engine of the dramatic improvement in living standards many economies have enjoyed over time. Progress through innovation is often embodied in new or improved goods and services. Yet the value of new goods, increased variety of goods, and improvements in quality of goods are not easily taken into account in productivity measurement; they pose challenges to the construction of price indexes used to deflate revenues and thus calculate "real" output growth and productivity.

There is continuing debate about the extent to which inflation measures are upwardly biased by inadequate treatment of new goods, new varieties, and quality improvements, and thus the extent to which real GDP (gross domestic product) and productivity growth might be understated. Although national statistical offices have made efforts to adjust price indexes for such advances, the debate about how to calculate deflators has recurred in recent years because of the "productivity puzzle," the slowdown in measured productivity growth in most OECD countries since the mid-2000s. This measured slowdown has occurred despite plentiful anecdotal evidence of continuing technological advances. These technological improvements in turn, raise the question of whether current adjustments to price indexes are

Diane Coyle is with the Bennett Institute, University of Cambridge.

With thanks to Karen Dynan, Richard Heys, Chad Jones, Cahal Moran, Leonard Nakamura, David Nguyen, Marshall Reinsdorf, Louise Sheiner, and all the participants in the Hutchins Center conference on productivity measurement in April 2020 for their helpful comments on an early draft. I also thank Julia Wdowin and Annabel Manley for their excellent research assistance. I am grateful for research funding from the Economic Statistics Centre of Excellence. Responsibility for any errors is all mine.

sufficient. In other words, is part of the answer to the productivity puzzle that mismeasured deflators lead official statistics to overstate inflation and underestimate the value of new and better goods and services?

This chapter discusses the significant role that new and improved goods and services—as well as increased variety—play in the modern economy and the challenge this poses to meaningful measurement of prices and productivity; summarizes the typical practices of national statistical offices (NSOs); describes a number of recent approaches in the academic literature to resolving measurement challenges, particularly due to digitalization; identifies broader questions about current approaches to measuring output and productivity; and concludes by suggesting that more radical approaches to accounting for progress may be needed to understand the ways new or improved goods affect living standards and productivity.

4.2 How Significant Are Introductions of New and Improved Goods and Services?

Productivity measurement relates economic production inputs to outputs, so the measure of GDP, the economy's aggregate output, is the starting point. GDP, the standard measure of a nation's or region's total economic activity, does not directly account for the range and novelty of products and services produced and consumed; these are assumed to be either captured by the price deflator used to convert nominal output into real output or allocated to unmeasured consumer surplus (that is, the amount consumers would have been willing to pay for a product above the market price they actually paid). Yet new goods or varieties offering consumers greater choice and better satisfying heterogeneous individual preferences are an indicator of improved quality, and thus of consumer welfare.

There are no clear distinctions between a new good, an additional variety of an existing good that increases consumer choice, and a quality change in an existing product. Nevertheless, the statistical treatments of these cases differ in practice. Changes in the specifications of items like laptops or cars tend to be treated by statistical agencies as quality changes, while new flavors of juice are treated as additional varieties. A big enough increment to the characteristics of a product means it can be characterized as a new good, such as a smartphone compared to a fixed line phone. Nordhaus (1996) refers to these major advances as "tectonic shifts." It is not possible to assess the value of a truly novel new good from past data on prices and characteristics,[1] whereas such an approach can work for a quality improvement of an existing good. But the distinctions are not always clear. If scientific progress brings personalized genomic treatment from an existing category of medication or a new use for an old medicine (such as mini-aspirin to prevent cardiovascular disease), which category of improvement is it?

Table 4.1 **Number of varieties, US consumer goods**

	Early 1970s	Late 1990s
Vehicle models	140	260
Personal computers	0	400
Websites	0	4,757,394
New book titles	40,530	77,446
Amusement parks	362	1,174
McDonald's menu items	13	43
Soft drink brands	20	87
Milk types	4	19
Pain relievers	17	141
Running shoe styles	5	285

Source: Extracted from Alm and Cox (1998).

Everyday experience makes it clear that the range of goods available in advanced economies has been increasing over time. Examples include the phenomenon of fast fashion, personalized biomedical treatments, new flavors of food items, the number of book titles published, and many others. Yet statistics on variety are not part of the standard suite of economic metrics, and it is difficult to find recent systematic data. Using websites, magazines, and various industry sources, Alm and Cox (1998) reported large increases in the number of varieties for a range of consumer goods from the early 1970s to late 1990s (table 4.1).

Similarly, the Economic Research Service of the US Department of Agriculture reports a broad upward trend in new product introductions (both food and beverages and nonfood) in retail outlets over the 1990s through 2010s (fig. 4.1). These data show an upward jump in introductions of goods other than food around the turn of the century with some tailing off in the late 2010s. For this to indicate improving productivity, the key question is whether the *proportion* of new goods is increasing, which would be reflected in an acceleration in figure 4.1. This acceleration seems to have occurred in the early 2000s, with some subsequent leveling off.

Other scanner datasets suggest the variety explosion has continued since then and may have accelerated. For instance, in its Breakthrough Innovation Reports, the market research company Nielsen uses the number of SKUs to estimate the net number of new product launches each year in different geographies. In 2014, there were 18,958 new product varieties launched in Europe, an 11 percent increase over 2011.[2] The following year, 2015, brought a further 9 percent increase over 2014[3] to about 20,000, and by 2019, the number of new SKUs had reached about 30,000.[4] There is, of course, vast churn, as many new varieties fail. In a large scanner dataset, Melser (2019) found 1,740 varieties of toothpaste available in 31 New York supermarkets

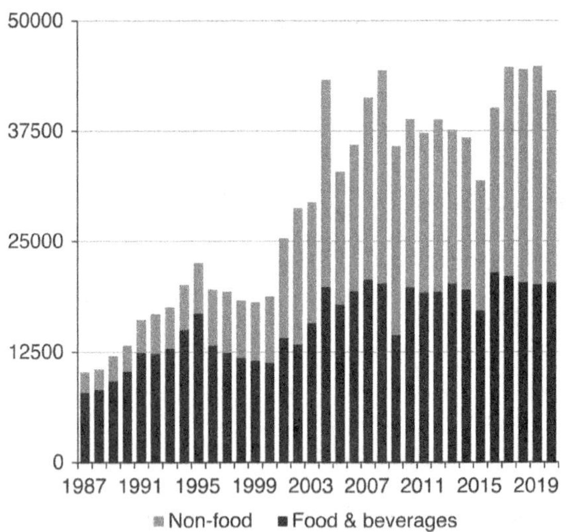

Fig. 4.1 Number of new products introduced in US retail outlets
Source: USDA ERS, https://www.ers.usda.gov/topics/food-markets-prices/processing-marketing/new-products.aspx (online from 1998, offline prior to then).

over the period 2001–2012. In a constant subset of supermarkets, the number of brands available increased from 408 to 519 over that period, with only 85 brands available consistently.

Bils and Klenow (2001) show that an increase in variety within a category of goods (as measured by the rate at which the Bureau of Labor Statistics, or BLS, replaces an item in the pricing basket because it is no longer available) tends to increase spending on that category. Using observed spending shifts across categories over time, they found that variety in the US increased an average of 1 percent per year from 1959 to 1999 and increased even faster from 1979 to 1999. There are some goods where variety ultimately manifests as personalization, ranging from the wide scope of tailoring specifications for personal computers to shoes produced to individual designs to "mass customized" 3D-printed items.

It is possible that additive manufacturing (3D printing) techniques will increase this scope in the future, including in categories such as medical devices ("orthopedic and cranial implants, surgical instruments, dental restorations such as crowns, and external prosthetics"[5]) and even human organs, where the welfare impact may be large (Culmone, Smit, and Breedveld 2019, Schubert, Van Langeveld, and Donoso 2014).

Widespread customization also increases the scope for personalized pricing, potentially allowing producers to capture much of the surplus created by customization by transforming consumer surplus into producer surplus (profits) via increased price discrimination. Of course, it is still important to adjust for the welfare benefits of customization—otherwise, price increases offset by quality increases are misrepresented as pure price increases.

Another reason increasing variety will not necessarily continue to increase consumer welfare is that, while better matching of products to preferences or needs improves welfare when tastes or circumstances are very varied (such as book or music titles), it does so less when preferences are less heterogeneous and/or new varieties are increasingly similar to each other (such as orange juice brands). For example, the model of gains from variety developed in Trajtenberg (1989) implies that consumer welfare tends to increase with the logarithm of the number of varieties so that the marginal benefit of an additional variety is inversely proportional to the number already present. In other words, while the initial introduction of differentiated varieties of orange juice—not from concentrate, for example—increases consumer welfare, as the variety space is filled in, each additional variety likely provides smaller welfare gains.

How much does the challenge posed by new goods and varieties matter for understanding real output and productivity growth? There have been several attempts to quantify how much difference the phenomenon might make to measurement. One well-known analysis of the upward bias to inflation and downward bias to real GDP growth and productivity, due in part to the introduction of new goods, is the Boskin Commission report (1996). The commission calculated that published US inflation was overstated by an average of up to 1.3 percentage points a year prior to 1996, of which the commission attributed about 0.6 percentage points a year to quality change and new product bias. The debate following the publication of the report, whose recommendations for changes to statistical practice had significant implications for the index linking of government payments, was but the last in a sequence of controversies about how inflation is calculated. The earlier Stigler Commission (1961) had similarly concluded that consumer price index (CPI) inflation in the 1950s was overstated due to failure to account for quality change; it explicitly recommended the construction of an index to measure a constant welfare basket of consumption. Moulton (2018) has updated the Boskin Commission approach and finds US CPI bias has fallen to 0.85 percentage points from its best estimate of 1.1 percentage points.

Estimated bias figures make a substantial difference to how growth and productivity statistics ought to be interpreted. Among important policy questions today, a high priority is whether mismeasurement of prices due to the way NSO indexes treat new goods, variety, and quality improvements can help explain the productivity puzzle. In other words, is the impact of new goods and innovation larger than in previous periods? The current balance of opinion is that there is probably some upward bias in price indexes (Ahmad, Ribarsky, and Reinsdorf 2017, Aghion et al. 2019, Reinsdorf and

Schreyer 2020) but that the extent of the bias has probably declined over recent years, so it does not help resolve the puzzle of declining productivity. However, as this chapter explores, this debate is far from settled.

4.3 Why New Goods and Varieties Make It Hard to Measure Prices and Productivity

In his classic *The Wealth and Poverty of Nations* (1998), David Landes writes that Nathan Mayer Rothschild, then the richest man in the world, died in 1836 of an infected tooth abscess for want of an antibiotic that had not yet been invented. That antibiotic today costs only around $10 and is routinely available to all. The tale is a vivid demonstration of the fundamental role that innovation and new goods play in economic progress, manifested in health, longevity, and quality of life. Can such progress be captured by the measurement of productivity?

The problem posed by the arrival of new and/or higher quality goods for the calculation of price indexes and, therefore, real activity is widely appreciated. As Diewert (1998) summarizes, "The basic problem is that index number theory assumes that the set of commodities is fixed and unchanging from period to period, so that like can be compared to like." This section provides the intuition for conceptual issues. The next section considers what NSOs do to address these challenges in practice.

The fundamental problem of a changing set of commodities is easily seen in classic price indexes like the Laspeyres and the Paasche. The Laspeyres price index (a variant of which is used to calculate most official price indexes) tracks the change in the cost of a basket of goods from the base period of the price comparison:

$$\text{Laspeyres} = \frac{\sum_i p_{it} q_{i0}}{\sum_i p_{i0} q_{i0}},$$

where p_i is the price of good i, q_i is its quantity, t is the current period, and 0 is the base period. Equivalently,

$$\text{Laspeyres} = \sum_i s_{i0} * \frac{p_{it}}{p_{i0}},$$

where s_{i0} are the base period expenditure shares. Thus, the Laspeyres price index is a weighted average of the price changes for every good and service purchased, with weights equal to the expenditure share of each good in the base period. The Laspeyres index asks, What has happened to the cost of yesterday's basket of goods?

An alternative price index is the Paasche index, which uses current period weights for its basket. The Paasche index asks, How has the cost of today's basket of goods changed since the base period?

$$\text{Paasche} = \frac{\sum_i p_{it} q_{it}}{\sum_i p_{i0} q_{it}}$$

The Fisher index—used by the Bureau of Economic Analysis when constructing price indexes to deflate GDP—combines the Laspeyres and Paasche indexes by taking their geometric mean.

$$\text{Fisher} = \sqrt{\left[\frac{\sum_i p_{it} q_{i0}}{\sum_i p_{i0} q_{i0}}\right] * \left[\frac{\sum_i p_{it} q_{it}}{\sum_i p_{i0} q_{it}}\right]}$$

For example, if the Laspeyres inflation rate is 6 percent and the Paasche inflation rate is 3 percent, the Fisher inflation rate would be $\sqrt{(1.06) * (1.03)} - 1 = 4.49$ percent.

Indexes like the Fisher index, known as superlative indexes, have the advantage of accounting for substitution between products over time (see chap. 1 by Dynan and Sheiner in this volume). If the same goods are available in both periods, superlative indexes closely approximate a true cost-of-living index that asks, How much would the consumer need this period compared to the previous one to keep a constant level of well-being?[6]

The challenge in measuring real output is how to deal with disappearing products, new products, and improved products. One approach to imputing the missing price of a disappearing or new product is to use Hicks's (1940) concept of the hypothetical "reservation price," the price that would make quantity demanded equal to zero. This concept can be used to impute current period prices for disappearing products and base period prices for new products or varieties in a superlative index.

This approach can also be used to impute the missing price of the old model in the Laspeyres index or the new model in the Paasche index. Consider the introduction of a new model of laptop in year 2 that displaces the model sold in year 1. Say the old model sold for $3,000 and the new and improved model sells for $3,200. To calculate the Laspeyres index, one would determine the price at which consumers would still buy the old model in year 2. If the new model is worth $400 more to consumers, then consumers would choose to purchase the old model if it were sold for $2,800. A Laspeyres index that imputes such a price to the disappearing laptop would register a price decline (from $3,000 to $2,800, a 6.7 percent decline).

Similarly, one could impute the period 1 price of the new laptop. In this example, the new laptop would not have been purchased in year 1 if its price were more than $3,400—and one could use $3,400 to impute a year 1 price for the new laptop in the Paasche index (that is, a price decline from $3,400 to $3,200, a 5.9 percent decline).

If the changes in characteristics between old and new models are valued differently by different consumers, the reservation price will reflect the highest willingness to pay. Using the reservation price for the disappearing item in the Laspeyres index will then tend to cause an overstatement of inflation (because some consumers might prefer the old item and be willing to pay a lot for it), while using the reservation price for the new model in the Paasche index will tend to cause an understatement of inflation (using the same logic). The Fisher index will still be a good approximation to the true cost-of-living index. For example, if the prices that different consumers would pay for the old model ranged from $2,700 to $2,950 and the prices that different consumers would pay for the new model ranged from $3,250 to $3,600, the Laspeyres index using the reservation price would show a small decline of ($3,000 – $2,950)/$3,000 = 1.67 percent; the Paasche index using the reservation price would show a large decline of ($3,600 – $3,200)/$3,600 = 11.1 percent, and the Fisher index would be show a decline of 6.5 percent.

Reservation prices of disappearing products tend to be lower than those of successful new products because inability to sell the old product at an acceptable price is generally the reason it disappears. The reservation prices of important new goods tend to be high. Consider, for example, the price people would have paid for antibiotics had they been available. If a deflator is estimated without taking account of new and disappearing goods, it will tend to overstate inflation and understate productivity growth. If statistical agencies do not include reservation prices—and they do not—their price indexes for goods with rapid technology progress are likely to be biased upward (Diewert, Fox, and Schreyer 2018).

4.4 How National Statistical Offices Compute Price Indexes in Practice

NSOs construct price indexes in two stages of aggregation: one aggregating price observations into indexes for narrow categories of goods and a second using these elementary indexes as the building blocks to calculate higher-level price indexes. In the US CPI, for example, phones, accessories, and smartwatches together compose one elementary index, and wireless phone service is another. Each stage of aggregation has its own measurement issues. For elementary indexes, the measurement problems are new and disappearing models and varieties, quality change, and potential obsolescence of samples of outlets and varieties. For higher-level aggregation, the main measurement problems are potential obsolescence of the basket used for higher-level weights, the inability of the Laspeyres index formula[7] to account for substitution between products, and the introduction of completely new products that do not fit in any existing elementary index.

4.4.1 The "Matched Models" Procedure for Constructing Elementary Indexes

The "matched models" procedure is the main method used by NSOs to compute elementary price indexes. A matched-model index compares prices of the same item at the same outlet over time. Disappearing items and new items are omitted from the calculation. For example, when a new refrigerator model with different features appears, its price is not be directly compared to the price of the old model. If the price impact of the different features cannot be estimated by the procedures used for explicit quality adjustments, and if the old model is still available, the price change of the old model is used to calculate inflation. If not, the NSO imputes a price, as described below.

4.4.2 Introduction of New Goods and Varieties

If a new product that is an improvement or is priced lower than existing products is introduced in a competitive market, the prices of existing products that continue to be sold will fall. The matched-model index then captures the price decline even though the new product has not yet entered the index's market basket. Yet in the real world, where withdrawals of old models, reduced competition due to product differentiation, and sluggish price adjustment are common, the matched-model index is likely to understate the benefits from the introduction of improved new goods or varieties. And when a product is truly new—the smartphone, for example—there are no obvious competitors, so the matched model simply misses its benefits.

In addition, any given sample of outlets and varieties used to calculate a matched-model index will become unrepresentative over time. Silver and Heravi (2005) use scanner data to show that the matched-model approach can cause the sample of goods whose prices are used in an index to be unrepresentative of what consumers are actually buying, as it does not take account quickly enough of substitution to more desirable products.[8] Sample refreshment is the periodic updating of retail outlets from which prices are collected, when new varieties often come into the index (Reinsdorf and Schreyer 2020). The updated sample is used to calculate change in the index once prices from outlets and varieties selected to be in the sample have been collected for the second time.[9] Overlapping prices are collected from the new and old samples in a link month; the implicit assumption is that the price differences between items in the new and old samples equal the value of their quality differences. For example, if the updated sample includes a new variety of cereal that is priced higher than the cereal in the old basket, that higher price does not show up as higher inflation—it is implicitly assumed that the higher price reflects a higher quality cereal. In other words, the real quality of cereal has increased when the consumer switches to a higher-priced brand or variety.

The assumption that price differences fully reflect quality differences can lead to understatement or overstatement of true price changes. For example, if manufacturers raise prices at the same time as they introduce new models or varieties, then this approach will understate inflation because it assumes that the entire price increase is offset by the improvement in quality associated with the new model.[10] In contrast, for products with improving technology, the approach is likely to overstate inflation because it does not account for any increase in value the consumer may be getting from the new model above and beyond that represented by the higher price.[11] The method assumes the consumer is indifferent between the lower-priced old model and the higher-priced new model, which is unlikely to be the case with such products.

For categories of products with advancing technology, new models often offer quality improvements that are not fully reflected in higher prices. The tendency of new models to come into the calculated price index during periodic sample refreshments rather than as specific replacements for models that have disappeared means that quality improvements in goods benefiting from technological progress are often overlooked (Moulton 2018). When new models are introduced as replacements, it is more likely that a quality adjustment will occur, as we describe below. Furthermore, long intervals between sample refreshments mean that new goods are often not introduced into the index in a timely way, so the index may miss the steep falls in price that sometimes occur early in a new good's life cycle.

4.4.3 Dealing with Disappearing Products

Of course, products often disappear between sample refreshments—perhaps because a company discontinues a line of products or introduces a new model/variety. Other times, the product is simply not in stock at the time of price collection.

Permanent disappearances require selection of similar replacement items. If a new model can be found that closely matches the disappearing model, their prices are directly compared—that is, the new model is simply treated as a continuation of the old model. Otherwise, the NSO must either explicitly adjust for the quality difference between the new and old items or treat the replacement item as noncomparable to the original item.

Treatment as noncomparable is more common. If an overlapping price of a replacement item is available from the period just before the original item disappeared, the price changes of the noncomparable replacement item immediately start to be used in the place of the price changes of the original item. For example, if dishwasher model A stops being sold in January 2020 and dishwasher model B is introduced in 2019, the percent change in the price of model B is used instead of the percent change in the price of model A beginning in December 2019. When overlapping prices are not available, as is usually the case, the price of the replacement item in the period when the original item was still present must be imputed in other ways.

The simplest and most common method of imputing the pre-entry price of the replacement item is to deflate its first observed price by an index calculated from other items in the same category—what the BLS calls the cell relative method. So, for example, if the price of similar items has increased

3 percent, the BLS assumes that the price of the replacement item was 3 percent lower in the previous period.

Producers of some types of products, such as motor vehicles, tend to time price increases to coincide with the introduction of new models. In these cases, the price changes of continuing items underpredict the price change associated with the introduction of a new model. If the new model's starting price must be imputed, BLS uses a method it calls class-mean imputation (Bureau of Labor Statistics 2020, chap. 17, 23). This method averages quality-adjusted price changes associated with the introduction of other new models (that is, using only the subset of similar products that are also new models).

4.4.4 Dealing with Quality Change

How do statistical agencies calculate price indexes when a good continues to be sold but its quality has changed? One of the techniques used is hedonic adjustment, which is based on fitting a model relating a good's characteristics to its price. Proposed first by Griliches (1961) and Adelman and Griliches (1961) as a method for official price indexes to take account of quality improvements in automobiles and subsequently applied to other types of products experiencing rapid technological or quality advance, this method requires data on quantifiable characteristics of quality—such as horsepower, heated seats, or automatic transmission for cars or memory and processing speed for computers. The hedonic regression estimates an implicit price for each characteristic, allowing price differential due to quality change to be used to adjust the index. For example, if a hedonic regression estimates that additional memory and a faster microprocessor increases the price of laptops by $500, then adjusting the price of the old model by this amount provides a prediction of what the new model would have sold for in the period when the old model's price was observed. Using this imputed price to calculate the index has the effect of deducting the value of the quality change from the difference between the price of the new computer model and the price of the model it replaced.

There is some arbitrariness with hedonic adjustment in practice. Only observable characteristics can be included in the hedonic model, but other, unobserved characteristics may be important (Erickson and Pakes 2011). Hausman (2003) notes other limitations on the ability of the method to isolate consumer utility, such as inability to distinguish a price rise due to market power from a genuine improvement in quality.

An alternative to hedonic adjustment for quality change is to estimate each new feature's contribution to price based on costs of production (option costing, in the terminology of the UK's Office for National Statistics, or ONS). For example, BLS obtains estimates from manufacturers of the price increments arising from features in new motor vehicle models and subtracts these increments (plus a markup) from the prices of new models to get quality-adjusted prices.[12]

4.4.5 How Common Are Quality Adjustments in Practice?

Groshen et al. (2017) state that from December 2013 to November 2014, a match was found for 73 percent of items in the US CPI; another 22 percent were temporarily missing for reasons such as seasonality. Of the remaining 5 percent, "three-fifths of those items were replaced by a similar good. For the remaining two-fifths, where the characteristics were judged to be insufficiently close, BLS staff made a quality adjustment to the replacement product's price."[13] The methods of quality adjustment include hedonic adjustment and adjustment based on costs of production.

For the UK, an analysis of the methods used in the CPIH (consumer price index including housing costs) found that direct comparison is used for 24.6 percent of the basket (based on spending), and imputation methods based on similar products, sometimes with adjustments for weight or size changes, are used for an additional 70 percent of the basket. Option costing (adjusting for the cost of new features) is used for 2.1 percent of the basket, and hedonic adjustment, adjustment for age (for used vehicles), or other methods are used for the remaining 3.3 percent.[14]

Reliance on hedonic adjustments varies widely across countries. In the CPI, the US BLS currently applies hedonic adjustment to a wide range of electronic goods and communications services (table 4.2—though for computers it adjusts for quality change using the option costing method). BLS also applies hedonics in the CPI to several clothing categories and uses both hedonics and option costing for rent and imputed rent.[15] It similarly adjusts internet access and semiconductor prices in the producer price index (PPI). This is a wider range of products than many other statistical agencies. For example, the UK's ONS hedonically adjusts prices only for a handful of

Table 4.2 **Electronic items BLS hedonically adjusts in the US CPI**

ED031	Wireless phone services
ED041	Landline telephone services
EE031	Internet access and other information services
EE041	Phones, accessories, and smartwatches
HK011	Refrigerators and freezers
HK012	Washers and dryers
HK013	Ranges and cooktops
HK014	Microwave ovens
RA011	Televisions
RA021	Cable and satellite television services
RA031	Other video equipment
RD012	Photographic equipment

Source: Quality Adjustment in the CPI, https://www.bls.gov/cpi/quality-adjustment/home.html.

consumer electronic items such as smartphones and laptops. Other countries either do not use hedonic adjustment at all (e.g., Denmark, Ireland, Norway) or adjust for quality change in different goods (e.g., used cars in Germany and Sweden, PCs, TV sets, and cameras in Japan).[16]

The general reason some countries opt to apply hedonic regressions to a relatively small proportion of items in price indexes is practicality; as Groshen et al. (2017) point out, the quality-adjustment methods used by agencies need to be cost effective, use timely data to fit with publication timetables, and be within the skill and information-processing capacity of the agencies. Hedonic methods often do not meet these criteria.

4.5 Alternative Methods to Account for Innovation

Researchers have proposed a number of methods beyond the standard practices of NSOs to estimate the value of new varieties, improved quality, and new goods. Three types are discussed here: unit value indexes, modeling of demand functions to impute missing prices, and methods to estimate the value of truly novel goods.

4.5.1 Unit Value Approaches

The innovation challenge is greatest in sectors where there is obvious technological advance. Recent work has proposed the use of unit value indexes—revenues divided by a volume metric—in some of these cases. Although generally discouraged in official statistics because their assumption that physical units of different items have the same value is usually unrealistic, unit value indexes are used by NSOs for homogeneous products (such as basic commodities) and sometimes when insufficient data is available, as with certain components of import price indexes.

Unit values have recently been applied to technology-related services where a physical volume measure is available. For example, Abdirahman et al. (2022) construct a unit value index for telecommunications services in the UK. The index, which is constructed by taking all services together (including fixed and mobile voice telephony, SMS, and other data services) and dividing revenue by total usage to get revenue per byte of data, declined 85 percent from 2010 to 2017. In contrast, the official price index for telecommunications services, which was not quality adjusted, was more or less flat over that period.[17]

The argument for a unit value index in telecommunications is that all bytes are equal, even though providers charge different prices for different services, such as high-price SMS messages as opposed to free instant message services. While there is valuable convenience in traditional services such as voice calls, consumers over time are steadily switching to the cheaper option; for instance, UK adults were as likely to use a service like WhatsApp as a traditional SMS by 2020.[18]

As there are still differences between services, though, another option would be to base a price index on narrower unit value indexes. For example, Byrne and Corrado (2020) construct a composite unit value price index for the services they call consumer digital access services: those delivering data, voice services, or digital content to consumers' homes. Their volume measure is total hours of usage, adjusted for quality. Byrne and Corrado argue that price per unit of data should differ for different categories of use. For services delivering data, they argue that data is a commodity and that unit values are appropriate to use without quality adjustment. But for cable and streaming services, consumers differentiate on grounds of quality, so they make an adjustment for the number of program channels available over time. Their price index declines by almost 12 percent a year from 1988 to 2018. In contrast, the matched-model indexes used for the US national accounts deflators rose by 1.2 percent a year on average over this 30-year period. In other work, Byrne and Corrado (2015, 2017) found similarly large declines in quality-adjusted indexes for digital goods.

The same question as to substitutability of different products arises in the contexts of entry by ride-sharing and generic pharmaceuticals. Aizcorbe and Chen (2022) found a steeper decline from 2015 to 2017 in a unit value index for local transportation services that treated taxi rides and rideshares as the same good than when taxi rides and rideshares were treated as distinct goods in a price index. This difference arises because taxi prices did not decline to fully match the lower prices of rides using Lyft and Uber—treating taxis and ride-sharing as the same good fully captures the lower cost from the introduction of ride-sharing, whereas treating them as different goods only captures the decline to the extent taxis matched Uber and Lyft prices or Uber and Lyft prices declined following entry. Similarly, in research on pharmaceutical prices, Griliches and Cockburn (1994) attributed half the price gap between patented and generic versions of pharmaceutical products to perceived quality differences and calculated a 48 percent decline in the average quality-adjusted price of pharmaceutical products, compared to a 14 percent rise in an index that linked generic versions in as new goods. After considering this research, BLS adopted unit values to capture cost savings from the substitution from patented to generic pharmaceuticals.

Nordhaus used a unit value approach to measure the price of lighting (Nordhaus 1996) and computer processing (Nordhaus 2007) over long periods of time. He constructed careful, long-run series of directly observed engineering measures of performance—lumens per watt or computations per second—and corresponding cost to obtain the service. By measuring the price of service provided instead of the price of good delivering the service, this approach should capture the value of new goods in these industries. In both examples, Nordhaus calculated price declines considerably greater than conventional price indexes suggest. The difference may be taken as an indication of what the conventional price index misses by omitting the initial impact of the introduction of new goods. For example, Nordhaus (2021) estimates that the price of a standard computational operation declined on average by 53 percent a year from 1940 to 2012. By comparison, the BLS PPI for 1990–2012 suggests prices of computers fell by 17.5 percent per year on average. The difference between measuring change in price of a service provided by a succession of products and products' prices can therefore be large. Constructing price indexes for the service received by consumers, as Nordhaus did, involves painstaking effort, but these indexes speak to the way innovations enhance human capabilities and why we consider them an engine of progress.

4.5.2 Estimating Demand Functions

Some researchers have sought to estimate the benefits consumers gain from having more varieties to choose from. The idea is that consumers are better off from access to new varieties even if varieties do not entail any objective improvement in a product, perhaps because they like to consume a wide variety of goods or because the more varieties there are, the easier for consumers to find products that match their tastes. An example of such variety is orange juice available with pulp, without pulp, with extra vitamin C, less sugar, and so on. Hedonic regressions are not helpful here because there is no quality characteristic to use, but Hicks's (1940) concept of hypothetical reservation price, as described above, is helpful. Using observations on today's prices and quantities, assuming a model of demand allows estimation of a demand curve and reservation price, and hence of the relevant consumer surplus. Consumer surplus is the additional amount consumers would have been willing to pay above the prevailing price—the triangle between the price line and the demand curve in the basic demand and supply diagram. (See Dynan and Sheiner, chap. 1 in this volume, on the relationship between reservation prices, consumer surplus, and GDP.)

Often this approach yields a large estimate of consumer surplus associated with variety and novelty. Hausman (1996) estimated a demand function for breakfast cereal and demand systems for brands of cereal and used the implied price elasticity of demand to approximate the reservation price of a new brand of cereal, Apple Cinnamon Cheerios. The reservation price was estimated to be twice the observed current price, so adding the reservation price to a Paasche index for breakfast cereal would cause this index to decline by approximately the share of current period spending going to the new variety, 1.6 percent. Hausman (1999) also estimated consumer surplus from the arrival of cell phones by fitting a demand model and found an upward bias of 1.9 percent per year in the US CPI for telecommunications services from omitted cell phones. Petrin (2002) carried out a similar exercise for the introduction of minivans. In the same spirit, Brynjolfsson, Hu, and Smith (2003) estimated consumer surplus from the increased variety of book titles available online, finding that the product variety available in online bookstores—with 23 times more titles available on Amazon than in a physical book superstore—increased US consumer welfare from book purchases from $731 million to $1.03 billion in 2000.

Feenstra (1994) introduced a simple method for incorporating gains from new varieties and losses from disappearing varieties into the price index for a good assuming a constant elasticity of substitution[19] between varieties. The method adjusts the matched-model price index, which includes only continuing varieties, to account for new and disappearing varieties. The adjustment depends on the market shares of continuing varieties (defined as the share of total spending on a particular category of good allocated to continuing varieties) in the periods compared and on the estimated elasticity of substitution between varieties (a measure of how interchangeable the existing and new varieties are from the consumer's perspective). If the expenditure share of new varieties in the final period exceeds the expenditure share of disappearing varieties in the initial period, so that continuing goods have a declining expenditure share, the adjustment to prices is downward, indicating that consumers became better off: if consumers choose to spend more on new varieties than they did on disappearing varieties, this suggests that they like the new varieties more. The magnitude of the welfare change (how much better off are consumers) implied by a given change in expenditure shares depends on how readily consumers substitute between varieties, as measured by the elasticity of substitution, with a higher elasticity of substitution implying a smaller welfare change for a given shift of expenditure shares.[20] Consumers may shift their purchases to a new variety, but if it is very similar to varieties they were purchasing before, the welfare gains will be small. For example, if consumers shift from juice with no pulp to juice with pulp, they will not be much better off if they only like juice with pulp a little bit more. Using this method, Feenstra (1994) found that import price indexes for the US were biased upward.

There have been many subsequent applications of Feenstra's (1994) method, most finding substantial consumer gains from new varieties. For example, Broda and Weinstein (2006) look at varieties of imports to the US, finding a threefold increase in the number of imported product varieties between 1972 and 2001 and an upward bias in the price index for imports of 1.2 percentage points a year. They estimate the gain to consumers from increased variety to be 2.6 percent of GDP over the period. Bils (2009) estimates that the inflation rate for consumer durables (excluding computers) in the US CPI was overstated by 2 percentage points a year from 1988 to 2006, while quality improvements were understated by about as much. Aghion et al. (2019) estimate that omitting new and disappearing varieties from the price index led economic growth in the US to be understated (and prices to be overstated) by about 0.5 percentage point a year between 1983 and 2013. However, they found the degree of mismeasurement did not increase much after 2005, so undercounting the benefits of new products could not explain the aggregate productivity growth slowdown that began at that time.

In another recent example, Melser (2019) used scanner data to examine the variety of products available in large, urban US supermarkets from 2001 to 2012. He estimates that the cost of living declined an average of 0.83 percent a year because of increases in quality and number of new products. Using detailed data from online retail, Goolsbee and Klenow (2018) estimate that inflation in goods and services purchased online in the US was 1.5 to 2.5 percentage points lower than suggested by the CPI over the 2014–2017 period. Their method used millions of online prices and quantities, far more granular data than the official index, and they conclude that entry and exit of products made a significant contribution; about half of online sales volume was for products that did not exist the previous year.

In a recent reconsideration of this approach, Diewert and Feenstra (2019) note that in the constant elasticity of substitution models, the reservation price is infinite, leading to unrealistically large implied gains from increases in variety. Using a different functional form for the consumer demand function, they find that upward bias from failure to account for increases in variety has been overstated in the literature. Indeed, whether some of the estimates of consumer surplus from increasing variety are implausibly high has long been debated.

4.5.3 Accounting for the Benefits of New Goods

As noted above, truly new goods pose a more difficult challenge than new goods that can be treated as quality change of an existing good. At least two methods have been proposed for dealing with truly new goods, both of which attempt to measure the benefit consumers receive from the new goods (in terms of equivalent monetary value).

Following the approach of Nordhaus (1996) and Cutler et al. (2001), a number of researchers have created quality-adjusted health care price indexes that attempt to account for the benefits of increased life expectancy and quality of life as a result of medical innovations. These approaches assess the impact of new technologies on quality-adjusted life years and measure the consumer surplus from additional life expectancy using estimated values of an additional year of life from the literature. For example, if a new drug costs $60,000 more than its replacement but provides an additional 1 year of life in good health, and if the value of a year of life is $100,000, then consumer surplus per patient is $40,000 higher from the introduction of the drug, and the price index for health care falls. Using this approach, researchers have found that official price statistics overstate quality-adjusted price increases in health care by up to 3 percent per year over the past few decades. (See chap. 6 in this volume on health productivity for more details and a discussion of other approaches to measuring quality-adjusted prices in health care.)

In a different approach aimed at measuring the benefits consumers get from digital goods, Brynjolfsson et al. (2019) measured the value of zero price digital goods like Twitter and Facebook using an adaption of the contingent valuation methods long used to estimate the value of nonmarket, free environmental goods. The authors used online and laboratory experiments to estimate participants' willingness to forgo certain free digital goods such as social media and online search engines. For example, Brynjolfsson (2019) reported that the median user needed compensation of about $48 to forgo Facebook for one month.

Brynjolfsson et al. (2019) conclude that the consumer surplus from digital goods is considerable and could be estimated through regular online surveys at reasonable cost.[21] Some argue that the estimated increment to consumer surplus from digital goods derived from these methods is implausibly large; Reinsdorf and Schreyer (2020) point out that it amounts to 30 percent of annual consumer expenditure in the US. Coyle and Nguyen (2023) suggest that the method can give a rank ordering of benefits from free digital goods but that the monetary valuations are not well-anchored because the survey answers are not constrained by a time budget for using various services and (as is common with survey-based methods) seem to differ substantially from willingness to pay for such goods. The literature on how to treat the phenomenon of free digital goods in productivity statistics remains an active research frontier.

If this method is considered reasonable for estimating welfare benefit from new digital goods, one obvious question is where to set the boundaries for free goods to be included, for there are many public goods whose consumer valuations are not currently included in estimates of GDP. Coyle and Nguyen (2023) show that some free public goods, such as parks and free-to-air radio, have comparable valuations (although their use has not been growing rapidly, unlike digital goods). This speaks to the debate about whether it is desirable and feasible to have a wider measure of economic welfare (Heys, Martin, and Mkandawire 2019). There are conceptual challenges in pursuing this route, however, including how to weight and aggregate such valuations (since there is no nominal spending to use as a weight).

Finally, it is worth noting that when new goods initially have high prices and are purchased in small volumes, as seems to be a fairly standard pattern, introducing them into a price index in a timely manner can capture most of the gains in consumer surplus as the prices subsequently fall. The initial price is likely close enough to the reservation price to capture most of the gains (Griliches and Cockburn 1994).

4.5.3.1 Improving on Official Statistics by Collecting Better Data

The alternative methods described above demonstrate that it is possible to adjust standard price indexes to better account for price declines (and standard of living gains) from new goods and varieties. Nevertheless, except for the unit value used by BLS to account for substitution of new generic products for patented pharmaceuticals, these methods are not used by statistical agencies. They have significant data requirements (including information on detailed characteristics or consumer expenditures), may be slow to calculate, and rely on uncertain assumptions.

New data sources and computational methods offer the prospect of innovation in the compilation of price indexes as well as data collection, including different ways of taking account of proliferation of varieties. Web-scraped data do not have quantity information, whereas scanner data provide price and quantity, so the sources of new types of data affect the kind of index that can be constructed.

New data sources and methods offer the potential for very frequent, even close to real time updating of items included in the price index, taking account of the arrival of new and improved varieties and the extent to which consumers are substituting them. For kinds of goods such as groceries that are generally covered by scanner data, this could resolve issues of introducing new varieties too slowly into the price index. Statistical agencies are exploring the use of these approaches, largely for supermarket scanner data (Cavallo and Rigobon 2016, Konny et al. 2019, Greenhough 2019, Mehrhoff 2019, Sands 2020).

As Groshen et al. (2017) underline, for new data to enter statistical production, there needs to be a straightforward, agreed on methodology able to handle large datasets on the monthly publishing schedule for official CPI data.[22] The practical implications of major changes in index methods also have to be considered: the widespread use of CPIs to escalate payments has led to an understandable reluctance by NSOs to revise CPI methods, and legislative barriers may even be present.

4.5.3.1.1 Could Improved Price Measurement Explain the Slowdown in Measured Productivity Growth?

How much difference potential adjustments such as those described in this section could make to the aggregate price index and thus the measurement of productivity is still debated. As noted above, previous commissions such as the Stigler and Boskin Commissions concluded that upward biases in price indexes, and therefore downward biases in output and productivity measures, were large. But unless the biases have been growing increasingly large, they do not explain the productivity slowdown since the mid-2000s. Byrne, Fernald, and Reinsdorf (2016) conclude that there is no evidence that biases have grown worse, and if anything, there is some evidence that they have declined since 2004. Reinsdorf and Schreyer (2020) combine a number of potential sources of bias due to failure to incorporate new goods, fully adjust for quality change, and capture the benefits of free goods related to digitalization. They suggest that because two-thirds of household expenditure is unaffected by such changes, impact on CPI or GDP deflator overall is limited. Their upper bound estimate of the annual overstatement of US consumer prices is 0.57 percentage points in 2015 (down from 0.68 percentage point in 2005). This is a large bias, but it has decreased over time, so it does nothing to help explain the productivity puzzle. However, it could be argued that not all items they categorize as unaffected by digitalization are correctly classified, particularly in the service sector. Feldstein (2017) argues that official data understate productivity and that there is not yet sufficient understanding of the extent of the biases. As the next section discusses, conceptual issues concerning productivity lead some authors to conclude that mismeasurement does account for a significant part of the productivity slowdown.

4.6 Broader Questions and Radical Approaches

The discussion so far has highlighted theoretical and practical challenges in the measurement of real output and productivity through deflating nominal output when the economy features increasing variety, new products, and quality change. I now turn to broader questions about the extent to which the standard construction of real GDP and productivity figures is too narrow to understand productivity and welfare improvements in a dynamic economy.

4.6.1 What Is "Real" Output?

At first blush, it seems obvious what a price deflator is meant to do, but it is inherently difficult to translate dollar revenues into "real" or volume terms. Thomas Schelling (1958) captured the essential point, writing that "what we call 'real' magnitudes are not completely real; only the money magnitudes are real. The 'real' ones are hypothetical." It is reasonably intuitive to think about the price and quantity of a physical product, say a liter of milk or a tractor, or of some services such as haircuts, but far from clear how to think of a volume unit of management consultancy, insurance, or nursing. Griliches (1994) highlighted this difficulty in dividing the economy into measurable (in his view, agriculture, mining, manufacturing, transportation, and utilities including communications) and unmeasurable (construction, trade, finance, other services, and government) categories. We might now shift communications and even much of manufacturing into the latter category (table 4.3). These hard-to-measure sectors include some that have had slow measured productivity growth, such as construction.

Griliches's measurable part of the economy has shrunk from about one in two to at most one in four or five current dollars spent. The challenge statisticians face is therefore how to measure changes in average cost of living when the concept of volume terms is unclear. The economy has become increasingly intangible in recent decades due to the trend toward services and the growing importance of intangible contributions to value

Table 4.3 **Distribution of US GNP/GDP by major industrial sector in current prices (%)**

Sector	1947	1959	1969	1977	1990	2019
Agriculture	8.8	4.1	3.0	2.8	2.0	0.8
Mining	2.9	2.5	1.8	2.7	1.8	1.5
Manufacturing	28.1	28.6	26.9	23.6	18.4	11.0
Transportation and utilities[a]	8.9	9.1	8.6	9.1	8.7	10.0
Construction	3.9	4.8	5.1	4.8	4.4	4.1
Wholesale trade	7.1	6.9	6.7	7.0	6.5	6.0
Retail trade	11.7	9.9	9.8	9.6	9.3	5.5
FIRE	10.1	13.8	14.2	14.4	17.7	21.0
Other services	8.6	9.7	11.5	13.0	18.9	27.8
Government	8.6	10.2	12.6	12.5	12.2	12.3
"Measurable"	48.7	44.3	40.3	38.2	30.9	23.3

Source: Griliches 1994 for first five columns (data break between 1969 and 1977), citing Tables 6.1 and 6.2 of the National Income and Products Accounts (1928–1982) and Survey of Current Business (May 1993); 2019 data from BEA, percent of GDP, https://www.bea.gov/data/gdp/gdp-industry (data break between 1990 and 2019). Shaded indicates "hard to measure."

[a] Information including telecommunications included here; we might now consider these (5.3 percent of GDP in 2019 nominal dollars) unmeasurable.

added, such as design (for example, to the iPhone) or after-sales services (for example, to Rolls Royce aero-engines) (Coyle 1997, Haskel and Westlake 2019, Xing 2020, Cavalieri et al. 2018). Even in a sector where physical product remains centrally important, such as agriculture, hedging against crop failure involves trade in ideas rather than older approaches such as crop diversification (Lloyd 2019).

In the case of agriculture, output is at least reasonably easy to quantify in homogeneous physical units. This is not the case with many recent innovations, whose output is not easy to measure or even conceptualize. For example, innovation in construction is improving the energy efficiency of buildings: the reduced consumption of energy occurs over time, not in one statistical accounting period and is unlikely to be captured in practice as a quality improvement in construction output. (The reduced energy intensity of output should, however, be a positive for future productivity.) The use of digital twins—virtual models from design through construction to operation stage—is gradually spreading in major construction projects, leading to process efficiencies, such as fewer engineering errors, that will not be directly measured against less-efficient counterfactual techniques. The ability of technology to monitor track failures will similarly result in efficiencies never captured in official statistics (Peplow 2016).

Other examples of welfare-improving ideas include the discovery that mini-aspirin can avert cardiovascular problems and the growing use of the cancer drug Avastin in place of the licensed, but more expensive, Lucentis to treat macular degeneration (Nakamura 2020). There are numerous intangible or nearly intangible innovations using pervasive digital technologies: parking sensors on cars avert minor bumps; apps such as Waze save time spent in traffic jams; smart thermostats keep heating bills down; apps advise runners areas to avoid to be able to social distance; smart watches can spot heart problems and send their owners promptly to the doctor for timelier treatment. These can be thought of as instances of process innovations in health or transportation services.

Quality-adjusting prices captures some of these types of innovation. For example, BLS used the manufacturers' cost of quality improvements to adjust the price of light trucks in model year 2022 by $138 for newly included sensors that facilitate parking and improve road safety and by $58 for infotainment system improvements.[23] These adjustments resulted in higher estimates of real output. Hedonic adjustment can indicate increasing real-terms output even when the physical quantity of an item is unchanged. An example would be real output of autos increasing due to adjustments for quality improvements while the number of units purchased does not change. The resolution of this apparent paradox lies in the difference between physical production and utility derived from consumption.

Another paradox is that hedonics, in seeking to measure true cost of living in utility terms, can also take the price index further away from a measure of literal cost of living. Not everyone is made better off to the same degree by quality improvements, and it is often impossible to buy older technology. A bottom-of-the-range washing machine costing $200 in 2019 might have considerably more features than a basic 1990 model costing $120, such that the hedonically adjusted price has risen far less than the $80 difference. But the 1990 model is not available to purchase, and the consumer still needs enough money in 2019 to buy the machine. Utility is not the same as affordability (see for example Cass 2020). Depending on overall rate of inflation, there may be other products whose relative prices have declined to which consumers can switch, potentially giving the same level of utility as previously. However, distributional implications are likely when the relative prices of hedonically adjusted products change.

A final reason it seems unlikely that a hedonic approach could be applied across the board is that underlying technologies are so pervasive. Is faster journey time thanks to GPS, Google Maps, and apps such as Waze an attribute of the vehicle, Google's (free) services, the reference geospatial data, or the US satellites providing the GPS system? In the case of medical innovations, where the outcome is improved longevity and/or quality of life, how can the contribution of an app on a smartwatch be accounted for separately from all other factors that contribute to health outcomes? While new technologies embedded in new goods have always involved a combination of existing technologies, the challenge with digital services in particular is that they are often process innovations providing utility due to broad outcomes (such as travel without delay) rather than innovations relating to a specific, priced product (such as a car or phone). Process innovations in consumption are hard to measure but should arguably be considered part of real value added and productivity.

4.6.1.1 Digital Goods and Consumer Welfare

A growing literature looks at the measurement of consumer welfare from digital goods, which seem to pose distinctive challenges. One is the proliferation of variety, especially in services such as music streaming. Looking directly at data on each year's online music consumption by year of a track's release and noting that new music is generally preferred to old, Waldfogel (2017) considers relative consumption of music adjusted for vintage using several detailed datasets. He finds that the flow of services adjusted from each annual vintage of music increased sharply after the late 1990s. He also notes that digitization has significantly increased the number of new creative products—music, movies, books, and TV programs—available to consumers, improved the quality of the best products, and increased consumer welfare through increased choice and serendipitous discovery. Similarly, Aguiar and Waldfogel (2018) observe that the internet has reduced entry cost for creative products such as music, resulting in increased production. They find that the unpredictability of the popularity of music under production increases welfare benefits from variety resulting from increased production of music. They do not quantify the increase in consumer surplus from new creative products, but whatever the parameters of an assumed demand function, they conclude it is a large increment.

Digital services for which users do not pay directly but spend many hours a week using, such as Google Maps or Twitter, have zero weight in consumers' expenditure. Dynan and Sheiner (2018) point out that these services are often funded by advertising and hence paid for indirectly via markups on advertised products, which are captured in national accounts, but aspects of the transaction providing additional utility are not captured. Various ways of addressing this issue have been proposed. One, described above, is the use of discrete choice experiments to elicit stated valuations by Brynjolfsson et al. (2019). Another treats the use of these services as a barter transaction between advertisers and consumers (Nakamura, Samuels, and Soloveichik 2017).

Hulten and Nakamura (2018, 2021) take a different approach. They argue that a new measure is needed to capture improvements in consumption technology made possible by digital goods and services. They call this measure Expanded GDP or E-GDP. They posit that free digital services enable improvements in consumption technology, allowing consumers to make more efficient use of income. The gains from the kinds of pervasive digital improvements described above are thus output saving technological change, as opposed to resource saving technological change embodied in directly measured goods. Just as with the measurement of consumer surplus through econometric techniques, this approach focuses on the wedge between growth in real production as traditionally measured and productivity and growth in consumer utility.

4.6.2 What Do We Mean by Progress?

The challenges discussed in this chapter arise from the desire to move from something conceptually easy to measure—aggregate economic transactions in dollars or pounds—to something much harder to conceptualize: a metric of progress. As soon as we deflate a nominal aggregate by a cost-of-living index intended to hold utility constant, an economic welfare concept has been introduced. The large and technical literature on price indexes has sought to reduce in ever more sophisticated ways bias in measurement of real activity ultimately linked to utility or social welfare. It is worth considering whether the debate about innovation should instead lead us to reflect on more fundamental questions about economic welfare.

Economic historians seeking to understand the standard of living in more distant times often look at the purchasing power of typical wages. For example, Brad DeLong (1998) compared the number of hours a median earner would need to work to buy certain standard goods from the Montgomery Ward catalog in 1895 compared to 1995. He concluded that the average American worker in 1995 needed to work one-sixth as many hours as their 1885 counterpart to pay for a representative selection of consumer goods available in both periods. The approach has distinguished precedents, for Keynes (1930) wrote: "If we want to compile a Consumption Index-Number for the value of gold or silver money over the past 3,000 years, I doubt if we can do better than to base on composite on the price of wheat and the price of a day's labor throughout that period. We cannot hope to find a ratio of equivalent substitution for gladiators against cinemas."

In this spirit, table 4.4 repeats the exercise for a few selected goods (extracted from a larger set) for 1990 to 2019. It suggests a mixed picture. There have been some significant relative price changes, with declines in prices of imported household appliances and basic items of clothing in particular, but increased prices in many services such as hairdressing or cleaning and in goods and durables where there has been quality improvement, such as cars, bicycles, or branded jeans or sneakers. Despite having Keynes's imprimatur as a way of assessing changes in living standards over longer periods, the labor hours approach to assessing changes in living standards for the typical person does not resolve the new goods problem. The table must be taken with a big pinch of salt as it lacks any attempt to adjust for the quality improvements under discussion here, focusing instead on afford-

Table 4.4 **Prices and hours in 1990 and 2019, selected goods**

	1990	Hours at median 1990 wage (£8.97)	2019 closest match	Hours at median 2019 wage (£14.31)
Small car	£8,000.00	891 hrs 52 mins	£15,000.00	1048 hrs 13 mins
Large white loaf of bread	£0.51	3.4 mins	£1.10	4.6 mins
Refrigerator/freezer	£279.95	31 hrs 13 mins	£229.99	16 hrs 4 mins
Bottom-of-range adult bike	£84.99	9 hrs 28 mins	£179.99	12 hrs 35 mins
Child's coat	£22.99	2 hrs 34 mins	£28.00	1 hr 57 mins
Washing machine	£269.99	30 hrs 6 mins	£279.99	19 hrs 34 mins
Microwave	£159.99	17 hrs 50 mins	£64.99	4 hrs 32 mins
Basic vacuum cleaner	£109.99	12 hrs 16 mins	£59.99	4 hrs 12 mins
Men's running shoes	£14.99	1 hr 40 mins	£90.00	6 hrs 17 mins
Men's haircut	£3.50	23 mins	£13.00	55 mins
Women's hairdressing cut and blow-dry	£8.50	57 mins	£34.00	2 hrs 23 mins

Source: Calculations based on ONS AWE (https://www.ons.gov.uk/employmentandlabourmarket/peopleinwork/earningsandworkinghours/datasets/averageweeklyearningsearn01), ASHE (https://www.ons.gov.uk/employmentandlabourmarket/peopleinwork/earningsandworkinghours/datasets/annualsurveyofhoursandearningsasheguidetotables), and consumer prices (https://www.ons.gov.uk/economy/inflationandpriceindices/datasets/consumerpriceindicescpiandretailpricesindexrpiitemindicesandpricequotes).

ability. But it does serve to underline the challenge of measuring change in deflators, and hence productivity, over time in an economy undergoing structural change with constant quality change and innovation. Conventional price indexes assume that there are no major shifts in expenditure patterns over time, whereas in reality these shifts are significant; consider for example the shrinking share of expenditure spent on food and increase in spending on health and education over many decades (Crawford 1994).

One way of assessing welfare gains that go beyond conventional measures involves treating new and free digital products as increases in household production, the economic activity undertaken by households outside the boundary of the market and excluded from GDP in the System of National Accounts (SNA) because no monetary transactions take place. Hulten and Nakamura (2018, 2021) consider the digital technologies we use in everyday life as utility-increasing, output-saving innovations in consumption (rather than increases in output). They argue that the increment from consumption technology improvements to E-GDP could be large. Schreyer (2021) proposes an Extended Measure of Activity (EMA) that would similarly add households' own-account production of digitally enabled leisure services, keeping gains outside the production boundary. He treats technological advances such as free digital goods as quality improvements reducing unit costs of leisure services for households. It makes sense to think of a spectrum of aggregate measures of the economy, ranging from market production alone to GDP (which adds government activity and an imputation for owner-occupied housing) to broader measures beyond the current production boundary, adding measures of consumer welfare such as E-GDP or EMA (Heys, Martin, and Mkandawire 2019). These approaches avoid the complexities of adjusting price deflators to calculate real output and productivity and are also consistent with the accounting framework of the SNA.

Another radical approach to measuring welfare changes would be to construct a monetary measure of people's well-being during the time they spend on different activities. As the digitalization of the economy is significantly changing production and household activity, Coyle and Nakamura (2022) argue that how we feel while working for pay, producing at home, or at leisure encompass all the possibilities for well-being. They advocate an extended utility framework combining time use with monetary measures of objective or subjective well-being for each activity. Implementation would require time use statistics as well as well-being data and direct survey evidence, such as the willingness to pay for leisure time. They advocate an experimental set of time and well-being accounts, with a particular focus on digitally driven shifts in behavior. A number of countries collect time use data periodically, and online collection would make this increasingly practical.

4.7 Conclusion

Evaluating in monetary terms either the utility provided by new or better goods or varieties or their contribution to productivity is an unresolved challenge. It is acutely felt at a time when, as now, there is considerable innovation and more in prospect—not only digital but biomedical, advanced materials, green energy, and more.

NSOs can improve price index compilation practices in three ways that would help measure more welfare gains from innovation and improving technology. First, increased use of quality adjustment techniques such as hedonics and option costing would enable indexes to reflect quality improvements involving characteristics whose value can be estimated. Second, increased utilization of new data sources, such as scanner data and web-scraped data, would help improve incorporation of new products and varieties in a timely way to better capture short-term price changes. Finally, in cases involving a relatively homogeneous product (such as generic and branded pharmaceuticals or bytes of data transmitted by telecommunications carriers), replacing the traditional matched-model index with a unit value index may enable gains from the entry of lower-priced alternatives to be measured.

Nevertheless, the conventional approach to constructing price indexes is not well suited to considering changes in either productivity or living standards over anything other than relatively short periods of time—although for purposes such as macroeconomic policy with short periods, indexes constructed with the conventional approach can be adequate. Some alternative methods of incorporating new goods or increased variety or quality provide case-by-case estimates of consumer surplus but are not suitable for regular statistical production.

When it comes to assessing somewhat longer-term changes in prices, and hence real output and productivity, how to respond to measurement challenges is not obvious. None of the radical alternatives discussed here is an obviously superior approach.

Quality adjustment methods that rely on strong assumptions or abstract modeling may be better suited to economic welfare analysis than to the day-to-day job of NSOs. Furthermore, the Hulten paradox (Hulten 1996, Reinsdorf and Schreyer 2020) suggests this approach's limitations; the paradox points out that projecting back in time the kinds of innovation-adjusted price declines generally found in the academic literature implies much higher price levels and therefore implausibly low living standards in the past. The utility construct underpinning economic welfare analysis may only be loosely correlated with economic well-being, leaving open the large question of how best to measure welfare changes. Efforts to expand the GDP framework to better account for economic welfare may be helpful but offer the promise of at best imperfect measures of well-being.

Notes

1. A different approach that may give an estimate of the impact of a truly novel new good is to fit a demand curve for the good and solve for the price at which demand would fall to zero (the Hicksian reservation price). However, inferring the reservation price may require relying on assumptions to extend the demand curve far outside the range of the data used to estimate it.
2. Nielsen (2015).
3. Nielsen (2016).
4. See https://nielseniq.com/global/en/insights/analysis/2019/bursting-with-new-products-theres-never-been-a-better-time-for-breakthrough-innovation/.
5. See https://www.fda.gov/medical-devices/products-and-medical-procedures/3d-printing-medical-devices.
6. Some statistical agencies, including the UK's Office for National Statistics (ONS), insist that they are not trying to measure cost of living (also known as the "economic approach" to price indices) at all, but rather the cost of goods. This approach may be understandable for a price index used for monetary policy purposes but makes it unclear why the agency would be concerned about adjustment for quality change or new goods.
7. Although NSOs use a variant of the Laspeyres index to calculate price indexes such as the CPI and producer price index, Fisher indexes are used for upper-level aggregation in the national accounts of the US and Canada.
8. The growing use of scanner data to supply price information offers the possibility of faster updating of items, albeit with challenges such as product classification.
9. Thus, in the overlap month, the NSO collects prices of the old sample to compute inflation in that period and of the new sample to compute inflation in the next period.

10. This scenario assumes that manufacturers raise prices only on new models; if they increase prices on old models as well, this price rise will be captured by the inflation measures.

11. Essentially, this method assumes that the reservation price, discussed above, is equal to the price at which the new model is introduced.

12. See https://www.bls.gov/ppi/quality-adjustment/, https://www.bls.gov/cpi/quality-adjustment/home.htm, and discussion in Groshen et al. (2017).

13. Groshen et al. (2017).

14. See https://uksa.statisticsauthority.gov.uk/wp-content/uploads/2019/06/APCP-T1904-Quality-adjustment-review.pdf.

15. See https://www.bls.gov/cpi/quality-adjustment/home.htm and https://www.bls.gov/ppi/quality-adjustment/.

16. See https://uksa.statisticsauthority.gov.uk/wp-content/uploads/2019/06/APCP-T1904-Quality-adjustment-review.pdf; https://www.stat.go.jp/nglish/data/cpi/1585.html.

17. ONS has since revised sectoral output and productivity data as well as GDP (ONS 2021a). The prices of detailed items in the deflator for telecommunication services are now measured by unit values, causing the deflator to decline substantially over that period (ONS 2021b).

18. See https://www.ofcom.org.uk/about-ofcom/latest/media/media-releases/2020/uk-internet-use-surges.

19. The elasticity of substitution is the percentage change in relative quantities caused by a 1 percent change in relative prices. Feenstra's method requires this elasticity to be greater than 1, meaning that the goods considered are good substitutes for one another.

20. Let C_1 be the market share of continuing varieties in period 1 and C_2 be the market share of continuing items in period 2 (the period when new varieties enter and disappearing varieties vanish). Feenstra (1994) shows that consumers' welfare gains from new varieties and welfare losses from disappearing varieties can be measured by multiplying the matched-model index (which considers only continuing varieties) by a factor equal to $(C_2/C_1)^{\sigma/(\sigma-1)}$, where σ is the (constant) elasticity of substitution. For example, if the new varieties have a market share of 12 percent, the disappearing varieties have a market share of 9 percent, and $\sigma = 4$, the matched-model index must be adjusted by factor of $(0.88/0.91)^{(1/3)}$, or 0.989.

21. They suggest that rather than replacing GDP, such approaches could be used to measure a GDP alternative, GDP-B, that accounts more thoroughly for new (digital) goods.

22. Groshen et al. (2017).

23. The average adjustment was of $138 (BLS 2021). For cars, BLS attributed 21.9 percent of the average over-the-year increase in list price to quality improvements.

References

Abdirahman, M., D. Coyle, R. Heys, and W. Stewart. 2020. "A Comparison of Deflators for Telecommunications Services Output." *Economie et Statistique / Economics and Statistics*, 517–518–519, pp. 103–22.

Abdirahman, M., D. Coyle, R. Heys, and W. Stewart. 2022. "Telecoms Deflators: A Story of Volume and Revenue Weights." *Economie et Statistique / Economics and Statistics*, 530–31, pp. 43–59. DOI: 10.24187/ecostat.2022.530.2063.

Adelman, I., and Z. Griliches. 1961. "On an Index of Quality Change." *Journal of the American Statistical Association* 56 (295): 535–48.

Aghion, P., A. Bergeaud, T. Boppart, P. J. Klenow, and H. Li. 2019. "Missing Growth from Creative Destruction." *American Economic Review* 109 (8): 2795–822.

Aguiar, L., and J. Waldfogel. 2018. "Quality Predictability and the Welfare Benefits from New Products: Evidence from the Digitization of Recorded Music." *Journal of Political Economy* 126 (2): 492–524.

Ahmad, N., J. Ribarsky, and M. Reinsdorf. 2017. "Can Potential Mismeasurement of the Digital Economy Explain the Post-Crisis Slowdown in GDP and Productivity Growth?" OECD Statistics Working Paper No. 2017/09, OECD Publishing, Paris. https://doi.org/10.1787/a8e751b7-en.

Aizcorbe, A., and J. Chen. 2022. "Outlet Substitution Bias Estimates for Ride-Sharing and Taxi Rides in New York City." Bureau of Economic Analysis Working Paper 0192. https://www.bea.gov/system/files/papers/BEA-WP2022-1.pdf.

Aizcorbe, A., and Y. Pho. 2005. "Differences in Hedonic and Matched-Model Price Indexes: Do the Weights Matter?" Bureau of Economic Analysis Working Paper WP2005–06. https://www.bea.gov/system/files/papers/WP2005-6.pdf.

Alm, R., and W. M. Cox. 1998. "The Right Stuff: America's Move to Mass Customization." In *Annual Report, Federal Reserve Bank of Dallas*, 3–26. https://fraser.stlouisfed.org/title/annual-report-federal-reserve-bank-dallas-475/1998-annual-report-596522.

Bils, Mark. 2009. "Do Higher Prices for New Goods Reflect Quality Growth or Inflation?" *Quarterly Journal of Economics* 124, no. 2 (May): 637–75.

Bils, M., and P. J. Klenow. 2001. "The Acceleration of Variety Growth." *American Economic Review* 91 (2): 274–80.

Boskin Commission. 1996. "Toward a More Accurate Measure of the Cost of Living." *Final Report*. https://www.ssa.gov/history/reports/boskinrpt.html#cpi5.

Broda, Christian, and David E. Weinstein. 2006. "Globalization and the Gains from Variety." *Quarterly Journal of Economics* 121, no. 2 (May): 541–58.

Brynjolfsson, E., Rock and C. Syverson (2018). "Artificial Intelligence and the Modern Productivity Paradox: A Clash of Expectations and Statistics." In *The Economics of Artificial Intelligence: An Agenda*, edited by A. Agrawal, J. Gans, and A. Goldfarb,23–57.Chicago: University of Chicago Press. http://www.nber.org/chapters/c14007.

Brynjolfsson, E., A. Collis, W. E. Diewert, F. Eggers, and K. Fox. 2019. "GDP-B: Accounting for the Value of New and Free Goods in the Digital Economy." Paper No. w25695, National Bureau of Economic Research.

Brynjolfsson, E., A. Collis, and F. Eggers. 2019. "Using Massive Online Choice Experiments to Measure Changes in Well-Being." *Proceedings of the National Academy of Sciences* 116 (15): 7250–5.

Brynjolfsson, E., Y. Hu, and M. D. Smith. 2003. "Consumer Surplus in the Digital Economy: Estimating the Value of Increased Product Variety at Online Booksellers." *Management Science* 49 (11): 1580–96.

Bureau of Labor Statistics. 2020. *Handbook of Methods: Consumer Price Index*. https://www.bls.gov/opub/hom/cpi/pdf/cpi.pdf.

Bureau of Labor Statistics. 2021. *Report on Quality Changes for 2022 Model Vehicles, November 2021*. https://www.bls.gov/ppi/quality-adjustment/report-on-quality-changes-for-2022-model-vehicles.pdf.

Byrne, D., and C. Corrado. 2015. "Prices for Communications Equipment: Rewriting the Record." Finance and Economics Discussion Series 2015–069. Washington, DC: Board of Governors of the Federal Reserve System. http://dx.doi.org/10.17016/FEDS.2015.069.

Byrne, D., and C. Corrado. 2017. "ICT Prices and ICT Services: What Do They

Tell Us about Productivity and Technology." *International Productivity Monitor* 33:150–81.

Byrne, D., and C. Corrado. 2020."The Increasing Deflationary Influence of Consumer Digital Access Services." *Economic Letters* 196 (November): 1–4. https://doi.org/10.1016/j.econlet.2020.109447.

Byrne, D., J. Fernald, and M. Reinsdorf. 2016. "Does the United States Have a Productivity Slowdown or a Measurement Problem?" *Brookings Papers on Economic Activity* (Spring): 109–83. https://www.brookings.edu/wp-content/uploads/2016/03/byrnetextspring16bpea.pdf.

Cass, O. 2020. *The Cost-of-Thriving Index: Reevaluating the Prosperity of the American Family*. American Compass, Manhattan Institute. https://media4.manhattan-institute.org/sites/default/files/the-cost-of-thriving-index-OC.pdf.

Cavalieri, S., Z. M. Ouertani, J. Zhibin, and A. Rondini. 2018. "Service Transformation in Industrial Companies." *International Journal of Production Research* 56 (6): 2099–102.

Cavallo, Alberto, and Roberto Rigobon. 2016. "The Billion Prices Project: Using Online Prices for Measurement and Research." *Journal of Economic Perspectives* 30 (2): 151–78.

Coyle, D. 1997. *The Weightless World: Strategies for Managing the Digital Economy*. MIT Press.

Coyle, D., and L. Nakamura. 2022. "Time Use, Productivity, and Household-Centric Measurement of Welfare in the Digital Economy." *International Productivity Monitor* no. 42 (Spring): 165–186.

Coyle, D. and D. Nguyen. 2023. "Free Digital Products and Aggregate Economic Measurement." *Economie et Statistique / Economics and Statistics*, no. 539: 27–50. https://doi.org/10.24187/ecostat.2023.539.2096.

Crawford, I. 1994. *UK Household Cost of Living Indices 1979–1992*. Institute for Fiscal Studies. https://ifs.org.uk/publications/uk-household-cost-living-indices-1979-1992.

Culmone, C., G. Smit, and P. Breedveld. 2019. "Additive Manufacturing of Medical Instruments: A State-of-the-Art Review." *Additive Manufacturing* 27:461–73.

Cutler, David, Mark McClellan, Joseph P. Newhouse, and Dahlia Remler. 2001. "Pricing Heart Attack Treatments." In *Medical Care Output and Productivity*, edited by David Cutler and Ernst Berndt, 305–62. Chicago: University of Chicago Press.

Dauda, S., A. Dunn, and A. Hall. 2022. "Are Medical Care Prices Still Declining? A Systematic Examination of Quality-Adjusted Price Index Alternatives for Medical Care." *Econometrica* 90 (2): 859–86.

DeLong, B. 1998. "How Fast Is Modern Economic Growth." *DeLong: Long Form* (blog). https://delong.typepad.com/delong_long_form/1998/03/how-fast-is-modern-economic-growth.html.

Diewert, W. E. 1998. "Index Number Issues in the Consumer Price Index." *Journal of Economic Perspectives* 12 (1): 47–58.

Diewert, W. E., and R. C. Feenstra. 2019. "Estimating the Benefits of New Products." In *Big Data for 21st Century Economic Statistics*, edited by K. Abraham, R. Jarmin, B. Moyer, and M. D. Shapiro. NBER Conference held March 15–16, 2019, forthcoming. Chicago: University of Chicago Press.

Diewert, W. E., K. Fox, and P. Schreyer. 2018. "The Digital Economy, New Products and Consumer Welfare." ESCoE Discussion Paper 2018–16, Economic Statistics Centre of Excellence (ESCoE).

Dynan, K., and L. Sheiner. 2018. "GDP as a Measure of Economic Well-Being." Brookings Institution, Hutchins Center Working Paper 43.

Erickson, T., and A. Pakes. 2011. "An Experimental Component Index for the CPI: From Annual Computer Data to Monthly Data on Other Goods." *American Economic Review* 101 (5): 1707–38.
Feenstra, R. 1994. "New Product Varieties and the Measurement of International Prices." *American Economic Review* 84 (1): 157–77.
Feldstein, M. 2017. "Underestimating the Real Growth of GDP, Personal Income, and Productivity." *Journal of Economic Perspectives* 31 (2): 145–64.
Goolsbee, A. D., and P. Klenow. 2018. "Internet Rising, Prices Falling: Measuring Inflation in a World of E-Commerce." *AEA Papers and Proceedings* 108:488–92.
Greenhough, L. 2019. "New Data Sources in Consumer Price Statistics." Office for National Statistics. https://www.ons.gov.uk/economy/nationalaccounts/uksectoraccounts/compendium/economicreview/july2019/newdatasourcesinconsumerpricestatisticsjuly2019.
Griliches, Z. 1961. "Hedonic Price Indexes for Automobiles: An Econometric Analysis of Quality Change." In *The Price Statistics of the Federal Government*, 173–96. National Bureau of Economic Research, General Series no. 73. New York: NBER.
Griliches, Z. 1994. "Productivity, R&D, and the Data Constraint." *American Economic Review* 84, no. 1 (March): 1–23.
Griliches, Z., and I. Cockburn. 1994. "Generics and New Goods in Pharmaceutical Price Indexes." *American Economic Review* 84 (5): 1213–32.
Groshen, E., B. C. Moyer, A. M. Aizcorbe, R. Bradley, and D. M. Friedman. 2017. "How Government Statistics Adjust for Potential Biases from Quality Change and New Goods in an Age of Digital Technologies: A View from the Trenches." *Journal of Economic Perspectives* 31 (2): 187–210.
Haskel, J., and S. Westlake. 2019. *Capitalism without Capital: The Rise of the Intangible Economy*. Princeton, NJ: Princeton University Press.
Hausman, J. A. 1996. "Valuation of New Goods under Perfect and Imperfect Competition." In *The Economics of New Goods*, edited by T. Bresnahan and R. J. Gordon, 207–48. Chicago: University of Chicago Press.
Hausman, J. A. 1999. "Cellular Telephone, New Products and the CPI." *Journal of Business and Economic Statistics* 17 (2): 188–94.
Hausman, J. A. 2003. "Sources of Bias and Solutions to Bias in the Consumer Price Index." *Journal of Economic Perspectives* 17 (1): 23–44.
Heys, R., J. Martin, and W. Mkandawire. 2019. "GDP and Welfare: A Spectrum of Opportunity." ESCoE Discussion Paper 2019–16, October.
Hicks, J. R. 1940. "The Valuation of Social Income." *Economica* 7 (26): 105–24. https://doi.org/10.2307/2548691.
Hulten, Charles R. 1996. "Quality Change in Capital Goods and Its Impact on Economic Growth." NBER Working Paper 5569, National Bureau of Economic Research.
Hulten, C., and L. Nakamura. 2018. "Accounting for Growth in the Age of the Internet: The Importance of Output-Saving Technical Change." NBER Working Paper 23315, National Bureau of Economic Research.
Hulten, C., and L. Nakamura. 2021. "Expanded GDP for Welfare Measurement in the 21st Century." In *Measuring and Accounting for Innovation in the 21st Century*. National Bureau of Economic Research, Studies in Income and Wealth, organized by C. Corrado, J. Haskel, J. Miranda, and D. Sichel, vol. 78. Chicago: University of Chicago Press.
Keynes, J. M. 1930. *Treatise on Money*. London: Macmillan.
Konny, Crystal, G. Brendan, K. Williams, and David M. Friedman. 2019. "Big Data in the U.S. Consumer Price Index: Experiences & Plans." Brookings Institute,

February. https://www.brookings.edu/wp-content/uploads/2019/02/Big-Data-in-the-U.S.-Consumer-Price-Index.pdf.

Landes, D. S. 1998. *The Wealth and Poverty of Nations: Why Some Are So Rich and Some So Poor*. London: Abacus.

Lloyd, S. 2019. "Learning How to Control Complex Systems." In *Worlds Hidden in Plain Sight*, edited by D. Krakauer, 51–61. Santa Fe Institute Press.

Mehrhoff, Jens. 2019. "Introduction—The Value Chain of Scanner and Web Scraped Data." *Economie et Statistique / Economics and Statistics* (509):5–11.

Melser, D. 2019. "Valuing the Quantity and Quality of Product Variety to Consumers." *Empirical Economics* 57(6): 2107–28.

Moulton, B. R. 2018. "The Measurement of Output, Prices, and Productivity: What's Changed Since the Boskin Commission?" Hutchins Center on Fiscal and Monetary Policy, Brookings Institution. https://www.brookings.edu/research/the-measurement-of-output-prices-and-productivity/.

Nakamura, L. 2020. "Evidence of Accelerating Mismeasurement of Growth and Inflation in the U.S. in the 21st Century." ESCoE Discussion Paper 2020–15. https://www.escoe.ac.uk/publications/evidence-of-accelerating-mismeasurement-of-growth-and-inflation-in-the-u-s-in-the-21st-century/.

Nakamura, L. I., J. Samuels, and R. Soloveichik. 2017. "Measuring the 'Free' Digital Economy within the GDP and Productivity Accounts." Working Paper No. 17–37, Federal Reserve Bank of Philadelphia.

Nielsen. 2015. *Nielsen Breakthrough Innovation Report, European Edition, December 2015*. https://www.mldk.org/pageimages/files/Nielsen%20Breakthrough%20Innovation%20Report%202015%20European%20Edition_digital.pdf.

Nielsen. 2016. *Nielsen Breakthrough Innovation Report, European Edition, December 2016*. http://www.abre.org.br/wp-content/uploads/2012/06/NielsenReport.pdf.

Nordhaus, W. D. 1996. "Do Real-Output and Real-Wage Measures Capture Reality? The History of Lighting Suggests Not." In *The Economics of New Goods*, edited by T. F. Bresnahan and R. J. Gordon, 27–70. Chicago: University of Chicago Press.

Nordhaus, W. D. 2007. "Two Centuries of Productivity Growth in Computing." *Journal of Economic History* 67 (1): 128–59.

Nordhaus, W. D. 2021. "Are We Approaching an Economic Singularity? Information Technology and the Future of Economic Growth." *American Economic Journal: Macroeconomics* 13 (1): 299–332.

ONS. 2021a. *Indicative Impact of a New Framework Including Double Deflation on Industry Volume Estimates of GDP: Blue Book 2021*. https://www.ons.gov.uk/economy/nationalaccounts/uksectoraccounts/articles/impactofdoubledeflationonindustrychainvolumemeasureannualestimates1997to2018/bluebook2021.

ONS. 2021b. *Double Deflation Methods and Deflator Improvements to UK National Accounts: Blue Book 2021*. https://fwww.ons.gov.uk/economy/nationalaccounts/uksectoraccounts/methodologies/doubledeflationmethodsanddeflatorimprovementstouknationalaccountsbluebook2021.

Peplow, M. 2016. "London's Crossrail Is a $21 Billion Test of Virtual Modeling." *IEEE Spectrum*, March 24. https://spectrum.ieee.org/transportation/mass-transit/londons-crossrail-is-a-21-billion-test-of-virtual-modeling.

Petrin, A. 2002. "Quantifying the Benefits of New Products: The Case of the Minivan." *Journal of Political Economy* 110 (4): 705–29.

Reinsdorf, M., and P. Schreyer. 2020. "Measuring Consumer Inflation in a Digital Economy." In *Measuring Economic Growth and Productivity*, edited by B. Fraumeni, 339–62. London: Academic Press.

Sands, H. 2020. "Using Statistical Distributions to Estimate Weights for Web-Scraped Price Quotes in Consumer Price Statistics." Office for National Statistics. https://

www.ons.gov.uk/economy/inflationandpriceindices/articles/usingstatistical distributionstoestimateweightsforwebscrapedpricequotesinconsumerprice statistics/2020-09-01.

Schelling, T. C. 1958. "Design of the Accounts." In *A Critique of the United States Income and Product Accounts*. NBER Conference on Research in Income and Wealth, 325–33. Princeton, NJ: Princeton University Press.

Schreyer, Paul. 2021. *Accounting for Free Digital Services and Household Production—An Application to Facebook*. OECD. https://iariw.org/wp-content/uploads/2021/08/Schreyer_paper.pdf.

Schubert, C., M. C. Van Langeveld, and L. A. Donoso. 2014. "Innovations in 3D Printing: A 3D Overview from Optics to Organs." *British Journal of Ophthalmology* 98 (2): 159–61.

Silver, M., and S. Heravi. 2005. "A Failure in the Measurement of Inflation: Results from a Hedonic and Matched Experiment Using Scanner Data." *Journal of Business & Economic Statistics* 23 (3): 269–81. http://www.jstor.org/stable/27638820.

Stigler, G. 1961. *The Price Statistics of the Federal Government*. NBER, Price Statistics Review Committee, National Bureau of Economic Research.

Trajtenberg, Manuel. 1989. "The Welfare Analysis of Product Innovations, with an Application to Computed Tomography Scanners." *Journal of Political Economy* 97 (2): 444–79.

Waldfogel, J. 2017. "How Digitization Has Created a Golden Age of Music, Movies, Books, and Television." *Journal of Economic Perspectives* 31 (3): 195–214.

Xing, Y. 2020. "Global Value Chains and the 'Missing Exports' of the United States." *China Economic Review* 61, 101429.

5

The Digital Economy and Productivity

David M. Byrne

5.1 Introduction

Since the mid-twentieth century, advances in information technology (IT) have relentlessly driven down the cost of gathering, storing, transforming, and transmitting information. The falling price of IT has fostered pervasive investment in equipment and software, exponential growth in digitally stored information, and soaring network traffic. In short, the economy has become more *digitalized*. Myriad productivity improvements have followed, from the word-processing software we now take for granted to the use of supercomputers to process seismic data and locate oil and gas reserves. Isolating and quantifying the contribution of digitalization to economic growth and productivity is a challenge. Like electrification in the early twentieth century, digitalization has become so widespread that it is in the background of essentially all economic activity; it is hard to distinguish a distinct *digital economy*.

Growth accounting makes it possible to capture the effects of digitalization throughout the economy without taking a stand on the boundary of the digital economy. It divides the economic effects of advances in IT into two components. The first is the contribution to economic growth from industries that *produce* IT; the second is the rise in labor productivity from the *use* of IT capital. Productivity in IT industries is driven by technical advances in solid-state electronics and other fundamental innovations. The

David M. Byrne is at the Federal Reserve Board of Governors.

The views expressed here are not represented to be the views of the Federal Reserve. The author is grateful for comments provided by Martin Fleming, Tina Highfill, Dale Jorgenson, Marshall Reinsdorf, Matt Russell, Jon Samuels, Louise Sheiner, Dan Sichel, and Rachel Soloveichik and for assistance from Joshua Dickey, Emily Green, and Molly Harnish with data curation and visualization.

use-of-IT contribution is a knock-on effect of the production effect: more efficient IT production drives down the price of IT capital, encouraging all industries to take a more IT-intensive approach.

In this chapter, we assess the plausible range of the effects of IT on productivity using the growth accounting approach with the economic statistics at hand. Despite extensive improvements in IT measurement by government and academic economists over many years, thorny measurement problems stand in the way of this exercise. The changing quality of IT goods and services is not well captured in many cases; measures from different parts of the statistical system are often mutually inconsistent; and some parts of IT output growth, such as data center equipment built for in-house use, appear to be omitted altogether.

After an overview of digitalization, this chapter reviews the state of play in these and other measurement issues that make efficiency gains in IT production and from the use of IT hard to quantify with precision. It then offers rough estimates of bias in reported output growth of the US economy and in reported contributions from IT to economic growth and productivity.

Although debates about these issues are far from settled, in the main, evidence supports a conclusion that mismeasurement of IT continues to contribute to understatement of GDP and productivity growth. Importantly, some of the sources of bias discussed in this chapter have worsened—indeed, some emerged only recently. These findings support the view that the slowdown in reported productivity growth since the mid-2000s is partly an artifact of IT mismeasurement. That said, the share of slowdown that can be disregarded as spurious is small. Nevertheless, measurement errors do significantly distort our estimates of the contribution of the IT sector to GDP growth. We suggest some steps statistical agencies could take to address these problems.

5.2 Overview of Digitalization

The increasing extent of digitalization—the collection, storage, transformation, and transmission of digital data—can be illustrated with two high-level indicators: spending on IT equipment and software and volume of data stored and transmitted.[1] Spending on IT capital tends to rise with digitalization because digital activity relies on electronic equipment and software. In the United States, the share of IT in total fixed capital investment excluding structures has moved up consistently from the dawn of electronic computing in the 1950s, reaching 40 percent in recent years. The share of IT in consumer durables spending began climbing in the 1980s and was 12 percent in 2021 (fig. 5.1a).[2]

The accumulation and circulation of data provides a barometer of the activity conducted using installed IT capital. Investment in data storage equipment has grown exponentially—reaching 10^{14} bytes per year in

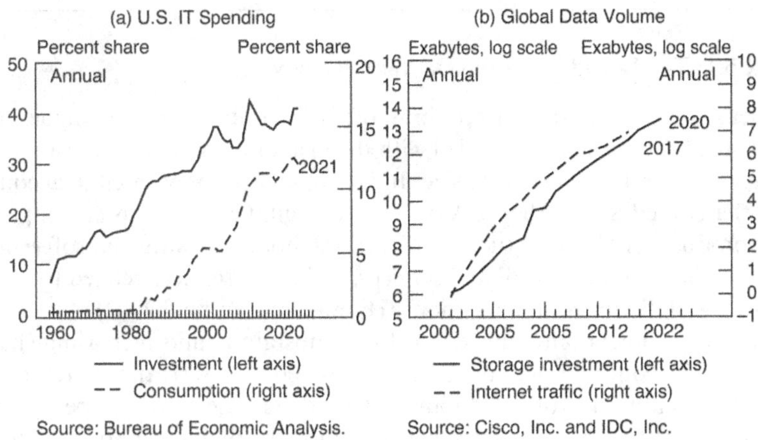

Fig. 5.1 Indicators of digital economy growth

Note: The figure on the left shows IT investment—computing and communications equipment, other information-processing equipment, software, and R & D in IT service industries—as share of nonstructures investment and shows households' spending on IT durable goods—computers, peripherals, software, mobile and other phones, and other information processing equipment—as a share of consumer durables spending. In the figure on the right, storage investment includes hard disk drives and solid-state drives. Internet traffic is estimated by Cisco for the point of end use.

2020—a sign of mushrooming amounts of stored digital data (fig. 5.1b).[3] Internet traffic has grown at a similar pace, roughly doubling every two years since 2000. This indicates the importance of interconnections among IT capital installations to the use of data (fig. 5.1b).

Additional indicators showing that rapid growth of the digital economy has continued are measures of the nominal and real value added of the digital economy as defined by the Bureau of Economic Analysis (BEA) in a satellite account discussed in box 5.1. Based on this definition, the digital economy accounts for a substantial and growing share of US GDP: over the period from 2005 to 2021, its nominal value added rose from 7.8 percent to 10.3 percent of GDP (fig. 5.2a), and its real value added grew at an average annual rate of 6.4 percent, nearly four times the rate of the total economy (fig. 5.2b).

5.3 A Growth Accounting Framework for Analyzing the Role of Digitalization in Productivity Growth

Analyses of sources of growth of US labor productivity using conventional tools of growth accounting imply that digitalization has played a prominent role in the pace of productivity growth in recent decades. These analyses consider both the growth of total factor productivity (TFP) in

Box 5.1: The Boundary of the Digital Economy

Discussions of the digital economy often leave its boundary vague, but statistical agencies have wrestled with the task of defining the concept precisely enough to quantify its size. In its digital economy satellite account for the United States, the BEA defines the digital economy as encompassing production of infrastructure (IT capital, both hardware and software), e-commerce, and priced digital services, which are services related to computing and digital communications (Highfill and Surfield 2022).

The digital economy thus defined is a substantial and increasing share of the US economy: over the period from 2005 to 2021, the share of the digital economy in total economy value added rose from 7.8 percent to 10.3 percent (fig. 5.2a). Real value added for the digital economy grew at an average annual rate of 6.4 percent over this period—nearly four times the rate of the total economy (fig. 5.2b).

To compile this account, BEA analysts identify products judged to be primarily digital from the hundreds of output types in the input-output accounts produced by BEA. The appropriate share of the value added of the industries producing these items is then assigned to the digital economy. Even with highly granular output data in hand, creating such a satellite account is a difficult undertaking. Some cases are straightforward, such as the production of cell phones; other categories contain both digital and

the production of IT capital and the contribution to output growth from the use of IT capital inputs as reflected in IT capital deepening—rising IT capital per worker. Estimates from the Bureau of Labor Statistics (BLS) Office of Productivity and Technology show that the 1.5 percentage point rise in US labor productivity growth in the mid-1990s can be attributed in great part to a rise in contributions of IT (fig. 5.3a). In this period, fast-rising TFP in IT capital–producing industries caused prices of IT capital to fall; increased investment in IT capital in response to falling prices resulted in IT capital deepening. The contribution from TFP growth in IT production declined dramatically in the mid-2000s, reflecting both a global slowdown in measured IT industry productivity and the negative effect of offshoring of IT capital production on this industry's weight in US GDP. IT capital deepening slowed as well. Together, these effects caused a slowdown in labor productivity growth of almost 2 percentage points.

Outside studies using arguably better price indexes and better accounting for capital utilization echo this qualitative takeaway—a substantial rise in the productivity contribution of IT in the mid-1990s and a subsequent

nondigital items and are excluded for lack of more detailed information. For example, ride-hailing services operating through digital intermediaries are excluded, as they cannot be separated from conventional taxi services (Barefoot et al. 2018).

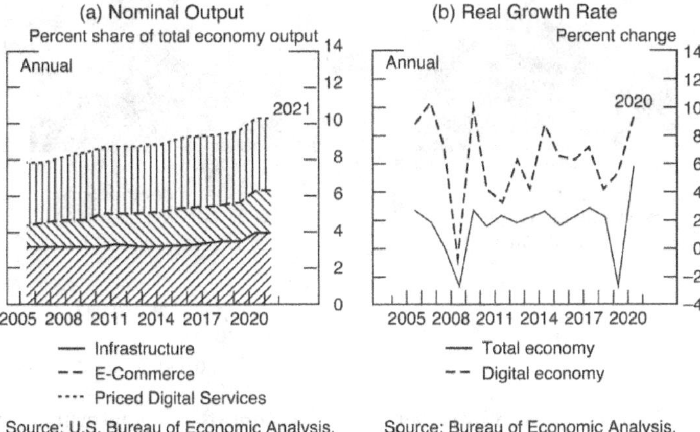

Fig. 5.2 BEA's measure of the US digital economy

Note: The BEA digital economy definition also includes federal nondefense digital services (very small and not shown), structures investment, and digital intermediary services.

drop—but find appreciably larger IT contributions to growth.[4] For example, Byrne, Oliner, and Sichel (2013) find the step up in productivity contributions from IT innovation and capital spending beginning in the mid-1990s to be twice as large as official estimates (fig. 5.3b). Even by official estimates, the contribution to economic growth from a relatively small sector of the economy is striking.[5]

Debate over the accuracy of official measures of the contributions of IT production and use to labor productivity growth highlights the fact that, as a practical matter, the accuracy of the growth accounting approach in quantifying the role of IT depends on the quality of the data used to implement it. In particular, the approach requires accurate measures of (a) output prices and value added for each IT-producing sector, (b) income shares of factors of production (labor, energy, capital inputs, etc.), (c) flow of real capital services supplied by each type of capital input, and (d) GDP.[6] We now turn to the degree to which these requirements can be met. After a journey through these details, we take stock of their collective effect on the accuracy of analysis.

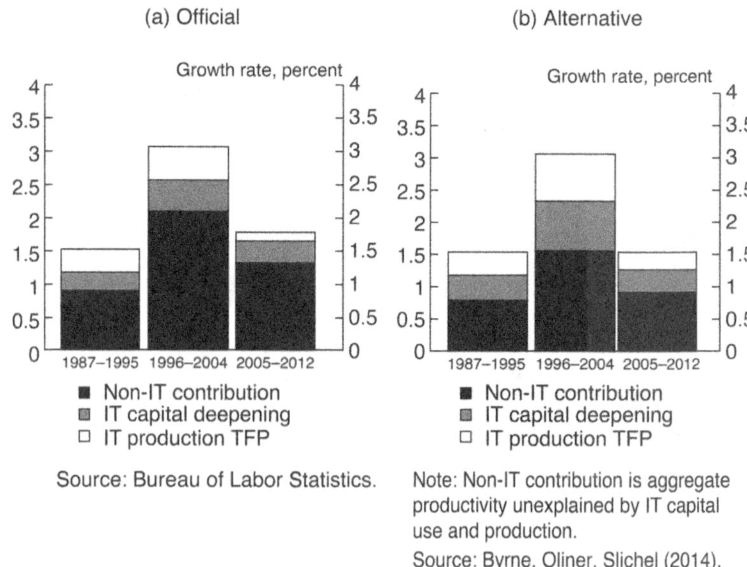

Fig. 5.3 Contribution of IT to labor productivity growth of nonfarm private business in the US

Note: The alternative growth decomposition differs with respect to IT price indexes and includes adjustment for varying capital utilization. The breakpoints of 1995 and 2004 were identified by Fernald (2015).

5.4 Measuring IT Capital Production

When a plant adopts techniques that yield more output from a fixed amount of inputs (labor, capital, materials, etc.), its TFP increases. TFP growth for the economy as a whole is the collective effect of TFP changes at individual plants plus the net effect of expansions and contractions in the size of plants with different productivity levels.[7] Thus, isolating the direct effect of IT innovation on economic growth and productivity boils down to accurately measuring in real (or volume) terms the output of IT capital products at the plant or sector level and the inputs used to produce that output.[8]

This section first discusses the measurement issues common to most IT products, including accounting for quality change, granularity (or detail) of available source data, and inconsistencies in methods over time, across countries, and across statistical programs within countries. Then, it separately considers the state of play of measurement for different types of capital, expanding the traditional scope of IT capital—computers, communications equipment, and software—to encompass the broader notion of digital economy most readers have in mind. To that end, this section considers the electronic systems embedded in seemingly all types of equipment, from robots to motor vehicles, and the value of data assets used in the provision of IT services.

5.4.1 Common Measurement Issues

Three issues that arise in measuring output growth of IT capital are common to many types of capital. First, many IT products experience a rapid pace of quality change, making the conversion of production at current prices (nominal output) into production at constant prices (real output) difficult. Second, collecting data on outputs and inputs with sufficient granularity to enable productivity estimation with minimal reliance on assumptions is a challenge for all types of IT capital. Finally, maintaining consistency in measurement methods over time and across statistical programs—necessary because productivity analysis synthesizes information from many statistical releases—requires careful attention.

5.4.1.1 Accounting for Quality Change

Rapid quality change is the norm for IT capital. New models of equipment and vintages of software typically embody quality improvements, such as engineering advances and design changes. They often enter the market at a lower quality-adjusted price—such as a new, higher performance phone with the same nominal price as the previous model. Ensuring that quality improvement is counted as an increase in real output is a job that falls to the price index used to deflate nominal output.

Official price indexes are most often calculated using the matched-model method: prices in a representative basket of product models are observed repeatedly over time, and price changes of the models present in both the current and previous period are averaged using weights reflecting their relative importance in production. Under the maintained assumption that the quality of each individual item in the basket is invariant over time, the price index often provides an accurate indicator of aggregate price trend even when new models enter (if the product market is competitive and price observations are reasonably frequent). In particular, in the presence of sufficient competition to ensure that the "law of one price" applies, when a new model enters with a lower price-performance ratio—more quality for a lower price, say—the prices of incumbent models fall, allowing the workhorse matched-model index to capture the correct price trend by tracking the prices of the incumbent models (fig. 5.4a). Thus, the matched-model index accounts for quality change indirectly.

Yet in the case of IT equipment, short product life cycles and imperfect product-market competition often undermine the accuracy of the matched-model approach. For product markets characterized by imperfect competition—such as when high cost of switching between products or platforms creates market power—price declines for incumbent items may not

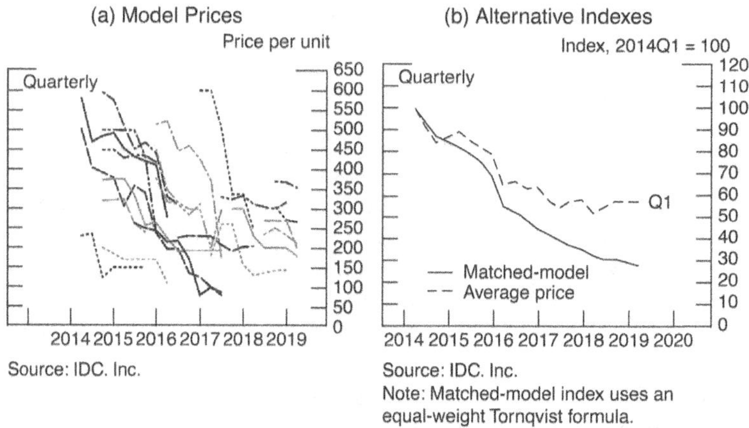

Fig. 5.4 Smartphone price cascade and index calculation
Note: Figures use models produced by the top three Android operating system smartphone manufacturers, sold in the United States, with initial prices between $200 and $600. Each line in the figure on the left represents the price evolution of a different model of phone.

capture the full difference in quality. For example, captive users of older systems may pay more for their equipment on a quality-adjusted basis because they are reluctant to switch to newer options. Markets for electronics often fall into this category, as many users are committed to a platform or IT "ecosystem" of devices with the same operating system.[9] In such cases, a method is needed to adjust for the portion of the premium or discount for the new product relative to the incumbent product caused by difference in quality to obtain a pure measure of price change.

One such method imputes the new product's price in the period just prior to its entry by fitting a hedonic regression model that relates product characteristics to product prices. The price change between the imputed price and the first observed market price is then folded into index calculations, reducing reliance on the induced price changes of incumbent models to capture quality change.[10] Provided the quality elements valued by the product's buyer, both observed and unobserved, correlate with the characteristics in the hedonic regression model, this approach can be expected to perform well.[11] The clock speed of a computer processor may, for example, serve as a proxy for unobserved characteristics of interest to the consumer, such as how fast the processor can render an image on the screen.

Personal computers and mobile phones are prime examples of goods for which BLS constructs constant-quality price indexes. However, other products have been harder to adjust for quality change because of source data limitations such as gaps in information on key quality characteristics or insufficient data granularity, a topic we turn to next.

5.4.1.2 *Data Granularity*

Source data granularity—the level of detail on a variety of dimensions—plays a crucial role in the precision of productivity measures for producers of IT capital. Short product life cycles, constant innovation, and varying industry structure create data needs that are difficult to meet with the current statistical system.

High-frequency, model-level information on prices, quantities, and product characteristics is the gold standard. Because data collection is costly, data collected by statistical agencies almost invariably fall short of that ideal. Productivity measurement research boils down to combining official statistics, other data sources, and judicious assumptions to construct imperfect but defensible price index estimates.

The list below provides some broad guidance on data requirements for precise estimates.

- **Model-level data on prices and characteristics** are essential for accounting for changing quality. When price information is available only at the product class level—as an average for a group of models—index results can be distorted by changes in average quality. As shown in figure 5.4b, following the average price for a class of products subject to entry and exit models of varying quality can lead to a markedly different price index than the conventional matched-model approach.[12] Fortunately, model-level price data are collected by statistical agencies for construction of producer and consumer price indexes, allowing these indexes to capture product life cycle price dynamics. In the presence of imperfect competition, information on models' characteristics is also needed to adjust for relative quality of models entering the market. For this information, researchers frequently turn to secondary sources.
- **Timely updates of the product baskets** used in price index construction are essential. Because collecting data is resource intensive, statistical agencies rely on periodically refreshed representative baskets of models in price construction. In highly dynamic product markets, waiting to update the basket can give unreliable results. The prices for the narrow class of computer processors shown in figure 5.5a illustrate this point. Fourteen models were sold over a four-year period, and price competition between entering and incumbent models was fierce, driving the price of the typical model down 16 percent over its first quarter in the market. As shown in figure 5.5b, a matched-model price index using the entire set of price information falls 38 percent per year on average for the first two years. In contrast, the annual basket index in figure 5.5b, whose basket is refreshed to include newly introduced models once per year, falls 7 percent per year for the first two years, 31 percentage points slower than the index that includes new models as soon as they appear.[13]

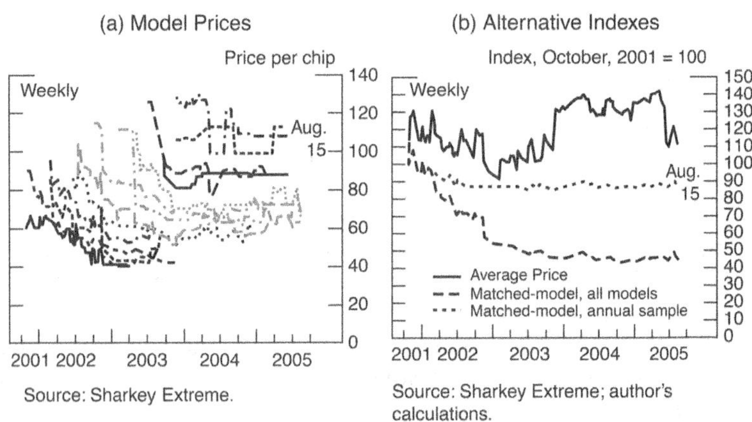

Fig. 5.5 Effect of sample updating frequency on microprocessor price indexes

Even annual basket updates are insufficient to capture price change accurately because new models' prices move dramatically shortly after their introduction. This example illustrates the importance of capturing price dynamics early in product life cycle.[14]

- **Fine product class data on output** is needed to capture the shifting composition of production. For example, offshoring has lowered the share of PCs in the output of the US computer industry dramatically, from roughly 40 percent prior to 2010 to roughly 5 percent in recent years in Census Bureau data from the Annual Survey of Manufactures. Statistical agencies construct price indexes at successively higher levels of aggregation. At the lowest level of aggregation, item-level price indexes are constructed from model-level prices, but no information about the evolving volume of sales for each model is collected.[15] Item-level indexes are aggregated using information on sales by product class (groups of similar models) in an earlier base period to produce higher-level indexes. Price trends differ significantly between personal computers and other computing equipment, so separate, up-to-date product class weights for PCs and other computer products are needed for an accurate deflator to convert nominal output into real output for the computer industry.
- **Input-output tables** provide information on inputs used in production. This information is essential for two reasons. First, because productivity growth is the difference between output growth and input growth, one cannot drill down to sectors or industries to understand their contribution to productivity without input-output detail. Unfortunately, the available level of product detail is not always adequate. For example, in the US statistical system, annual industry input-output tables contain a single category of inputs of electronic materials, but prices for microprocessors used in PCs tend to fall far faster than prices for the

hundreds of discrete sensor chips used in motor vehicles. Using a single semiconductor price index for inputs used by both industries leads to overstatement of TFP growth in the PC industry and understatement in the motor vehicle industry. Second, due to the in-house production of equipment in certain industries, some IT equipment is missed by capital stock measures unless it is imputed. Detailed information on inputs facilitates this estimation because in-house production of IT equipment may be assumed to be proportional to input of electronic materials.[16] Furthermore, in-house production of software is often assumed to be proportional to labor inputs from relevant job categories, making data on employment by occupation and industry essential, as discussed below.

5.4.1.3 Methodological Consistency

Tracking the impact of new general-purpose technologies such as IT requires long-term perspective. The effects of new general-purpose technologies—those that have a transformative effect throughout the economy, such as electrification and solid-state digital electronics—diffuse slowly as new firms appear and exploit the innovation, incumbent firms exit or adapt, and capital and labor are reallocated to more productive firms. To study the transformative effects of IT, long time series on IT production and use based on consistent methodology are needed. However, constructing these long time series involves several challenges, listed below.

- **Innovative new platforms may embody quality changes that are impossible to quantify.** To control for quality change, one must split price differences between old and new types of equipment into quality change and pure price change components. As noted above, with model-level data on prices and characteristics, one can usually construct a serviceable constant-quality price via hedonic analysis of the price impact of the new model's differences in characteristics from the incumbent models. But when an entirely novel platform enters the IT market, the value of differences in characteristics may be impossible to estimate. For example, a smartphone is not simply a digital camera, cell phone, and tablet computer bundled together.
- **Consistency in granularity of available data is needed to enable historical consistency** of methods used. For example, model-level information on prices and characteristics is available back to the introduction of the PC, providing an opportunity to consistently account for quality change in measuring real growth of PC production. In contrast, similar information is hard to come by for mainframes.[17] Estimates of the growth of real output of mainframes may therefore fail to account for quality improvements, causing the acceleration in computer production when the industry shifted from mainframes to PCs to be overstated.

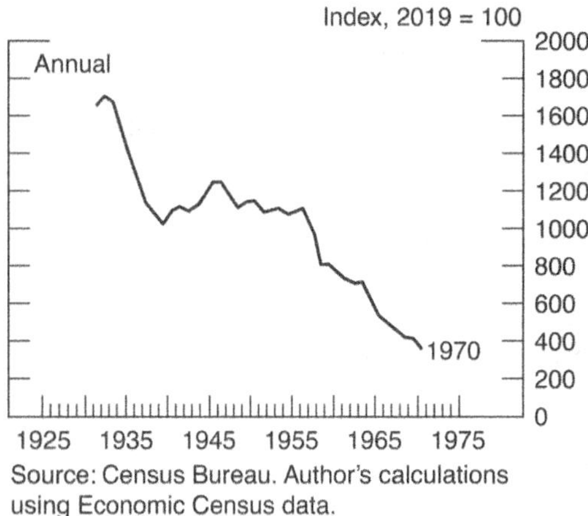

Fig. 5.6 Adding machine price index

Note: The index shown is an equal-weight Törnqvist index of average prices for electronic and hand-powered ten-key adding machines.

- **Failing to construct plausible estimates of output of products based on earlier IT tends to overstate the relative productivity effect of semiconductor-based equipment**. Earlier IT performed many of the same functions, broadly defined, as solid-state electronics (semiconductors) and need to be accounted for in any analysis of the *relative* impact of newer IT on productivity. Nordhaus (2007) identifies 1944 as the break point where rapidly falling computing costs began—a time when computers relied on vacuum tube technology, not semiconductors. Other IT predated the solid-state transistor as well, including adding machines, whose prices fell by a factor of four between 1930 and 1970 (fig. 5.6).
- **The consistency of the data on output; inputs of labor, capital, and materials; and prices** is crucial for accuracy of productivity estimates. For example, output of a product is sometimes deflated with a price index that contains different products. In the US statistical system, different sources provide data on output (the Annual Survey of Manufactures published by the Census Bureau), hours worked (the BLS Current Employment Statistics), prices (BLS Producer Price Program and International Price Program), and inputs of capital and materials (BEA GDP by industry program). These and other sources are integrated into the growth accounting framework to answer questions about sources of growth in output and productivity. Because of the need to combine data from both agencies, BEA and BLS jointly construct the Integrated Industry-Level Production Account (KLEMS). Such collaboration helps reduce inconsistencies in data used to calculate productivity.

- **Cross-country consistency** in the measurement of IT is crucial for understanding the roles of individual countries in the global IT sector, for comparing the relative success of individual countries in harnessing IT for productivity gains, and for analyzing international supply chain risks. Although countries generally adhere to the internationally accepted conceptual guidelines of the *System of National Accounts 2008*, practical estimation methods are beyond the scope of these guidelines. Price and volume estimation practices vary significantly across countries in areas such as quality adjustment of IT prices in the construction of deflators.[18] Mobile phones, for example, are to a great extent produced by a single global supply chain, suggesting that mobile phone price trends should be similar across individual markets except for small differences due to variation in market structure and costs of transportation and distribution (Byrne 2019). Yet there is a wide, sustained divergence in mobile phone price trends (fig. 5.7a). Another striking example of dissonance across national statistical systems is the semiconductor industry. Implicit chip quality, calculated as the real output reported in national statistics divided by a measure of the raw silicon wafer capacity of the national industry, doubled in the United States between 2011 and 2019 (fig. 5.7b). Over the same period, chip quality calculated with official measures declined by 50 percent in South Korea—an obviously erroneous indicator for a country at the leading edge of the global industry.

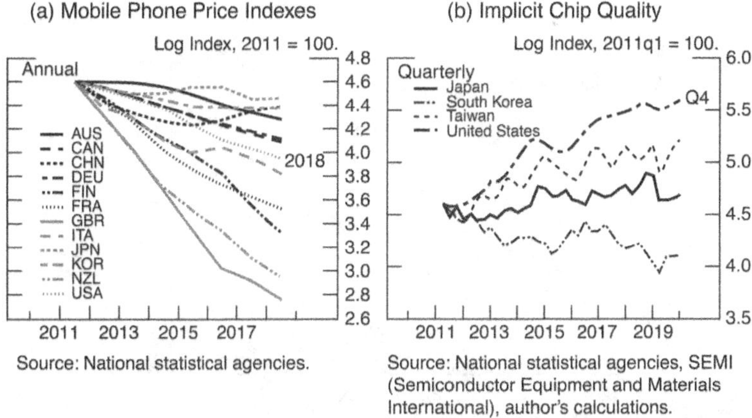

Fig. 5.7 Cross-country tension in IT measurement

Note: In the figure on the left, mobile phone CPI divided by overall CPI is shown. CPIs for Australia, Canada, New Zealand, and the United States are for broader categories. In the figure on the right, implicit quality index is real output of semiconductors divided by chip plant capacity measured in wafers.

These broad measurement challenges—quality adjustment, data granularity, and historical and global consistency—are discussed in the context of specific capital types below.

5.4.1.4 Mismeasurement of Real Value Added Due to "Factoryless Manufacturing"

A substantial portion of the value added in IT equipment produced abroad is the value of design and management taking place in the United States (fig. 5.8), but the associated US export may omit quality improvements embedded in designs (see Dynan and Sheiner, chap. 1, for further discussion). How such service exports are measured has been the subject of recent scrutiny.[19] US "factoryless manufacturing" establishments—those that outsource fabrication of products but maintain control of the production process, own associated intellectual property, and bear the entrepreneurial risk—are classified as wholesale trade in official statistics (Murphy 2009). And while the NIPA (National Income and Product Accounts) are not sufficiently granular to determine with certainty what price index is used to deflate exports from these establishments, wholesale trade prices do not, as a rule, behave in a way that suggests noteworthy quality change: the official price index for the output of the wholesale trade sector moved up 2 percent, on average, in the 10-year period ending in 2018. In effect, absent intervention to ensure the real value of exports includes the value of domestically produced design improvements, the entirety of quality change in electronic equipment may well be implicitly attributed to greater efficiency in offshore assembly activity.

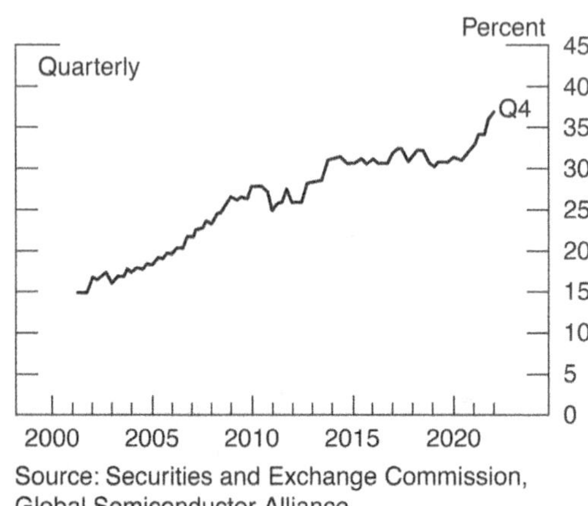

Fig. 5.8 "Factoryless" semiconductors

Note: The figure shows the ratio of the revenue of factoryless semiconductor companies (those that design but do not fabricate chips) to the revenue of all semiconductor companies.

Table 5.1 **IT equipment by type in the US economy**

Equipment Type	Production	Percent share of Investment	Consumption
Computing	9.7	28.1	35.8
Communications	16.7	39.1	26.6
Special-purpose	73.6	29.7	47.4

Source: US Census Bureau and Bureau of Economic Analysis.

Note: Shares are for 2019. Special-purpose equipment is navigational, measuring, electromedical, and control instruments—industry 3345 in the North American Industry Classification System (NAICS).

5.4.2 IT Capital Production by Type

The contribution of IT capital production to aggregate US productivity growth comes solely from *domestic* production of equipment and intangible assets. For equipment, the composition of US manufacturing is rather different from the composition of the global industry. Because general-purpose electronic equipment—computing and communications equipment—is now heavily supplied by imports, its impact on US productivity comes primarily through its *use* (the subject of the next section) rather than its production. Computing equipment, for example, accounts for one-third of global IT equipment production but only one-tenth of the US industry.[20] Special-purpose electronics—devices such as navigational and electromedical equipment (table 5.1) account for roughly three-quarters of the value of US electronic equipment production. These devices can be considered IT capital because they incorporate embedded electronic systems; indeed, accounting for the IT embedded in them is central to understanding IT capital production in the United States.

IT intangibles—software, data, and IT research and development (R&D)—present different measurement challenges than equipment. They are typically not exchanged at arm's length, so the assessment of their quality change cannot rely on market prices.

5.4.2.1 Computing Equipment

Computing equipment includes computers proper (a housing containing central processing unit, memory, and connections to input and output devices) and related equipment for data storage, collection, and reporting. Substantial research has gone into measuring computing equipment, making it arguably the most accurately measured category of IT.[21] Quality-adjusted PC prices in particular have been the subject of a great number of studies.[22] Many statistical agencies devote attention to them, and the BLS producer price program has long adjusted computer prices for quality change using hedonic analysis.

Concerted effort to get these prices right notwithstanding, price declines for computers have been surprisingly slow, or even stopped, in recent years. Slow price declines for the domestic industry are not necessarily indicative of mismeasurement; they may reflect the unusual composition of US computer industry, which now focuses on storage systems, peripherals, and servers rather than PCs and hard drives. Nevertheless, corroboration from outside research would be reassuring on several fronts:

- Relative to 2005–2009, the BLS producer price index (PPI) for single-user and multiuser computers (PCs and servers) fell, on average, 15 percentage points per year more slowly in the 2010–2019 period. Regular publication of the results of hedonic calculations behind BLS prices would be of great value to researchers in the study of this shift.
- The PPI for computer storage equipment edged down only 1 percent per year on average in 2015–2019. Yet a private IT consulting company, IDC, Inc., reports that storage equipment prices (per megabyte) plunged in this period an average of 24 percent and 37 percent per year for hard disk drives (HDDs) and solid-state drives (SSDs), respectively. HDDs and SSDs are the core of computer storage systems, raising the question of why their prices do not pass through to the system prices used in the calculation of PPI.
- The computer peripherals PPI moved down at a 3 percent annual rate, on average, for 2015–2019. Over the same period, the BLS consumer price index (CPI) for televisions fell 18 percent per year; this product is technologically quite similar to computer terminals, an important type of peripheral. Aizcorbe and Pho (2005) found prices based on retail scanner data fell significantly faster than official indexes for an array of peripheral types.

This apparent regime change in computing equipment prices, combined with the slow decline in MPU prices, raises the question of whether advances in computing have slowed since the late 2000s. Answering that question is made more complicated by the shift from PCs and local networks to cloud computing providers, but available evidence suggests this shift has entailed efficiency gains and lower prices. The performance of large-scale computing installations has continued to move up rapidly in recent years, and a number of studies find that prices for cloud computing have fallen quite rapidly.[23]

5.4.2.2 Communications Equipment

Communications equipment encompasses the wireline networks connection of computing equipment in local area networks and over the internet, long-haul and local data transmission equipment, and cellular and other wireless systems. Communications equipment prices have been studied extensively, with particular attention to the data networking and transmission equipment that supported the IT boom of the 1990s and the mobile networking equipment central to more recent IT advances.[24] The Federal Reserve publishes price indexes for these products, and BEA uses them as deflators in the national accounts. In a major step forward, the BLS recently adopted a hedonic approach with frequent updates to the models in the basket for constructing its price index for smartphone consumption.[25]

However, major gaps in our understanding remain. Price-performance trends for satellite equipment and a variety of radio-wave base station equipment are not well understood, due in part to obscurity of relevant prices within complicated contracts.[26] And there has been no research on prices for broadcast and studio equipment for radio and television, a major component of communication equipment spending and an important area of the ongoing transition to solid-state electronics from legacy technologies. These are products produced at lower volumes in less competitive markets, so they might be expected to have slower falling prices. Unfortunately, the composition of US production has shifted away from well-measured products—cell phones, routers—toward satellites and other products where quality-adjustment of output has been limited.

5.4.2.3 Other Electronics

In the wake of a massive wave of offshoring in the 2000s, US manufacturing of electronics has primarily focused on special-purpose equipment for narrow applications rather than computing and communications equipment designed for general purpose use (fig. 5.9a). Prominent examples include medical imaging machines (MRI, CT, radiographic, and ultrasound equipment), military equipment (reconnaissance and surveillance, electronic

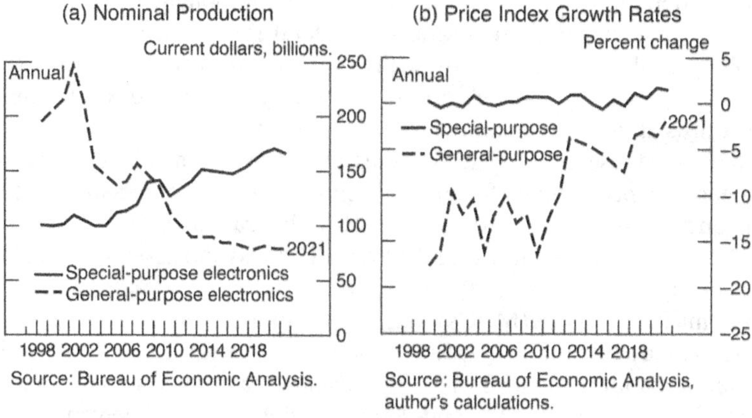

Fig. 5.9 US general-purpose and special-purpose electronics production

Note: The general-purpose price index is a Törnqvist aggregate of computer and peripheral equipment and communications equipment from BEA's underlying detail tables on gross output by industry. The special-purpose index contains navigational, measuring, electromedical, and control instruments manufacturing.

warfare, and missile guidance equipment), and industrial process control equipment (instruments, displays, etc.).

The special-purpose portion of the electronics industry raises questions that have not yet been explored in the research on economic measurement (Byrne 2015). BEA's deflator for special-purpose equipment production rose 0.5 percent per year on average for 2015–2019—markedly different behavior from general-purpose electronics, whose prices *fell* 7.4 percent per year over this period (fig. 5.9b).[27] This sharp contrast in behavior is puzzling because the extensive use of electronic components in the manufacture of special-purpose equipment items suggests that, like general-purpose electronics, there should be downward pressure on their prices from advances in semiconductor technology.[28] To be sure, these industries differ in ways that may affect their prices, such as market structure and scale economies, but the contrast in price trends between general-purpose and special-purpose electronics is so pronounced that research to corroborate the official price indexes is merited.

Complicating matters further for analyzing the effect of IT production on productivity, semiconductors seem to be embedded in almost all types of equipment. Ideally, an account of the role of IT in the economy would consider electronic systems found within devices of all kinds as production of IT capital but not count the entire device—the dashboard navigation system but not the entire automobile, say. The semiconductor manufacturing industry is a reasonable proxy for the production of embedded systems (Byrne, Oliner, and Sichel 2013). Taking this approach, the key measurement question becomes whether we are properly measuring the output of the semiconductor industry.

Considerable research into US electronic component prices has been conducted at the BLS, BEA, and the Federal Reserve Board (FRB), but publicly available data only allow price indexes to be estimated for some product types in some time periods.[29] In fact, the price indexes for nearly two-thirds of global semiconductor production have not been corroborated with detailed research.[30] Whereas researchers have been able to make solid estimates of price trends for memory chips and microprocessors, suitable data on more specialized processors, such as the graphics processors (GPUs) used in advanced computing, and on circuit boards and assemblies are hard to come by.

For microprocessors (MPUs)—the most important product in the domestic semiconductor industry—how to adjust prices for quality change is a matter of dispute. The BLS MPU PPI displayed a marked step down in the pace of price declines in the mid-2000s, slowing from a 48 percent average annual decline in the 2000–2004 period to a 7 percent average annual decline in the 2009–2013 period (fig. 5.10a). To investigate this dramatic flattening out of the BLS index, Byrne, Oliner, and Sichel (2018) construct hedonic price indexes that control for chip performance as measured by a suite of

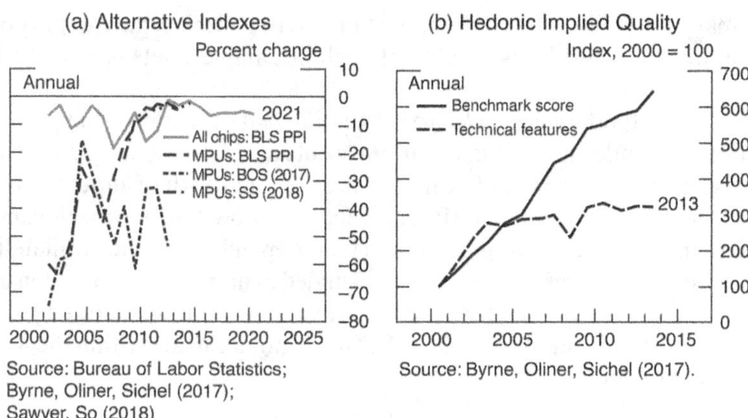

Fig. 5.10 MPU price index quality adjustment

Note: In 2015, BLS stopped publishing a separate price index for MPUs due to confidentiality concerns. In the figure on right, implied quality is constructed from hedonic regression coefficients and average characteristics for Intel microprocessors.

benchmark tests and conclude that quality-adjusted prices of MPUs continued to decline by roughly 40 percent per year after 2009. The BLS has since implemented a hedonic approach for its price index, finding 8 percent per year price declines for the 2009–2013 period (Sawyer and So 2018). The primary difference between the two hedonic indexes lies in the approach to quality adjustment: Byrne, Oliner, and Sichel (2018) treat performance scores as a sufficient statistic for quality and omit technical characteristics (clock speed, for example). They also test an alternative specification of the hedonic regression model using only chip technical characteristics and argue that it implies a spuriously flat path for chip quality in the post-2009 period (fig. 5.10b). Sawyer and So (2018) prefer a specification with both performance scores and technical characteristics and arrive at much slower price declines.

5.4.2.4 *Intangible IT Capital*

Intangible capital plays a growing role in the global economy. Corrado (chap. 3 in this book) discusses the types of intangible investment that are excluded from GDP. A substantial share of the intangible investment included in GDP consists of software and other IT assets (Haskel and Westlake 2017; Corrado, Haskel, Jona-Lasinio, et al. 2022).

The measurement of IT intangible capital investment is complicated by two common challenges. The creation of intangible assets often takes place within the firm that will use them, and in cases of own-use or own-account production, no transaction occurs whose price and value can be observed. Second, unlike IT equipment, which usually has standardized characteristics, many intangible capital assets are tailored to a specific, narrow purpose, and efforts to quantify the quality of such intangible assets have met with limited success.

When the standard approach to calculating real output growth by deflating by a price index for that same output is not feasible, national accountants often measure the growth of real output through growth of inputs plus an adjustment for changes in TFP. The details of how this approach can be implemented vary by intangible capital type, depending on data availability.

The intangible investment currently included in national accounts consists of software and databases, R&D, mineral exploration, and artistic originals. Of these, software, databases, and R&D in IT industries are within the scope of IT investment.

- **Software and databases:** The US national accounts distinguish three types of software: prepackaged, custom, and own account. Prepackaged and custom software have sales data that can be used to estimate their nominal output, but nominal output of own-account software (produced in-house for the firm's own use) must be measured by production costs. To do this, BEA assumes that a portion of the time of employees in relevant occupations is devoted to own-account software creation and estimates the production cost by the wage bill for employee time plus the cost of intermediate inputs and capital services. To estimate real output of prepackaged software, BEA deflates nominal output by the price index for this product from BLS,[31] but measuring the deflator of custom and own-account software is a longstanding challenge. BEA constructs this deflator by averaging the price index for prepackaged software and an index of input prices including wages and adjusting for an assumed rate of TFP growth in software production.[32] Databases—specifically, database management systems—are included in the software investment estimation process. The data contained within databases are not currently included in national accounts intangibles, as discussed below.
- **R&D of IT-producing industries:** In US national accounts, estimates of nominal investment in R&D are based on survey data on R&D spending from the National Science Foundation. The deflator for this investment is an input price index developed at BEA (Robbins et al. 2012) that incorporates a downward adjustment for TFP growth in the performance of R&D. Estimates of R&D investment include some of the costs of creating software originals (the original source code) because distinguishing between these two types of intangible investment can be difficult in practice. This chapter treats only the R&D of IT-producing industries as IT intangible investment.

Data is the main IT intangible asset currently excluded from national accounts.[33] Corrado (chap. 3 in this book) explains an analytical framework

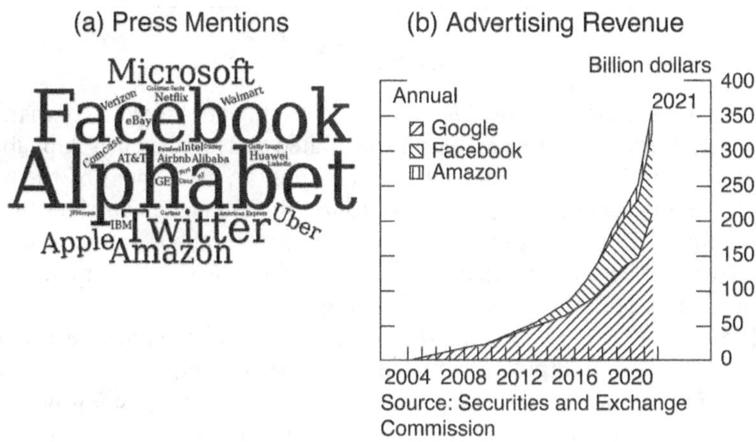

Fig. 5.11 Digital economy companies

Note: Company name size is proportional to frequency of mentions in articles in the business press that reference the "digital economy."

for the value of data with three stages: ingestion of raw records to create data stores, transformation of data (cleaning, transforming, and formatting) to create databases, and integration of data using analytical tools to create data intelligence. Corrado, Haskel, Iommi, et al. (2022) use a measurement approach analogous to the approach used for software in the national accounts and treat a portion of the wage bill for relevant occupations as the cost of production of data. They find that investment in data not covered by software and database estimates in national accounts is on the order of 3.5 to 5.7 percent of GDP for six European countries. They note, however, that data intelligence, the outcome of the analysis of data, is difficult to separate from investment in R&D. Calderón et al. (2022) use a similar approach for the United States but employ machine learning techniques to estimate the share of time spent on data investment by job category. (Other authors rely on judgmental estimates.) They find that investment in data assets amounted to about 1 percent of business sector value added and grew at an annual rate of 4.2 percent from 2003 to 2020, little different from the growth rate of investment in other intangible assets.

5.5 Measuring the Use of IT

The use of IT in production or by consumers reduces costs in numerous ways—including in activities such as searching, transportation, tracking, and verification (Goldfarb and Tucker 2019). Furthermore, IT usage by consumers and producers created space for the emergence of online platforms and merchants often refer to as "the digital economy" (box 5.2).

This section analyzes IT inputs to production and household consump-

Box 5.2: Digital Economy Companies

The term "digital economy" is often used to refer to a set of companies that play a prominent role in digitally mediated daily life, such as Alphabet/Google and Meta/Facebook (fig. 5.11a). Thus, an assessment of the role of the digital economy in productivity should include the contribution of these digital economy companies.[1] Conventional methods capture the use of IT capital by these companies, but measuring their TFP—or efficiency in producing output—is more challenging.

Measuring the TFP of digital economy companies requires a full accounting of their output. The revenue measure of output for these companies in the national accounts includes advertising revenue—which has grown rapidly, as shown in figure 5.11b—and other revenue sources such as retail markups from e-commerce and subscription content from streaming services. Services provided to households by these companies for free are not recorded as output, and whether these services should be counted as consumption is an area of active research and debate.

These companies produce, receive from users, or purchase content such as media files (Netflix), reference information (Wikipedia), social media posts (Twitter), and reviews (Yelp). This content can be considered as data assets, including the free content received from platform users. In principle, investment in long-lived self-produced and purchased media should already be captured in the national accounts.

Digital economy companies also invest in distinctive user interfaces and back-end software connecting users to content through "recommendation engines" that take user queries and combine them with content characteristics, information on the particular user, and information about the user base as a whole to predict content likely to match the user's interests, often using machine learning (Schrage 2020; Resnick and Varian 1997). Business clients query the platforms as well, seeking the users most suited to their products. This form of intangible investment should be captured under investment in software and databases in national accounts.

1. What counts as a digital economy company? Arguably, these companies' core competency is mediation of access to the sprawling information landscape, connecting users quickly to information matching their needs. Their technology may be used to improve the matching process for items of almost any kind—goods, web pages, and images are examples—provided they can be digitally described. So, while these digital economy firms have varied product lines, they share a production process.

Each of these capital types—content, information on users, recommendation engines, and user interfaces—is a stock of intangible capital that provides a stream of capital services. Digital economy companies receive revenue from some, but not all, of the services provided to households by these assets. Only the services that users pay for, such as streaming services, are directly captured in the household consumption expenditures component of GDP.[2]

A value of consumption can be imputed for free services, such as social networking, but doing so requires simultaneously imputing both the extra output and the household income used to purchase that output. This is a requirement because one should arrive at the same estimate of GDP whether one aggregates across value added of industries in the economy, across types of expenditure, or across types of income. So if one imputes a consumption expenditure for the seemingly free services provided by websites, one must also impute the additional income that funded the spending. However, the objection to this move is that imputed income is fundamentally different in character from money income, as it cannot be saved or divided among a range of alternative consumption choices.

If the full value of the stream of services produced by the intangible capital held by digital economy companies is not accounted for in some fashion—whether revenue is generated or not—the TFP of digital economy companies will be understated and the digital economy will appear less productive than one might expect from observation of the rapid innovation at these companies.

Proposed changes to the international standards for national accounts in the 2025 System of National Accounts would provide a cost-based estimate of the value of the free services that households obtain from digital platforms in a satellite account (Digitalization Task Team 2022a). In the satellite account, households would fund imputed purchases of the platforms' free services with imputed payments received from the platforms for the data the platforms collect on them. Although the imputed value of the free services consumed by households would not be included in GDP, the platforms' investment in data assets may be included in GDP under the proposed international standards.

2. The advertising expenditures of firms purchasing advertising from digital economy companies are ultimately recovered in the sale of their final products, ensuring this portion of digital economy company output is reflected in GDP.

tion using a conceptual framework in which IT use takes the form of a flow of capital services. Treating producers' stocks of IT capital as supplying a flow of services is standard in growth accounting, and the same sort of approach can be applied to households' stocks of consumer durables like IT equipment. In addition, treating the IT capital services embodied in capital-intensive final products such as telecommunications services as directly consumed by households is convenient for analytical purposes.

Mismeasurement of IT as an input to production affects the share of productivity growth attributable to IT but does not affect measured GDP (or productivity) because GDP is calculated from data on final expenditures. In contrast, measurement errors involving final consumption—like network access services consumed by households—*do* have a direct effect on the accuracy of GDP estimates. We discuss the measurement of both types of service flows in this section.

5.5.1 Broad Measurement Issues Involving IT Capital

Estimating capital stock is the first step in measuring capital service flows because the service flow from a capital asset is estimated as the product of the value of the capital stock and the gross rate of return on that capital stock. Here, "gross" means that the rate of return includes a component that covers the cost of depreciation and other adjustments in addition to providing the required rate of return on investment. Capital stocks are built up by cumulating real investment net of depreciation, so estimating the stock of each type of capital requires data on nominal investment, a suitable investment price index, and a rate of depreciation. The main issues that affect the measurement of nominal investment have been discussed above; they are the uncertainty of estimates of own-account investment in software and the omission of own-account investment in data center equipment.[34] The issues involved in measurement of price indexes and depreciation are discussed next.

5.5.1.1 Investment Price Indexes

Investment price indexes in the US national accounts are typically estimated as a weighted average of the relevant PPI and import price index.

Using this approach, the effect of shifts between domestic and foreign sources of supply on prices paid for investment items is not captured. That is, if foreign sources of supply are cheaper and the share of investment derived from foreign sources increases, investment prices will not decline because foreign and domestic supplies are considered different goods. Houseman et al. (2011) demonstrate that this shortcoming is a first-order issue for the measurement of manufacturing inputs in the US economy; the analogous problem for IT equipment investment is likely large given the shift to offshore production in recent years. And, as discussed in section 5.6, the increases in import price indexes for IT equipment from BLS seem inconsistent with the flat or falling trends of the price indexes for domestic production, suggesting that import price indexes are underadjusting for quality change. These last two problems would cause overestimation of investment deflators and underestimation of real investment. This, in turn, could tend to cause underestimation of the contribution of IT to output and overestimation of TFP growth.

5.5.1.2 Depreciation Rates

Depreciation, broadly defined to include both physical deterioration and obsolescence, wears away the value of capital stock with the passage of time (Schreyer et al. 2009). For IT equipment, which has tended to suffer little physical deterioration over time since the advent of solid-state electronics, and for intangibles, which have no physical component, obsolescence is the preeminent driver of depreciation.

Depreciation rates in the national accounts are based on occasional studies rather than ongoing data collection (Herman et al. 2003). Prices for used equipment provide the variation needed to identify depreciation rates (Doms et al. 2004; Oliner 1993). Unfortunately, the foundational studies for IT equipment depreciation rates are somewhat out of date. In addition to differences in mix of IT equipment types, differences in rate of price change for new equipment matter, as rate of obsolescence is closely related to new equipment inflation.[35] More frequent updating of the estimation of depreciation rates is needed to account for changing conditions.[36]

Estimating the rate of obsolescence of intangible assets is a more challenging problem; no "blue book" with prices for used custom software and R&D exists. Economists have made substantial headway on the problem by clever use of financial data (company market valuations, for example) and economic modeling. Li and Hall (2020) use R&D investment data, industry output, and a model of declining contribution to profits as R&D depreciates. They find that depreciation rates for R&D in IT industries are appreciably higher than previously assumed.

5.5.2 Use of IT Capital Services by Producers

The procedure for deriving the services supplied by each type of capital begins with the construction of a capital stock time series using the perpetual inventory method. This method builds the current stock by starting from a point in the distant past and cumulating annual investment and depreciation flows. Then the gross rate of return (user cost) on capital is estimated as an interest cost adjusted for anticipated depreciation, taxes, and capital gains on the asset. The flow of capital services used as an input in production is calculated by multiplying the value of the stock of capital stock by the gross rate of return. Faster depreciation therefore implies a higher gross return and a higher ratio of capital services to capital stock, which tends to increase the weight on capital assets with a high depreciation rate in TFP calculations.

Full accounting of IT capital services and their modeled contribution to output would incorporate the electronic capital embedded in equipment of all types, not just the computing and communications equipment that constitute the standard measure of IT capital. For example, the capital service flow from transportation equipment includes various electronic systems in machinery whose capital services could be isolated and shown separately. This additional step would provide a more complete accounting of the contribution of the digital economy to growth and productivity. Importantly, it would not change overall GDP; additional contributions from IT would be treated as a separately reported part of overall capital services. Considering that about one-quarter of global semiconductor production is used in the manufacture of industrial, automotive, and military equipment and that this share has risen over time (fig. 5.12), making this calculation would be worthwhile.

5.5.3 IT Capital Services Used by Households

The network access services that enable households to visit websites, stream videos or sound, watch cable television, make phone calls, and send emails and messages are physically produced by IT capital, including networks, equipment, and software. Furthermore, many digital services supplied over the internet are themselves physically produced by a digital economy company's software, equipment, and network capital. Households can be viewed as using IT capital services when they consume telecommunication and digital services physically produced by IT capital.[37] Also, by extending the national accounts approach of owner-occupied housing to households' stocks of IT durable goods (such as smartphones and laptops), the capital services of IT consumer durable goods can be included. This approach recognizes that consumer durables yield a flow of services over their lifespan.

Network access services are the most important of the IT capital services used by households in this analytical framework, as they account for a notable share of personal consumption expenditures. Researchers have found that the real growth of network access services is being substantially understated, and alternative approaches (using data volume measures) could potentially be adopted for GDP (Byrne and Corrado 2020; Abdirahman et. al 2020). Alternative treatments of free services provided by digital economy companies and services provided by consumer IT durables also have the potential to significantly change the picture of economic growth under an expanded concept of economic activity.

5.5.3.1 Digital Network Access Services

Digital access services—including internet, mobile phone, video and audio streaming, cable television, and cloud services—comprise a large fraction of directly consumed services of IT capital of the telecommunications

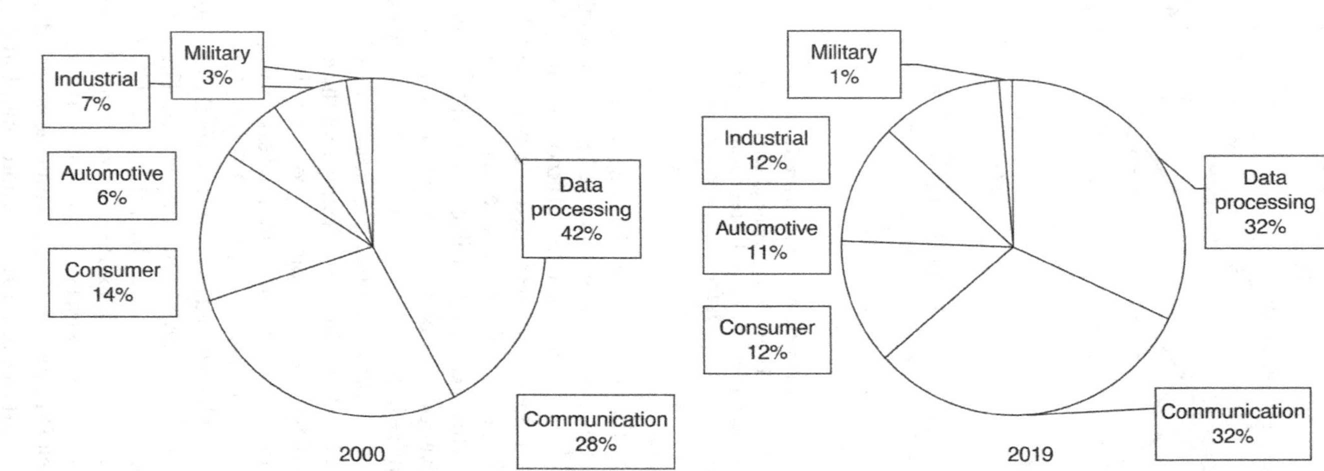

Fig. 5.12 End uses for global semiconductor production

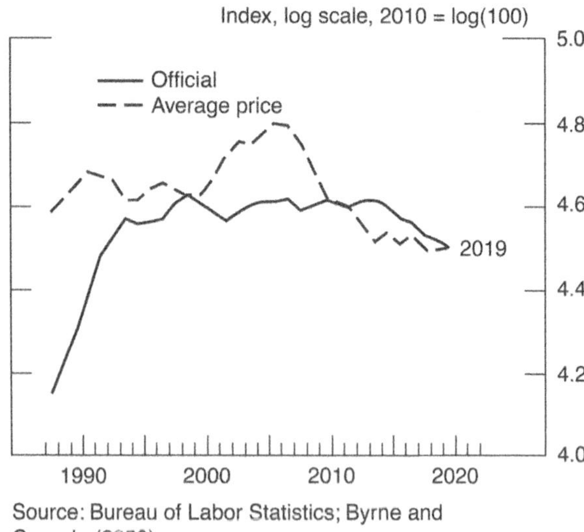

Source: Bureau of Labor Statistics; Byrne and Corrado (2020).

Fig. 5.13 Price index of consumer digital access services

Note: The average price index is a Törnqvist aggregate of service spending per user for smartphone, feature phone, internet access, cable, and three streaming services. The official price index is a Törnqvist aggregate of the CPIs for those IT services.

sector. Consequently, the falling prices of IT capital should exert downward pressure on the price of digital access services. Yet, surprisingly, an average of the official price indexes from the national accounts for various consumer digital access services as a whole (the dotted line in fig. 5.13) has been flat in recent years, implying the quality of services received per dollar spent has changed very little. This seems implausible in a world seemingly filled with digital service innovation. For comparison purposes, Byrne and Corrado (2020) construct a price index with *no adjustment for quality* by aggregating the raw average monthly price paid by households for each service and get a similarly flat index (the black line), suggesting that the price indexes in US national accounts fail to capture quality improvements.

In constructing price indexes for digital access services, the choice of quantity unit is crucial. Byrne and Corrado (2020) find that data usage per telecom service contract has soared in recent years in the United States, while contract subscription prices have been fairly stable. Thus, if the quantity of services supplied can be measured by volume of data sent or received, quality-adjusted prices for telecom services have plunged.[38] They find that their price index for digital access services falls, on average, at a similar rate to the price index for related capital assets, as would be expected from the theoretical relationship between capital services and capital stocks. In contrast, official prices use price *per contract*, and the CPI for mobile phones—though hedonically adjusted in some cases—yields a noticeably slower falling price index than does pricing per unit of data consumed.

Similarly, for video streaming services, if the quantity of services of, say, Netflix, is invariant to the number of shows actually watched, the official price indexes seem accurate, but if hours of programming consumed is the proper measure of the quantity of services consumed, prices have plunged in recent years. In effect, in the NIPAs, real consumption of streaming services is the same for a subscriber *regardless of the number of programs watched.* Edquist, Goodridge, and Haskel (2022) examine music streaming services accounting for volume of use and find a striking overstatement of inflation. Cloud services, some of which are consumed by households (to store photos and documents, for example) have rapidly falling prices as well. All told, official and alternative prices are markedly different.

5.5.3.2 Free Services

A variety of approaches have been proposed to account for free consumption of the services provided by digital companies in an expanded measure of GDP. A direct approach to determining the valuation of free services is to conduct experiments designed to elicit participants' willingness to pay. Brynjolfsson et al. (2019) fold this approach into national accounting to provide a method of constructing an expanded measure of GDP. Furthermore, proposed updates to the international standards for national accounts include a satellite account that would measure the value of free services consumed by households by cost of production.

Groshen et al. (2017) argue that consumption of these services is nonmarket activity properly excluded from GDP and that, in any case, one may reasonably expect the cost of production of these services to be reflected in the price of final goods if these platform firms are to remain solvent—Facebook receives advertising revenue, and the prices of advertised products reflect that cost. Although one may expect GDP to move sympathetically with free consumption as a result, serving as an *indicator* of free household consumption, it remains the case that households consume *both* the final good *and* the free digital platform service, which is not counted as consumption.

5.5.3.3 Consumer Durables

In conventional national accounting, residences are treated as investments that provide a stream of services to their owner. A treatment of consumer durables as also providing a stream of capital services would be consistent with the treatment of residences and theoretically sound. The argument for differing treatments is that if residences were not treated as investments, the trends, cyclical variation, and international comparisons of GDP would be distorted by movement between owning and renting. The shift in ownership of IT equipment capital stock shown in figure 5.14a poses a similar risk of distortion. Byrne and Corrado (2020) calculate the effect of capitalizing

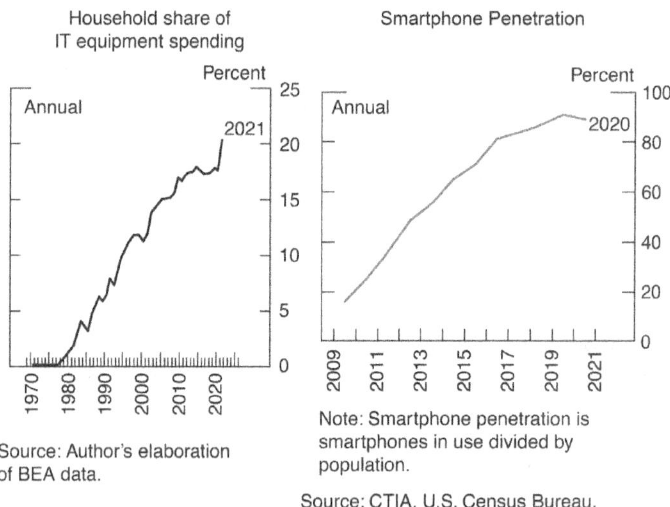

Fig. 5.14 Household IT spending

Note: Equipment spending in the figure on the left includes investment in computing, communications, and other information-processing equipment and consumption of computers, peripherals, and telephones and related equipment. The figure on the right shows smartphones in use divided by population.

this equipment and find an increasing effect on GDP growth in recent years, from a contribution of 0.06 percentage points in the 1997–2007 period to 0.17 percentage points in the 2007–2017 period.[39]

5.6 Lessons for Digital Economy Measurement

The challenges and assumptions involved in measuring IT production and IT use mean that official estimates of productivity growth must be viewed as imprecise. Moreover, estimates of growth of labor productivity related to IT are likely to be biased downward because of uncounted quality improvements, own-account production of equipment and intangible capital, and failure to capture the rapid growth of household consumption of IT capital services.

How much do these measurement issues matter and what can be done about them? We consider first the question of the productivity slowdown, apparent in figure 5.3, which techno-optimists have treated with skepticism. We then offer some concrete ideas for tackling the measurement issues at statistical agencies.

5.6.1 The Productivity Slowdown

The productivity slowdown of the 2000s has been a subject of great concern. The resumption of rapid productivity growth in the late 1990s and early 2000s turned out to be a relatively short interruption in a long era of comparatively weak productivity growth that began in the early 1970s.[40] Was such a brief hopeful interlude really all we should expect from the IT revolution?

Some observers have found the anemic reported rate of productivity growth since the mid-2000s to be implausible in light of the growing penetration of IT into economic life. For example, the smartphone-to-population ratio in the US had climbed to more than 90 percent by the tenth anniversary of the 2007 invention of the iPhone (fig. 5.14b); computing has shifted to the cloud; extensive embedded electronics give motor vehicles new safety, entertainment, and convenience features; and both video entertainment streaming services and the large digital economy companies have experienced phenomenal growth (fig. 5.11).

Yet many of the IT measurement problems discussed above, including inadequate adjustment for quality change, have existed almost as long as IT. Measurement issues present beforehand that are not getting worse cannot be the explanation for the productivity slowdown. To dismiss the productivity slowdown as measurement error, one must identify newly emerged measurement issues or reasons to believe that preexisting ones became more significant.

A few of the issues identified in this chapter fit the bill. Among these are the shift toward own-account hardware production, surging investment in data, rapidly growing consumption of free services provided by digital economy companies, and increased specialization of US domestic IT production in poorly measured intangible investment, including IT equipment designs (fig. 5.8) and special-purpose IT hardware.

In addition, embedded IT inputs such as semiconductors and software often enable new capabilities or features in types of equipment not classified as IT products, such as motor vehicles. These quality improvements may not be captured in the price indexes for the affected products, resulting in increased measurement error in real GDP as an indirect effect of the fast-growing use of IT inputs.[41] However, the slowdown in overall productivity can only be *directly* attributed to mismeasurement of IT if the mismeasurement involves products used for final consumption or investment.[42]

A coarse estimation of the magnitude of contributions to the productivity slowdown from measurement issues that directly involve IT is attempted in table 5.2, which compares productivity mismeasurement in 1996–2004 to productivity mismeasurement in 2005–2015.[43] All told, a mere 13 basis points of the 150-basis-point slowdown are attributed to increased undermeasurement of productivity caused by these issues. As should be abundantly apparent from the long discussion of challenges to IT measurement, this conclusion is highly uncertain—a point estimate with very large confidence interval, perhaps. The reasoning for each component is provided below.

Table 5.2 **Adjustments to the aggregate labor productivity slowdown, by industry (percentage points)**

Industry	Primary Issues	Adjustment
IT hardware equipment	Quality adjustment, in-house production	0.02
Semiconductors	Quality adjustment, embedded systems	–0.07
IT intangibles software	Quality adjustment, in-house production	0.08
Product design	"Factoryless" manufacturing	–0.02
Data	User and item information	unknown, likely positive
IT services telecom	Quality adjustment, utilization	0.12
Web	"Free" content	unknown, likely positive
Total adjustment	*(A moderately smaller slowdown)*	0.13 plus data investment and service effects

Source: Author's judgmental assessment as described in the text.

Note: Slowdown estimated between the 1996–2004 and 2005–2015 period. A positive adjustment figure represents raising the second period's productivity growth rate relative to the first.

- **IT equipment** production grew faster than measured due to overlooked quality change, but its weight in GDP fell. In the case of computing and communications equipment, the shift in composition toward hardware types that are more difficult to measure means that overstatement of price change would have been roughly 50 percent larger in the slowdown period if nothing else changed. But at the same time, offshoring reduced the value-added weight of IT equipment industries by almost enough to keep the contribution of mismeasurement of these industries to aggregate productivity's measurement error from growing. The effect of this source of mismeasurement on the reported productivity slowdown is therefore negligible.
- **Semiconductor** production growth becomes appreciably higher when adjusted for unmeasured quality improvements, but this has little effect on the productivity slowdown for two reasons. First, semiconductors are an intermediate input, and upward adjustments to output growth of an intermediate input come at the expense of the productivity of industries that use that input. Second, although a faster decline in semiconductor price indexes raises the growth rate of real exports, it also raises the growth rate of real imports. Because trade in semiconductors is nearly balanced, revising their price indexes has little net effect on GDP growth. However, the growth of semiconductor production was *more* understated before the slowdown, and adjusting for this slightly *increases* the size of the productivity slowdown.
- **Software** and IT product design R&D investment is difficult to assess. While Byrne and Corrado (2017a) note that the bias in prepackaged software inflation has worsened, the bulk of investment is in own-account software and custom software, for which inflation estimates are highly uncertain. R&D inflation rates present a similar challenge.

- **Data** is currently not recorded as an asset in national accounts. An estimate of the value of data is not attempted here. Moderation of the productivity slowdown from this source seems a natural expectation in light of the burgeoning digital economy. However, it bears repeating that an *acceleration* in data investment is needed to mitigate the slowdown, and while the level of data investment was clearly lower prior to the slowdown, as seen in figure 5.1b, growth in stored data was rapid prior to the slowdown as well.
- **IT services** have a noteworthy effect on the productivity slowdown. Adjusting the estimates of real digital access services, as discussed above, reduces the slowdown by 12 basis points. Other information services, such as the cloud, constitute a much smaller share of consumption and have little effect on the slowdown.
- **Free digital economy company services** consumed by households—which have grown in importance in recent years—may be expected to have a moderating effect on the productivity slowdown if an estimate of their value were added to the real GDP. An estimate of the value of these services is not attempted here. Again, as noted in the bullet on data above, free service consumption would need to have accelerated, not just risen.

The resulting revision to the slowdown is modestly different from the effect found by Byrne, Fernald, and Reinsdorf (2016), who found that understatement of IT durables production was substantial but had not gotten worse during the slowdown. The present study adds estimates of issues not quantified in the earlier work, including product design, data investment, and telecommunications services. Of these, telecommunications service production is the only correction that materially affects the conclusion.[44]

5.6.2 Recommendations for Addressing the Measurement Challenges

To improve measurement of the production and use of IT and its effects on productivity, statistical agencies could use new methods for quality adjustment, improve data granularity, and better coordinate among the programs that produce the various types of data needed to calculate productivity growth, ensuring consistency, better international harmonization of detailed methods, and international comparability of the growth statistics.

5.6.2.1 Accounting for Quality Change

Some recently introduced methods have the potential to make quality adjustment of prices of IT products more accurate or more likely to take place when needed. Benchmark test scores (which summarize the amount of time it takes a chip to complete a battery of common computing tasks) for IT products such as semiconductors have the potential to improve hedonic models, and regular checks for evidence of bias using market share information and private data from IT consulting companies should enable price index compilers to identify problem areas quickly.

Benchmark performance scores should be more widely utilized as a measure of quality in constructing hedonic price indexes for IT equipment such as semiconductors. They provide a direct measure of relevant aspects of performance.[45] Quality adjustments of prices of IT capital have traditionally been based on physical characteristics, such as the clock speed of MPUs. However, physical features may not have a strong, stable relationship with the aspects of performance that matter to the product's buyers.[46] If benchmark scores on relevant tasks are available, they will allow price analysts to take a more direct approach to controlling for quality, as benchmark tests are usually designed to represent common uses for equipment. Examples of electronic products with benchmark scores that still lack plausible price indexes are graphics processor units (GPUs), used in a host of computing applications, and industrial robots, a class of special-purpose equipment.

Machine learning (ML) techniques have emerged as a valuable tool for constructing quality-adjusted price indexes from large datasets with product prices and descriptions.[47] Identifying price-determining equipment characteristics and developing a satisfactory model of how they affect price are time-consuming processes. ML has the potential to speed up the process, lower its cost, and improve the accuracy of hedonic indexes, enabling much wider use of hedonic techniques. ML offers an opportunity to expand the types of characteristics used in quality adjustment as well.[48] A drawback of ML approaches for sensitive, published statistics is their limited interpretability.[49]

Market share information about products and services has increasingly been exploited to provide insight into product valuations (Feenstra 1994; Redding and Weinstein 2020). In particular, an opportunity to structurally identify constant-quality price trends is provided by changes in product market shares under the assumption that these shifts reflect choice behavior in response to changing relative prices. Using data with simultaneous prices and volumes at a high level of detail, Ehrlich et al. (2019) demonstrate the feasibility of this approach. A methodological challenge that remains to be addressed is the heavy influence of structural assumptions about the demand system on resulting price indexes. Because statistical agencies typically collect market share information independently of price surveys, at a lower frequency, and at a lower level of product granularity, this technique is of limited use except in conjunction with an expansion of statistical programs or use of alternative data sources.

5.6.2.2 Data Granularity

New and traditional measurement techniques can be made more effective by leveraging commercially available point-of-sale information and incorporating more administrative data. In addition, a reorientation of business surveys toward collecting multiple items of interest—such as prices for both inputs and outputs—in a single survey would be beneficial for productivity analysis.

Point-of-sale data, whether scanner data collected in stores or data "scraped" from retail websites, expand the range of feasible areas of price measurement research and may be a supplemental data source for official price measurement programs.[50] The use of point-of-sale data, collected by barcode scanners in retail establishments, is hardly new in economics, dating at least back to Guadagni and Little (1983). However, fully exploiting scanner data to produce constant-quality price indexes at scale remains a work in progress.[51] Ehrlich et al. (2019) demonstrate the feasibility of an array of price index techniques with scanner data, including hedonic indexes with no manual curation of the hedonic regression for each product. Further, they exploit current period expenditure weights, product characteristics, and comprehensive (not sampled) coverage of available products.[52] New avenues for price collection via the internet include projects to refine price estimation across a wide range of products, such as electronics.[53]

Like scanner data, web-scraped data has the appeal of high-frequency observations, product characteristics information, and extensive product coverage. However, it lacks weights indicating how often products are sold at the observed prices, if at all. And, though freely available (subject to website license restrictions), web-scraped data requires extensive knowledge of the price posting practices of the online source to be effectively employed.

Administrative data provided by corporations to statistical agencies has improved measurement of prices for such items as prescription drugs (Konny, William, and Friedman 2019). In particular, real-time information on the volume of items sold at a particular price is a noteworthy improvement over agency survey measures, which typically collect prices alone and rely on less frequent surveys to provide weights. Konny, William, and Friedman (2019) discuss the challenges that statistical agencies face when working with corporate administrative data (as well as scanner and web-scraped data).

Regular firm-level production surveys on inputs to production (values and prices) and outputs (values and prices) would be invaluable, addressing many of the shortcomings of the current measurement system for productivity analysis.[54] Such surveys would enable the construction of indexes of prices paid by buyers for investment goods and intermediate inputs, *which are not currently produced by the US statistical system*.[55] Absent this sort of information at the firm level, a host of assumptions is needed to study the impact of firm dynamics—entry, exit, expansion—on productivity (Foster et al. 2019).

5.6.2.3 *Consistency of Definitions and Methods*

Productivity analysis requires a diverse array of economic data drawn from many corners of the statistical system, which is fragmented across

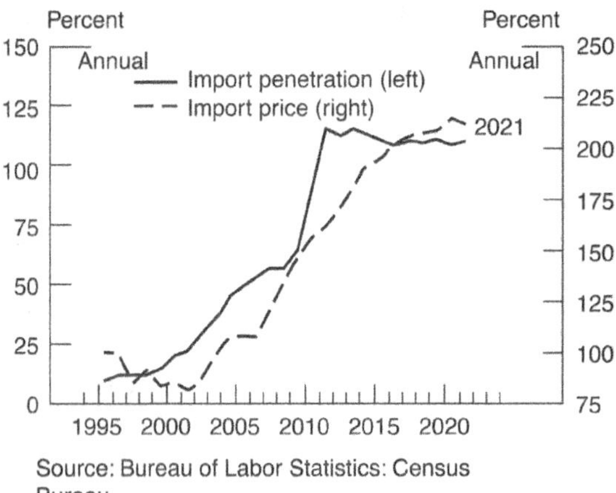

Fig. 5.15 Computer import penetration and prices

Note: Computer import price is the ratio of the computer import price index to the computer (domestic) producer price index. Import penetration is the ratio of imports to imports plus domestic production less exports.

multiple agencies in the case of the US. Inconsistencies within the system of statistics often occur. One area of inconsistency in particular need of attention is the price index used for imports of IT goods and services. A massive shift in US spending on computing equipment toward imports occurred from 2000 to 2010, when import penetration rose from minimal to nearly complete (the dotted line in fig. 5.15). At the same time, the ratio of the US import price index to the (domestic) PPI, an indicator of the relative price of imports, roughly doubled (the solid line). A tension of this magnitude between relative prices and consumer behavior sustained over a long period—a pronounced shift toward a reportedly higher-priced alternative—is puzzling. Although other factors may be in play, this tension suggests the presence of inconsistent price measurement across separate BLS programs that produce prices for imports and domestic production.

Similarly, inconsistencies appear between flat digital service prices (fig. 5.13) and rising digital traffic volume (fig. 5.1b), between prices for different types of electronic equipment (fig. 5.9b), and between measures of mobile phone prices around the world (fig. 5.8a). Regular comparisons of price behavior between related items would help reveal weaknesses in estimates that could be prioritized for methodological improvements and harmonization.

Input prices are used to measure the deflator for investment in own-account and custom software. These are derived from the hourly cost or price of labor inputs and other inputs, with adjustment for an assumed rate of TFP growth (Grimm, Moulton, and Wasshausen 2009). A similar approach based on input costs could provide a useful plausibility check, or even a replacement, for the methods currently used for output deflators for special-purpose IT equipment (table 5.1). Quality-adjusted prices are hard to measure for this type of equipment. An adjustment for productivity growth would be needed, but fortunately, in the electronics industry, a wide array of products are designed and assembled under similar conditions by a small set of contract manufacturing firms. Estimates of TFP growth from products where both inputs *and* outputs are well measured, such as personal computers, may serve as plausible indicators for TFP growth in the production of a host of electronic devices that lack plausible output indexes.

Capital asset and service prices are, in theory, closely tied to one another (Jorgenson and Griliches 1967). In the presence of sufficient competition, prices for IT investment and IT services should generally move sympathetically. This expected relationship can be used to check the plausibility of price indexes of capital-intensive IT services. Byrne and Corrado (2020) do so for digital access services (internet, mobile phone, cable TV, and streaming) and demonstrate that the flat price indexes for digital access services in recent years are inconsistent with the theoretical cost of services of capital assets of the industry.

The global supply chain for electronic equipment is highly integrated, so there is little room for differences in production costs to explain the wide cross-country variation in inflation for mobile phones shown in figure 5.7a and in implied quality growth for semiconductors shown in figure 5.7b. These examples suggest that national statistical agencies could improve measurement through harmonization of methods and investigation of cases of widely divergent price indexes.

5.7 Summary and Conclusion

Rather than attempting to define a boundary for the digital economy in a world where nearly everything seems digitized, this chapter has focused on the measurement challenges involving production and use of IT that may affect estimates of real GDP growth. Although many of these challenges tend to result in underestimation of productivity growth, the suspected sources of measurement error that emerged or worsened around the time of slowdown—which include unmeasured own-account production of IT equipment, software, and data assets and underestimation of the rapid growth of household consumption of digital access services—can explain only a small fraction of the 2 percentage point slowdown in US labor productivity growth that started in the mid-2000s.

Some steps that would yield substantial progress on these IT measurement challenges have also been identified. These range from use of private datasets based on transaction data (big data) and of ML techniques in hedonic quality adjustments to the more mundane regular reestimation of IT depreciation rates. Finally, as IT supply chains sprawl across the globe, harmonizing measurement procedures and aligning the mirror import and export prices from pairs of trading partners could improve the measurement of IT. Indeed, in light of the global nature of production and the long time it has taken for IT innovations to show through to aggregate productivity, harmonization of statistics across space and time is essential to understanding the digital economy.

Taking this long perspective, many questions emerge. When should we consider the IT revolution to have started—how important were innovations prior to the solid-state transistor? How does the IT revolution compare to the rollout of earlier general-purpose technologies like electricity? Is the IT revolution losing its impetus? How much of the productivity boom in the late 1990s can be attributed to IT? To what extent is the slowdown since the boom overstated because we are mismeasuring IT? Is the United States special, or do we just measure the economy differently—how has the IT revolution played out in productivity in other countries? What effect has industrial policy had on the pace of the IT revolution and the location of various links in the global supply chain?

Most of these questions are difficult to tackle with the statistics in hand. Cross-country comparisons and a full historical understanding of the IT revolution are not currently possible, for example. That said, with the radical increase in mobile data use, the shift to cloud computing, the explosion of data investment, and the advances in artificial intelligence in recent years, it seems clear that the IT revolution is not over; whether we are capturing the latest developments is less clear. Reports of a productivity slowdown since the mid-2000s are not false, though at least a modest amount of the slowdown is spurious due to IT measurement problems.

Appendix

Growth Accounting

The mathematics of the decomposition of economic growth and productivity into contributions from the digital economy and other factors is laid out in this appendix, serving to clarify exactly which economic quantities need to be measured. The growth accounting approach exploits the fact that in the presence of competitive markets and an assumption about production (namely, constant returns to scale), economic growth at an aggregate level can be decomposed into contributions from inputs to production weighted by income shares plus contribution from the efficiency with which inputs are combined to produce outputs (Solow 1956; Jorgenson and Griliches 1967; Hulten 2010).

Under these assumptions, we can write production as a function of labor input, IT capital services, and other capital services,

$$(1) \qquad Y = \mu F(L, T, K),$$

where μ is total factor productivity (TFP), which is assumed to shift the production capacity of the economy proportionally regardless of the mix of inputs.[56]

The growth rate (represented by a dot) of output per hour worked, $\dot{y} = \dot{Y} - \dot{H}$, is a linear combination of TFP growth and growth in inputs *per unit of labor*, weighted by income shares (α):

$$(2) \qquad \dot{y} = \dot{\mu} - \alpha_L \dot{q} + \alpha_T \dot{t} + \alpha_K \dot{k}.$$

Here, $\dot{t} = \dot{T} - \dot{L}$ represents IT capital deepening (the growth in IT capital per worker), $\dot{k} = \dot{K} - \dot{L}$ represents other capital deepening,and $\dot{q} = \dot{L} - \dot{H}$ represents labor quality growth. The contribution of digitalization—the use of IT capital throughout the economy—to productivity is accounted for through $\alpha_T \dot{t}$.

The effect of changes in the efficiency of IT capital production—the portion of $\dot{\mu}$ contributed by the IT industry—is isolated by decomposing total output into the sum of the value added of IT capital goods production and the production all other goods and services, X.[57] Assuming each sector produces according to a production function with separable TFP, TFP growth for the economy as a whole is the suitably aggregated productivity growth in the component industries:

$$(3) \qquad \dot{\mu} = \delta_T \dot{\mu}_T + \delta_X \dot{\mu}_X,$$

where the weights, δ, correspond to the gross output of the sector divided by aggregate value added for the economy and account for both the direct contribution of the industry and the indirect effect via the use of its output in other industries (Domar 1961; Hulten 2010).

The contribution of the digital economy to labor productivity growth, $\dot{y}_D$, can be written as the sum of contribution from IT capital production and contribution of IT capital deepening:

$$(4) \qquad \dot{Y}_D = \delta_T \dot{\mu}_T + \alpha_T \dot{t}.$$

To calculate the TFP of the IT production industry, found in the first term on the right side of equation (4), requires real output of IT and associated factor inputs. Industry inputs are readily available from the national accounts, as are nominal input and the industry price index.

To calculate the weight component of the contribution of IT capital deepening, α_T in the second term, requires a capital service price, the user cost of capital. Abstracting from the effect of taxes, the user cost, r_T is a function of the investment price for IT capital, P_T^I, the depreciation rate for IT capital

d_T, the risk-free rate of return, i, and the inflation rate for IT assets, $\dot{P}_t$ (Jorgenson and Griliches 1967):

$$(5) \qquad r_T = (i + d_T - \dot{P}_T^I)P_T^I$$

Among these terms, debate over the accuracy of productivity measurement centers around the accuracy of the industry price index for IT and the price index for IT investment, which are closely related. (The rate of depreciation receives less attention, though it merits examination.)

Note that the capital terms are service flows, not stocks. The product of user cost of capital and stock of capital yields the capital service flow used in the calculation of the IT contribution:

$$(6) \qquad T = r_T \kappa_t,$$

where κ_t is the stock of IT capital, which is typically not measured directly but follows from information on investment flows via the perpetual inventory method,

$$(7) \qquad \kappa_t = \kappa_{t-1}(1 - \delta_t) + I_t.$$

where I_t is investment at time t.

Notes

1. For other indicators, such as the effects of digitalization on human capital accumulation, income inequality, and R&D, see OECD 2020.
2. In the interest of brevity, we focus on the US economy. For a global perspective, see OECD 2020.
3. Visualizations were created using R (R Core Team 2021) supplemented with packages *wordcloud*, *policyPlot*, and *tidyverse* (Capital Markets et al. 2017; Pennec and Slowikowski 2019; Wickham et al. 2019).
4. See Oliner and Sichel 2000; Jorgenson, Ho, and Stiroh 2003. For analysis of other countries, see Ark, Inklaar, and McGuckin 2003; Gordon and Sayed 2019.
5. Byrne, Oliner, and Sichel (2013) estimate the effects of IT on productivity directly and the non–IT contributions as the residual amount of GDP growth not explained by the effects of IT.
6. Details of the growth accounting approach are laid out in the appendix.
7. Because industries use one another's outputs as intermediate inputs, aggregating to economy-wide productivity requires summation using Domar weights rather than a straight sum of industry-level TFP. See discussion in the appendix.
8. Analysis of productivity at the level of individual firms and plants is a growing field of work not covered here. Syverson (2011) is a discussion of early work in this area. Foster et al. (2019) demonstrate the deeper insights into the dynamics of productivity growth that come from drilling down to the firm level.
9. See the discussion of the computer market in Dulberger (2007), for example.
10. In some circumstances, a menu of option prices is available with which one can construct a hypothetical price in the pre-entry period without resorting to re-

gression analysis. Personal computer manufacturers often provide system "configurators" on their websites, for example.

11. A hedonic index may adequately adjust for quality change even when the full set of price-determining characteristics is rarely available. As Griliches (1961) notes, discussing motor vehicles, "only a few of the observed quality changes come in discrete lumps with an attached price tag."

12. Whether price dynamics within product cycles *should* be reflected in aggregate price indexes is a matter of judgment. It may not be appropriate to link prices paid by early adopters and late adopters, for example (Williams and Sager 2019). See the discussion of the choice between unit values (average prices), which obscure life cycle dynamics, and matched-model indexes in Silver (2010).

13. Annual basket updating is more frequent than is typical for statistical agencies. Importantly, the annual basket index outperforms the average price index, which roughly moves sideways in the period shown. Considering that these processors are distinguished from one another almost entirely by one characteristic—clock speed—and that the last model introduced performed calculations nearly three times as fast as the first, the unit value index is clearly unsuitable.

14. Note that even with comprehensive data, conventional indexes may fall short. Byrne, Oliner, and Sichel (2018) show that even in the presence of comprehensive model-level data, when incumbent prices do not respond to new model entry, matched-model indexes will perform poorly.

15. The statistical sampling process accounts for lagged differences in relative importance across models to some degree, but these implicit weights remain static between samples.

16. For plant-level productivity, analysis has yielded useful insights in recent years but has even greater data demands. Analysts must collect or estimate input-output relationships at the plant level.

17. This is partly a by-product of market structure. IBM dominated the mainframe industry, limiting the audience for market studies. With the introduction of the IBM PC "clone" market, a flurry of manufacturers entered the business, creating a need for market research that could be exploited for productivity measurement. Further complicating the measurement exercise, IBM marketed mainframe time bundled with other services, making zeroing in on the price of the computer itself difficult.

18. On cross-country consistency in IT measurement, see Ahmad, Ribarsky, and Reinsdorf (2017).

19. See the discussion of this activity in Doherty (2013), Kamal, Moulton, and Ribarsky (2013), and Bayard, Byrne, and Smith (2015).

20. These figures are based on data from the 2019 *Reed Yearbook of World Electronics Data.*

21. Long before the effect of data processing on productivity came to the foreground, economists had begun to account for the rising efficiency of computing in academic research on prices and to incorporate falling price-to-performance ratios for computers into economic statistics (Chow 1967; Cartwright 1986). The BEA, in collaboration with IBM, introduced performance-adjusted price indexes to the national accounts for computing equipment in 1985, with coverage beginning in 1972. Later work pushed coverage back to 1959.

22. See, for example, Berndt and Rappaport (2001), Chwelos (2003), and Pakes (2003).

23. See the data on large-scale computing from the TOP500 project, available at http://www.top500.org. Wu et al. (2018) construct a hedonic price index for Amazon Web Services (AWS) computation products that falls at an annual rate of

20 percent, on average, between 2008 and 2017. Byrne, Corrado, and Sichel (2017), using a smaller set of controls, find AWS computation prices fell at an annual rate of 7 percent between 2009 and 2016, with some acceleration coinciding with the entry of Microsoft into the market. Coyle et al. (2018) find computation prices in the United Kingdom fell at annual rates ranging from 6 to 22 percent between 2010 and 2018 depending on the type of compute product considered. Cloud computing, which allows more efficient use of IT capital assets, is difficult to analyze because much of the infrastructure is built by the provider rather than purchased at arm's length. See the discussion in Byrne, Corrado, and Sichel (2018a).

24. See the seminal work on data networking and transmission in Doms (2009) and analysis of prices for the entire scope of communications equipment in Byrne and Corrado (2015).

25. During the first three years after BLS began publication of this CPI, it fell at an annual rate of 18.4 percent. In communication with the author, analysts have confirmed that the index's behavior resembles that of Aizcorbe, Byrne, and Sichel (2020).

26. Work is underway on satellites at BEA (Highfill and MacDonald 2022).

27. These prices from the GDP-by-industry accounts differ from PPIs published by BLS in that BEA supplements BLS producer prices with internal price research results and communications equipment prices produced by the Federal Reserve Board. Strassner and Wasshausen (2017) outline the IT equipment prices in use and under development for national accounts in the United States.

28. The share of electronics in the intermediate inputs used in special-purpose equipment manufacturing was 10.8 percent in 2012, the latest year for which data is available from BEA input-output tables, and the share for general-purpose electronics was 15.5 percent.

29. See, for example, Grimm (1998), Holdway (2000), and Aizcorbe, Corrado, and Doms (2003).

30. According to data published by the Semiconductor Industry Association, production of memory chips and microprocessors—the well-measured semiconductors—has accounted for under 40 percent of global production in recent years.

31. Byrne and Corrado (2017b) review the literature on software price measurement.

32. The debate over approaches to quantifying software productivity—lines of code, "function points," and many others—is discussed in Berlin et al. (2009).

33. Additional categories of intangibles not currently included in the accounts, using the taxonomy of Corrado, Hulten, and Sichel (2009) as updated by Corrado (chap. 3 in this book), are attributed designs (industrial), financial product development, brand and market research, business processes and organizational practices, and employer-provided training.

34. This own-account investment in equipment is only partially missed in US national accounts because BEA treats some purchases of data center operators labeled as electronic components as equipment and may include the in-house design of this equipment in R&D investment.

35. Byrne, Dunn, and Pinto (2016) show that depreciation rates for tablet PCs differ from those used in the national accounts.

36. Giandrea et al. (2021) show that substituting depreciation rates estimated by Statistics Canada, which were more recently estimated than those in the US accounts, would noticeably reduce estimates of US capital stock.

37. By treating households as users of IT capital services, this approach unpacks the production process of the standard growth accounting framework, in which

capital services are inputs into firms' production of outputs (such as telecommunications services) supplied to customers.

38. Abdirahman et al. (2020a, 2020b, 2022) find similar results for the United Kingdom.

39. See discussion of alternative approaches to capitalizing consumer durables in Karz (1983) and a vision of more complete, internally consistent national accounts in Jorgenson and Landefeld (2007).

40. Baily et al. (1988), among many others, were puzzled over the productivity slowdown already in the 1980s and explored many of the measurement issues discussed in the present chapter.

41. The BLS price indexes for new motor vehicles incorporate cost-based adjustments for quality changes, but these may not fully capture value to consumers. These adjustments accounted for about one-third the new model year price increase for cars and one-quarter of the price increase for light trucks from 2014 to 2023.

42. Mismeasurement of exports and imports of IT materials used as inputs in production matters for estimates of GDP growth and aggregate productivity growth.

43. Fernald (2015) identifies 2004 as the break point between productivity regimes.

44. Byrne, Fernald, and Reinsdorf (2016) discuss the issue in terms of final expenditure components of GDP rather than industry components and, consequently, do not include measures of the production of IT components directly in their calculations. In principle, they would have arrived at the same estimates had they taken an industry approach, but empirical estimates of GDP growth based on the industry and final expenditure approaches do not always match despite theoretical equivalence.

45. Ohta and Griliches (1976) state succinctly that "ideally, quality adjustments should be based on performance variables, which presumably enter the utility function directly, not physical characteristics." See extensive discussion of computer performance and benchmarks in Jorgenson and Wessner (2005), especially Triplett (2005) in that volume.

46. Clock speed for high performance MPUs is a well-known example of a breakdown in the relationship between physical characteristics and performance. Advances in clock speed stalled in the early 2000s, yet performance continued to climb (Byrne, Oliner, and Sichel 2018).

47. Ehrlich et al. (2019) and Bajari et al. (2021) use ML for model specification. Illustrating the feasibility of ML for statistical agencies, the BLS has recently adopted an ML approach to model selection in its PPI for MPUs, allowing it to be agnostic about which characteristics to employ as it controls for quality change (Sawyer and So 2018).

48. Ehrlich et al. (2019) use supervised learning to group products according to product description codes that would be unintelligible to human analysts. Bajari et al. (2021) discern product characteristics in the unstructured text descriptions and images available in listings on Amazon.com using unsupervised ML—without guidance from the analyst.

49. For example, a quality adjustment based on ML that reduces the consumer price for reasons that cannot be explained might not win public acceptance. Lipton (2018) discusses formalization of the "interpretability" concept. Athey (2019) notes that issues of fairness, nondiscrimination, and manipulability of ML models naturally arise.

50. After many years of analysis, the data from IT consultancies and product catalogs used in many price studies have fewer and fewer secrets left to reveal. Also,

in the case of IT, point-of-sale data does not have exhaustive coverage. Data is available for data processing consumer durables as well as high-volume, moderately priced business equipment like PCs but typically not for high-priced items such as large-scale computing equipment and special-purpose electronics.

51. Feenstra and Shapiro (2003) noted these data provide a "tidal wave of information" but are only now becoming manageable after nearly 20 years of improvement in computing efficiency and development of big data techniques. An early example of their use is Reinsdorf (1999).

52. Updated results are available in Ehrlich et al. (2021).

53. Examples include the Billion Prices Project (http://www.thebillionpricesproject.com) and the Adobe Digital Economy Index (https://business.adobe.com/ru/resources/digital-economy-index.html).

54. Quarterly frequency collection would suffice, as this is the level at which productivity statistics are produced by the BLS, and higher-frequency data on a slow-moving process is unnecessary.

55. The weighted average of production and import indexes currently used for investment omits consequential effects of substitution toward imported intermediates (Houseman et al. 2011).

56. This "Hicks-neutral" technology parameter assumes that innovation is not biased in favor of any particular input to production.

57. X includes non−IT capital K and final goods and services.

References

Abdirahman, Mohamed, Diane Coyle, Richard Heys, and Will Stewart. 2020. "A Comparison of Deflators for Telecommunications Services Output." *Economie et Statistique / Economics and Statistics* 517 (1): 103–22.

Abdirahman, Mohamed, Diane Coyle, Richard Heys, and Will Stewart. 2022. "Telecoms Deflators: A Story of Volume and Revenue Weights." *Economie et Statistique / Economics and Statistics* 530 (31): 43–49. https://www.insee.fr/en/statistiques/6328083?sommaire=6328099.

Ahmad, Nadim, Jennifer Ribarsky, and Marshall B. Reinsdorf. 2017. "Can Potential Mismeasurement of the Digital Economy Explain the Post-Crisis Slowdown in GDP and Productivity Growth?" OECD Statistics Working Papers, 2017/09.

Aizcorbe, Ana M., David M. Byrne, and Daniel E. Sichel. 2020. "Getting Smart about Phones: New Price Indexes and the Allocation of Spending Between Devices and Services Plans in Personal Consumption Expenditures." In *Measuring Economic Growth and Productivity*, edited by Barbara Fraumeni, 387–411. Cambridge, MA: Academic Press/Elsevier.

Aizcorbe, Ana M., Carol A. Corrado, and Mark E. Doms. 2003. "When do Matched-Model and Hedonic Techniques Yield Similar Measures?" FRB of San Francisco Working Paper 2003–14.

Aizcorbe, Ana M., and Yvon Pho. 2005. "Differences in Hedonic and Matched-Model Price Indexes: Do the Weights Matter?" Bureau of Economic Analysis Working Paper WP2005–06, September. https://www.bea.gov/system/files/papers/WP2005-6.pdf.

Ark, Bart van, Robert Inklaar, and Robert H. McGuckin. 2003. "ICT and Productivity in Europe and the United States Where Do the Differences Come From?" *CESifo Economic Studies* 49 (3): 295–318.

Athey, Susan. 2019. "The Impact of Machine Learning on Economics." In *The Economics of Artificial Intelligence: An Agenda*, edited by Ajay Agrawal, Joshua Gans, and Avi Goldfarb, 507–52. Chicago: University of Chicago Press.

Baily, Martin Neil, Robert J. Gordon, William D. Nordhaus, and David Romer. 1988. "The Productivity Slowdown, Measurement Issues, and the Explosion of Computer Power." *Brookings Papers on Economic Activity* 1988 (2): 347–431.

Bajari, Patrick L., Zhihao Cen, Victor Chernozhukov, Manoj Manukonda, Jin Wang, Ramon Huerta, Junbo Li, Ling Leng, George Monokroussos, Suhas Vijaykunar, and Shan Wan. 2021. "Hedonic Prices and Quality Adjusted Price Indices Powered by AI." Technical Report, CEMMAP Working Paper CWP04/21. https://www.cemmap.ac.uk/wp-content/uploads/2021/02/CWP0421-Hedonic-prices-and-quality-adjusted-price-indices-powered-by-AI-1.pdf.

Barefoot, Kevin, Dave Curtis, William Jolliff, Jessica R. Nicholson, and Robert Omohundro. 2018. *Defining and Measuring the Digital Economy*. Washington, DC: US Department of Commerce, Bureau of Economic Analysis.

Bayard, Kimberly, David M. Byrne, and Dominic Smith. 2015. "The Scope of U.S. 'Factoryless Manufacturing.'" In *Measuring Globalization: Better Trade Statistics for Better Trade Policy*, edited by Susan Houseman and Michael Mandel, 81–120. Kalamazoo, MI: Upjohn Press.

Berlin, Stanislav, Tzvi Raz, Chanan Glezer, and Moshe Zviran. 2009. "Comparison of Estimation Methods of Cost and Duration in IT Projects." *Information and Software Technology* 51 (4): 738–48.

Berndt, Ernst R., and Neal J. Rappaport. 2001. "Price and Quality of Desktop and Mobile Personal Computers: A Quarter-Century Historical Overview." *American Economic Review* 91 (2): 268–73.

Bi, Z. M., Zhonghua Miao, Bin Zhang, and Chris W. J. Zhang. 2020. "The State of the Art of Testing Standards for Integrated Robotic Systems." *Robotics and Computer-Integrated Manufacturing* 63, 101893.

Brynjolfsson, Erik, Avinash Collis, W. Erwin Diewert, Felix Eggers, and Kevin J. Fox. 2019. *GDP-B: Accounting for the Value of New and Free Goods in the Digital Economy*. Technical Report, National Bureau of Economic Research.

Byrne, David M. 2015. "Domestic Electronics Manufacturing: Medical, Military, and Aerospace Equipment and What June 2. Washington, DC: Board of Governors of the Federal Reserve System (US).

Byrne, David M. 2019. "The Mysterious Cross-Country Dispersion in Mobile Phone Price Trends." *National Institute Economic Review* 249 (1): R39–R46.

Byrne, David M., and Carol A. Corrado. 2015. "Prices for Communications Equipment: Rewriting the Record." *Finance and Economics Discussion Series (FEDS)* 2015–069. Washington, DC: Board of Governors of the Federal Reserve System (US).

Byrne, David M., and Carol A. Corrado. 2017a. "ICT Asset Prices: Marshaling Evidence into New Measures." Finance and Economics Discussion Series (FEDS) 2017–016. Washington, DC: Board of Governors of the Federal Reserve System (US.).

Byrne, David M., and Carol A. Corrado. 2017b. "ICT Services and Their Prices: What Do They Tell Us about Productivity and Technology?" *International Productivity Monitor* 22 (33): 150–86.

Byrne, David M., and Carol A. Corrado. 2018. "Accounting for Innovation in Consumer Digital Services: IT Still Matters." Technical Report, National Bureau of Economic Research Working Paper 26010, revised 2020.

Byrne, David M., and Carol A. Corrado. 2020. "The Increasing Deflationary Influence of Consumer Digital Access Services." *Economics Letters* 196.

Byrne, David, Carol Corrado, and Daniel Sichel. 2017. "The Rise of Cloud Computing: Minding Your Ps, Qs and Ks." In *Measuring and Accounting for Innovation in the 21st Century*, edited by Carol A. Corrado, Jonathan Haskel, Javier Miranda, and Daniel E. Sichel, 519–551. Chicago: University of Chicago Press.

Byrne, David M., Wendy E. Dunn, and Eugenio Pinto. 2016. "Prices and Depreciation in the Market for Tablet Computers." *FEDS Notes*, December 5. Washington, DC: Board of Governors of the Federal Reserve System (US).

Byrne, David M., John G. Fernald, and Marshall B. Reinsdorf. 2016. "Does the United States Have a Productivity Slowdown or a Measurement Problem?" *Brookings Papers on Economic Activity* 2016 (1): 109–82.

Byrne, David M., Stephen D. Oliner, and Daniel E. Sichel. 2013. "Is the Information Technology Revolution Over?" *International Productivity Monitor* 25 (Spring): 20–37.

Byrne, David M., Stephen D. Oliner, and Daniel E. Sichel. 2018. "How Fast Are Semiconductor Prices Falling?" *Review of Income and Wealth* 64 (3): 679–702.

Calderón, José Bayóan Santiago, Dylan G. Rassier, et al. 2022. "Valuing the US Data Economy Using Machine Learning and Online Job Postings." NBER Books and Chapters. https://www.nber.org/books-and-chapters/technology-productivity-and-economic-growth/valuing-us-data-economy-using-machine-learning-and-online-job-postings.

Capital Markets section of the Research and Statistics division of the Federal Reserve Board and Collin Harkrader. 2023. *policyPlot: Functions to make easy Tealbook style plots* (software).

Cartwright, David W. 1986. "Improved Deflation of Purchases of Computers." *Survey of Current Business* 66, March, 7–10.

Chow, Gregory C. 1967. "Technological Change and the Demand for Computers." *American Economic Review* 57 (5): 1117–130.

Chwelos, Paul. 2003. "Approaches to Performance Measurement in Hedonic Analysis: Price Indexes for Laptop Computers in the 1990's." *Economics of Innovation and New Technology* 12 (3): 199–224.

Corrado, Carol, Jonathan Haskel, Massimiliano Iommi, and Cecilia Jona-Lasinio. 2022. "Measuring Data as an Asset: Framework, Methods and Preliminary Estimates." OECD Economics Department Working Paper No. 1731. https://doi.org/10.1787/b840fb01-en.

Corrado, Carol, Jonathan Haskel, Cecilia Jona-Lasinio, and Massimiliano Iommi. 2022. "Intangible Capital and Modern Economies." *Journal of Economic Perspectives* 36 (3): 3–28.

Corrado, Carol A., Charles R. Hulten, and Daniel E. Sichel. 2009. "Intangible Capital and U.S. Economic Growth." *Review of Income and Wealth* 55 (3): 661–85.

Coyle, Diane, David Nguyen, et al. 2018. "Cloud Computing and National Accounting." Economic Statistics Centre of Excellence Discussion Paper 2019.

Digitalization Task Team. 2022. "Recording and Valuing 'Free' Products in an SNA Satellite Account." Guidance Note DZ.4. https://unstats.un.org/unsd/nationalaccount/aeg/2022/M20/M20_4_DZ3_DZ4.pdf.

Doherty, Maureen. 2013. "Reflecting Factoryless Goods Production in the U.S. Statistical System." In *Measuring Globalization: Better Trade Statistics for Better Trade Policy*, edited by Susan Houseman and Michael Mandel, 13–44. Kalamazoo, MI: Upjohn Press.

Domar, Evsey D. 1961. "On the Measurement of Technological Change." *Economic Journal* 71 (284): 709–29.

Doms, Mark E. 2009. "Communications Equipment: What Has Happened to Prices?" In *Measuring Capital in the New Economy*, edited by Carol A. Corrado, John C. Haltiwanger, and Daniel E. Sichel, 323–62. Chicago: University of Chicago Press.

Doms, Mark E., Wendy E. Dunn, Stephen D. Oliner, and Daniel E. Sichel. 2004. "How Fast Do Personal Computers Depreciate? Concepts and New Estimates." *Tax Policy and the Economy* 18: 37–79.

Dulberger, Ellen R. 2007. "Sources of Price Decline in Computer Processors: Selected Electronic Components." In *Price Measurements and Their Uses*, edited by Murray F. Foss, Marilyn E. Manser, and Allan H. Young, 103–24. Chicago: University of Chicago Press.

Edquist, Harald, Peter Goodridge, and Jonathan Haskel. 2022. "The Economic Impact of Streaming Beyond GDP." *Applied Economics Letters* 29 (5): 403–8.

Ehrlich, Gabriel, John Haltiwanger, Ron Jarmin, David Johnson, Ed Olivares, Luke Pardue, Matthew D. Shapiro, and Laura Yi Zhao. 2021. "Quality Adjustment at Scale: Hedonic vs. Exact Demand-Based Price Indices." *NBER Working Papers*, No. w31309. National Bureau of Economic Research.

Ehrlich, Gabriel, John Haltiwanger, Ron Jarmin, David Johnson, and Matthew D. Shapiro. 2019. "Re-engineering Key National Economic Indicators." In *Big Data for 21st Century Economic Statistics*, edited by Katharine G. Abraham, Ron G. Jarmin, Brian Moyer, and Matthew D. Shapiro, 25–68. Chicago: University of Chicago Press.

Executive Office of the President and Office of Management and Budget, eds. 2022. *North American Industry Classification System: United States, 2022*. Blue Ridge Summit, PA: Bernan Press.

Feenstra, Robert C. 1994. "New Product Varieties and the Measurement of International Prices." *American Economic Review* 84 (1): 157–77.

Feenstra, Robert C., and Matthew D. Shapiro. 2003. "Introduction to 'Scanner Data and Price Indexes.'" In *Scanner Data and Price Indexes*, edited by Robert C. Feenstra and Matthew D. Shapiro, 1–14. Chicago: University of Chicago Press.

Fernald, John G. 2015. "Productivity and Potential Output before, during, and after the Great Recession." *NBER Macroeconomics Annual* 29 (1): 1–51.

Foster, Lucia, Cheryl Grim, John Haltiwanger, and Zoltan Wolf. 2019. "Innovation, Productivity Dispersion, and Productivity Growth." In *Measuring and Accounting for Innovation in the 21st Century*, edited by Carol A. Corrado, Jonathan Haskel, Javier Miranda, and Daniel E. Sichel, 103–36. Chicago: University of Chicago Press.

Giandrea, Michael D., Robert J Kornfeld, Peter B. Meyer, Susan G. Powers, et al. 2021. *Alternative Capital Asset Depreciation Rates for US Capital and Multifactor Productivity Measures*. Technical report, Bureau of Labor Statistics.

Goldfarb, Avi, and Catherine Tucker. 2019. "Digital Economics." *Journal of Economic Literature* 57 (1): 3–43.

Gordon, Robert J., and Hassan Sayed. 2019. "The Industry Anatomy of the Transatlantic Productivity Growth Slowdown: Europe Chasing the American Frontier." *International Productivity Monitor* 37 (Fall): 3–38.

Griliches, Zvi. 1961. "Hedonic Price Indexes for Automobiles: An Econometric of Quality Change." In *The Price Statistics of the Federal Government*, edited by Price Statistics Review Committee, 173–96. Cambridge, MA: NBER.

Grimm, Bruce T. 1998. "Price Indexes for Selected Semiconductors." *Survey of Current Business* 78 (2): 8–24.

Grimm, Bruce T., Brent R. Moulton, and David B. Wasshausen. 2009. *Information-Processing Equipment and Software in the National Accounts*. Chicago: University of Chicago Press.

Groshen, Erica L., Brian C. Moyer, Ana M. Aizcorbe, Ralph Bradley, and David M. Friedman. 2017. "How Government Statistics Adjust for Potential Biases from Quality Change and New Goods in an Age of Digital Technologies: A View from the Trenches." *Journal of Economic Perspectives* 31 (2): 187–210.

Guadagni, Peter M., and John D. C. Little. 1983. "A Logit Model of Brand Choice Calibrated on Scanner Data." *Marketing Science* 2 (3): 203–38.

Haskel, Jonathan, and Stian Westlake. 2017. *Capitalism without Capital*. Princeton, NJ: Princeton University Press.

Herman, Shelby, Arnold Katz, Leonard Loebach, and Stephanie McCulla. 2003. "Fixed Assets and Consumer Durable Goods in the United States, 1925–97." Mimeo, Bureau of Economic Analysis.

Highfill, Tina C., and Alexander C. MacDonald. 2002. "Estimating the United States Space Economy Using Input-Output Frameworks." *Space Policy* 101474.

Highfill, Tina, and Christopher Surfield. 2022. *New and Revised Statistics of the U.S. Digital Economy, 2005–2020*. Washington, DC: Bureau of Economic Analysis.

Holdway, Michael. 2000. "An Alternative Methodology: Valuing Quality Change for Microprocessors in the PPI." Unpublished paper presented at Issues in Measuring Price Change and Consumption Conference, Bureau of Labor Statistics, Washington, DC, June.

Houseman, Susan, Christopher Kurz, Paul Lengermann, and Benjamin Mandel. 2011. "Offshoring Bias in US Manufacturing." *Journal of Economic Perspectives* 25 (2): 111–32.

Hulten, Charles R. 2010. "Growth Accounting." In *Handbook of the Economics of Innovation*, edited by Bronwyn H. Hall and Nathan Rosenberg, 2:987–1031. Amsterdam: Elsevier.

Jorgenson, Dale W. 1963. "Capital Theory and Investment Behavior." *American Economic Review* 53 (2): 247–59.

Jorgenson, Dale Weldeau, and Zvi Griliches. 1967. "The Explanation of Productivity Change." *Review of Economic Studies* 34 (3): 249–83.

Jorgenson, Dale W., Mun S. Ho, and Kevin J. Stiroh. 2003. "Lessons from the U.S. Growth Resurgence." *Journal of Policy Modeling* 25 (5): 453–70.

Jorgenson, Dale W., and Steven J. Landefeld. 2007. "Blueprint for Expanded and Integrated U.S. Accounts: Review, Assessment, and Next Steps." In *A New Architecture for the U.S. National Accounts*, edited by Dale W. Jorgenson, J. Steven Landefeld, and William D. Nordhaus, 13–112. Chicago: University of Chicago Press.

Jorgenson, Dale W., and C. Wessner, eds. 2005. *Deconstructing the Computer*. Washington, DC: National Academy Press.

Kamal, Fariha, Brent R. Moulton, and Jennifer Ribarsky. 2013. "Measuring 'Factoryless' Manufacturing: Evidence from U.S. Surveys." US Census Bureau Center for Economic Studies Paper No. CES-WP-13-44.

Karz, Arnold J. 1983. "Valuing the Services of Consumer Durables." *Review of Income and Wealth* 29 (4): 405–27.

Konny, Crystal, Brendan Williams, and David Friedman. 2019. "Big Data in the U.S. Consumer Price Index: Experiences & Plans." In *Big Data for 21st Century Economic Statistics*, edited by Katharine G. Abraham, Ron G. Jarmin, Brian Moyer, and Matthew D. Shapiro, 69–98. Chicago: University of Chicago Press.

Li, Wendy C. Y., and Bronwyn H. Hall. 2020. "Depreciation of Business R&D Capital." *Review of Income and Wealth* 66 (1): 161–80.

Lipton, Zachary C. 2018. "The Mythos of Model Interpretability: In Machine

Learning, the Concept of Interpretability Is Both Important and Slippery." *Queue* 16 (3): 31–57.

Murphy, John. 2009. "Classification of Units That Outsource Manufacturing Transformation Activities." Mimeo, April. Washington, DC: US Census Bureau.

Nakamura, Leonard I., Jon Samuels, and Rachel H. Soloveichik. 2018. "'Free' Internet Content: Web 1.0, Web 2.0 and the Sources of Economic Growth." *Federal Reserve Bank of Philadelphia Working Paper* 17.

Nordhaus, William D. 2007. "Two Centuries of Productivity Growth in Computing." *Journal of Economic History* 67 (1): 128–59.

OECD. 2020. "A Roadmap toward a Common Framework for Measuring the Digital Economy." In *Report for the G20 Digital Economy Task Force*. Saudi Arabia.

Ohta, Makoto, and Zvi Griliches. 1976. "Automobile Prices Revisited: Extensions of the Hedonic Hypothesis." In *Household Production and Consumption*, edited by Nestor E. Terleckyj, 325–98. Cambridge, MA: NBER.

Oliner, Stephen D. 1993. "Constant-Quality Price Change, Depreciation, and Retirement of Mainframe Computers." *Price Measurements and Their Uses*, edited by Murray Foss, Marylin Manser, and Allan Young, 19–62. Cambridge, MA: NBER.

Oliner, Stephen D., and Daniel E. Sichel. 2000. "The Resurgence of Growth in the Late 1990s: Is Information Technology the Story?" *Journal of Economic Perspectives* 14 (4): 3–22.

Oliner, Stephen D., and Kevin J. Stiroh. 2007. "Explaining a Productive Decade." *Brookings Papers on Economic Activity* 1: 81–137.

Pakes, Ariel. 2003. "A Reconsideration of Hedonic Price Indexes with an Application to PC's." *American Economic Review* 93 (5): 1578–96.

Pennec, Erwan Le, and Kamil Slowikowski. 2019. *ggwordcloud: A Word Cloud Geom for 'ggplot2'* (software).

R Core Team. 2021. *R: A Language and Environment for Statistical Computing* (software). R Foundation for Statistical Computing.

Redding, Stephen J., and David E. Weinstein. 2020. "Measuring Aggregate Price Indices with Taste Shocks: Theory and Evidence for CES Preferences." *Quarterly Journal of Economics* 135 (1): 503–60.

Reinsdorf, Marshall B. 1999. "Using Scanner Data to Construct CP1 Basic Component Indexes." *Journal of Business & Economic Statistics* 17 (2): 152–160.

Resnick, Paul, and Hal R. Varian. 1997. "Recommender Systems." *Communications of the ACM* 40 (3): 56–58.

Robbins, Carol, Olympia Belay, Matthew Donahoe, and Jennifer Lee. 2012. "Industry-Level Output Price Indexes for R&D: An Input-Cost Approach with R&D Productivity Adjustment." BEA Working Paper.

Sawyer, Steven D., and Alvin So. 2018. "A New Approach for Quality-Adjusting PPI Microprocessors." *Monthly Lab. Rev.* 1, 1–31.

Schrage, Michael. 2020. *Recommendation Engines*. Cambridge, MA: MIT Press.

Schreyer, Paul, et al. 2009. *Measuring Capital: OECD Manual 2009*. Paris: OECD Publishing.

Silver, Mick. 2010. "The Wrongs and Rights of Unit Value Indices." *Review of Income and Wealth* 56: S206–S223.

Solow, Robert M. 1956. "A Contribution to the Theory of Economic Growth." *Quarterly Journal of Economics* 70 (1): 65–94.

Strassner, Erich H., and David Wasshausen. 2017. "BEA Deflators for Information and Communications Technology Goods and Services: Historical Analyses and Future Plans." In *Measuring and Accounting for Innovation in the 21st Century*, edited by Carol A. Corrado, Jonathan Haskel, Javier Miranda, and Daniel E. Sichel, 553–72. Chicago: University of Chicago Press.

Syverson, Chad. 2011. "What Determines Productivity?" *Journal of Economic Literature* 49 (2): 326–65.

Triplett, Jack E. 2005. "Performance Measures for Computers." In *Deconstructing the Computer*, edited by Dale W. Jorgenson and Charles W. Wessner, 99–143. Washington, DC: National Academy Press.

West, Jeremy, Anne Carblanc, and Sarah Ferguson. 2019. "An Introduction to Online Platforms and Their Role in the Digital Transformation." In *OECD Draft Report*. Paris: OECD Publishing,.

Wickham, Hadley, Mara Averick, Jennifer Bryan, Winston Chang, Lucy D'Agostino McGowan, Romain Franois, Garrett Grolemund, Alex Hayes, Lionel Henry, Jim Hester, Max Kuhn, Thomas Lin Pedersen, Evan Miller, Stephan Milton Bache, Kirill Müller, Jeroen Ooms, David Robinson, Dana Paige Seidel, Vitalie Spinu, Kohske Takahashi, Davis Vaughan, Claus Wilke, Kara Woo, and Hiroaki Yutani. 2019. "Welcome to the Tidyverse." *Journal of Open Source Software* 4 (43): 1686.

Williams, Brendan, and Erick Sager. 2019. "A New Vehicles Transaction Price Index: Offsetting the Effects of Price Discrimination and Product Cycle Bias with a Year-Over-Year Index." Economic Working Paper No. 514. Washington, DC: Bureau of Labor Statistics.

Wu, Caesar, Adel Nadjaran Toosi, Rajkumar Buyya, and Kotagiri Ramamohanarao. 2018. "Hedonic Pricing of Cloud Computing Services." *IEEE Transactions on Cloud Computing* 9 (1): 182–96.

6

Measuring Prices and Productivity in the Health Care Sector

Louise Sheiner and David M. Cutler

6.1 Introduction

Health care is a large and growing share of GDP. In 1987, health care comprised just 10.6 percent of GDP, while today it accounts for roughly 18 percent.[1] Measured productivity growth in health care has been low. Over the 1987–2019 period, official measures show a *decline* in multifactor productivity in the health sector, with growth averaging between -0.3 percent and -0.6 percent per year depending on the measure used—well below the economy-wide rate of 0.8 percent.

Some argue that health care productivity is low because health care is very labor intensive and there is little scope for substituting capital for labor to boost productivity, as is done in other industries (Shatto and Clemens 2011). In that view, health costs increase rapidly over time because wages in the sector have to increase to compete with rising wages in sectors where productivity growth is higher: without the cost savings from higher productivity, prices in the health care sector have to rise to accommodate those higher wages. This phenomenon is often termed Baumol's cost disease. And, indeed, using official measures, health care prices have increased rapidly, rising 4.2 percent from 1980 to 2019 compared to 2.5 percent for personal consumption prices.[2] As a consequence, real health consumption—calculated using official deflators—increased just 2.7 percent per year over that time

Louise Sheiner is with the Hutchins Center on Fiscal and Monetary Policy, the Brookings Institution.

David M. Cutler is with Harvard University and NBER.

We are grateful to Elijah Asdourian, Sophia Campbell, Lorae Stojanovic, and Kadija Yilla for excellent research assistance and to Marshall Reinsdorf and David Wessel for valuable comments.

period, equal to the rate of increase of real GDP, even as nominal health spending as a share of GDP doubled.

The conclusion that health care is necessarily a low productivity growth sector is premature. The services provided by the health care system have changed dramatically over time, but little attempt has been made to adjust official price measures for changing quality and the introduction of new technologies. Consider, for example, that the age-standardized premature heart disease mortality rate decreased by 70 percent from 1968 to 2017,[3] that death rates for infants fell by over 50 percent from 1980 to 2017,[4] that cancer death rates decreased 28 percent from 2000 to 2020,[5] and that hepatitis C, which used to lower life expectancy among sufferers by an average of 15 years,[6] is now curable. None of these health improvements is accounted for in the official statistics for health spending. Nor—as an important counter-example—is the increase in mortality stemming from the overprescription of opioids, which is an example of technological regress.[7]

Further, the official statistics have a difficult time accounting for substitution of one form of treatment for another. For example, as a result of the development of statin drugs, antihypertensive, and other pharmaceutical agents, many fewer people have serious cardiac events. But because pills and hospitalization are different products in separate industries, the shift from inpatient stays to medication is not captured as a productivity improvement, but rather is implicitly accounted for as a shift in tastes. For all these reasons, it seems likely that the official statistics do a poor job of capturing actual productivity growth in the health care sector.

Given health care's large and growing share of GDP, mismeasurement of health care productivity growth may significantly distort both the level and the trends in aggregate productivity. With health care projected to continue rising as a share of GDP over time, distortions are likely to increase.

The question of whether health care productivity is rising also speaks to a number of debates in health care policy. If the quality of health care has increased significantly over time, it is more likely that the large increase in expenditures on health care will be deemed to have been "worth it."[8] Looking forward, understanding productivity growth in health care is important to understanding the trade-offs society faces in trying to cut back on health care spending growth. If health care productivity growth is inherently low and prices rise over time as a result, reductions in spending are more likely to lead to actual reductions in the quality of health care than if productivity growth is high—in which case spending cuts might simply slow the rise in quality increases.[9]

Much progress has been made in recent years in properly measuring health care prices and real health care expenditures, and most analyses suggest that health care productivity is higher than suggested by official estimates. However, some estimates suggest adjusting for quality would have only a small effect on health prices, while others suggest that properly measured health care price inflation could be 2 to 3 percentage points lower than official measurements suggest. More work is necessary to understand the source of the variation across studies and to reach consensus among researchers and the statistical agencies on the best approaches and assumptions.

In this chapter, we review measures of health care productivity and prices in the official statistics, discuss various approaches to quality adjustment, review the implementation challenges associated with quality adjusting health prices, and survey recent research. We discuss how an ideal national accounting system would account for health care—discussing, for example, whether health care is a final good or an intermediate good. We conclude with recommendations for the statistical agencies and suggestions for further research.

6.2 Measures of Health Care Productivity Using Official Statistics

Traditional measures of health care productivity—real output per unit of input—define real output as spending on health goods and services (physician services, hospital services, drugs, etc.) deflated by appropriate price indexes for that spending, the same method used for other goods and services. The Bureau of Economic Analysis (BEA) constructs the deflator for health care output from the producer and consumer prices indexes (PPIs and CPIs) for individual medical goods and services produced by the Bureau of Labor Statistics (BLS). These price indexes measure the change in price for the same service at the same location paid for by the same payer—for example, a hip replacement or a doctor's visit at provider X paid by payer Y.[10] Thus, real output will capture the number of hip replacements, the number of doctor's visits, and so on, and productivity will measure the number of hip replacements that can be produced for a given level of inputs.

Using BEA's measure of output as the basis of productivity calculations, productivity in the health care industry appears much slower than in many other industries. Figure 6.1a shows the estimates of multifactor productivity (MFP) growth (growth in real output less growth in real inputs, including both labor and capital) for health services. Over the entire 1987 to 2019 period, MFP in ambulatory health services[11] and hospitals, nursing, and residential care facilities was negative on average—meaning that inputs grew faster than output. In contrast, MFP for private business rose an average of 0.8 percent per year during this period. Over the past decade or so, productivity growth for ambulatory health services has been fairly robust, while MFP for hospitals and nursing homes has remained negative.

Figure 6.1b shows growth in labor productivity in the health sector.[12] Productivity growth for ambulatory care was extremely weak in all time periods examined, averaging about 0 over the 1987–2019 period; however, in recent

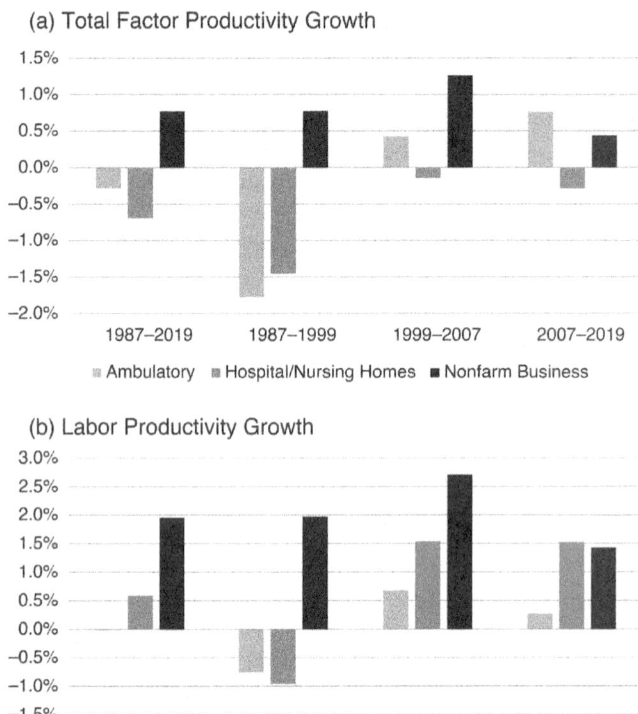

Fig. 6.1

years, labor productivity growth in hospitals has been relatively strong. This discrepancy between labor productivity and MFP at hospitals likely reflects a large increase in capital inputs in the sector.

The corollary of slow productivity growth is faster price growth. Health care price inflation in the official statistics has been higher than GDP inflation. Figure 6.2 shows change in health care prices as measured by the national account deflator for health services since 1987 compared to price growth for overall GDP. Health care prices increased 3.3 percent per year from 1987 to 2019, compared to just 2.1 percent for overall GDP prices. Health care prices rose particularly rapidly from 1987–1999 but the rise has been fairly muted since 2007.[13]

6.3 Adjusting Health Care Prices and Output for Quality Changes

As discussed above, the deflators constructed for health care goods and services measure the change in price for a particular service at the same

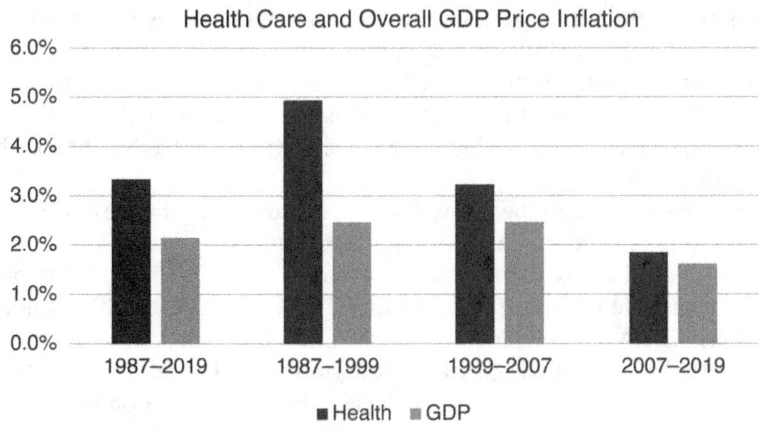

Fig. 6.2 Health care and overall GDP price inflation
Source: BEA

location paid for by the same payer. Incremental changes in the quality of health care—for example, improvements in anesthesia, imaging, or other equipment—are generally not taken into account. To the extent incremental improvements raise prices or costs, they are counted as price and cost increases in the official statistics. The prices of *new* treatments (or of significantly changed existing treatments) are not compared to previous prices; new treatments enter the basket during a sample rotation, and only changes in their prices that occur after they enter the sample affect measured inflation.[14]

In a very few cases, BLS does adjust prices for changes in the quality of health care services. For example, in calculating the PPI for nursing homes, BLS subtracts estimates of the costs of changes in staffing levels.[15] (We discuss the use of a cost-based approach to quality adjustment below.) But in general, there is little attempt to measure quality changes in health care.[16] In addition, because the PPI is based on particular services—such as an office visit or a knee replacement—it misses price changes that arise when a treatment for a disease shifts from one care setting to another. We discuss this issue first, before returning to the larger issue of how to account for changes in quality over time.

6.3.1 Accounting for Substitutions between Settings

A shift in treatment from one care setting to another—from inpatient to outpatient, from surgery to medical management, from talk therapy to pharmaceuticals—affects the price of treatment. For example, if the introduction of a new medication means that some patients with depression are successfully treated with medication instead of therapy, and if medication is less costly than therapy, then the price of treatment has decreased. But because official price indexes only capture changes in the price of the same treatment—changes in the price of a therapist visit or changes in the price of a medication—they do not capture these savings as price declines.[17] One exception is generic drugs, which BLS considers to be perfectly substitutable for brand-name drugs.[18]

The approach researchers have taken to capture price changes associated with changes in the modality of care is to categorize health spending by disease instead of by treatment. For example, since 2015, BEA has published a satellite account for health care that categorizes health spending by illness. (BEA uses satellite accounts to allow in-depth analysis of special topics not easily seen within BEA's core statistics.) The account combines data from large medical claims databases with survey data on private and public insurance spending, as well as household out-of-pocket expenditures, to measure total spending by condition from 2000 onward. Similarly, using the Medicare Beneficiary Survey, Cutler et al. (2022) construct an account of spending on the elderly to treat 80 conditions from 1999 to 2012. The key to the disease-based price index is that all spending is considered in the same bucket. No distinction is made between one category of treatment or another.

Switching to a disease-based price index that treats spending per case as the price can lower estimates of price growth by capturing within-condition shifts to less expensive treatment options. The growth of spending per case using disease-based indexes for cataracts, heart disease, and depression, for example, has all been less than the growth of service-based price indexes (Shapiro and Wilcox 1996, Cutler et al. 1998, and Berndt, Busch, and Frank 2001). For many other conditions, patients have received an increasing quantity of services per disease as medical care advances. On net, the BEA's satellite account shows spending by disease increasing at an annual rate 0.9 to 1.3 percentage points faster than official service-based price indexes (Dunn, Rittmueller, and Whitmire 2015), driven largely by the introduction of expensive technologies and increased preventative, imaging, and rehabilitation services to treat the same conditions (Dunn et al. 2018).[19]

Yet if greater intensity of treatment or a new technology improves outcomes for patients, the higher costs of providing these services should not be counted as price increases. To properly capture changes in the price of care, it is important to adjust for changes in the quality of care. Categorizing spending by disease is an essential first step in examining the relationship between increased spending and improved outcomes, but the resulting estimate of spending by disease cannot be viewed as a price index, since it conflates price increases with quantity/quality increases stemming from increases in treatment intensity. Like the disease-based indexes produced by BEA, the BLS experimental disease-based price indexes also measure total spending by disease and are thus not really capturing price of care in the sense of the changing price of constant-quality treatment.

6.3.2 Accounting for Changes in Treatments and Outcomes

Consider the following example: A hospital changes the type of stent used in all its coronary angioplasties from one that is uncoated to one that is coated with antibiotics so as to prevent infections. The switch raises costs by $3,000 but increases life expectancy by one month. Assume that the price of the angioplasty in period 1 using the uncoated stent is $20,000, and the price in year 2 with the coated stent is $23,000—that is, for the purposes of this example, the increased cost of the stent is passed on to the consumer with no markup (table 6.1, panel A).

Without accounting for the change in the quality of the stent, a price deflator would show the price of an angioplasty increasing 15 percent, from $20,000 to $23,000 (panel B). But, of course, the product sold in the second period is different from the one sold in the first period, so a direct comparison is not appropriate—an adjustment for quality change is necessary.[20]

Three basic methods have been suggested to make this sort of adjustment: the cost-of-living approach, the unit value approach, and the cost approach.[21] These are compared mathematically in box 6.1 but discussed intuitively here. Note that for many goods, these approaches yield the same result, but for reasons discussed below, they can yield very different results for health care.

6.3.2.1 Method 1: The Cost-of-Living Approach

A cost-of-living index measures the change in income necessary to achieve the same level of utility over two periods. For example, if one needs 5 percent more income to achieve the same utility in period 2 as in period 1, then prices are said to have increased 5 percent. Conceptually, this is the approach used by BLS to make decisions about the CPI and by BEA to calculate deflators for personal consumption. To the extent that GDP is aimed at capturing standards of living, this perspective seems appropriate for measuring prices, output, and productivity. (See Dynan and Sheiner, chap. 1 of this volume, for a discussion of GDP as a measure of well-being.)

As shown by Cutler et al. (1998), the correct price adjustment for a change in health care treatment using this approach is to subtract the increased value of the health service from the change in price. In our example, if consumers value a year of life expectancy at $100,000 (we discuss this valuation below), the new stent is worth $8,333 more to them than the old stent. Rather than increasing 15 percent from $20,000 to $23,000, a quality-adjusted price using the cost-of-living approach would fall from $20,000 to $14,667, a 27 percent reduction.[22] (See panel B.) This makes intuitive sense—the increased value of the angioplasty in period 2 is worth $8,333, as if the consumer

Table 6.1 Example

Panel A: Basic Setup

	Stent Type	Angioplasty Price	Life Expectancy Increase from Treatment
Period 1	Uncoated	$20,000	30 months
Period 2	Coated	$23,000	31 months

Panel B: Comparing Quality-Adjusted Prices across the Three Methods

	No Quality Adjustment	Cost-of-Living	Unit Value	Cost
Period 2 price	$23,000	Price less increase in value: $23,000 – $8,333 = $14,667	Price prorated for increased life expectancy: $23,000 * 30/31 = $22,258	Price less increase in cost $23,000 – $3,000 = $20,000
Health price inflation	15%	–27%	11%	0%

Note: This table compares the three methods to adjust health care prices for quality adjusted discussed in this text. For the purposes of this example, the assumed value of a year of life is $100,000, and the increase in cost for the coated stent is $3,000.

paid $23,000 but then got a rebate of $8,333 (which was spent on health care improvement), leaving the net price at $14,667. Another way to frame the comparison is to recognize that, if the price of the angioplasty with the *uncoated* stent were $14,667, the consumer would be indifferent between it and the angioplasty with the coated stent—thus the quality adjustment imputes the price at which the period 1 good would be purchased alongside the new good.[23] This imputed price can be used in a Laspeyres price index, which calculates the changing cost of a fixed basket of goods.

6.3.2.2 *Method 2: The Unit Value Approach*

The unit value approach measures the changing price of what consumers ultimately value; rather than pricing treatments, it prices outcomes like increases in life expectancy or the ability to live in the community. Just as one might calculate the price per ounce of cereal to compare prices over time when cereal boxes are made smaller (rather than measuring the cost of a box of cereal regardless of its volume), or price per megabyte of data when internet service becomes better, one can calculate the price per additional year of life expectancy or other outcome measure, such as improvement in quality of life.

Many researchers have employed this approach to quality adjust health care—including Berndt, Busch, and Frank (2001), Romley, Goldman, and Sood (2015), and Hult, Jaffe, and Philipson (2018). While this method seems appealing, it is not likely to fully capture the benefits from many innovations in health care. The reasoning—discussed more fully in box 6.1—is as follows: In the case of cereal being sold in 16-ounce boxes in period 1 and 14-ounce boxes in period 2, consumers in each period can buy as much cereal as they want at the same price. If the price per ounce of cereal increases from period 1 to period 2, then consumers are clearly worse off, because they could have bought as much cereal as they wanted at a lower price in period 1.[24]

That is not the case with health care. One cannot buy as many years of increased life expectancy as one wants at the current average price per year of life. In many cases, consumers would be willing to pay more for an extra month of life than the average price paid for the survival improvements they are currently able to buy, so new technologies that allow consumers to purchase more years of life at an increased price per life year can leave consumers better off.

As described in box 6.1, the unit value method is the same as the cost-of-living method *if* the average price charged per year of life is equal to the consumer's valuation. If the consumer values a year of life at more than the average price charged, the cost-of-living measure shows a bigger decline in prices for innovations that increase life expectancy.[25] On the other hand, if people choose to undergo low-value health care treatments where the value to the consumer is less than the price charged—for example because of health insurance, lack of information, or other frictions—the cost-of-living approach would show smaller price declines than the unit value approach.

Returning to the example above, one can see from table 6.1 that using a unit value approach, the adjusted period 2 price of the angioplasty is \$22,258, meaning that the price increase using the unit value method would be 11 percent. This is less than the 15 percent price increase calculated when no adjustment is made for quality but still a much higher price increase than obtained using the cost-of-living method (panel B). This difference reflects the fact that the average cost per year of life from angioplasty—around \$9,000—is less than 10 percent of what consumers would pay for a year of life.[26]

6.3.2.3 Method 3: The Cost Approach

As discussed in Diane Coyle's chapter in this volume, one approach BLS sometimes uses when a product has changed quality is to add the cost of that improvement to the previous period's price—for example, if a new model of a car has heated seats, BLS might add the manufacturer's cost plus markup of the seats to the price of the previous car model to give an apples-to-apples comparison with the older model. Similarly, as discussed above, BLS uses a cost-based approach in its PPI for nursing homes. This approach can be viewed as taking the producer's perspective—it measures the price a producer would have charged last year for this year's model.

The cost method ensures that price-increasing quality improvements are not counted as price increases, but it misses entirely the *benefits* consumers get from effective new treatments.[27]

In the example above, the increase in the price of the angioplasty is entirely accounted for by the higher price for the coated stent; adding that cost to last year's angioplasty price would result in no change in price (panel B). Thus, the price would not increase 15 percent—as it would if no quality adjustment were made—but it would not fall as it does under the cost-of-living method.

6.3.2.4 Summary

The cost method can help ensure that changes in the way care is delivered are not counted as prices increases, but it is unable to capture the value of health care innovations to consumers. As we discuss below, although the cost approach is not ideal from the perspective of consumer welfare, it is better than counting cost-increasing quality improvements as price increases, which likely occurs in many cases under current approaches.

To fully adjust for changes in health care quality, it is necessary to focus on their impact on outcomes. The literature has used two methods of adjusting health care prices for changes in outcomes—the cost-of-living method and the unit value method. The cost-of-living method is more appropriate from the perspective of consumer welfare. One potential disadvantage to the approach is that it requires measuring the monetary value people place on outcomes—which may not be able to be learned from the health care market itself. The unit value approach requires no such information, although, as noted by Dunn, Hall, and Dauda (2022), it implicitly assumes that the consumer values health outcomes at their average price.

6.4 Putting a Dollar Value on Outcomes

To implement the cost-of-living approach to quality adjustment, it is necessary to put a monetary value on increased life expectancy and quality of life. What are improvements to health worth in monetary terms? Such calculations are fraught but nonetheless important in many situations. For example, many government agencies use the value of a statistical life (VSL) in cost-benefit analysis of regulations like improving highway safety (DOT 2021)[28] and air and water quality (EPA 2023).[29]

As discussed in Muller (chap. 7 in this volume), two approaches have been used to estimate the value of life: those derived from hedonic studies that examine the wage premium required to induce people to take risky jobs or the price premium people are willing to pay for safer products (these are called revealed preference studies), and those based on surveys asking people how much they would pay for small reductions in mortality risk (these are called stated preference or contingent valuation studies).

The VSL is calculated by assuming a linear relationship between the willingness to pay for a change in death and the probability of death. As HHS (2021) explains: "If each of 10,000 individuals is willing to pay $1,000 for a 1 in 10,000 reduction in his or her chance of dying in a given year, the total expected value of that risk reduction is $10 million (10,000 × $1,000) and one less person would be expected to die that year (10,000 × 1/10,000)."[30] Thus, the VSL would be $10 million, and a 1 percent reduction in the probability of death would be valued at $100,000.[31]

6.4.1 Accounting for the Quality of Life

To capture the changing value of health care, it is not only the quantity of life that matters but also the quality (Hall and Jones 2007). Much of health care is aimed at treating illnesses that are not life threatening but cause pain and suffering. In these cases, the outcome of health spending is improved quality of life, not quantity. Even for illnesses that are life threatening, it is as important to capture the quality of life after treatment as the quantity.

The health economics literature has a long tradition of valuing health improvement using quality-adjusted life years (QALYs). QALYs range between 0 and 1, with 0 representing death and 1 representing perfect health.

Box 6.1 Three Approaches to Adjusting Health Care Prices for Quality Changes

As discussed in the main text, three approaches have been used to account for quality improvements in health care: the cost-of-living approach, unit value approach, and cost approach.

To compare these approaches, we start with a categorization of health spending by disease and define the following terms:

- P_1 and P_2 are the per person spending on the disease in periods 1 and 2—the price of treatment unadjusted for quality.
- LE_1 and LE_2 are the QALYs (quality-adjusted years of life) from treatment in periods 1 and 2, respectively.
- $\Delta Cost$ and ΔLE are the changes in costs and QALYs between the two periods.
- M is the value of each additional year of life (assumed to be constant for this example).
- μ is a markup between costs and prices (also assumed to be constant).
- $\hat{P}_t^{CostofLiving}$, $\hat{P}_t^{UnitValue}$, and $\hat{P}_t^{Cost}$ are the quality adjusted prices in period t using the three methods.

Assume for this example that in period 1, all the prices are the same.[1]

The **cost-of-living approach** is consistent with a true cost-of-living index: it is measured as the change in income needed to obtain the same utility from one period to the next when prices change. Sheiner and Malinovskaya (2016) show that, under this method, the change in the quality-adjusted price of treatment is health spending less the additional value received by the consumer with the second period treatment, which is equal to the value per QALY multiplied by the increase in QALYs.[2] Intuitively, it is as if a person is purchasing a service for price P but then receiving a rebate worth $M\Delta LE$, leaving the true price change as the stated price change less the rebates:

$$\hat{P}_2^{CostofLiving} = P_2 - M\Delta LE.$$

The **unit value method** adjusts the price in period 2 for change in QALYs, just as one would adjust the price of a box of cereal for changes in the number of ounces:

1. To perfectly implement the utility and cost methods, it would be necessary to do the adjustments starting with the time the treatments were first introduced.

2. This adjustment would be used for a Laspeyres price index, which prices the items in the period 1 basket. It corresponds to the compensating variation in utility. For a Paasche index, one would compute the increase in period 1 price that would make the consumer as well off as they are in period 2—corresponding to the equivalent variation measure of utility change

$$\hat{P}_2^{UnitValue} = P_2 \frac{LE_1}{LE_2},$$

which can be rewritten as

$$\hat{P}_2^{UnitValue} = P_2 - P_2 \frac{\Delta LE}{LE_2}$$

The **cost method** subtracts the change in the cost (plus markup) of treatment from the price:[3]

$$\hat{P}_2^{Cost} = P_2 - Cost(1 + \mu).$$

This method ensures that any additional costs associated with changing the treatment are not captured as price increases. It is a method BLS uses for some quality improvements (see Diane Coyle, chap. 4 in this volume, for a discussion).

Comparing the methods

Cost-of-Living versus Unit Value Method

The difference between the quality-adjusted prices using the two methods is as follows:

$$\hat{P}_2^{CostofLiving} - \hat{P}_2^{UnitValue} = P_2 \frac{LE}{LE_2} - M\Delta LE = \Delta LE\left(\frac{P_2}{LE_2} - M\right).$$

The cost-of-living and unit value methods yield the same quality-adjusted price if

$$\frac{P_2}{LE_2} = M.$$

When the price paid by the consumer per QALY is equal to the value to the consumer, then the cost-of-living method and the unit value method yield the same outcome. For most goods, this is the normal result of utility maximization—the consumer keeps buying health until the value received just equals the price. Thus, for most goods that have only one characteristic (as is assumed to be the case with health care since QALYs incorporate both quantity and quality of life), the unit value method captures the change in consumer surplus.

But when the average price paid per QALY is less than the value of a QALY, $\hat{P}_2^{CostofLiving}$ is lower than $\hat{P}_1^{UnitValue}$.

3. As noted above, when the BLS implements the cost method, it adds the cost of the improvement from last year's price instead of subtracting it from this year's. For ease of comparison across methods, we implement the cost method here as a subtraction from the current period price; in practice, the two methods yield similar results.

(*continued*)

Box 6.1 ***(continued)***

Why would the price paid for years of life be less than the value? The unique aspect of health is that in most cases, people cannot buy as many QALYs as they like at a given price per QALY. If you double the dose of chemotherapy, for example, a person does not live twice as long. Thus, if a new innovation allows people to buy more QALYs—even if it is at a higher price per QALY—the consumer can be better off.

Figure 6.3 provides a simple example of a consumer's maximization problem under a budget constraint. The budget constraints are the straight (panel A) or kinked (panel B) lines, and the curves are indifference curves. The consumer must decide between two goods: QALYs and all other consumption. In panel A, the consumer can buy as many QALYs as she wants at the same price per QALY. In this situation, an increase in the price per

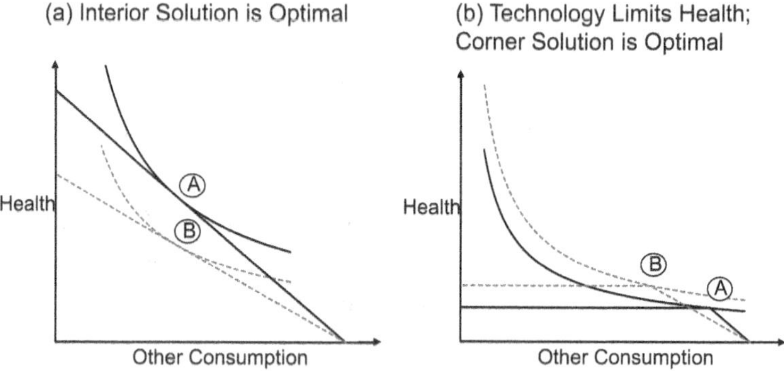

Fig. 6.3 Budget constraints and optimal health consumption

QALY, shown by the inward shift of the budget constraint, makes the consumer worse off—as shown by the move from point A to point B.

Panel B shows a case where the consumer is constrained by technology—she would like to buy more health, but medical technology is not capable of delivering it. The budget constraint has a kink at the maximum amount of health that can be purchased. (As shown in Dauda, Dunn, and Hall 2022, the basic result and intuition are the same if the consumer *can* buy more health, but only at a higher price.)

The optimal consumption mix in period 1, given the constraint, is shown by point A. In period 2, technology has improved so that more years of life are possible, although the price per year of life is higher than previously. Nonetheless, people are better off and move to a higher indifference curve. In period 2, one would have to take away income for people to have the same utility they had in period 1. The cost-of-living index captures this improvement in welfare. A quality adjustment that simply measures the price of an additional year of life expectancy does not.

Utility versus Cost Method

The difference between the period 2 quality-adjusted price using the two methods is as follows:

$$\hat{P}_2^{CostofLiving} - \hat{P}_2^{Cost} = \Delta Cost(1 + \mu) - M\Delta LE.$$

These two methods yield the same quality adjustment if the change in cost (plus markup) is equal to the change in value received by consumers. If the value of an innovation exceeds its cost (that is, if MFP increases), then the cost-of-living method shows a steeper price decline than the cost method. In other words, the cost method *assumes* that there is no MFP associated with changes in treatment.

The QALY allows the quantity and quality of life to be combined into a single index. For example, if someone has health impairments that reduce their QALY to 0.5, that means that two years of living with this impairment provides them with the same utility as one year of living in perfect health. QALYs are typically derived from surveys of patient attitudes about the quality of life associated with various health impairments combined with an assumption about how those attitudes map into year-of-life equivalents. Cutler et al. (2022) assume a linear relationship between the utility from life quality and the utility from a year of life. For example, they assume that when someone rates their quality of life a 10 on a 0 to 100-point scale, each year of life is worth 10 percent of what a year of life would be worth for someone in perfect health.

6.4.2 Variation in VSL by Age and Health Status

Although the environmental literature has settled on the concept of the VSL—typically not adjusted for age or health status—the health economics literature focuses on the value of a statistical life *year* (VSLY), calculated as the flow of annual values over a person's expected lifetime that has the same present value as the VSL.[32] Although in much of the literature the VSLY is itself not explicitly conditioned on age, the VSLY approach nonetheless values lifesaving medical treatments more highly for younger than older people because older people have a shorter life expectancy and also tend to be in worse health, so their quality of life remaining is also worse.[33]

Ketcham, Kuminoff, and Saha (2022) note that most estimates of the VSL and VSLY come from studies of people younger than 65. Using a revealed preference approach focused on the elderly's willingness to spend on medical care, they estimate much smaller VSLYs for older people.[34] The question of how the VSLY varies with age is important given the large fraction of health spending accounted for by the elderly; more work in this area would be helpful.

6.4.3 Variation in the VSL and VSLY over Time

Another question with the VSLY is whether it should be constant over time (in real dollars) or whether it should increase with real income. Theoretical analyses of the VSL, like those in Murphy and Topel (2006) and Jones and Klenow (2016), suggest that the VSL should increase with income—the higher the income, the greater the enjoyment in life and the more valuable additional life becomes relative to an increase in consumption within a fixed lifetime. Hall and Jones (2007) argue that health spending rises over time as societies get richer exactly *because* of this phenomenon. The Environmental Protection Agency (EPA) and Department of Transportation (DOT) assume that the VSL increases proportionally with aggregate (national) earnings, while other studies suggest it should rise more rapidly than income (Costa and Kahn 2004). Most of the recent health literature, however, assumes a constant, inflation-adjusted VSLY. Thus, these studies arguably underestimate the growth in real (quality-adjusted) health benefits over time.

6.5 Implementation Challenges

Implementing an outcomes-based quality adjustment requires addressing a number of challenges, including the following:

- Finding useful data
- Classifying spending by disease
- Linking health spending directly to outcomes

We discuss each of these in turn.

6.5.1 Source Data

Researchers have used a variety of datasets to create quality-adjusted price indexes, each of which has advantages and limitations.[35]

Medicare Claims Data: A number of researchers (e.g., Dauda, Dunn, and Hall, 2022, Romley et al. 2020) have used Medicare claims data to create quality-adjusted price indexes. These records include information on health spending (Medicare paid and out-of-pocket spending for Medicare covered services); patient demographics (age, sex, and zip code); and certain outcomes (mortality and readmissions) for the universe of Medicare beneficiaries enrolled in Medicare fee-for-service insurance. While the sample is very large, it is only representative of the population ages 65 and older, which accounts for roughly one-third of health spending (Centers for Medicare & Medicaid Services 2014).[36] Furthermore, the data only capture outcomes that can be gleaned from claims data.

Private insurance claims: Similar information for the nonelderly population is available from data on commercial claims. For its satellite health accounts, BEA uses information from Truven Health MarketScan to capture spending for the nonelderly commercially insured population. Berndt, Busch, and Frank (2001) use a database of private claims to study improvements in treatments for depression.

Medicare Community Beneficiary Survey (MCBS): The MCBS, used by Cutler et al. (2022), is a nationally representative survey of the Medicare population. It includes much more extensive information than available in claims data, including complete data on health spending and financing sources, detailed data on demographics and income/wealth, and information on quality of health and health outcomes. The sample is much smaller than that represented in claims data, however, and also only representative of the elderly population.

Medical Expenditure Panel Survey (MEPS): The MEPS is the only nationally representative (of the noninstitutionalized population) dataset that contains detailed data on health spending, but it covers just a fraction of the observations available in claims data. The BEA uses the MEPS (for some of its estimates, in conjunction with claims data) in its satellite health accounts. The BLS also uses the MEPS to allocate spending by disease in its experimental disease-based price indexes.[37]

Data from the Institute for Health Metrics and Evaluation (IHME): IHME has produced two datasets that can be used to measure quality-adjusted prices in health care. The *Disease Expenditure Project (DEX)* estimates health spending in the US by payer and condition from 1996 to 2016. The *Global Burden of Disease (GBD)* study measures changes in mortality and disability associated with diseases over time.

Tufts Cost-Effectiveness Analysis (CEA) Registry: The CEA registry is a database of the clinical trial results of over 10,000 cost-effectiveness studies covering a broad range of conditions and treatments. Dauda, Dunn, and Hall (2022) and Hult, Jaffe, and Philipson (2018)[38] use these studies to calculate the impact of technological innovations on health prices. A limitation of this approach is that it is difficult to know how to weight the various innovations because they are not linked to spending in the database—that is, the innovations are simply listed, and it is unclear the extent to which any innovation is responsible for changes in health spending observed over time. In addition, the database cannot capture changes in the price of providing existing treatments over time.

6.5.2 Classifying Spending by Disease

The first step to creating outcomes-based price indexes that weight changes in outcomes by condition is to classify spending by condition. As discussed above, this step is necessary to account for substitution between treatment modalities. It also allows researchers to create separate quality-adjusted prices series for each disease.

Exactly how to classify spending by disease is not obvious when patients have multiple conditions. If a patient visits the doctor seeking treatment for diabetes and cardiovascular disease, to which condition should the cost of the appointment be attributed?

The encounter-based approach to classifying spending by disease, used by the BEA healthcare satellite account, assigns expenditures using the primary diagnosis code associated with individual medical claims (Dunn et al. 2014).[39] This method is the easiest to apply but can miss relevant secondary diagnoses.[40] Sometimes, secondary conditions are not even recorded. For example, depression may make treatment of heart disease more costly, but a cardiologist may not record mental illness as a comorbid condition when seeing a patient.

When diagnosis codes are missing, such as for certain prescription drug claims, the BEA satellite account instead uses the person-based approach. This method regresses a patient's total spending on indicators that they currently have various conditions, capturing the marginal effect of each disease on spending. The coefficients of the regression are used to apportion total spending across conditions.

The episode-based approach, on the other hand, assigns spending to distinct bouts of disease across time. This can be done using software algorithms that assign medical claims to conditions based on a patient's medical history, as in Dunn et al. (2014). Alternatively, Romley, Goldman, and Sood (2015), Gu et al. (2019),[41] and Romley et al. (2020) use diagnostic codes to identify the condition associated with an initial visit (such as an unexpected acute-care hospital stay) and then assign all associated spending within a certain time period to that condition, regardless of the primary diagnoses listed on each individual claim.

Dunn et al. (2014) compare these three approaches and find that, while relative price growth across conditions is sensitive to the choice of methodology, overall disease-price inflation is fairly insensitive to the exact approach taken.

Cutler et al. (2022) implement the person-based approach using propensity scores to categorize spending by disease, which is possible because their data include much more information than what is found on an insurance claim. In particular, in a first stage, they compare spending on people with a particular illness to spending on people who have the same attributes but do not have that illness and attribute the difference in health expenditures to the illness. In a second stage, they reallocate spending on some illnesses to other conditions that they find are the fundamental drivers of those illnesses—for example, from heart disease to hypertension.

6.5.3 Linking Outcomes to Health Spending

The final step in producing quality-adjusted health price indexes is to determine outcomes and link them to spending.

Population health changes over time because of a wide array of forces, including changes in the environment (air quality, nutrition, stress, pandemics), changes in behavior (fitness, diet, smoking), and advances in medicine. To measure the output of the health care sector, it is important to know which changes in outcomes are directly attributable to changes in treatment and which reflect other societal changes. Researchers have taken a variety of approaches to try to account for changes in health outcomes that are not the result of health spending, although there is more work to be done in this area.

Most researchers attempt to control for changes in the health of patients over time. With claims data, the only information available are basic demographics (age, sex, and often race) and data on other conditions for which people have been treated (and for which Medicare has paid providers). Claims data do not include factors such as smoking history and BMI except to the extent they are reported in a patient's medical history. Some researchers (e.g., Romley et al. 2020)[42] control for the average attributes of people living in patients' zip codes, which are likely to be predictive of a particular patient's health status.

Cutler et al. (2022) link spending to outcomes by comparing spending and outcomes of people with a particular disease to those of similar people without the disease. Their data allow them to ensure that changes in outcomes deriving from changes over time in things they have data on, like smoking and obesity, are not inappropriately attributed to the health system. Still, they do not control for other changes that could affect outcomes—for example, exposure to pollution or stress—though information on some of these could be added.

Much of the research discussed above takes disease prevalence as given—it assumes that the number of people with any particular condition is exogenous and the impact of medical care is shown by changes in outcomes for people with the condition.[43] This assumption is not always justifiable—we noted above that the opioid epidemic can be traced back to loose prescribing practices of physicians, so some of the prevalence of addiction should be attributed to the health system (although no researchers have attempted this yet). Similarly, widespread cancer screening likely affects prevalence. For some cancers, like colon cancer, screening reduces prevalence because it catches and treats diseases in precancer stages—in this case, screening is responsible for improved outcomes. But screening can also increase prevalence by catching early-stage cancers that may never have affected health (because they are too slow growing, for example). In that case, outcomes given a cancer diagnosis appear better even if overall outcomes do not change—that is, prevalence increases and outcomes per case improve, with no net effect on health. The literature has not accounted for this possibility yet and so might be overstating the benefits of health care related to cancers.

6.6 Empirical Estimates of Quality-Adjusted Health Deflators

Table 6.2 reports estimates of the effects of quality adjustment on health spending deflators from some recent studies. The table is organized by type of quality adjustment: cost-of-living (panel A), unit value (panel B), and cost-based (panel C). The table includes the period covered, the data source, the type of spending analyzed, the assumed VSLY (for the cost-of-living method) and the resulting quality-adjusted health price inflation. These results are either reported in the studies themselves or calculated by us using a chained Fisher deflator.[44] Research that uses the cost-of-living approach has found that relative health prices (health prices relative to general inflation) have either declined over time or been roughly constant. For example, the data from Cutler et al. (2022) suggest that relative prices of the elderly's health care declined 3 percent per year from 1999 to 2012, perhaps 2–3 percentage points less than what official prices show.[45]

Using data from the Institute of Health Metrics and Evaluation to examine quality changes in health prices for the full population, Weaver et al. (2022) find that relative health spending prices rose 0.2 percent per year from 1996–2016 when the VSLY is assumed to be $100,000 but fell 0.7 percent per year when the VSLY is assumed to be $150,000. This compares to a rise of just 0.6 percent over the period in official health prices, suggesting that quality adjustment had little effect on inflation under an assumption of a $100,000 VSLY but lowered it by 2 percentage points using a $150,000 VSLY. The relatively small effect compared to Cutler et al. (2022) merits further research—why are the results so different? How much is associated with different methodologies, different time periods, or different populations?

The difference between approaches to quality measurement is highlighted by a comparison between the results in Dunn, Hall, and Dauda (2022)—who use the Tufts CEA registry of new innovations and the cost-of-living approach—and Hult, Jaffe, and Philipson (2018), who use the same registry but the unit value approach. Dunn et al. find that quality-adjusted price of median innovation is about 18 percent lower than the price of previous treatments, whereas Hult, Jaffe, and Philipson find that new innovations cost about 4 percent more than previous treatments.[46] Some researchers using the unit value method for narrow sets of treatments find significant price reductions—Romley et al. for diabetes and Berndt, Busch, and Frank (2001) for depression—while Howard et al. (2015) find significant increases in the price of cancer drugs using the unit value approach.

Matsumoto (2021) uses data on hospital quality collected by CMS to adjust inpatient prices for changes in quality over time.[47] These quality measures include elements like patient satisfaction, outcomes for certain conditions, and the degree to which hospitals comply with recommended actions. Using Medicare claims data and Medicare hospital cost reports, he is able to relate changes in quality to changes in cost. Because his estimation strategy relies on random ambulance assignment to control for patient selection, he can only estimate the effect of quality improvements for emergency admissions. Still, he finds that accounting for the costs of these quality improvements lowers the inpatient PPI by 0.19 to 0.26 percentage point per year from 2010 to 2016.

The implications for labor productivity are straightforward: productivity estimates using official price estimates would be adjusted by the deviation between official price inflation and quality-adjusted price inflation. For example, if quality-adjusted prices rise 2 percent less per year than official prices suggest, real health care productivity rises 2 percent more per year than official estimates suggest. The implications for MFP are less obvious, because to the extent the improvements in outcomes are the result of better capital—better MRIs, robotic surgical tools, and so on—one would want to adjust the prices of capital inputs downward and hence the quantity of capital upward, lessening or eliminating any effect on MFP.[48]

6.7 Accounting for Health Care in GDP and Productivity

The preceding section explored appropriate price indexes for deflating nominal health care expenditures. In this section, we consider how these real expenditures on health care fit into a GDP framework. Our discussion is somewhat speculative because the literature has not grappled with these questions in depth. We ask three questions:

1. Which health outcomes belong in GDP, and which are outside the boundary?
2. How much of health care is an intermediate good?
3. How should services provided by nonprofit and government health providers be deflated?

6.7.1 GDP Boundary

A reasonable approach to valuing the effect of population health on well-being is to simply multiply expected QALYs by the value of a year of life

Table 6.2 Results from selected studies

Authors	Time Period	Data Source	Condition	Quality Measure	Value of a Life Year	Annual Decline in Quality-Adjusted Health Prices (Relative to Economy-Wide Deflator)
Panel A: Cost-of-Living Approach						
Cutler et al. (2022)	1999–2012	Medicare Current Beneficiary Survey	All health spending	Quality-adjusted life years (QALYs) gained	$100,000 in 2010	–3%[a]
Weaver, Joffe, Ciarametaro, Dubois, Dunn, Singh, Sparks, Stafford, Murray, and Dieleman (2022)	1996–2016	Institute of Health Metrics and Evaluation for changes in outcomes; Disease Expenditure Project on spending by condition	All health spending	Disability adjusted life years (DALYs) averted	$100,000 or $150,000 in 2016	+0.4% with $100,000; –1.4% with $150,000
Dauda, Dunn, and Hall (2022)	2001–2014	Medicare Cost Reports	Acute myocardial infarction, congestive heart failure, and pneumonia	Life expectancy gained	$50,000, $100,000, and $150,000	–3.1% with $50,000, –7.4% with $100,000, –12.0% with $150,000
Eggleston, Shah, Smith, Berndt, and Newhouse (2011)	1999–2009	Sample of patients combined with results from clinical studies	Diabetes	Life expectancy gained	$200,000	~0%
Panel B: Unit Value Approach						
Romley, Goldman, Sood, and Dunn (2020)	2004–2012	CMS Medical Claims	Chronic type 2 diabetes	No deterioration in quality of life two years after diagnosis	N/A	–1.3% Price per successful (high quality) treatment

Hult, Jaffe, and Philipson (2018)	1976–2014	Tufts CEA Registry	Sixty-five disease categories	QALYs gained	N/A	+4% Price per QALY increased for median innovation
Howard, Bach, Berndt, and Conti (2015)	1995–2013	Clinical trials	Cancer drugs	Increased life expectancy	N/A	+10% Average increase in price of cancer drugs per year of life expectancy gained (results not weighted by spending)
Berndt, Bir, Busch, Frank, and Normand (2002)	1991–1996	Private Claims Database along with expert opinion about treatment success	Major depression	Probability of remission	N/A	–1.66% to –2.13% Price per successful treatment
			Panel C: Cost Approach			
Matsumoto (2021)	2010–2016	Medicare Cost Reports/ Hospital Compare for quality indicators	Acute myocardial infarction, congestive heart failure, and pneumonia	CMS Hospital Quality Indicators	N/A	Inpatient PPI increased 0.19 to 0.26 percentage point less per year when adjusted for costs of quality improvement

[a] Cutler et al. (2022) do not calculate a price deflator and instead use a measure of productivity that is the percentage change in consumer surplus. We use their data to estimate a price deflator using a Fisher index (geometric mean of Laspeyres and Paasche price indexes) using the methodology described in box 6.1.

in perfect health. Jones and Klenow (2016) value differences in well-being across countries using this approach.

But for measuring real GDP growth, only improvements in health that derive from goods and services supplied by the health sector are relevant.[49] Approaches that explicitly link outcomes to health expenditures by controlling for other changes seem appropriate for GDP measurement.

The implication of this approach is that exogenous changes in health—from a pandemic, for example—would have no effect on GDP except to the extent they affect labor supply (which we discuss next), while efforts to combat those changes—COVID-19 treatment or vaccinations—could show large positive effects on properly measured GDP. This is especially true in the case of the COVID-19 vaccine, which saved hundreds of thousands of lives during the pandemic at very low resource costs. Thus, despite the huge increase in mortality during the pandemic and the clear reduction in well-being, the approach to quality adjusting health care prices discussed here would have the effect of boosting GDP. Note that this is the same treatment as natural disasters, in which destruction of property from the disaster does not lower GDP but spending for repairs increases it. In this case, the property is people's health.

6.7.2 Intermediate versus Final Goods

Part of the reason people value health is because good health allows them to work and earn income they can use for consumption. Consider, for example, the COVID-19 vaccine that enabled people to go back to work. Assume for this example that people must be vaccinated at least once a year to be protected—that is, that the benefits are short lived. (We discuss the treatment of health spending with long-lasting benefits below.)

The increased economic activity associated with the vaccine is fully captured in GDP *as currently measured*—wages and profits from economic activity on the income side and consumption and investment financed by those wages and profits on the product side. While the return to the vaccine was enormous because it allowed a burst of economic activity (in addition to saving lives), one would not want to add the value of the additional earnings made possible by the vaccine to GDP because that would be double counting. The vaccine is an intermediate input into the production function.

Of course, people value their health for reasons other than the income they can earn from being healthy, and *these* benefits of the vaccine are not currently captured by GDP. These benefits *are* final goods that should be included in a quality adjustment for health prices.

Note, however, that when valuing the productivity of the health sector itself, additional earnings resulting from improved health care *should* be counted—that is, the vaccine was enormously valuable, and any evaluation of the spending on R&D, production, and distribution of the vaccine, as well as funds allocated toward treating COVID-19, should account for the effects on earnings and on improved health and life expectancy.[50]

None of the studies summarized in table 6.2 include direct estimates of the effects of health care on earnings. A key question, then, is how much of the VSL discussed above, typically derived from people's willingness to accept lower wages for a safer job or pay higher prices for a safer car, reflects the pure enjoyment of life and how much it reflects the preservation of future earnings.

The models of willingness to pay for life expectancy show three sources of benefits from longer life: (a) higher lifetime earnings and thus higher lifetime consumption; (b) more lifetime leisure; and (c) greater lifetime enjoyment from any given level of lifetime consumption. This final benefit results from the assumption that the marginal utility of consumption declines as annual consumption increases, so a person is better off with lower annual consumption but more years in which to enjoy it.[51]

Thus, one might imagine that measures of the VSLY do include future earnings. However, it seems likely that VSLs based on wage studies mostly reflect people's valuation of life itself rather than future earnings because between workers' compensation and life insurance, most workers are fairly well insured for income losses associated with a work-related fatality.[52] On the other hand, when the EPA or DOT uses the VSL in a cost-benefit analysis, it is attempting to account for the entire benefit of additional life, which includes forgone earnings. (Indeed, the VSL was introduced in the early 1980s at OSHA as a replacement for an old method that only counted forgone earnings.[53]) Becker (2007) calculates that about one-quarter of the value of life likely stems from the future earnings component, so the question of whether earnings are included is significant.[54] More broadly, the question of how to properly account for the benefits of health care that stem from higher earnings is one that merits more attention in the literature.

6.7.3 Nonprofit Institutions in the NIPAs

About half of health care services are provided by nonprofit and public providers. The System of National Accounts (SNA) specifies that the output of nonmarket producers be measured by their expenses. The SNA identifies nonmarket producers by whether they operate like for-profit businesses rather than by their legal status. However, the National Income and Product Accounts (NIPAs) identify nonmarket producers by their legal status. Thus the real output of health care providers legally organized as nonprofit institutions and the real output of most government services is measured by their expenditures (not revenues) deflated by an input price deflator (e.g., the Employment Cost Index for labor costs). This means that there is an assumption of zero productivity growth in these sectors.[55] The rationale is that market prices are not meaningful for nonprofits and governments and therefore cannot be used to deflate revenues. However, for health care, that assumption is not reasonable, as the prices charged by nonprofits and governments are economically significant, and these institutions operate very much like for-profit health providers (Gee and Waldrop 2022).[56]

What are the implications of not using output prices for this sector? First, the output of the health sector is understated. If prices do not rise as quickly as costs because of productivity improvements, then real output increases faster than real costs. Second, because the PPI is only used to deflate nominal output for for-profits, changes to markups (the difference between prices and costs) at nonprofit and public providers are counted in personal consumption expenditure (PCE) and GDP prices.[57] Markups could have increased in recent years because of provider consolidation or decreased as a result of the subdued growth rate of Medicare and Medicaid reimbursements. Third, any improvements made to the PPI for health care to better account for quality have limited impact on GDP and PCE quantities and prices. This includes improvements that have been made over the past few decades, discussed in Moulton (chapter 2 of this volume), and any future improvements (like those discussed in this chapter) to account for improved outcomes. From 2003 to 2021, the input-cost deflator for nonprofit health services increased 2.6 percent per year, compared to 2.4 percent for the PPI-based deflator.[58]

6.8 Conclusion and Recommendations

Health care is a large and growing share of the economy, so getting measurement right in this sector is important. Doing so requires adjusting prices for quality. The rapid declines in quality-adjusted health prices found in some studies would have a significant effect on overall inflation. Spending on health care goods and services averaged roughly 16 percent of personal consumption expenditures from 1999 to 2012, so a reduction in health price growth of 2 percent per year would reduce measured PCE inflation by about one-third percentage point. But numerous issues—both empirical and theoretical—still need to be worked out before outcomes-based quality adjustments in health can be included in official estimates of GDP and aggregate productivity.

The methodological approach advocated in this chapter for measuring real health care spending—using the value of a QALY gleaned from other contexts—represents a significant departure from standard procedures used in national income and product accounting and BLS price measurement. As discussed above, this method captures the consumer surplus from every new health care innovation, essentially treating each innovation as a new good. While many advocate such an approach for new goods in general, statistical agencies view it as too experimental (Groshen et al. 2017).[59] Furthermore, the methods that have been considered to account for consumer surplus (e.g.,

Hausman 1996, Redding and Weinstein 2016) have used information on demand for the product being introduced rather than relying on exogenous measures like the VSLY concept used here. The VSLY approach is most similar to one proposed by Brynjolfsson et al. (2019) to value free digital goods like Facebook, which uses online auctions and other methods to gauge consumers' willingness to pay for such innovations. Because that approach is so different from the one used in the regular accounts, Brynjolfsson et al. (2019) have advocated the creation of a concept called GDP-B—basically a satellite account of a more inclusive measure of GDP to supplement but not replace official GDP.

The statistical agencies have made great strides in health care measurement in recent years. Going forward, we recommend they pursue a two-pronged strategy: They should work on improving the treatment of health spending in the NIPAs and the official prices for medical care while continuing to work on creating fully quality-adjusted real health spending by disease in the satellite accounts. BLS should consider terminating its experimental prices by disease series. There is no reason for BEA and BLS to both produce data on health spending by disease, and because BLS needs to produce price indexes in real time—and does not revise history—official BLS price indexes for medical care will probably never incorporate quality adjustments based on outcomes. BEA has much more flexibility in this regard.

6.8.1 Improving Health Spending in the NIPAs

For the time being, the NIPAs remain the basis of national estimates of health care inflation and productivity. These accounts do not do explicit quality adjustment. Still, several changes could be made to improve the accounts.

- As discussed above, BEA should treat most nonprofit and government health providers in the same manner as they treat for-profit entities, deflating revenues by PPIs rather than costs.[60]
- BLS should work on improving the PPIs used for health care using a traditional methodology—like adjusting for the costs of quality improvement. As described above, BLS does not try to adjust for changes in the mix of services provided in an encounter like a hospital visit for a given diagnosis-related group code. Matsumoto (2021) shows that statistics available in close to real time can be a good proxy for hospital quality and that, for the variety of services he was able to study, current methods overstate health care inflation.

Further work in this area—covering other parts of health care or working on implementing Matsumoto's approach for hospital services, for example—would be valuable. One approach BLS might take to get a handle on the scope of the problem would be to choose a subset of items that account for a large share of health services and do a detailed analysis of how inputs that affect patient well-being have changed over time. If the changes are significant, this type of analysis would have to be done on a continuous basis.

6.8.2 Improving the Health Satellite Accounts

Simultaneously, BEA should continue its work on satellite health accounts, which promise a more accurate measure of productivity and inflation in the medical care sector.

- BEA should aim to produce a health satellite account that includes nominal and real spending by disease, where deflators to calculate real spending account for the benefits of changes in quality using a cost-of-living (utility based) approach. The cost-of-living approach fits well into a GDP framework (see Dynan and Sheiner, chap. 1, this volume) and has the strongest theoretical justification of all the approaches that have been suggested (Sheiner and Malinovskaya 2016). The ultimate goal of such an endeavor is to develop an alternate set of accounts that could fit into a GDP framework at an appropriate time.
- BEA needs to decide which approach to follow. The Cutler et al. (2022) approach is the only one thus far that has managed to do quality adjustments for the full set of medical conditions, and we think it is a reasonable approach for BEA to adopt, perhaps with some modifications.
- As part of this approach, BEA should expand the set of medical conditions currently tracked in the satellite accounts to include a set of risk factors—factors like cholesterol, hypertension, mood disorders, immunizations, diabetes, and cancer screening. Accounting for risk factors is important because treating risk factors is a key part of medical care and could lead to a large increase in productivity over time.
    - For example, if cholesterol levels fall over time because of more widespread use of statins, contributing to lower incidence of heart disease and hence mortality, that reduction in mortality should be counted as an increase in the quality of medical services; without explicitly accounting for the reduction in cholesterol attributable to statins, that reduction in the incidence of heart disease would be counted as an exogenous change in disease incidence, thus understating the role of medical care in health improvement.
- BEA should consider whether the approach used to monetize quality of life in the literature (including in the Cutler et al. (2022) method) is appropriate. That approach uses a linear transformation between individual ratings of the quality of health and the value of life—for example, someone rating their health as 50 on a 0–100 scale has a value of life only half as large as someone claiming to be in perfect health.

This deserves further thought and research. Undoubtedly, other factors besides health affect quality of life, so this linear transformation likely understates the value of increased longevity for people in less than perfect health.

- BEA should plan on doing extensive validation of its findings before publication using the results from clinical trials and disease models. Does the literature suggest that the kinds of benefits ascribed to treatment are plausible? Cutler et al. show that for heart conditions and some cancers, their method produces results that are consistent with the medical literature. Validation across all medical conditions would help instill confidence in the results.
- BEA should consider the question of how quality-adjusted health spending accounts fit into a GDP framework.
    - *Splitting intermediate from final output:* The health sector improves GDP by producing valuable consumption goods and increasing people's ability to work. From the perspective of the productivity of health spending, both types of benefits should be included. But from the perspective of GDP, only the consumption value of higher length and quality of life should be considered, because goods and services purchased with the increase in income afforded by improved medical treatment are already counted in GDP. BEA should consider trying to separately identify these benefits.
    - *Timing of the health benefits:* The NIPAs treat spending on health goods and services as final consumption even if the benefits of that spending span more than one year. This is how other nonhousing durables are treated. With the Cutler et al. method of calculating quality-adjusted real health spending, part of the value of health spending is captured in the year the spending occurs, but part may not be captured until years later.[61]
    - One possible approach BEA could consider would be to calculate the flow of consumption arising from health spending rather than the present value—that is, to treat health consumption in the same way that owner-occupied housing is treated, where the flow of services is captured and not the purchase of the house itself. That might entail measuring investment in health spending, as is done with residential construction.
- Because of the detailed medical knowledge required to produce high-quality estimates of quality-adjusted health prices and the complexity of the challenges, BEA should consider setting up a working group to advise it. That working group should include economists (from within BEA and BLS and from outside the government) and medical professionals (including from NIH).

Notes

1. CMS, National Health Accounts, "National Health Expenditures as a Share of GDP." (https://www.cms.gov/research-statistics-data-and-systems/statistics-trends-and-reports/nationalhealthexpenddata/nationalhealthaccountshistorical).

2. Health prices increased much more rapidly than other prices from about 1970 to 2010, but health price inflation has been more muted since then. These prices are from BEA Table 2.5.4, "Price Indexes for PCE by Function." As we discuss below, the prices used to calculate GDP have increased a bit faster because of the way the NIPA treats public and nonprofit health care.

3. See https://www.ncbi.nlm.nih.gov/pmc/articles/PMC7098848/.

4. See https://www.cdc.gov/nchs/hus/contents2019.htm#Table-003.

5. See https://seer.cancer.gov/statistics-network/explorer/application.html?site=1&data_type=2&graph_type=1&compareBy=sex&chk_sex_1=1&race=1&age_range=1&advopt_precision=1&advopt_show_ci=on&hdn_view=0&advopt_show_apc=on&advopt_display=2#graphArea.

6. See https://www.emedicinehealth.com/ask_how_long_can_a_person_live_after_hepatitis_c/article_em.htm.

7. See https://apps.bea.gov/scb/issues/2020/06-june/0620-beyond-gdp-deaton.htm.

8. If health care prices increase because of low productivity growth, increasing spending on health care will still be worth it if the marginal value we receive from health care exceeds its cost. The finding of low productivity growth in health care thus is not sufficient to judge health care not worth it.

9. See the report from Medicare Technical Panel 2010 for a discussion of the implications of slower growth in Medicare provider payments on health care quality. Of course, if health care productivity is low because of wasteful spending, and policies are enacted that reduce this type of spending, spending can decrease without reduction in quality.

10. Providers are supposed to tell BLS if quality has improved and, if so, at what cost, but that adjustment rarely happens in practice (personal communication with BLS analysts). In any case, as we show below, an adjustment based on cost is not likely to capture all the value of improvements in health care quality.

11. Ambulatory health services include offices of physicians and other health providers, home health care services, medical labs, and other outpatient services.

12. Other researchers have examined MFP and labor productivity for different time periods or different subsectors of the health care industry, including Cylus and Dickensheets 2007; Nghiem, Coelli, and Barber 2011; Chansky, Garner, and Raichoudhary 2018; Spitalnic et al. 2016. Their results are discussed in Sheiner and Malinovskaya 2016.

13. The chart understates the price increases for health care actually used in the NIPAs because the deflator for services of nonprofit health providers is larger, an issue we discuss below.

14. Moulton (chap. 2) and Coyle (chap. 4) discuss the entry of new goods into the basket during sample rotations, or sample refreshments.

15. See https://www.bls.gov/ppi/quality-adjustment/quality-adjustment-in-the-producer-price-index.pdf. For a short while, the BLS used a cost-based approach to adjusted hospital prices for changes in quality indicators gathered by the Center on Medicare and Medicaid Services; however, this quality adjustment has been discontinued. See http://conference.nber.org/confer/2008/si2008/PRCR/murphy2.pdf. It had little impact on measured prices in any case.

16. For example, BLS simply uses Medicare payment updates to adjust prices for Medicare-paid hospital stays (personal communication, BLS staff).

17. This may be seen as a form of outlet substitution bias—bias that arises from the fact that BLS does not count as a price decline the savings consumers get when a new lower-cost outlet, like Walmart, enters a market (unless that entry also lowers prices at existing stores, in which case it does). It could also be seen as a problem with capturing the value of new goods—in this case, a new treatment modality—because welfare gains associated with the introduction of new goods are generally not captured in official statistics. See the chapter by Dynan and Sheiner and the chapter by Coyle for further discussion.

18. Prior to 1995, the introduction of a generic drug did not lower measured drug price inflation because the brand-name drug and the generic drug were treated as different goods. Now, six months after the introduction of a generic drug, BLS resamples the prices of brand versus generic drugs based on relative shares sold at the pharmacy being sampled and treats any difference in price between the two as a price change of the same good. See https://www.bls.gov/opub/mlr/1999/06/art4full.pdf.

19. See https://www.healthaffairs.org/doi/pdf/10.1377/hlthaff.2017.1688.

20. Exactly how the BLS would adjust prices in this scenario, or others like it, is unclear. If the two angioplasties were viewed as comparable, then the entire change in cost would be called a price increase. If they were viewed as too different to compare, and if angioplasties with bare mesh stents were no longer used in period 2, the item would likely be dropped. See Coyle in this volume for a discussion of the various approaches BLS uses to adjust for changes in the items it prices.

21. Different authors have used various names for what we call the unit value approach: Sheiner and Malinovskaya call it the "redefine the good" approach and Dauda et al. call it the "treatment endpoint" approach.

22. The subtraction method is appropriate for the Laspeyres price index; for a Paasche index, one would add the increased value of health services to the prior year's price.

23. But producers likely would not choose to offer angioplasty with the uncoated stent at this price.

24. This is a slight oversimplification, as the ability to purchase cereal in smaller quantities might be valued by consumers.

25. Another way of thinking about the quality adjustment is that it essentially treats the new treatment as a new good and captures the consumer surplus from its introduction.

26. Life expectancy in period 2 is 31 months, or 2.5 years, so the average cost per life year is 23,000/2.58 = $8,803. An alternative approach would examine the marginal cost of a life year (akin to a hedonic regression of cost on life expectancy)—in this example, the price per marginal life year is $36,000, still much less than what consumers would be willing to pay.

27. If the cost method uses a markup, and if producers are able to capture the entire consumer surplus through prices, then the cost method yields the same result as the cost-of-living method. But if producers cannot capture all the benefits, the cost method results in higher prices than the cost-of-living method.

28. See https://www.transportation.gov/sites/dot.gov/files/2021-03/DOT%20VSL%20Guidance%20-%202021%20Update.pdf.

29. See https://www.epa.gov/environmental-economics/mortality-risk-valuation.

30. See https://aspe.hhs.gov/sites/default/files/2021-07/hhs-guidelines-appendix-d-vsl-update.pdf.

31. The environmental literature stresses the idea that the assumption of a linear

relationship may not be valid when annual willingness to pay becomes a substantial portion of income. Without health insurance, for example, many people would have to forego valuable medical treatments because they could not afford them, and hence the revealed willingness to pay would be lower. However, our society has clearly shown a willingness to pay for expensive health treatments, and people choose to purchase health insurance that allows them to make those choices.

32. As noted by Kniesner and Viscusi (2019; https://law.vanderbilt.edu/phd/faculty/w-kip-viscusi/368_Value_of_Statistical_Life_Oxford.pdf), in an analysis in the early 2000s the US Environmental Protection Agency (EPA) used evidence from stated preference studies to reduce the VSL for those 65 and over by 37 percent; this led to public outcry from senior citizen groups and led EPA to abandon age adjustments. The Department of Transportation (DOT) also uses the same VSL for people regardless of age.

33. The Affordable Care Act and the Inflation Reduction Act both contain language that specifically prohibits the secretary of Health and Human Services from using QALYs in determining the effectiveness of particular services or drugs because such an approach does not value all patients' lives equally (Basu, Carlson, and Veenstra 2020; Frank and Nichols 2023). See https://www.brookings.edu/blog/usc-brookings-schaeffer-on-health-policy/2023/03/15/threats-to-medicares-new-drug-negotiation-power/; https://www.sciencedirect.com/science/article/pii/S1098301519351873.

34. An additional question is whether the VSLYs gathered from individuals overstate the social value of life because they do not account for the increased cost of additional longevity from higher Social Security and Medicare expenditures.

35. See Dunn, Rittmueller, and Whitmire 2015 for a more extensive discussion of these data sources (https://apps.bea.gov/scb/pdf/2015/01%20January/0115_bea_health_care_satellite_account.pdf).

36. Medicare provides coverage to those 65 and older and to some nonelderly with disabilities. Even within that population, only people enrolled in Traditional Medicare are represented—a share that has declined steadily from over 80 percent in 2007 to only about 50 percent in 2022 (https://www.kff.org/medicare/issue-brief/medicare-advantage-in-2022-enrollment-update-and-key-trends/). In the future, the data may include claim equivalents for people enrolled in Medicare Advantage.

37. See https://www.bls.gov/pir/disease/technical-documentation_2022.pdf.

38. See https://www.journals.uchicago.edu/doi/abs/10.1162/ajhe_a_00109.

39. See https://www.bea.gov/system/files/papers/WP2014-4.pdf.

40. This approach is also used by BLS. In one version, its experimental price indexes by disease; in a second version, it distributes spending from an encounter across each of the listed diagnosis codes. See https://www.bls.gov/pir/disease/technical-documentation_2022.pdf.

41. See https://pubmed.ncbi.nlm.nih.gov/31002706.

42. See https://www.brookings.edu/wp-content/uploads/2020/05/WP61-Romley-et-al_5.14.2020.pdf.

43. One exception is Cutler et al. (2022), who assign some of the decreased prevalence of cardiovascular disease to improved treatments of risk factors like hypertension and high cholesterol.

44. We use the method described in box 6.1 to calculate the Laspeyres and Paasche price indexes and take the geometric mean. We are unable to calculate price deflators holding constant the mix of medical conditions from year to year, so our estimates should be viewed as rough estimates of what a true Fisher deflator would show.

45. There is no official price index for total Medicare services or for health care

of the elderly. There is a PPI for hospital services for Medicare beneficiaries, which rose 1 percent more than the GDP deflator over this time period. Using various CMS Medicare Trustees reports, we calculate that real Medicare payments (using the GDP deflator) for physician services fell almost 1 percent per year over this time period. Thus, the price inflation for Medicare services without quality adjustment was likely between -1 percent and 1 percent.

46. Overall, Dauda, Dunn, and Hall (2022) find that improvements in technology cause quality-adjusted health care prices to fall about 1.3 percent per year.

47. See https://www.bls.gov/osmr/research-papers/2021/ec210090.htm.

48. Exactly how one would determine which outcomes are the result of improved capital versus MFP is unclear; no researcher has attempted this decomposition.

49. Health benefits derived from externalities and unintended impacts of product changes are beyond the scope of the standard measure of GDP, but an extended measure of GDP growth that includes health effects of pollution abatement from process improvements is discussed in Nicholas Muller's chapter (chap. 7).

50. Intermediate inputs that allow health care workers to go back to work would not be part of the output that that sector delivers to the rest of the economy.

51. This assumption requires consumption be above some minimum subsistence level. The intuition is as follows: Compare having $10,000 in consumption each year for two years with $20,000 in consumption in one year. Because the marginal utility of consumption declines as consumption increases, the loss in utility from lowering consumption from $20,000 to $10,000 is less than the gain in utility from raising consumption from 0 to $10,000 in the second year. A person would pay to live an extra year even if that meant no additional increase in lifetime resources. Of course, lifetime resources often increase because of improved health, either because of higher earnings capacity or because of annuities like Social Security and Medicare. From a social point of view, the increased annuity income is being financed by others and so does not represent a net benefit—the private value of extending life may exceed the social value. On the other hand, increased earnings results in higher tax collections, which means that the individual may place too low of a value on their life. These questions have not received sufficient attention.

52. Although workers' comp typically covers only about two-thirds of prior wages, this may be sufficient to ensure that workers' survivors are able to maintain the same level of consumption. https://www.gerberholderlaw.com/employee-death-benefits-by-state/.

53. See https://law.vanderbilt.edu/phd/faculty/w-kip-viscusi/articles/324_The_Value_of_Individual_and_Societal_Risks_to_Life_and_Health.pdf, 435.

54. Another issue is whether there is a wedge between the public and private valuation of a year of life because of the taxes and benefits that people pay and collect in their lifetimes.

55. Productivity growth is the difference between growth of real output and growth of real input. When real output is defined to be real input, productivity growth is zero.

56. See https://www.americanprogress.org/article/policies-to-hold-nonprofit-hospitals-accountable/.

57. The accounting is not straightforward: In calculating real household services in PCE, spending at all health providers (public, private for-profit, and private not-for-profit) is counted and deflated using PPIs. However, PCE also includes services provided by nonprofit institutions serving households (NPISH). These are calculated as total output of NPISH less sales to other sectors; sales to other sectors equal the amount purchased by consumers and included in PCE services. In calculating real PCE, total output of NPISH is deflated using input costs, while

the subtracted sales to other sectors are deflated using PPIs. Thus, in PCE, health services provided by NPISH are deflated using input costs, but health services provided by public and for-profit health providers are deflated using PPIs. In GDP, however, the output of state and local health providers is included as government output and deflated using input costs, with sales to other sectors subtracted and deflated using PPIs. Thus, in the GDP deflator, PPI is only used for health services provided by for-profits.

58. US Bureau of Economic Analysis, "Table 2.4.4U. Price Indexes for Personal Consumption Expenditures by Type of Product" (accessed May 17, 2023). These are calculated by comparing the growth rates in line 342 and line 355 in NIPA's Underlying Detail Table 2.4.4U.

59. See https://pubs.aeaweb.org/doi/pdfplus/10.1257/jep.31.2.187.

60. BEA treats some government agencies, which it calls "government enterprises," in the same way as for-profit institutions. Highfill 2022 (https://www.bea.gov/system/files/papers/BEA-WP2022-8.pdf) suggests that public hospitals be designated as government enterprises.

61. The Cutler et al. method calculates the value of health spending as the present value of changes in mortality and quality of life as a result of that health spending. If improvements to health occur coincidentally with health spending, then the value of spending is captured in the same time frame as the spending. However, if improvements do not fully show up in the data until outside the time window—which is likely for many preventative measures—there is a lag between when the spending occurs and when the benefits are captured.

References

Basu, Anirban, Josh Carlson, and David Veenstra. 2020. "Health Years in Total: A New Health Objective Function for Cost-Effectiveness Analysis." *Value in Health* 23 (1): 96–103.

Becker, Gary. 2007. "Health as Human Capital: Synthesis and Extensions." *Oxford Economic Papers* 59 (3): 379–410.

Berndt, Ernst, Susan Busch, and Richard Frank. 2001. "Treatment Price Indexes for Acute Phase Major Depression." In *Medical Care Output and Productivity*, edited by David M. Cutler and Ernst Berndt, 463–508. Chicago: University of Chicago Press.

Brynjolfsson, Erik, Avinash Collins, W. Erwin Diewert, Felix Eggers, and Kevin Fox. 2019. "GDP-B: Accounting for the Value of New and Free Goods in the Digital Economy." NBER Working Paper w25695. National Bureau of Economic Research.

Centers for Medicare & Medicaid Services. 2014. "Health Expenditures by Age and Sex." https://www.cms.gov/data-research/statistics-trends-and-reports/national-health-expenditure-data/age-and-sex.

Chansky, Brian, Corby Garner, and Ronjoy Raichoudhary. 2018. "Measuring Output and Productivity in Private Hospitals." In *Measuring and Modeling Health Care Costs*, edited by Ana Aizcorbe, Colin Baker, Ernst R. Berndt, and David M. Cutler. Chicago: University of Chicago Press. Costa, Dora, and Matthew Kahn. 2004. "Changes in the Value of Life, 1940–1980." *Journal of Risk and Uncertainty* 29 (2): 159–80.

Cutler, David, Kaushik Ghosh, Kassandra Messer, Trivellore Raghunathan, Allison

Rosen, and Susan T. Stewart, et al. 2022. "A Satellite Account for Health in the United States." *American Economic Review* 112 (2): 494–533.

Cutler, David, Mark McClellan, Joseph Newhouse, and Dahlia Remler. 1998. "Are Medical Prices Declining? Evidence from Heart Attack Treatments." *Quarterly Journal of Economics* 113 (4): 991–1024.

Cylus, Jonathan, and Bridget Dickensheets. 2007. "Hospital Multifactor Productivity: A Presentation and Analysis of Two Methodologies." *Health Care Finance Review* 29, no. 2 (Winter): 49–64.

Dauda, Seidu, Abe Dunn, and Anne Hall. 2022. "A Systematic Examination of Quality-Adjusted Price Index Alternatives for Medical Care." *Journal of Health Economics* 85, 102662, ISSN 0167-6296. https://doi.org/10.1016/j.jhealeco.2022.102662.

DOT. 2021. Departmental Guidance on Valuation of a Statistical Life in Economic Analysis. https://www.transportation.gov/sites/dot.gov/files/2021-03/DOT%20VSL%20Guidance%20-%202021%20Update.pdf.

Dunn, Abe, Eli Liebman, Lindsey Rittmueller, and Adam Shapiro. 2014. "Defining Disease Episodes and the Effects on the Components of Expenditure Growth." Bureau of Economic Analysis paper. https://www.bea.gov/research/papers/2014/defining-disease-episodes-and-effects-components-expenditure-growth.

Dunn, Abe, Lindsey Rittmueller, and Bryn Whitmire. 2015. "Introducing the New BEA Health Care Satellite Account." Survey of Current Business, January. Bureau of Economic Analysis, Washington, DC.

Dunn, Abe, Bryn Whitmire, Andrea Batch, Lasanthi Fernando, and Lindsey Rittmueller. 2018. "High Spending Growth Rates for Key Disease in 2000–14 Were Driven by Technology and Demographic Factors." *Health Affairs* 37 (6): 915–24.

Eggleston, Karen, Nilay Shah, Steven Smith, Ernst Berndt, and Joseph Newhouse. "Quality Adjustment for Health Care Spending on Chronic Disease: Evidence from Diabetes Treatment, 1999–2009." *American Economic Review* 101, no. 3 (May): 206–11.

EPA. 2023. "Mortality Risk Valuation." *Environmental Economics*, https://www.epa.gov/environmental-economics/mortality-risk-valuation.

Frank, Richard, and Len Nichols. 2023. "Threats to Medicare's New Drug Negotiation Power." USC-Brookings Schaeffer Initiative for Health Policy, March 15. https://www.brookings.edu/articles/threats-to-medicares-new-drug-negotiation-power.

Gee, Emily, and Thomas Waldrop. 2022. "Policies to Hold Nonprofit Hospitals Accountable." Center for American Progress Report, October 18. https://www.americanprogress.org/article/policies-to-hold-nonprofit-hospitals-accountable.

Groshen, Erica, Brian Moyer, Ana Aizcorbe, Ralph Bradley, and David Friedman. 2017. "How Government Statistics Adjust for Potential Biases from Quality Change and New Goods in an Age of Digital Technologies: A View from the Trenches." *Journal of Economic Perspectives* 31 (2): 187–210.

Gu, Jing, Neeraj Sood, Abe Dunn, and John Romley. 2019. "Productivity Growth of Skilled Nursing Facilities in the Treatment of Post-Acute-Care-Intensive Conditions." *PLoS ONE* 14 (4): e0215876. https://doi.org/10.1371/journal.pone.0215876.

Hall, Robert, and Charles Jones. 2007. "The Value of Life and the Rise in Health Spending." *Quarterly Journal of Economics* 122 (1): 39–72.

Hausman, Jerry. 1996. "Valuation of New Goods under Perfect and Imperfect Competition." In *The Economics of New Goods*, edited by Timothy F. Bresnahan and Robert J. Gordon, 207–48. Chicago: University of Chicago Press.

HHS. 2021. "Guidelines for Regulatory Impact Analysis. Appendix D: Updating Value per Statistical Life (VSL) Estimates for Inflation and Changes in Real Income." US Department of Health and Human Services. https://aspe.hhs.gov/sites/default/files/202107/hhs-guidelines-appendix-d-vsl-update.pdf.

Highfill, Tina. 2022. "Better Reflecting Transitions in Market Production by Government Functions Over Time: Updating the Classification of State and Local Government Enterprises in the National Income and Product Account." BEA Working Paper 2022–8.

Howard, David, Peter Bach, Ernst Berndt, and Rena Conti. 2015. "Pricing in the Market for Anticancer Drugs." *Journal of Economic Perspectives* 29 (1): 139–62.

Hult, Kristopher, Sonia Jaffe, and Tomas Philipson. 2018. "How Does Technological Change Affect Quality-Adjusted Price in Health Care? Systematic Evidence from Thousands of Innovations." *American Journal of Health Economics* 4 (4): 433–53.

Jones, Charles, and Peter Klenow. 2016. "Beyond GDP? Welfare across Countries and Time." *American Economic Review* 106 (9): 2426–57.

Ketcham, Jonathan, Nicolai Kuminoff, and Nirman Saha. 2022. "Valuing Statistical Life Using Seniors' Medical Spending." https://www.public.asu.edu/~nkuminof/KKS_working_paper.pdf.

Kniesner, Thomas, and W. Kip Viscusi. 2019. "The Value of a Statistical Life" Vanderbilt Law Research Paper No. 19–15.

Matsumoto, Brett. 2021. "Producing Quality Adjusted Hospital Price Indexes." BLS Working Paper No. 543.

Murphy, Kevin, and Robert Topel. 2006. "The Value of Health and Longevity." *Journal of Political Economy* 114 (5): 871–904.

Nghiem, Hong Son, Tim Coelli, and Scott Barber. 2011. "Sources of Productivity Growth in Health Services: A Case Study of Queensland Public Hospitals." *Economic Analysis and Policy* 41 (1): 37–48.

Redding, Stephen J., and David Weinstein. 2016. "A Unified Approach to Estimating Demand and Welfare." NBER Working Paper 22479, National Bureau of Economic Research.

Romley, John, Dana Goldman, and Neeraj Sood. 2015. "US Hospitals Experienced Substantial Productivity Growth During 2002–11." *Health Affairs* 34 (3): 511–18.

Romley, John, Dana Goldman, Neeraj Sood, and Abe Dunn. 2020. "Productivity Growth in Treating a Major Chronic Health Condition." Hutchins Center on Fiscal and Monetary Policy Working Paper No. 61.

Shapiro, Matthew, and David Wilcox. 1996. "Mismeasurement in the Consumer Price Index: An Evaluation." *NBER Macroeconomics Annual* 11.

Shatto, John D., and M. Kent Clemens. 2011. "Projected Medicare Expenditures under an Illustrative Scenario with Alternative Payment Updates to Medicare Providers." Centers for Medicare & Medicaid Services, memo, May 13. https://www.cms.gov/Research-Statistics-Data-and-Systems/Statistics-Trends-and-Reports/ReportsTrustFunds/Downloads/2011TRAlternativeScenario.pdf.

Sheiner, Louise, and Anna Malinovskaya. 2016. "Productivity in the Health Care Sector." Hutchins Center on Fiscal and Monetary Policy at Brookings Working Paper.

Spitalnic, Paul, Stephen Heffler, Bridget Dickensheets, and Mollie Knight. 2016. "Hospital Multifactor Productivity: An Updated Presentation of Two Methodologies." Centers for Medicare & Medicaid Services, memo, February 22. https://www.cms.gov/Research-Statistics-Data-and-Systems/Statistics-Trends-and-Reports/ReportsTrustFunds/Downloads/ProductivityMemo2016.pdf.

Weaver, Marcia, Jonah Joffe, Michael Ciarametaro, Robert Dubois, Abe Dunn, Arjun Singh, Gianna Sparks, Lauryn Stafford, Christopher Murray, and Joseph Dieleman. 2022. "Health Care Spending Effectiveness: Estimates Suggest that Spending Improved US Health from 1996 to 2016." *Health Affairs* 41, no. 7 (July): 994–1004.

7

Productivity and the Environmental Accounts

Nicholas Z. Muller

7.1 Introduction

Environmental quality in the United States has changed significantly since the early 1970s, when major federal environmental laws such as the Clean Air Act (CAA) were enacted.[1] As a result of this legislation and subsequent policies, the US has enjoyed significant improvements in quality of air and water. Still, significant challenges remain, particularly with respect to emissions of greenhouse gases, which have increased substantially since the 1970s.

The environmental legislation of the 1970s and subsequent laws and regulations led to changes in the economy that were likely a contributing factor to the post-1970 slowdown in productivity documented by Robert Gordon (2016). Capital, labor, and intermediate goods used in production were allocated to the provision of environmental protection services and, therefore, away from market activities. This change in the composition of output adversely affected measures of growth and productivity because most benefits from investments in environmental quality do not count in gross domestic product (GDP) growth, while costs of environmental policy (which manifest as opportunity costs in the form of foregone production of market goods) do. Over time, increased investment in environmental quality shows up as a drag on growth, even if the benefits from such investment exceed the costs (National Academies of Science, and National Research Council 1999; Muller 2014a; 2014b; 2020). In other words, the increased investment in environmental protection since the 1970s has lowered measured GDP

Nicholas Z. Muller is with Carnegie Mellon University and NBER.

The author appreciates the comments and feedback provided by Louise Sheiner, David Wessel, Marshall Reinsdorf, and other participants at the authors' conference hosted by the Brookings Institution's Hutchins Center on Fiscal and Monetary Policy.

growth even as it has raised living standards and welfare. Properly accounting for environmental damages is important not only to better understand underlying productivity but also to properly inform policymakers about the effects of environmental regulation on well-being.

This chapter discusses the integration of environmental considerations into an expanded measure of economic output that accounts for the benefits of environmental protection. It summarizes the literature on the intersection between environmental pollution and productivity, characterizes a conceptual framework for integration of environmental pollution damage into the national accounts, and computes a measure of productivity growth from 1957 to 2016 in the US economy that incorporates empirical pollution damage estimates from the literature.

The analysis finds that the economic cost of air pollution damage in the US is large but falling relative to GDP. As a percent of GDP per hour worked—a standard measure of productivity—air pollution damage has declined sharply since the passage of the CAA in 1970. In contrast, the social cost of greenhouse gases (GHGs) relative to GDP is small but rising from a base of about 1 percent of GDP in the 1960s. Combined damage from air pollution and GHGs amounted to 30 percent of GDP in the 1960s, 20 percent in the 1980s, 15 percent in the 1990s, 10 percent in the 2000s, and around 5 percent in 2016. Incorporating the benefits of environmental protection would have significant effects on economy-wide productivity growth. Between 1957 and 2016, environmentally adjusted productivity (EAP) expanded 2.4 percent per year while market output per hour worked grew at a 1.7 percent pace. Furthermore, taking account of environmental damages changes the trajectory of productivity growth: the official measure of productivity growth slows after 1970, while environmentally adjusted measures rise.

The remainder of this chapter is structured as follows. Section 7.2 provides a brief review of the literature. Section 7.3 gives a conceptual model for accounting for pollution damage when measuring output and output growth. Section 7.4 discusses approaches that have been taken to place a monetary value on environmental damage. Section 7.5 explores data on pollution trends. Section 7.6 presents empirical methods used in damage calculations and time series trends in damage from local air pollution and GHGs. Section 7.7 reports adjusted productivity measures, and section 7.8 concludes.

7.2 Brief Literature Review

The damage estimates in this chapter build on an earlier empirical literature. Nordhaus and Tobin (1973) present possibly the first empirical estimates of monetary damage from environmental pollution. Since then, a few notable papers estimate cross-sectional extended accounts (Bartelmus

2009; Muller, Mendelsohn, and Nordhaus 2011) and time series augmented accounts (Muller 2014a; 2014b; 2020; Tschofen, Azevedo, and Muller 2019). Muller (2014a) reports that environmentally adjusted value added (EVA)—defined as GDP less pollution damage—grew by between 0.3 and 0.6 percent per year more rapidly than GDP in the US from 1999 to 2008. Muller (2020) shows that, especially prior to and just after passage of the CAA, EVA grew at significantly different rates than GDP. Prior to the passage of the CAA, when pollution concentrations and damage were rising, the growth rate of EVA was 100 basis points less than that of GDP. Yet following the passage and enactment of the CAA, EVA outpaced GDP by an approximately equal margin (Muller 2020). By failing to account for the benefits of cleaner air, the US has been understating output and productivity growth since the 1970s.

While most of the extant literature on pollution damage focuses on the US economy because of data constraints, a recent paper estimates environmental accounts, including air pollution and GHGs, for 163 countries from 1998 to 2018 (Mohan et al. 2020). This paper finds an appreciable effect on growth of including pollution damage in an adjusted output measure. For example, from 1998 to 2012, China's pollution-adjusted growth was as much as 50 basis points less than its GDP growth. Western European countries exhibited pollution-adjusted growth well in excess of their GDP growth, as pollution levels fell. Lower income countries tended to show very little difference between pollution-adjusted growth and GDP growth rates, as pollution damage changed proportionately with output (Mohan et al. 2020).

In addition to work on growth and environmental accounting, recent papers have found that air pollution, by negatively affecting health, reduces labor supply (Hanna and Oliva 2015) and decreases labor productivity (Graff Zivin and Neidell 2012; Chang et al. 2016). These effects should already be reflected in the output statistics in national accounts. Similarly, Deschênes, Greenstone, and Shapiro (2017) report substantial investments by households in pharmaceuticals to mitigate effects from pollution exposure. Such expenditures count as consumption in standard national accounts.

7.3 Conceptual Model

This section of the analysis employs a national income accounting framework to characterize the effect of including pollution damage in measures of output and growth. The model is presented formally in the box. The main ideas are as follows:

- First, the model assumes that the production measured by GDP leads to pollution but that pollution can be reduced by either (a) switching to less polluting (but possibly more costly) production technologies or (b) spending money on pollution abatement. Spending money on pollution abatement or using more expensive production techniques to limit pollution raises firms' costs, hence lowering final output of market goods and services.[2] This drag on market output is already captured in current measures of GDP. However, the benefits to society from less air pollution or CO_2 are emissions are not.[3]

- The model then introduces environmentally adjusted GDP, a measure of output that accounts for the damage produced by *unabated pollution*. For example, if measured market GDP is \$2 trillion but pollution produced by that production lowers well-being by \$200 billion, then environmentally adjusted GDP is \$1.8 trillion.
- Third, the model explores the effects of pollution on GDP growth. The effect of pollution damage on environmentally adjusted GDP growth depends on how damage changes through time. If damage from pollution is falling as a share of GDP, then growth rate of environmentally adjusted GDP will be higher than growth rate of market GDP. To continue the example from above, if in the next period, measured market GDP is \$2.2 trillion, a 10 percent increase, and damage is \$205 billion, only a 2.5 percent increase, environmentally adjusted GDP increases from \$1.8 trillion to \$1.995 trillion—a 10.8 percent rate of increase. Because pollution damage rose less than GDP, the measure of GDP that subtracts the cost of pollution showed more growth. If, on the other hand, damage had been rising faster than GDP, then environmentally adjusted GDP would have increased at a lower rate than market GDP.
- Finally, the model shows that the growth effect of a constant damage policy depends on the beginning level pollution intensity. If initial pollution intensity is lower, the boost to growth from having damage increase at a slower pace is also lower. In the example above, if pollution caused \$20 billion of damage in the base year and \$20.5 billion in the next period, environmentally adjusted GDP would increase only slightly more rapidly than market GDP—10.1 percent versus 10 percent.

7.4 Putting a Monetary Value on Environmental Damage

The framework discussed above incorporates nonmarket environmental "bads" (damage) that lie outside the market boundary into a measure of productivity.[4] The most economically important of these extramarket effects is premature mortality risk from exposure to fine particulate matter, or $PM_{2.5}$ (US EPA 1997; 1999; 2011). The increasing adverse effects on the climate from emissions of carbon dioxide (CO_2) are also taken into consideration. In this section, we discuss approaches that have been taken to value benefits from reduction in pollution (section 7.4.1) and costs of increased GHG emissions (section 7.4.2).

Box 7.1 Modeling the Growth Rate of Environmentally Adjusted GDP

Market output, or GDP, in period t is denoted Y_t^m. Damage from pollution is reduced by spending on abatement. If A_t denotes expenditure on pollution abatement in period t, then $A_t = \gamma_t Y_t^m$, where $(0 \leq \gamma_t < 1)$. Let D_t denote pollution damage from period t production, net of abatement: $D_t = \alpha_t Y_t^m - \beta_t(\gamma_t Y_t^m)$. The pre-abatement pollution intensity of output is given by α_t. The term β_t shows the responsiveness of pollution damage to spending on abatement. Combining these terms, damage falls with increasing abatement effort γ_t and with greater responsiveness of damage to abatement, and it rises with greater pollution intensiveness of output α_t (Muller 2020).

Environmentally adjusted GDP (Y_t^e) deducts postabatement pollution damage from emissions in period t from output in period t. Expression (1) presents this augmented characterization of output:

$$(1) \qquad \begin{aligned} Y_t^e &= Y_t^m - D_t \\ &= Y_t^m[1-(\alpha_t - \beta_t\gamma_t)]. \end{aligned}$$

Growth in adjusted output between periods t and $t + 1$ is shown in equation (2):

$$(2) \qquad \begin{aligned} \frac{Y_{t+1}^e - Y_t^e}{Y_t^e} &= \frac{Y_{t+1}^m - Y_t^m - (D_{t+1} - D_t)}{Y_t^m - D_t} \\ &= \frac{Y_{t+1}^m}{Y_t^m}\frac{[1-(\alpha_{t+1} - \beta_{t+1}\gamma_{t+1})]}{[1-(\alpha_t - \beta_t\gamma_t)]} - 1. \end{aligned}$$

The effect on growth of pollution damage depends on how damage changes through time (Le Kama and Schubert 2007; Hoel and Sterner 2007; Heal 2009; Gollier 2010; Baumgärtner et al. 2015; Six and Wirl 2015; Muller 2019). Rising damage depresses growth since damage acts as a drag on output. If this drag is falling, growth is enhanced.

The central thrust of this chapter is that adjusting for pollution damage appreciably affects productivity growth. The next step, therefore, compares adjusted growth as measured in equation (2) to GDP growth, which, for the purposes of this chapter, can be treated as the output growth concept used for productivity statistics:[1]

1. The main output concept used in practice to measure productivity omits the parts of GDP covering nonmarket output of government and nonprofit institutions. This distinction is not material to the purposes of this chapter.

(*continued*)

Box 7.1 ***(continued)***

$$(3)\qquad \frac{Y_{t+1}^e - Y_t^e}{Y_t^e} - \frac{Y_{t+1}^m - Y_t^m}{Y_t^m} = \frac{Y_{t+1}^m}{Y_t^m}\frac{[(\alpha_t - \beta_t\gamma_t) - (\alpha_{t+1} - \beta_{t+1}\gamma_{t+1})]}{[1-(\alpha_t - \beta_t\gamma_t)]}.$$

The sign of the growth rate correction in equation (3) is determined by change in the postabatement pollution intensity of output. If pollution intensity is rising, the numerator of the correction term is negative, and GDP growth exceeds the growth of Y_t^e. And if the economy is becoming cleaner, growth in Y_t^e outpaces GDP growth.

The conditions under which the growth rates of market output and adjusted output Y_t^m are the same are also worth noting. Expression (4) shows that for the growth rates to equate, *damage intensity must be fixed:*

$$(4)\qquad \frac{Y_{t+1}^m}{Y_t^m} = \frac{Y_{t+1}^m[1-(\alpha_{t+1} - \beta_{t+1}\gamma_{t+1})]}{Y_t^m[1-(\alpha_t - \beta_t\gamma_t)]}.$$

In this case, damage grows at the GDP growth rate, and growth of Y_t^e equals that of Y_t^m. Only under the special circumstance that pollution damage changes at the same rate as GDP are the growth rates of Y_t^e and GDP the same.

In the US and other advanced economies, policies for air pollution establish standards that are held fixed over several years. How does growth in Y^e and Y^m differ if emission constraints are binding and equally stringent over time? That is, how do growth rates compare if the level of damage D_t is constant over time? In that case,

$$\alpha_{t+1} - \beta_{t+1}\gamma_{t+1} = \frac{Y_t^m}{Y_{t+1}^m}(\alpha_t - \beta_t\gamma_t),$$

and the growth differential given by equation (3) becomes

$$\frac{Y_{t+1}^e - Y_t^e}{Y_t^e} - \frac{Y_{t+1}^m - Y_t^m}{Y_t^m} = \left(\frac{Y_{t+1}^m - Y_t^m}{Y_t^m}\right)\left(\frac{\alpha_t - \beta_t\gamma_t}{1-(\alpha_t - \beta_t\gamma_t)}\right).$$

This expression shows that when damage is constant and GDP growth is positive, the growth rate of Y^e exceeds that of Y^m. Also, the growth effect of a constant damage policy depends on the beginning (period t) level of pollution intensity. If initial pollution intensity is higher, the boost to growth from holding damage constant is also higher. When pollution intensity is low, as in the US economy and other developed countries currently, the growth differential from holding damage fixed is small.

7.4.1 Valuing the Benefits of Improved Health from Reduction in Pollution

One of the distinctive challenges associated with building environmental pollution damage into an adjusted measure of productivity centers on valuation. In contrast to goods and services traded in markets, for which prices can be used to estimate a value at the margin, environmental goods and services leave no such convenient trace. Therefore, economists must resort to alternative approaches to elicit marginal values. As this issue pertains to local air pollution, techniques may be grouped into two categories: revealed preference methods, based on what people do, and stated preference methods, based on what people say (Viscusi and Aldy 2003). Both are discussed below.

7.4.1.1 Revealed Preference Techniques

Revealed preference techniques estimate marginal willingness to pay (WTP) for environmental services from market transactions (Viscusi and Aldy 2003). One common approach is to use the relationship between wages and risk of job-related injury and fatality to estimate the marginal rate of substitution between money (wages) and mortality risk (Viscusi and Aldy 2003). This is also referred to as the value of a statistical life (VSL).[5] Though not a direct measure of the monetary value of risk from pollution, academic researchers and regulatory agencies routinely use this approach to value mortality risk from pollution exposure (US EPA 1997; 1999; 2011; Muller, Mendelsohn, and Nordhaus 2011; Tschofen, Azevedo, and Muller 2019).

Although these models use actual market transactions and hence give an estimate of society's valuation of mortality risk, their application to risk associated with environmental pollution does pose methodological concerns. First, mortality risk preferences vary over the life cycle. Researchers have estimated the functional form of the VSL-age relationship, finding an inverted U-shape that reaches its maximum between 35 and 45 years of age (Aldy and Viscusi 2008). The samples on which these estimates are based are, by definition, dominated by working-age persons. Yet environmental pollution risks are most acutely focused on the very young and the very old (US EPA 1999; 2011; Muller 2020). In part to address heterogeneity in the age-risk relationship, researchers have applied an annualized VSL to value life years lost from environmental pollution exposure implied by actuarial tables (Muller, Mendelsohn, and Nordhaus 2011). The approach based on life years yields damage estimates on the order of one-half the magnitude of a uniform VSL applied to all persons.

An additional methodological concern is that most deaths on the job are associated with accidents: vehicle accidents, falls, and electrocution, for example. However, the largest share of mortality risk from environmental pollution is due to chronic exposure (US EPA 1999; 2011). It is conceivable that WTP for reductions in long-term mortality risk from chronic exposure differs from WTP for reductions in sudden mortality risk from accidents.

Third, the literature on estimation of the VSL finds that the VSL is greater for people with higher income (Hammitt and Robinson 2011). Nonetheless, in cross-sectional contexts, standard procedure in the context of federal benefit-cost analyses or regulatory impact analyses is to apply the VSL uniformly, regardless of income. While this necessarily abstracts away from a known determinant of individuals' VSL, the practice reflects sensible ethical and political considerations.

7.4.1.2 Stated Preference Methods

In contrast to revealed preference techniques, stated preference methods survey people directly about their valuation of risks or of environmental goods and services. The most common such approach is contingent valuation (CV), in which researchers design structured surveys to elicit WTP holding potential confounding factors fixed. For example, people may be asked to state their WTP for a numerically specified risk reduction. Often, survey respondents are educated about the magnitude of the risk changes they are being asked about on the survey instrument.

CV studies, broadly, suffer from the basic flaw that the survey response is necessarily hypothetical. This results in skepticism among some economists about the reliability of the technique (Hausman 2012) and potential biases in the VSL estimate (Edwards and Anderson 1987). However, CV studies can target more relevant age populations than hedonic wage studies. Moreover, CV studies can be designed to focus on risks that may manifest after years of exposure, more suitable to the valuation of environmental pollution risks than accidents in the hedonic studies. While CV analyses could, of course, estimate different VSLs for different income groups, the ethical and political constraints to their use in policy evaluation or design noted above would apply.

Typically, stated preference studies report VSLs that are about one-third of the magnitude of revealed preference studies (Kochi, Hubbell, and Kramer 2006). The US EPA employs a sample of both hedonic wage and CV studies to develop its VSL estimate, which is employed in this chapter.

7.4.2 Calculating the Costs of Greenhouse Gas (GHG) Emissions

Although the argument for valuation of damages from GHG emissions is analogous to that for local pollution, the empirical approach is substantively different. For valuing CO_2-equivalent (CO_2e)[6] damage, a widely used metric is the social cost of carbon (SCC), defined as marginal damage per ton of GHG emissions. The SCC is the discounted present value of damage caused by emitting one ton of CO_2e. SCC estimates are produced by integrated assessment models (IAMs), which combine a neoclassical growth model with a representation of the climate system. A mathematical function links temperature change to future damage, typically expressed as a fraction of global GDP.

There is now extensive literature on IAMs and the SCC.[7] Much of the current debate centers on the functional form of the temperature-damage relationship, the choice of social discount rate used in IAMs, and the treatment of the possibility of catastrophic damage (Pindyck 2013; Drupp et al. 2018; Weitzman 2011; Nordhaus 2011). The SCC used in this chapter was produced in a meta-analysis conducted by the US Federal Inter-Agency Working Group on the Social Cost of Carbon (FWG 2021). That analysis includes results from three prominent IAMs (Page, DICE, and Fund) and several different choices for the key parameters listed above (FWG 2016). The FWG (2016) demonstrates that the SCC increases over time as CO_2 accumulates in the atmosphere. Thus, researchers' assumptions regarding future economic growth play a central role in SCC calculations, because the higher the economic growth, the greater the projected emissions and accumulation of CO_2 in the atmosphere. Further, sensitivity of the SCC to the social discount rate is quite high: using a 2.5 percent discount rate rather than 3 percent (used in the default case) increases the SCC by 50 percent. This sensitivity occurs because much of the damage, in nominal terms, manifests far in the future. Reflecting the high costs of catastrophic outcomes, the SCC corresponding to the ninety-fifth percentile of the empirical distribution of SCC values is three times larger than the mean estimate.

7.5 Secular Trends in Emissions, Ambient Pollution, and Damage

Changes in the amount of pollution and the damage it causes determine the effect on productivity of including environmental considerations in an expanded GDP. This chapter discusses two of the most important types of pollution: local air pollution and long-lived GHGs. Because monetary damage has not been estimated for water pollution, this type of pollution is not addressed here.[8]

7.5.1 Air Pollution Emissions

Over the past three decades, emissions of most local air pollutants have fallen (US EPA 2020); emissions of carbon monoxide (CO), sulfur dioxide (SO_2), and nitrogen oxides (NO_x) declined the most. Table 7.1 reports that CO and NO_x dropped by roughly 3 percent annually over the 28-year period from 1990 to 2018. Releases of SO_2 plummeted by over 7 percent per year over the same period. Emissions of primary particulate matter ($PM_{2.5}$) and volatile organic compounds (VOCs) exhibited more modest declines. Ammonia (NH_3), which is largely unregulated, declined least of all.

What induced these changes? Holland et al. (2020) demonstrate that the exit of coal-fired power plants and the installation of SO_2 control technology on remaining coal-fired plants contributed significantly to this decline.

Further, Holland et al. (2020) show that the penetration of renewables in the power sector led to large declines in emissions and damage. In the US manufacturing sector, Shapiro and Walker (2018) report that between 1990 and 2008, emissions of local air pollution fell considerably despite significant growth in real output. The authors highlight three possible explanations for these trends: trade and offshoring of emissions, domestic policies requiring abatement, and efficiency improvements at facilities. Shapiro and Walker (2018) find that increasing stringency of domestic environmental policy accounts for most of the observed emission reductions. In the transportation sector, fuel pollution content regulations substantially contributed to reduced emissions (US EPA 2020).

7.5.2 Air Quality

Prior research on the damage, or social costs, from exposure to ambient air pollution emphasizes the importance of exposure to fine particulate matter ($PM_{2.5}$) to total damage (Muller and Mendelsohn 2007; US EPA 1999; 2011; Shindell et al. 2012). Thus, the present summary of air quality conditions in the US economy focuses on this pollutant.

$PM_{2.5}$ is an amalgamation of many constituent species that derive from emissions of the pollutants listed in table 7.1, excluding CO_2. It includes sulfates, particles formed from emissions of SO_2 (a gas), and ammonium nitrate, particulates formed in the atmosphere after NH_3 and NO_x gases are emitted. Other common components of $PM_{2.5}$ include organic and elemental carbon, a variety of metals, and biogenic dusts. Thus, ambient $PM_{2.5}$ serves as a useful index, or summary statistic, for air quality since it depends on emissions of a variety of air pollution species and accounts for a large share of the damage from pollution.

Muller (2020) has assembled a long time series of $PM_{2.5}$ data for the US spanning the years 1957 to 2016.[9] These data reveal a considerable reduc-

Table 7.1 Emission trends from 1990 to 2018

Pollutant	Annual Rate of Change (%)	Total Change (%)
Carbon monoxide (CO)	–3.42	–62.28
Nitrogen oxide (NO_X)	–3.18	–59.54
Particulate matter <=2.5 micrometers in diameter ($PM_{2.5}$)	–1.25	–29.70
Sulfur dioxide (SO_2)	–7.33	–88.15
Volatile organic compounds (VOC)	–1.46	–33.74
Ammonia (NH_3)	–0.69	–17.63
Carbon dioxide (CO_2)	1.08	86.44

Source: https://www.epa.gov/air-emissions-inventories/air-pollutant-emissions-trends-data for local air pollution.
CO2 (USDOE 2019).

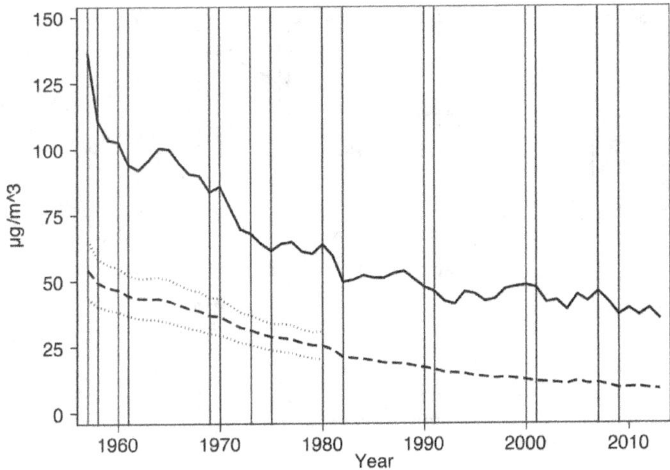

Fig. 7.1 Total suspended particulates (TSP) and PM2.5 national average concentrations

Dash = PM2.5 (95 percent confidence intervals on predicted values prior to 1980); solid = TSP Vertical lines demarcate NBER recessions.

Source: Muller (2020).

tion in national annual average $PM_{2.5}$, which is evident in figure 7.1. In 1957, annual average $PM_{2.5}$ was just over 50 micrograms per cubic meter ($\mu g/m^3$), a level comparable to China in 2014 (Mohan et al. 2020). This level fell to roughly 30 $\mu g/m^3$ by the energy crisis in the middle 1970s. The annual average dropped to 20 $\mu g/m^3$ in the early 1980s, and in 2016, the national average was under 10 $\mu g/m^3$. As of 2018, the national average $PM_{2.5}$ level has been between 7 and 8 $\mu g/m^3$. An important pattern evident in figure 7.1 is that large and persistent reductions in ambient $PM_{2.5}$ tend to coincide with troughs in the business cycle. This is especially apparent in the early 1980s double-dip recessions and the Great Recession of 2008 (Muller 2020). Connecting figure 7.1 to table 7.1, the declining trend in ambient $PM_{2.5}$ is a result of emission reductions of the pollutants listed in table 7.1.

7.5.3 Emissions of GHGs

Both past and present emissions of GHGs are key contributors to climate change. Scientists measure GHGs (which consist of CO_2, methane, and nitrous oxide, among other species) by their CO_2 equivalent, or CO_2e. Total atmospheric CO_2 depends on global emissions because these gases mix globally, and thus changes in US emissions are only weakly correlated with global concentrations.

Table 7.1 reports that US CO_2 emissions, produced from combustion and other releases, have increased 1.1 percent per year on average since 1990.[10] Figure 7.2 displays total, economy-wide emissions of CO_2e (all GHGs con-

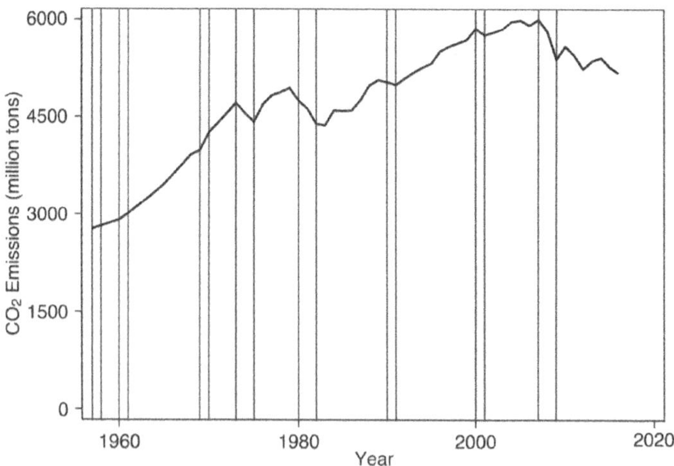

Fig. 7.2 CO2 emissions in the US economy
Source: US DOE 2019.

verted to their CO_2 equivalent). Emissions increased rapidly from the late 1950s through the 1970s. Following the disruptive period of recessions in the early 1980s, emissions rose at a more moderate pace until the Great Recession in 2008. CO_2e emissions have been falling in the US since then. Although discharges of GHGs have essentially been unregulated at the federal level, air quality policies (which target the air pollutants discussed earlier) and market forces have contributed to the leveling off of emissions growth in the US economy. Specifically, air pollution policies that limit discharges of SO_2, NO_x, and $PM_{2.5}$ have curtailed the use of coal in power generation and manufacturing and have led to the use of pollution control technology (Holland et al. 2020; Shapiro and Walker 2018). Further, the rapid expansion of natural gas production resulted in price decreases for natural gas, leading firms to substitute away from coal to natural gas where possible. Because coal is more carbon intensive than natural gas, CO_2 emissions fell.

Additionally, steep declines in the cost of renewable power generation—due to technological advancements, learning by doing, and federal subsidies—contributed to reduced reliance on coal. Overall, changes in the mix of coal and natural gas in the power generation sector and in emission rates at existing plants contributed more to the decline in emissions than renewable penetration (Holland et al. 2020).

Market forces led to the second pattern evident in figure 7.2: CO_2 emissions are strongly procyclical. CO_2 emissions are the product of business activity and household consumption. Thus, as economic activity ebbs and flows over the business cycle, CO_2 fluctuates as well. The vertical lines in the figure demarcate recessions.[11] One can clearly see significant reductions in

CO_2 emissions during contractionary periods. In particular, emissions fell precipitously during the middle 1970s recession during the energy crisis, the double-dip recession in the early 1980s, and the Great Recession. Since peaking at about 6 billion tons in 2008, emissions have not returned to that level.

As noted above, CO_2 is a globally mixed pollutant. As such, trade is an important determinant of global concentrations of CO_2 and, ultimately, damage caused by emissions. Shapiro (2016) reports that international trade increased CO_2 emissions by 5 percent but that the welfare consequences (benefits) of trade far outweigh environmental costs from emissions of CO_2. Relatedly, Shapiro (2021) finds that tariffs and other trade barriers provide an implicit subsidy to CO_2 emissions by protecting cleaner downstream industries. This reinforces the point that both market and policy forces shape CO_2 emission trends.

7.6 Calculating the Damage from Pollution: $PM_{2.5}$ and GHGs

Methods to integrate environmental considerations into the national accounts have been developed by the academic literature[12] and international standards for official statistics.[13] The literature concludes that, just as goods and services traded in markets are valued by their price, emissions of pollution should be valued according to their marginal damage. Therefore, total pollution damage should be valued as the marginal damage of emissions times the quantity of physical discharges.[14]

7.6.1 Damage from $PM_{2.5}$

$PM_{2.5}$ causes multiple types of damage, including premature mortality, short-term illness, and reduced worker productivity. Of these, premature mortality risk comprises the bulk of monetary damage from air pollution (US EPA 1997; 1999; 2011; Muller and Mendelsohn 2007; Muller, Mendelsohn, and Nordhaus 2011).

One component of ambient $PM_{2.5}$ is lead (Pb). About 10 percent of the benefits from the CAA are from avoided lead exposure—direct emissions of which have been essentially eliminated by reduction in use of leaded gasoline (US EPA 1997). Benefits from avoiding lost IQ points from lead exposure are considerably smaller than monetized benefits from avoided premature death (US EPA 1997). In addition, nonmonetized effects of current lead exposure from polluted topsoil include reduced fertility (Clay, Portnykh, and Severnini 2021).

This section calculates the premature mortality damage from air pollution from 1957 to 2016 using a time series of national, annual average $PM_{2.5}$ concentrations from 1957 to 2016 (Muller 2020). The basic approach to measuring the damage from air pollution exposure is to multiply an estimate of the number of lives lost from pollution exposure by the VSL. Equation (5) demonstrates a standard approach used for this calculation:

(5) $$\text{Damage}_{pm,t} = \text{VSL}_t \times \text{MR}_t \times \text{Pop}_t \times (1 - \exp^{-\beta PM_{2.5,t}}),$$

where

$\text{Damage}_{pm,t}$ = damage from $PM_{2.5}$ at time t

MR_t = mortality rate time (t)

Pop_t = population time (t)

β = statistically estimated parameter from Krewski et al. 2009.

The functional form in (5) stems from the epidemiological literature, which finds that $PM_{2.5}$ exposure is more harmful in populations with high mortality rates. The mechanism for this relationship is that relatively unhealthy populations are less able to withstand exposure than healthier populations. Mortality damage from exposure to $PM_{2.5}$ therefore depends on baseline incidence rates of death, size of exposed population, and annual average concentrations.[15] Further, baseline mortality rates depend on the age, gender, and race[16] of the exposed population (US EPA 1999; 2011). Standard practice in both academic research and benefit-cost analyses is to calculate (5) for distinct age groups but not for different races and genders (US EPA 1999; 2011; Muller, Mendelsohn, and Nordhaus 2011). The parenthetical term in (5) is the concentration-response function reported in Krewski et al. (2009), which is an updated version of Pope et al. (2002). It measures the share of mortality risk attributable to $PM_{2.5}$ exposure. This function is commonly used in US EPA regulatory impact analyses for modeling mortality risk from $PM_{2.5}$ exposure (US EPA 1999; 2011). The product of mortality rates and population yields total deaths. Then, deaths multiplied by ($1\text{-}\exp^{-\beta PM2.5,t}$) is the number of deaths due to $PM_{2.5}$. Multiplying by the VSL converts deaths to monetary damage.

Because of the long time series in this study, income adjustments to the VSL are necessary. Guidance on precisely how and why to do these adjustments is found in the literature (Costa and Kahn 2004; Hammitt and Robinson 2011). In this chapter, the decadal VSLs from 1950 until 1980 are those reported in Costa and Kahn (2004). From 1980 through 2016, the VSL series is derived from the US EPA's preferred VSL using an income elasticity of 0.4. The US EPA's preferred VSL was about $11 million by 2016 ($11.4 million in 2020).

7.6.2 Damage from GHGs

Emissions of CO_2 are typically converted into monetary damage using the SCC, which is the discounted present value of the damage resulting from one ton of CO_2e. Total, or gross, external damage for CO_2e is thus computed as the product of the SCC (dollars/ton) and emissions (tons). While the SCC is invariant across space because CO_2 is a globally mixed pollutant, it does vary through time according to the global accumulation of atmospheric CO_2. This analysis uses an SCC of $36/metric ton CO_2e corresponding to the estimate for 2015 from the FWG (2016). This value is adjusted to earlier years in the analysis using real rates of change in the FWG document (FWG 2016).

Figure A7.2 displays a time series of national annual combined damage from average $PM_{2.5}$ concentrations and CO_2e emissions from 1957 to 2016 to demonstrate pollution damage intensity in the US economy.[17] Damage was quite substantial in the 1960s prior to the enactment of the federal CAA, totaling between 30 percent and 40 percent of GDP. Damage fell to 20 percent of GDP in the 1980s, 15 percent in the 1990s, 10 percent in the 2000s, and around 5 percent in the modern era. Importantly, while ambient concentrations of $PM_{2.5}$ were declining over this period, the key monetization parameter, the VSL, was rising along with real per capita income (see fig. A7.1). Rising valuation per unit of pollution-induced mortality risk counteracts the decline in risk from the reduction in ambient air pollution. The sensitivity of the damage calculations to the VSL is discussed below.

Figure 7.3 shows real (in 2021 dollars) per capita damage for local air pollution and GHGs (discussed below). The air pollution damage increased rapidly from the late 1950s until the passage of the CAA in 1970. Following the act's passage, damage plateaued and then began to decline. The drop in damage, from a peak of approximately \$10,000 right around 1970 down to about \$5,000 in the modern era, is characterized by numerous, notable discrete changes. A few of these correspond directly with the business cycle. For example, damage fell by about \$1,000 over the recessions in the middle 1970s and early 1980s. And as the economy rebounded out of these recessions, importantly, real per capita damage did not rebound. Following a long period of relatively steady decline from the late 1980s to 2007, the Great

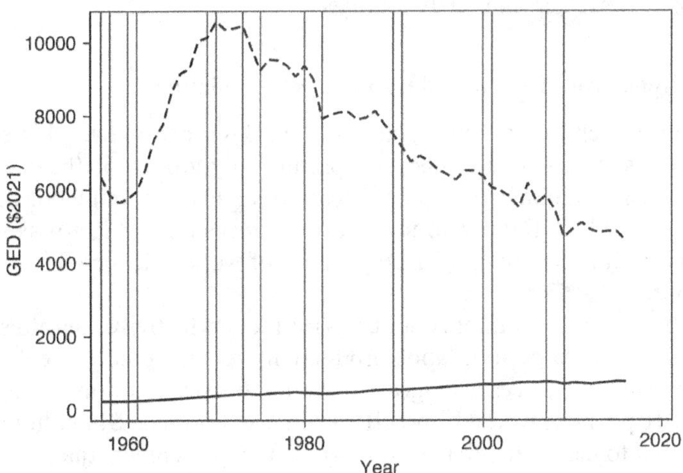

Fig. 7.3 Per capita damage from air pollution and greenhouse gas emissions
Source: Author's calculations. Dash = local air pollution. Solid = CO2e.

Recession in 2008 was also associated with a large discrete decrease in per capita damage.

In addition to damage from local air pollution, figure 7.3 shows per capita damage from annual emissions of CO_2e. There are two central patterns in figure 7.3 worth reinforcing. First, CO_2e damage is a small fraction of local air pollution damage. Second, damages have increased over time. In 1957, damage amounted to just \$200 per person, less than 5 percent of the damage caused by air pollution. In the 1950s, emissions exerted little damage because global concentrations of GHGs were much lower than in the modern era. In 2016, per capita monetary damage was over \$750, still only 16 percent of the damage caused by air pollution.

It may surprise readers to see the relative magnitudes of GHG and air pollution damage. It is important to bear in mind that the SCC represents the present value of global damage from one ton of CO_2e emissions and that the cumulative global total of CO_2e emissions is much greater than the annual additions to this total from the US. Further, severe damage occurring decades in the future are discounted. The GHG damage shown in figure 7.3 employs an SCC estimated with a 3 percent discount rate. Some analysts take the position that the discount rate in this context should be lower, which increases damage significantly. Using a 2.5 percent discount rate, damage from GHGs in 2016 would amount to over \$1,100 on a per capita basis. It is also important to recognize that damage may simply be much higher than the central SCC estimates suggest. Using the SCC from the ninety-fifth percentile of the distribution reported by the Inter-Agency Working Group results in per capita damage over \$2,100 in 2016 (FWG 2016). Though these alternative assumptions increase the GHG damage, air pollution damage is consistently greater than GHG damage.

7.7 Productivity Growth and Environmental Pollution

Using the empirical approach and data described above, this section provides estimates of the effects on productivity growth of the decline in environmental damage over time. Conventionally measured labor productivity is given by GDP per hour of work. To measured EAP, gross external damage pollution damage (GED) per hour of work is deducted from GDP per hour.[18]

Table 7.2 reports summary statistics for the productivity measures. Over the entire sample period, labor productivity as measured by real output per hour in 2021 prices averaged just over \$50. Air pollution damage was about \$10 per hour worked, and GHG damage was under \$1 per hour. EAP amounted to just over \$40 per hour—about 20 percent less than measured productivity.

Looking over time, the costs of environmental damage fell sharply. In the late 1950s and 1960s, EAP was less than 70 percent of measured productiv-

Table 7.2 **GDP, gross external damage (GED), and environmentally adjusted productivity (EAP) per hour worked by decade**

	1957–2016 (1)	1960s (2)	1970s (3)	1980s (4)	1990s (5)	2000s (6)	2010s (7)
GDP	54.94[A]	35.42	44.07	50.68	59.22	72.64	81.43
	(15.96)[B]	(3.23)	(2.01)	(2.76)	(2.80)	(4.44)	(0.87)
GED	10.07	11.41	14.01	11.08	8.63	7.34	6.53
Air	(2.76)	(2.15)	(1.08)	(0.88)	(0.61)	(0.42)	(0.32)
GED	0.70	0.43	0.61	0.64	0.76	0.91	0.98
GHG	(0.19)	(0.05)	(0.03)	(0.03)	(0.04)	(0.05)	(0.02)
GED	10.77	11.84	14.62	11.72	9.40	8.25	7.52
Total	(2.63)	(2.19)	(1.05)	(0.86)	(0.57)	(0.40)	(0.32)
EAP	44.17	23.58	29.45	38.96	49.82	64.39	73.91
	(17.98)	(1.21)	(2.99)	(3.57)	(3.33)	(4.69)	(1.17)

[A] = $/hour worked (real 2021 dollars)
[B] = standard deviation

Table 7.3 **Annual growth in productivity and pollution damage**

	GDP (1)	GED (2)	EAP (3)
	1957–2016		
Annual Growth	1.68***[A]	–1.04***	2.38***
	(0.021)[B]	(0.153)	(0.037)
	1957–1970		
Annual Growth	2.27***	4.57***	1.10***
	(0.0914)	(0.353)	(0.230)
	1971–2016		
Annual Growth	1.64***	–1.76***	2.44***
	(0.0255)	(0.0531)	(0.0479)

[A] = growth expressed in (%). Coefficients from log-linear, OLS regression of GDP, GED, and EAP on year.
[B] = standard errors in parentheses.
* $p < 0.10$; ** $p < 0.05$; *** $p < 0.01$
Column (1) regresses GDP/hour worked in natural log form on year.
Column (2) regresses EAP/hour worked in natural log form on year.
Column (3) regresses GED/hour worked in natural log form on year.
Gross external damage (GED), environmentally adjusted productivity (EAP)

ity, meaning that accounting for the environmental damage associated with production would lower measured labor productivity by over 30 percent. By 2010, EAP was 90 percent of measured productivity. Reflecting aggregate trends, air pollution GED per hour fell by 45 percent, and GHG damage per hour increased by 127 percent.

Table 7.3 reports empirical growth rates in real (inflation adjusted) GDP, GED, and EAP per hour. As shown in the top panel of the table, GDP per hour increased at a real rate of about 1.7 percent per year from 1957 to 2016. GED per hour fell by 1.0 percent per year. Combining the two in EAP results in a marked increase in apparent productivity growth; EAP expanded 2.4 percent annually compared to the 1.7 percent rise in GDP. The large adjustment to productivity growth evident in EAP manifests because, in the early years of the sample, the GED amounted to a large share of GDP. Recall from table 7.2 how large GED per hour worked was relative to GDP prior to 1970. This *relative* magnitude fell precipitously from 1970 to 2016. Figure 7.1 demonstrates that a key reason for this large pollution damage burden was the very high ambient levels of pollution before passage of the CAA. Annual average $PM_{2.5}$ in 1957 was on par with that in China in 2014 (Mohan et al. 2020).

The conceptual model in the box above provides intuition for orientation between EAP and GDP growth rates. If GED is rising more rapidly than GDP per hour, EAP growth falls short of GDP. In contrast, if GED is rising less quickly than GDP, productivity growth as measured by EAP per hour surpasses productivity growth as measured by GDP per hour. This is precisely what table 7.3 shows. Over the 1957 to 2016 period, GED fell while output per hour increased. Thus, EAP outpaced GDP per hour worked.

The bottom two panels of table 7.3 break the 60-year sample up into the 14 years before the CAA was enacted and the 46 years between its enactment and the end of the sample. From 1957 to 1970, conventionally measured GDP per hour worked expanded at a rate of 2.3 percent per year. In this preregulatory state, GED per hour worked grew even more rapidly, at 4.6 percent. So not only was productivity growing, but the pollution intensity of output was also rising. As a result, EAP increased at a rate of just 1.1 percent while GDP per hour expanded at 2.3 percent. Building the GED into the measure of output per hour lowers productivity growth before the passage and implementation of the CAA.

In marked contrast, after the passage and beginning of enactment of the CAA, the GED fell by about 1.8 percent per year. Over this time period, as is well known, conventionally measured productivity growth slowed: from 2.3 percent prior to 1971 to 1.6 percent afterward. This chapter argues, in part, that this is due to mismeasurement of output. Over this post-CAA period, with the GED deducted from output per hour, EAP suggests productivity grew at 2.4 percent per year. The contrast to market-based productivity growth could not be more stark. With GDP per hour as the metric, indeed, productivity growth appears to have attenuated following 1970. However, with the more comprehensively defined EAP, productivity *increased* after 1970.

Figure 7.4 provides a graphical depiction of these trends. The top-left panel plots GDP per hour worked (the solid line) together with EAP (the dashed line). Prior to the passage of the CAA in 1970, GDP per hour climbed

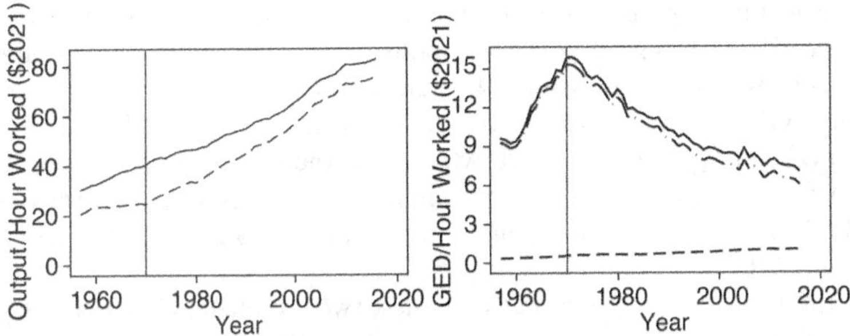

Fig. 7.4 Productivity, wages, and pollution damage

The left panel plots GDP/hour worked and EAP/hour worked. The right panel plots total pollution damage GED/hour worked (solid), air pollution GED/hour worked (dash-dot), and CO2e GED/hour worked (dash).

Source: FRED (2021a, 2021b, 2021c, 2021d) and author's calculations.

more rapidly than EAP. Then, following the CAA, EAP increased rapidly, partially catching up to GDP per hour through the 1990s and early 2000s.

The top-right panel of figure 7.4 plots GED per hour worked. The solid line combines local air pollution (dash-dot) and CO_2e (dash) damage. Beginning at roughly \$9 per hour worked, the GED rose to over \$15 by 1970. Following the CAA, GED per hour fell steadily to about \$6 by 2016. The decomposition of local air pollution and CO_2e damage is especially instructive. Only local air pollution was effectively regulated at the federal level over this time period. As such, it is intuitive that CO_2e damage, strongly correlated with economic activity, increased over time, while the regulated air pollution damage fell.

7.7.1 Sensitivity Analysis

Table A7.1 reports the results from a partial sensitivity analysis that focuses on the VSL. The default approach relies on decadal VSL estimates from Costa and Kahn (2004) and then uses the US EPA's VSL-income elasticity of 0.4 and labor market data on income to impute the series forward to 2016. The sensitivity analysis uses a 1.0 income elasticity throughout the 60-year sample and does not rely on the estimates from Costa and Kahn (2004). Figure A7.1 depicts both VSL series in nominal terms. Prior to 1980, the alternative VSL rises less rapidly than the VSL estimated from labor market data by Costa and Kahn (2004). After 1980, it rises more rapidly than the default VSL. The top panel of table A7.1 reports that EAP computed with the alternative VSL rises at 2.2 percent annually, compared to 2.4 percent with the default VSL. The orientation between GDP and EAP growth rates is not appreciably affected by the alternative VSL.

The GED series is more appreciably affected, with damage falling by

1 percent and 0.3 percent with the default and alternative VSLs, respectively. Prior to 1971, the GED rises less rapidly (1.2 percent) with the alternative VSL than with the default VSL (4.6 percent). The result is that EAP growth exceeds GDP per hour growth, whereas in the default case, EAP growth falls short of GDP per hour worked. After 1971, the results are quite similar to the default case, with EAP rising more rapidly than GDP per hour worked and GED per hour worked falling, but at a more modest rate than with the default VSL.

Thus, the key discrepancy between these two parameter choices is the rate of increase in GED per hour worked prior to 1971. Given that Costa and Kahn (2004) estimate VSLs directly from labor market data over this time period, it is likely that the rate of change in the VSL from the late 1950s to 1970 is better reflected in their approach than in the uniform application of the alternative VSL examined here.

7.8 Conclusions and Recommendations

Since the late 1960s and early 1970s, the US has allocated considerable resources to the provision of environmental public goods. GDP, which, by definition, measures economic activity within the market boundary or activity that is a close substitute for market production, forms the basis of metrics often used by growth and productivity scholars, such as output per worker and output per hour. Accounts with a market-centric perspective at best only partially reflect returns to society's investments in environmental public goods. And, in fact, the extant literature demonstrates that the vast majority of damage from remaining pollution (or benefits from policy-induced reductions in emissions) lies outside the scope of markets; these damages consist of premature mortality risk and the present value of future monetary damage from GHG emissions (US EPA 1999; 2011; Muller, Mendelsohn, and Nordhaus 2011).

The present analysis contends that omission of the *very large* monetary benefits from environmental quality improvements creates the illusion that the trillions of US dollars allocated to environmental cleanup have only had the effect of reducing GDP. The empirical section of this chapter, drawing from previous work (Muller 2020) and conducting new analysis, demonstrates the dramatic effect that counting the value of reduced pollution damage has on productivity growth estimates. From 1957 to 2016, EAP grew at 2.4 percent per annum, whereas conventionally measured GDP per hour worked expanded at 1.7 percent. What is more, prior to the enactment of the CAA in the early 1970s, EAP growth lagged GDP per hour worked because pollution damage was on the rise. Investments in pollution control, essentially without a signature in GDP per hour, induced a dramatic reversal in the relationship between EAP and GDP productivity growth.

While there are certainly other dimensions of environmental quality not captured in the present analysis (water quality, for instance), this chapter shows that expanding the national accounts and the metrics used to gauge productivity growth to include environmental quality has the potential to (1) appreciably affect productivity estimates and (2) influence macrolevel trends in productivity growth in the US economy. Air pollution's clear downward trend in emissions, ambient pollution levels, and damage have had the largest effect on EAP thus far. However, productivity as measured by EAP may encounter new headwinds if CO_2e emissions remain largely unregulated. Figure 7.3 shows the growing importance of CO_2e damage relative to air pollution. If damage proves worse than expected, or if emissions rise rapidly as the developing world's incomes grow, EAP will suffer setbacks from rising external cost. The bottom line from this study is the need to expand the national accounts to provide a more complete picture of productivity growth.

7.8.1 Recommendations for Implementation

The following recommendations are offered to statistical agencies focused on productivity measurement that are planning to implement or have implemented an augmented set of accounts inclusive of environmental goods and services.[19]

1) Begin by including pollutants that stand to make the greatest impact on productivity measures. These likely include $PM_{2.5}$ and CO_2e.
   i. Later, as data and models improve, include water pollution, toxics, and solid waste.

2) Estimate monetary damage rather than physical emissions to facilitate incorporation directly into monetary productivity measures. Use peer-reviewed techniques to translate emissions and concentrations into monetary damage.
   i. These include the VSL, the SCC, and the $PM_{2.5}$ adult-mortality concentration response function.

3) Deduct the present value of damage caused from current emissions from current measures of output, then express in productivity terms (i.e., per unit labor).

4) Conduct sensitivity analysis on the parameters and functions in 2.i.

5) Policymakers who use productivity or growth measures in policy evaluation should include environmentally adjusted output and productivity. An example of such an application is the legislation scoring process developed and used by the Congressional Budget Office.

Appendix

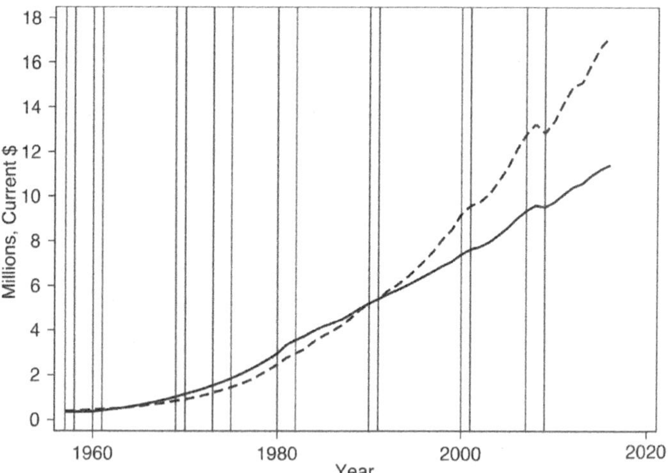

Fig. A7.1 VSL under various assumptions
Solid: default variable income elasticity; dash: income elasticity = 1.0.
Source: Muller (2020).

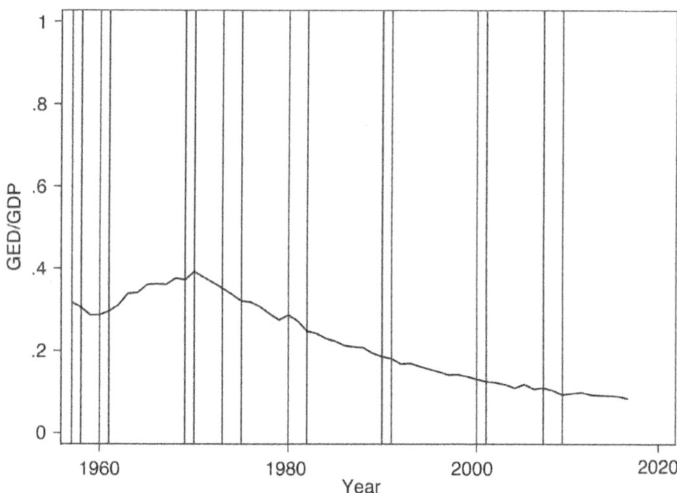

Fig. A7.2 Pollution damage intensity: Gross external damage (GED)/GDP
Vertical lines demarcate NBER recessions.
Source: Muller (2020).

Table A7.1 Sensitivity analysis on VSL-income elasticity, productivity, and damage growth rates

	GDP	EAP	EAP unit VSL	GED	GED unit VSL
All Years					
Year	0.0168***	0.0238***	0.0224***	–0.0104***	–0.00302***
	(0.000212)	(0.000367)	(0.000342)	(0.00153)	(0.000415)
Constant	–29.56***	–43.66***	–41.01***	22.78***	8.251***
	(0.421)	(0.730)	(0.679)	(3.052)	(0.827)
R^2	0.994	0.991	0.992	0.558	0.462
N	60	60	60	60	60
Before 1971					
Year	0.0227***	0.0110***	0.0280***	0.0457***	0.0121***
	(0.000914)	(0.00230)	(0.00144)	(0.00353)	(0.00138)
Constant	–41.09***	–18.53***	–52.02***	–87.36***	–21.38***
	(1.792)	(4.511)	(2.835)	(6.931)	(2.716)
R^2	0.983	0.754	0.980	0.934	0.811
N	14	14	14	14	14
1971 and After					
Year	0.0164***	0.0244***	0.0208***	–0.0176***	–0.00248***
	(0.000255)	(0.000479)	(0.000311)	(0.000531)	(0.000651)
Constant	–28.76***	–44.89***	–37.73***	37.24***	7.170***
	(0.508)	(0.952)	(0.617)	(1.057)	(1.299)
R^2	0.991	0.991	0.994	0.964	0.283
N	46	46	46	46	46

Gross external damage (GED) and environmentally adjusted productivity (EAP)

Notes

1. These landmark laws also include the National Environmental Policy Act (NEPA), the Clean Water Act (CWA), and the Safe Drinking Water Act (SDWA).

2. Pollution abatement expenditures are intermediate goods and services that are not counted directly in GDP so as to avoid double counting. For example, when a bakery buys flour to make a cake, the flour is not in final demand, but the cake is. In the environmental context, the service produced by the inputs used to lessen environmental damage—environmental protection—is missing from GDP.

3. In aggregate, damages are deducted from GDP. At the level of an industry or business sector, damages are subtracted from value added.

4. Pollution is an externality—a by-product of economic activity that affects others without their consent. The international standards for national accounts of the *System of National Accounts 2008* (paragraph 3.92) exclude externalities from GDP calculations because an externality is not a transaction.

5. It is important to emphasize that the VSL is a marginal concept. That is, it reflects tradeoffs between money and small changes in mortality risk. There is a common misperception that the VSL reflects the value of avoiding certain death. This is incorrect, as hedonic wage models estimate the marginal implicit price for risk changes on the job. When applied to environmental pollutants, deaths attributable

to exposure are estimated by multiplying the (typically small) changes in mortality risk from exposure times the exposed population. The resulting change in *expected* deaths is then valued using the VSL.

6. CO_2e is a means of standardizing the damage from emissions of CO_2, methane (CH_4), and nitrous oxide (N_2O). These principal GHGs each have different atmospheric lifetimes, warming potential, and, hence, impacts at the margin.

7. A good summary of the SCC, models used to estimate the SCC, and associated issues is provided by the US Inter-Agency Working Group on the Social Cost of GHGs (FWG 2021).

8. The lack of estimates on monetary damage from water pollution represents a key unmet challenge to the development of comprehensive environmental accounts. Keiser, Kling, and Shapiro (2019) provide an excellent review of the issues associated with the estimation of water pollution damage.

9. These data consist of two series spliced together. From 1957 to 1980, the $PM_{2.5}$ estimates are imputed from readings of total suspended particulate matter (TSP), a broad classification of ambient particulate matter that includes $PM_{2.5}$ as a subset. The TSP readings are from early state and municipal monitoring networks located mostly in large cities. The imputation procedure is discussed in Muller (2020). From 1980 to 2016, the series consist of satellite and modeled $PM_{2.5}$ estimates provided by Meng et al. (2019). These data are reported at 1o x 1o resolution across the entire US and are collapsed to a population-weighted average in Muller (2020).

10. Purchases by US-based economic agents of goods from abroad also embody CO_2 emissions and could be ascribed to the US. However, standard emissions accounting practices attribute emissions to the country in which the discharge occurs.

11. These are periods reported to be recessions by the National Bureau of Economic Research.

12. Nordhaus and Tobin 1973, Hamilton 1994; 1996; Weitzman and Lofgren 1997; Asheim and Weitzman 2001; Cairns 2002; Abraham and Mackie 2006; Nordhaus 2006.

13. System of Environmental Economic Accounting (https://www.seea.un.org/).

14. For long-lived pollutants, the marginal damage is the present value of expected future damage. This is akin to how durable goods are valued; their price reflects the discounted flow of benefits from the goods' use.

15. The damage calculations for premature mortality risk from $PM_{2.5}$ exposure employ age-specific national population counts, baseline mortality rates, and annual VSL estimates. All data sources are provided in Muller (2020).

16. Recent work demonstrates that race-specific mortality rates can have a significant effect on total damage estimates (Spiller et al. 2021).

17. The air pollution damage in this series was estimated in Muller (2020).

18. For a discussion of the conceptual basis for the term "GED," see Muller, Mendelsohn, and Nordhaus (2011).

19. When this chapter was being written, the US Bureau of Economic Analysis was gathering feedback on a set of regulations to launch a system of natural capital accounts and environmental statistics (White House 2022).

References

Abraham, Katherine G., and Christopher Mackie. 2006. "A Framework for Nonmarket Accounting." In *A New Architecture for the U.S. National Accounts*. NBER

Studies in Income and Wealth, edited by D. W. Jorgensen, J. S. Landefeld, and W. D. Nordhaus, vol. 66. Chicago: University of Chicago Press.
Aldy, J. E., and W. K. Viscusi. 2008. "Adjusting the Value of a Statistical Life for Age and Cohort Effects." *Review of Economics and Statistics* 90 (3): 573–81.
Asheim, Geir B., and Martin L. Weitzman. 2001. "Does NNP Growth Indicate Welfare Improvement?" *Economics Letters* 73 (2): 233–9.
Bartelmus, Peter. 2009. "The Cost of Natural Capital Consumption: Accounting for a Sustainable World Economy." *Ecological Economics* 68 (6): 1850–7.
Baumgärtner, S., A. M. Klein, D. Thiel, and K. Winkler. 2015. "Ramsey Discounting of Ecosystem Services." *Environmental and Resource Economics* 61 (2): 273–96.
Cairns, Robert D. 2002. "Green Accounting Using Imperfect, Current Prices." *Environment and Development Economics* 7 (2): 207–14.
Chang, Tom, Joshua Graff Zivin, Tal Gross, and Matthew Neidell. 2016. "Particulate Pollution and the Productivity of Pear Packers." *American Economic Journal: Economic Policy* 8 (3): 141–69.
Clay, K., M. Portnykh, and E. Severnini. 2021. "Toxic Truth: Lead and Fertility." *Journal of the Association of Environmental and Resource Economists* 8 (5): 975–1012.
Costa, D. L., and M. E. Kahn. 2004. "Changes in the Value of Life, 1940–1980." *Journal of Risk and Uncertainty* 29 (2): 159–80.
Deschênes, Olivier, Michael Greenstone, and Joseph S. Shapiro. 2017. "Defensive Investments and the Demand for Air Quality: Evidence from the NOx Budget Program." *American Economic Review* 107 (10): 2958–89.
Dockery, D. W., C. A. Pope, X. Xu, J. D. Spengler, J. H. Ware, M. E. Fay, B. G. Ferris, and F. E. Speizer. 1993. "An Association between Air Pollution and Mortality in Six U.S. Cities." *New England Journal of Medicine* 329 (1993): 1753–9.
Drupp, Moritz A., Mark C. Freeman, Ben Groom, and Frikk Nesje. 2018. "Discounting Disentangled." *American Economic Journal: Economic Policy* 10 (4): 109–34.
Edwards, Steven F., and Glen D. Anderson. 1987. "Overlooked Biases in Contingent Valuation Surveys: Some Considerations." *Land Economics* 63 (2): 168–78.
Federal Reserve Economic Data (FRED). 2019a. "Hours Worked by Full-Time and Part-Time Employees, Millions of Hours, Annual, Not Seasonally Adjusted." B4701C0A222NBEA. Economic Research Division, Federal Reserve Bank of St. Louis.
Federal Reserve Economic Data (FRED). 2019b. "Employed Full Time: Median Usual Weekly Real Earnings: Wage and Salary Workers: 16 Years and Over, 1982–84 CPI Adjusted Dollars, Quarterly, Seasonally Adjusted." LES1252881600Q. Economic Research Division, Federal Reserve Bank of St. Louis.
Federal Reserve Economic Data (FRED). 2019c. "Real Gross Domestic Investment: Consumption of Fixed Capital, Billions of Chained 2012 Dollars, Annual, Not Seasonally Adjusted." A264RX1A020NBEA. Economic Research Division, Federal Reserve Bank of St. Louis.
Federal Reserve Economic Data (FRED). 2021a. "Average Hourly Earnings of Production and Nonsupervisory Employees, Utilities, Dollars per Hour, Monthly, Seasonally Adjusted." CES4422000008. Economic Research Division, Federal Reserve Bank of St. Louis.
Federal Reserve Economic Data (FRED). 2021b. "Average Hourly Earnings of Production and Nonsupervisory Employees, Manufacturing, Dollars per Hour, Monthly, Seasonally Adjusted." CES3000000008. Economic Research Division, Federal Reserve Bank of St. Louis.
Federal Reserve Economic Data (FRED). 2021c. "Average Hourly Earnings of

Production and Nonsupervisory Employees, Transportation and Warehousing, Dollars per Hour, Monthly, Seasonally Adjusted." CES4300000008. Economic Research Division, Federal Reserve Bank of St. Louis.

Federal Reserve Economic Data (FRED). 2021d. "Farm Output: Compensation of Employees: Wage and Salary Accruals, Billions of Dollars, Annual, Not Seasonally Adjusted." B1019C1A027NBEA. Economic Research Division, Federal Reserve Bank of St. Louis.

Gollier, Christian. 2010. "Ecological Discounting." *Journal of Economic Theory* 145 (2): 812–29.

Gordon, Robert J. 2016. *The Rise and Fall of American Growth*. Princeton, NJ: Princeton University Press.

Graff Zivin, Joshua, and Matthew Neidell. 2012. "The Impact of Pollution on Worker Productivity." *American Economic Review* 102 (7): 3652–73.

Griliches, Zvi, ed. 1971. *Price Indexes and Quality Change*. Cambridge, MA: Harvard University Press.

Hamilton, Kirk. 1994. "Green Adjustments to GDP." *Resources Policy* 20 (3): 155–68.

Hamilton, Kirk. 1996. "Pollution and Pollution Abatement in the National Accounts." *Review of Income and Wealth* 42 (1): 13–33.

Hammitt, James, and Lisa A. Robinson. 2011. "The Income Elasticity of the Value per Statistical Life: Transferring Estimates between High and Low Income Populations." *Journal of Benefit-Cost Analysis* 2 (1): 1–27.

Hanna, Rema, and Paulina Oliva. 2015. "The Effect of Pollution on Labor Supply: Evidence from a Natural Experiment in Mexico City." *Journal of Public Economics* 122: 65–79.

Hausman, Jerry. 2012. "Contingent Valuation: From Dubious to Hopeless." *Journal of Economic Perspectives* 26 (4): 43–56.

Heal, Geoffrey. 2009. "The Economics of Climate Change: A Post-Stern Perspective." *Climatic Change* 96:275–97.

Hoel, M., and T. Sterner. 2007. "Discounting and Relative Prices." *Climatic Change* 84:265–80.

Holland, Stephen P., Erin T. Mansur, Nicholas Z. Muller, and Andrew J. Yates. 2020. "Decompositions and Policy Consequences of an Extraordinary Decline in Air Pollution from Electricity Generation." *American Economic Journal: Economic Policy* 12 (4): 244–74.

Keiser, David A., Catherine L. Kling, and Joseph S. Shapiro. 2019. "The Low but Uncertain Measured Benefits of US Water Quality Policy." *Proceedings of the National Academies of Science* 116 (12): 5262–9.

Kochi, Ikuho, Bryan Hubbell, and Randall Kramer. 2006. "An Empirical Bayes Approach to Combining and Comparing Estimates for the Value of a Statistical Life for Environmental Policy Analysis." *Environmental and Resource Economics* 34:385–406.

Krewski, D., et al. 2009. "Appendix C: Extended Follow-Up and Spatial Analysis of the American Cancer Society Study Linking Particulate Air Pollution and Mortality." *Research Report (Health Effects Institute)*. DOI: 10.1002/(SICI)1096-8652(199905)61:1<1::AID-AJH1>3.0.CO;2-J.

Lave, Lester B., and Eugene P. Seskin. 1973. "An Analysis of the Association between U.S. Mortality and Air Pollution." *Journal of the American Statistical Association* 68 (342): 284–90.

Le Kama, Alain Ayong, and Katheline Schubert. 2007. "A Note on the Consequences of an Endogenous Discounting Depending on the Environmental Quality." *Macroeconomic Dynamics* 11 (2): 272–89.

Meng, J., C. Li, R. V. Martin, A. van Donkelaar, P. Hystad, and M. Brauer. 2019.

"Estimated Long-Term (1981–2016) Concentrations of Ambient Fine Particulate Matter across North America from Chemical Transport Modeling, Satellite Remote Sensing and Ground-Based Measurements." *Environmental Science and Technology*. DOI: 10.1021/acs.est.8b06875.

Mohan, A., N. Z. Muller, A. Thyagarajan, R. Martin, M. Hammer, and A. von Donkelaar. 2020. "The Growth of Nations Revisited: Global Environmental Accounting from 1998 to 2018." NBER Working Paper No. 27398, National Bureau of Economic Research.

Muller, Nicholas Z. 2014a. "Boosting GDP Growth by Accounting for the Environment: Including Air Pollution and Greenhouse Gas Damage Increases Estimated U.S. Growth." *Science* 345 (6199): 873–4.

Muller, Nicholas Z. 2014b. "Towards the Measurement of Net Economic Welfare: Air Pollution Damage in the US National Accounts—2002, 2005, 2008." In *Measuring Economic Sustainability and Progress*, edited by D. W. Jorgensen, J. S. Landefeld, and P. Schreyer, vol. 72. NBER Book Series in Income and Wealth. Chicago: University of Chicago Press.

Muller, Nicholas Z. 2017. "Environmental Benefit-Cost Analysis and the National Accounts." *Journal of Benefit-Cost Analysis*. http://dx.doi.org/10.1017/bca.2017.15.

Muller, Nicholas Z. 2020. "Long-Run Environmental Accounting in the United States Economy." In *Environmental and Energy Policy in the Economy*, 1, edited by Matthew J. Kotchen, James H. Stock, and Catherine D. Wolfram, 158–91. Cambridge, MA: National Bureau of Economic Research.

Muller, Nicholas Z., and Robert O. Mendelsohn. 2007. "Measuring the Damage Due to Air Pollution in the United States." *Journal of Environmental Economics and Management* 54 (1): 1–14.

Muller, Nicholas Z., Robert O. Mendelsohn, and William D. Nordhaus. 2011. "Environmental Accounting for Pollution in the U.S. Economy." *American Economic Review* 101 (5): 1649–75.

National Academies of Science, and National Research Council. 1999. *Nature's Numbers*. Washington, DC: National Academies Press.

Nordhaus, William D. 2006. "Principles of National Accounting for Non-Market Accounts." In *A New Architecture for the U.S. National Accounts*. NBER Studies in Income and Wealth, edited by D. W. Jorgensen, J. S. Landefeld, and W. D. Nordhaus, vol. 66. Chicago: University of Chicago Press.

Nordhaus, William D. 2011. "The Economics of Tail Events with an Application to Climate Change." *Review of Environmental Economics and Policy* 5 (2): 240–57.

Nordhaus, William D., and James Tobin. 1973. "Is Growth Obsolete?" In *Economic Research: Retrospect and Prospect-Economic Growth*. Fiftieth Anniversary Colloquium V. New York: Columbia University Press for National Bureau of Economic Research.

Pindyck, Robert S. 2013. "Climate Change Policy: What Do the Models Tell Us?" *Journal of Economic Literature* 51 (3): 860–72.

Pope, C. Arden, Richard T. Burnett, Michael J. Thun, Eugenia E. Calle, Daniel Krewski, Kazuhiko Ito, and George D. Thurston. 2002. "Lung Cancer, Cardiopulmonary Mortality, and Long-Term Exposure to Fine Particulate Air Pollution." *Journal of the American Medical Association* 287 (9): 1132–41.

Robinson, L., Ian Mitchell, and Atousa Tahmasebi. 2021. "Valuing Climate Liabilities: Calculating the Cost of Countries' Historical Damage from Carbon Emissions to Inform Future Climate Finance Commitments." CGD Policy Paper 233. Washington, DC: Center for Global Development. https://www.cgdev.org/publication/valuing-climate-liabilities-calculating-cost-countries-historical-damage-carbon.

Sanders, Nicholas J., Alan I. Barreca, and Matthew J. Neidell. 2020. "Estimating Causal Effects of Particulate Matter Regulation on Mortality." *Epidemiology* 31 (2): 160–7.

Shapiro, Joseph S. 2016. "Trade Costs, CO_2, and the Environment." *American Economic Journal: Economic Policy* 8 (4): 220–54.

Shapiro, Joseph S. 2021. "The Environmental Bias of Trade Policy." *Quarterly Journal of Economics* 136 (2): 831–86.

Shapiro, Joseph S., and Reed Walker. 2018. "Why Is Pollution from US Manufacturing Declining? The Roles of Environmental Regulation, Productivity, and Trade." *American Economic Review* 108 (12): 3814–54.

Shindell, Drew, Johan C. I. Kuylenstierna, Elisabetta Vignati, Rita van Dingenen, Markus Amann, Zbigniew Klimont, Susan C. Anenberg, Nicholas Muller, Greet Janssens-Maenhout, Frank Raes, Joel Schwartz, Greg Faluvegi, Luca Pozzoli, Kaarle Kupiainen, Lena Höglund-Isaksson, Lisa Emberson, V. Ramanathan, Kevin Hicks, Kim Oanh N. T., George Milly, Volodymyr Demkine, Martin Williams, David Streets, and David Fowler. 2012. "Simultaneously Mitigating Near-Term Climate Change and Improving Human Health and Food Security." *Science* 335 (6065): 183–9.

Six, Magdalena, and Franz Wirl. 2015. "Optimal Pollution Management When Discount Rates Are Endogenous." *Resource and Energy Economics* 42: 53–70.

Spiller, E., J. Proville, A. Roy, and N. Z. Muller. 2021. "Mortality Risk from PM2.5: A Comparison of Modeling Approaches to Identify Disparities across Racial/Ethnic Groups in Policy Outcomes." *Environmental Health Perspectives* 129 (12): 127004-1–127004-12.

Tschofen, Peter, Ines L. Azevedo, and Nicholas Z. Muller. 2019. "Fine Particulate Matter Damage and Value Added in the United States Economy." *Proceedings of the National Academy of Science*. https://doi.org/10.1073/pnas.1905030116.

United States Department of Energy, Energy Information Agency. 2019. "Environment." https://www.eia.gov/environment/data.php.

United States Environmental Protection Agency. 1997. *The Benefits and Costs of the Clean Air Act: 1970 to 1990 Retrospective Study*. EPA report to Congress. Washington, DC: Office of Air and Radiation, Office of Policy. https://www.epa.gov/sites/default/files/2015-06/documents/contsetc.pdf.

United States Environmental Protection Agency. 1999. *The Benefits and Costs of the Clean Air Act: 1990–2010.* EPA report to Congress. EPA 410-R-99-001. Washington, DC: Office of Air and Radiation, Office of Policy.

United States Environmental Protection Agency. 2010a. *Guidelines for Preparing Economic Analyses*. Washington, DC: National Center for Environmental Economics, Office of Policy.

United States Environmental Protection Agency. 2010b. "Regulatory Impact Analysis for the Proposed Federal Transport Rule." Docket ID No. EPA-HQ-OAR-2009-0491. Washington, DC: Office of Air and Radiation.

United States Environmental Protection Agency. 2011. *The Benefits and Costs of the Clean Air Act: 1990–2020*. Final report. Washington, DC: Office of Air and Radiation, Office of Policy.

United States Environmental Protection Agency. 2020. "National Emissions Inventory." Air Emissions Inventories. https://www.epa.gov/air-emissions-inventories/national-emissions-inventory-nei.

United States Environmental Protection Agency. 2023. "Previously Published PACE Survey Data (1973-1993)." Pollution Abatement Cost and Expenditures (PACE). https://www.epa.gov/environmental-economics/previously-published-pace-survey-data-1973-1993.

United States Interagency Working Group on Social Cost of Greenhouse Gases (FWG). 2016. "Technical Support Document: Technical Update of the Social Cost of Carbon for Regulatory Impact Analysis Under Executive Order 12866."

United States Interagency Working Group on Social Cost of Carbon (FWG). 2021. "Technical Support Document: Social Cost of Carbon, Methane, and Nitrous Oxide Interim Estimates Under Executive Order 13990." https://www.whitehouse.gov/wp-content/uploads/2021/02/TechnicalSupportDocument_SocialCostofCarbonMethaneNitrousOxide.pdf.

Viscusi, W. Kip, and Joseph E. Aldy. 2003. "The Value of a Statistical Life: A Critical Review of Market Estimates throughout the World." *Journal of Risk and Uncertainty* 27 (1): 5–76.

Weitzman, Martin L. 2011. "Fat-Tailed Uncertainty in the Economics of Global Climate Change." *Review of Environmental Economics and Policy* 5 (2): 275–92.

Weitzman, Martin L., and Karl-Gustav Lofgren. 1997. "On the Welfare Significance of Green Accounting as Taught by Parable." *Journal of Environmental Economics and Management* 32: 139–53.

White House. 2022. "National Strategy to Develop Statistics for Environmental-Economic Decisions." Office of Science and Technology Policy, Office of Management and Budget, and Department of Commerce. https://www.whitehouse.gov/wp-content/uploads/2022/08/Natural-Capital-Accounting-Strategy.pdf.

8

Modernizing Measurement of Productivity with Nonstandard Data
Opportunities, Challenges, and Progress

Erica L. Groshen, Michael W. Horrigan, and Christopher Kurz

8.1 Introduction

For official statistics to achieve their mission as public goods, they must be of high quality and earn the trust of data users. These requirements are particularly germane in the case of productivity growth, which is hard to measure—especially for the burgeoning service sector and in a granular way for any sector. For example, former Federal Reserve Chair Alan Greenspan's skepticism of productivity measures during the late 1990s can be seen in his question: "With all the extraordinary technological advances of the past couple of decades, why have our recent productivity data failed to register any improvement?"[1] Greenspan's comments convey some doubt that was based, in part, on potential price mismeasurement, including adjusting for quality change, and the challenges of measuring services output and technological change. This doubt led the Federal Reserve to a different view of economic conditions and monetary policy than relying on the statistics uncritically.[2]

Since their inception in 1959, official US productivity measures have improved markedly in timeliness, granularity, and accuracy. Yet today, nonstandard data present opportunities to make further improvements. Currently, most official statistics rely heavily on surveys conducted by statistical

Erica Groshen is with the Cornell University ILR School. She acknowledges the hardworking, top-notch national statisticians at the BLS and BEA.

Michael Horrigan is with the W.E. Upjohn Institute for Employment Research. He acknowledges his research analysts.

Christopher Kurz is with the Federal Reserve Board. He acknowledges the Industrial Output group at the Federal Reserve.

The analysis and conclusions set forth here are those of the authors and do not indicate concurrence by other members of the research staff or the Board of Governors.

agencies. These surveys generate statistical agencies' "standard" data, which have known statistical properties and answer questions designed precisely to meet measurement objectives. Such surveys are expensive, and many are subject to declining response rates. Increasingly, statistical agencies are seeking ways to tap into burgeoning nonstandard data, including government and private sector administrative data, corporate records, transactional files, web-scraped data, and private sector aggregations.

This chapter addresses the particular question of how nonstandard data could help improve productivity measures. Section 8.2 assesses the current state of productivity measures. In section 8.3, we provide an overview of general opportunities and challenges in using nonstandard data. Section 8.4 describes particularly promising efforts and opportunities for tapping into these data. Section 8.5 discusses changes in statistical agency organization that could promote more use of nonstandard data. The final section concludes with a summary and policy recommendations.

8.2 What Is the Current State of Productivity Measurement?

Productivity, despite being one of the most important metrics of a country's well-being, is also one of the most difficult to estimate properly. Productivity measures the ability to change various inputs into output. This single factor accounts for a substantial portion of the increase in a country's standard of living. Elements that influence productivity growth include technological advances, increases in human capital, intangible investment, and expanded use of information technology (IT). The contributions of these factors can be captured in the economy's production function (if properly measured) to guide forecasts and policy.

There are two primary sets of productivity statistics in the United States, both publicly provided by the Bureau of Labor Statistics (BLS): *labor productivity* and *multifactor productivity*. Levels of both are calculated as ratios of real output to real inputs, so productivity growth is the difference between growth in output (the numerator) and growth in inputs (the denominator).

Labor productivity growth is equal to rate of growth in output minus rate of growth in labor hours.[3] Figure 8.1 presents a time series of US labor productivity growth from 1959 until 2019, with several subperiods broken up to account for periods of high and low growth in labor productivity, such as the IT boom or the recent period of low productivity growth. Due to productivity growth's year-to-year volatility, analysts and policymakers tend to compare averages over time, such as the subperiods shown in figure 8.1.[4]

BLS derives the numerator in the labor productivity ratio for manufacturing from industry sectoral output estimates provided by Bureau of Economic Analysis (BEA) and Census Bureau data.[5] Output measures for other sectors are derived from National Income and Product Account (NIPA) data from BEA. Both are deflated by BLS price indexes. The denominator

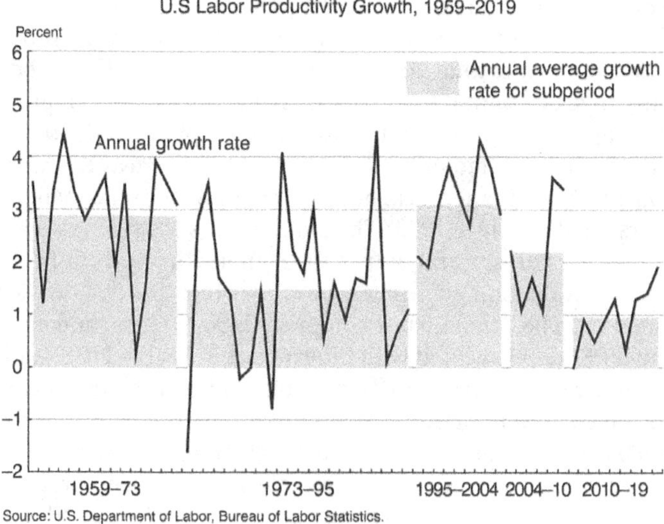

Fig. 8.1 US labor productivity growth, 1959–2019

includes hours and labor inputs from the Current Employment Statistics (CES), the Current Population Survey (CPS), and the National Compensation Survey (NCS), all from BLS. The data are quarterly and released two months after the end of each quarter.

Labor productivity is estimated for the major sectors, including nonfarm business, business, nonfinancial corporate, manufacturing, and for more disaggregated industries.[6] One challenge in the construction of labor productivity estimates is measuring total value of output for the relevant industry sector. The relative ease with which statistical agencies can properly measure the output of goods-producing sectors as opposed to service-providing sectors causes two problems. First, productivity statistics are not produced for as many service sector industries as goods sector industries. Second, the difficulty in quantifying what services produce means that for certain sectors that the BEA measures, sectoral output is proxied by labor input (such as hours of house cleaning, nursing care, consulting, or legal advice). Using a labor input proxy implies (by construction) zero growth of labor productivity over time.[7] Even when it is possible to construct a measure of output in a hard-to-measure service-providing industry, the proxy measure may be less than ideal, such as counting number of transactions in the banking sector. A natural question (addressed later in this chapter) is the extent to which alternative forms of data can help develop measures of output in service-providing industries that improve the coverage and quality of labor productivity measures in those sectors.

In addition to labor, other inputs to the production process include various forms of capital and intermediate inputs of materials, energy, and purchased services, leading to the need to estimate multifactor productivity (MFP), also known as total factor productivity (TFP).[8] MFP is the ratio of a quantity index of output to a quantity index of combined inputs, that is, labor and capital for business output and labor, capital, energy, services, and materials for the manufacturing sector (together known as KLEMS).[9] BLS has published MFP for nonfarm business major sectors and manufacturing subsectors regularly since 1983. The numerator is the real value added for private business and sectoral output for manufacturing from BEA NIPAs and Census production aggregates, both of which are deflated with BLS price deflators. The denominator comprises labor hours (sourced from the CES and CPS, supplemented with information from the NCS) and capital services (sourced from BEA NIPA data on land and capital stocks). MFP data are annual and released three months after the end of year for major nonfarm business sectors, with a two-year lag for manufacturing subsectors.

As one can see from the description above, measuring productivity is technically complex due to the varying concepts employed and the importance of capturing correct inputs into the production process. This complexity includes estimating and calculating factors for numerous KLEMS categories—each of which embodies technical assumptions to arrive at estimates. For example, BLS calculates the depreciation rate of capital for 42 different types of equipment and software and aggregates hours of work for more than 1,000 types of workers. The complexity of the numerous inputs requires widely disparate source data, often as varied as the inputs themselves.[10] For example, motor vehicle production is measured in units, and electricity output is measured in kilowatt hours. Meanwhile, physical output estimates—when available—derive from surveys and nonstandard data sources provided by the Departments of Energy, Interior, and Transportation, the Federal Reserve Board, the Federal Deposit Insurance Corporation, and the US Postal Service, to name a few.

Complexity of sourcing and estimation undoubtedly contribute to the persistent volatility of productivity estimates, as seen in the first figure. The components of these estimates also exhibit volatility. Indeed, both the numerator and denominator for MFP and labor productivity are more volatile than the ratio estimates. Figure 8.2 decomposes the growth in labor productivity since 1959 into the growth of its two underlying components. As the series are measured in growth rates, their difference is the growth rate in labor productivity. The component parts are roughly twice as volatile as their ratio over the 1959 to 2019 timeframe. Importantly, strong comovement in output and hours results in productivity growth having a lower variance than its components. One implication of a high degree of comovement in the numerator and denominator is that very minor differences between the components can produce noticeable movements in measured productivity growth.

The components of the ratio are indexed to account for changes in price

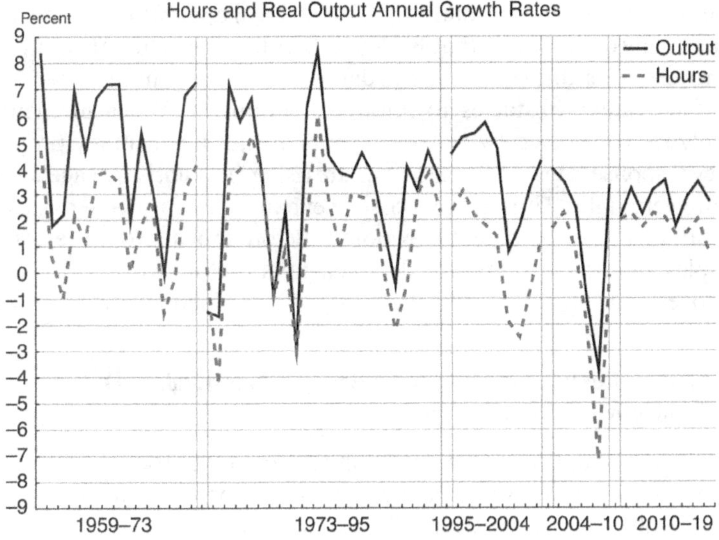

Fig. 8.2 Hours and real output annual growth rates

over time. When not measured in units, output is translated into real terms using data from the PPI and CPI programs. All the well-known problems of price measurement affect the quality of productivity measurement: specifically, input price mismeasurement, substitution bias, new goods, and challenges of hedonic and other quality adjustments. For example, if price declines associated with the shift to low-cost foreign suppliers are not captured in price indexes, then growth in the input price index is overstated. During the period of rapid import substitution following China's 2001 accession to the World Trade Organization, this effect could have caused growth of productivity in the US to be overstated by 0.1 to 0.2 percentage point per year and the real value added growth to be overstated by 0.2 to 0.5 percentage point per year (see Houseman et al. 2011).[11] Moulton's (chap. 2) review of what has changed since the Boskin Commission highlights that the most critical issues in productivity measurement involve price measurement.

Taking all of this complexity together, calculating productivity is nontrivial, subject to measurement issues, and relies on data from disparate sources. It is telling and impressive that with all these challenges, our current productivity estimates can convey such compelling stories and are consistent with other trends that underpin the American economy. Production of useful productivity measures requires considerable effort. It must be guided by a conceptual framework that ensures methodological consistency in all stages of constructing and combining an extensive array of source data.

These source data are produced by the statistical apparatus of the US and include many data sources that BEA and BLS tap to produce their inputs to the process.[12] Yet this success leaves data users wanting more.

Unfortunately, obstacles to improved productivity measurement are unlikely to be resolved by new or expanded traditional survey programs. Survey response rates are falling, costs are rising, and statistical agency budgets are very tight. Thus, newly possible expansions of the role for nontraditional data must be urgently explored. Before moving to more concrete examples and avenues, we provide a general structure with which to view how to leverage nonstandard data to improve productivity measurement.

8.3 Getting Real: A Framework for Bringing Nonstandard Data to Productivity Measurement

Nonstandard data offer the opportunity to improve production of official statistics in important ways. Data gathered from organic sources—such as from payroll providers or electronic scanners—may improve the granularity of products (by location, industry, or occupation, for example) and may boost timeliness, coverage, precision, or accuracy. Nonsurvey sourcing may also allow agencies to discontinue, shorten, or merge existing surveys, reducing respondent burden and counteracting falling response rates.

This section provides a framework for thinking about the uses of nonstandard data in the measurement of productivity. The benefits of improved productivity statistics ultimately accrue to the many users of the data, to the taxpayers who fund the statistical agencies, and to everyone affected by decisions of public and private data users. These benefits, though ultimate goals, are hard to assess specifically and directly. Thus, our framework focuses largely on intermediate benefits and costs (that is, to the statistical agencies and their products). In particular, we examine the incentives for the use of such data and the challenges and opportunities they present, focusing first on data quality and then on other critical aspects of operating data collection and estimation programs. These aspects include access to source data, respondent protection, operational challenges, comparability over time, and mission compatibility.

8.3.1 Benefits of Using Nonstandard Data for Productivity Statistics

Statistical agencies have many incentives to develop procedures for acquiring and using nonstandard data. Incentives include the potential to significantly improve granularity, capture a significant fraction of the full universe, and provide more precise operational measures of the desired target concept. Some of these may be accomplished by combining standard and nonstandard data via new modeling approaches. The sheer volume and ready availability of nonstandard data may significantly improve timeliness and precision of estimates. Another possible benefit is to greatly reduce respondent burden and help mitigate the impact of falling response and cooperation rates from both businesses and households. And, of course, statistical agencies benefit if replacing traditional survey data collection with nonstandard data significantly reduces overall operational costs.

8.3.2 Framework for Assessing the Use of Nonstandard Data in Official Statistics

Nonstandard data opportunities vary greatly in their potential to achieve the benefits we list above. And the extent to which a source achieves some benefits and not others must be weighed in the calculus for its use. There are three fundamental questions to address a priori in terms of the impact of using nonstandard data: (1) Are the estimates consistent with the conceptual measurement objective? (2) What types of errors are introduced, and what is their impact? (3) Does the use of nonstandard data introduce other significant improvements?

8.3.2.1 Consistency with Theoretical Framework

An immediate question is whether the nonstandard data fit into the existing theoretical framework for data collection or estimation. For example, the BLS consumer price index (CPI) program uses a matched-model strategy to measure inflation, with the objective of repricing the same good or service each month.[13] In practice, there may be difficulties in achieving this objective, such as changes to qualities of a good or service or an item no longer being available to be repriced. Numerous data collection and statistical procedures exist to handle these challenges, such as direct pricing of changes in quality characteristics, use of hedonic models, and data collection procedures for item substitution. While the matched model is not always achieved perfectly in practice, this does not obviate the need to ask whether a nonstandard source of data is consonant with this approach. And, if not, are the compromises required with the alternative method currently deemed appropriate for use?

Absent this possibility, is there a new estimation approach that is both feasible for use with the nonstandard data and acceptable within the overall estimation framework? For example, suppose there is a new nonstandard source of data that provides very granular and timely measures of output and labor input for every establishment in a specific industry. How could such detailed data be used to measure labor productivity for that industry? It may be possible to transform these data to develop a measure of sectoral level output and labor used in traditional productivity statistics. Or is there value in replacing the current estimation framework with new frameworks that are more consonant with these detailed establishment level data? Could one think of adding a new series to the current suite of products? Whatever the answer, perhaps what is most important is that all statistical agencies be methodologically transparent about their choices and subject decisions to the rigors of peer review.

8.3.2.2 Challenges in Measuring the Target Concept under Study and Accepting Some Bias in Estimation

A second hallmark of standard estimation procedures is whether the collected data, while adhering to a strict theoretical estimation framework, measures the target concept precisely and produces unbiased estimates with sufficiently small standard errors. This is often not the case with nonstandard data. Stated plainly, nonstandard data can be messy. Perhaps they measure a target concept imprecisely, including units not in the target population or excluding units in the target population—for example, the problem of outlets or products that disappear or, in other cases, newly appear and are not captured in the current item/outlet sample. Perhaps the format of data does not fit easily into existing classification systems, making data curation and estimation problematic.

Fortunately, workarounds may be available, but some may introduce bias. Statistical agencies need to study, justify, and account for the extent of bias in releases, standard error estimates, and documentation. Small amounts of bias can be acceptable in return for important benefits such as broader coverage, lower burden, more granularity, and so on.

For example, consider an administrative database of wages that includes job titles used by firms instead of occupation titles from the OMB Standard Occupational Classification (SOC) system. Consistent use of classification schemes for occupations is needed to merge data across sources.[14] A statistical agency may be able to solve this issue by using high-powered text-learning models to do the assignments from job title to SOC (which would have the added benefit of reducing response burden).

Or perhaps the alternative data do a great job of capturing the measurement concept but include units that are out of scope for the target population.[15] This could produce biased estimates of the population under study. For example, the CPI uses point-of-sale information from the Energy Information Agency (EIA) to prorate consumer expenditure data on total gasoline purchases to estimate expenditures for regular, mid, and premium gasoline purchases. The EIA data, from the CPI point of view, are biased as they include sales to businesses (because anyone can buy at a retail pump and businesses may have special discounts or prefer certain outlets). The CPI is intended to capture only sales to consumers. However, the business share of gasoline purchases is probably modest enough to keep purchases by businesses from causing a significant bias in the estimates of the proportions of consumers' spending going to different grades of gasoline.

Viewed in this way, the use of nonstandard data to fill in prorated detail from high-level, unbiased, survey-based estimates may be a very useful approach to marrying traditional and nonsurvey sources of data.

8.3.2.3 Other Means of Improving Statistics

The opportunities from nonstandard data are not limited to estimation. They can affect all stages of the process of producing statistics, including sample frame selection; strata identification; sample weighting and selection; data collection, edit/review, and coding; development of estimates; and publication and analysis.

Consider the selection of a sampling frame—the choice of which items to price and how to weight them—for deflators employed in the estimation of productivity. Because BLS lacks access to the Census Bureau's Business Register—the dataset that includes product sales revenue—BLS's producer price index (PPI) program cannot select a sample based on product revenue. Instead, BLS uses the employment in Quarterly Census of Employment and Wages (QCEW) as a sampling frame, which implicitly assumes that revenue is proportional to employment. The possible bias introduced by such a sampling frame becomes more acute as firms import more intermediate inputs, affecting input prices but not employment. Whether this is an acceptable alternative may depend on a number of factors, such as the age of Census Bureau frames (up to five years old) versus the timeliness of QCEW data (six months old at the time of sample selection) and whether better coordination between agencies would be feasible. Also, without BLS access to Internal Revenue Service (IRS) records (which would require Congress to amend tax law), only the segment of the Census Bureau universe that is directly collected (generally, units with employment of 50 or more) would be available for use by BLS. Would mixing QCEW-based employment information from smaller firms with possibly much older information on product information from Census Bureau firms be preferred to the current full sample draw from QCEW?

Numerous examples cover the full spectrum of the survey methods process. Each opportunity creates its own set of methodological challenges. Consider, for example, having access to a rich database of credit card purchases, including detail on the characteristics of items purchased. Using these data to estimate consumer expenditures may pose significant problems in understanding the impact of non–credit card purchases, especially among low-income individuals. Simply being transparent about the differences may not be sufficient to judge such a choice as statistically fit for use. Similar to the spirit of nonresponse bias analysis, the use of large-scale nonstandard data for sample selection and estimation should be accompanied by studies of potential bias in terms of unit or concept coverage of nonstandard data.

8.3.3 Challenges and Risks Posed by Incorporation of Alternative Data

The preceding section suggests that not all good ideas pan out for official statistics. A high bar is essential to maintain quality and trust. For successful use in an ongoing official statistic, a data stream must survive six key challenges: adequate quality, ongoing access, respondent protection, operational suitability, comparability, and provider mission compatibility. Cases where the data successfully pass the bar can be quite valuable, even though these issues may need continual management. When a promising source fails to meet acceptable thresholds by one or more criteria, the source may still be useful for validating other sources or for research purposes.

We have already noted many real-life data quality hurdles. For example, the data must accurately represent the desired target population of people, firms, or products. The measurements must be consistent with existing concepts and with existing or newly sought measures. The specific characteristics of the alternative data must be available at the desired level of granularity, frequency, and timeliness. Data collection must be adequately consistent across respondents. To ensure accuracy, datasets must be well documented, and it must be possible to curate them (that is, check for and resolve outliers, missing information, and errors) in a timely way.

Critically, the agency must have a way to validate and benchmark the alternative data. For validation, past patterns in new data may be compared to other data with which the new data have an expected relationship. When the new data are timelier than survey data, microdata from units that appear in both series can be compared. Such validation exercises are important for choosing a new data series and are necessary for assessing and maintaining quality on an ongoing basis. Validation typically goes on behind the scenes, although the results may be posted or published. In one example from the BLS payroll job series, validation takes the form of comparing business cycle properties, particularly during downturns, or estimating seasonal factors and comparing them.[16]

By contrast, benchmarking is more visible to data users because it leads to periodic revision. When high-frequency data are informative but sparse or not fully representative, estimates of trends for the whole economy or sectors are the product of models. Models apply weights and other adjustments to incoming data to approximate what is happening more broadly or more locally. But models are always imperfect because they oversimplify reality. So when more complete and reliable information comes out, the agency replaces modeled estimates with better measures. These are called benchmark revisions. Thus, the agency needs continuing access to information from a more complete or reliable source for periodic rebenchmarking.

Assured ongoing access is another key criterion. When running a survey, the statistical agency controls the design of the sample, questionnaire, timing, frequency, and data gathered. Data acquired from other sources may not be legally accessible. In one glaring example, BLS lacks ongoing access to data originating with the IRS that could improve its establishment survey programs and make its business register consistent with that of the Census Bureau. Notably, the recommendations of the Commission on Evidence-Based Policymaking and subsequent passage of the Evidence Act of 2018 aim to expand statistical agencies' access to federal government administrative data. This long overdue and promising development for official statistics offers a potentially important source of nonstandard data that may not have the same challenges of using data from the private sector. If the data come from a private source, the purchase price may be too high.[17] Investing in developing the IT infrastructure—and investing in the personnel to identify, negotiate, and manage data acquisition, curation, and integration of data into production frameworks—can be very expensive. Even after a satisfactory agreement and incorporation are completed, agencies face the risk that current providers of alternative data will become unable or unwilling to continue the relationship in the future.

Whether the nonstandard data derive from private or administrative sources, challenges remain. Statistical agencies are responsible for protecting the confidentiality of respondents to their surveys. This responsibility becomes quite murky with nonstandard data. For example, what is the concept of informed consent for web-scraped data? Currently, some statistical agencies (including BLS) seek permission to web scrape in advance, while others do not. It is also unclear what responsibilities statistical agencies have to respondents in purchased microdata beyond any specified in the purchase contract. Who has liability for inadvertent disclosure? Using administrative data, including combining different sources of administrative data, requires considering the confidentiality promises made for each source in terms of sharing and statistical uses. The ability to identify individuals or establishments directly or indirectly through combinations of statistical and corporate or administrative releases must be taken into account. All these questions involve managing disclosure control, which can require a significant and increasing investment of personnel and IT resources over time.

Data inputs must also be suitable for ongoing operations. Challenges include how to integrate alternative data into a production environment; potential investments in data storage, secure transmission, and computational capacity; managing ongoing data curation as input data specifications change or new sources are added; achieving appropriate frequency and timeliness; and validating and benchmarking estimates derived from data sources.

Data requirements for linking and modeling can be substantial. Often an agency seeks data comparable in some way with those obtained previously or from other sources. To be useful for granular estimates or merging, there must be a way to apply consistent identifiers or classification systems (particularly those used by the government) such as location, occupation, industry, products and services, firm structure, and so on. In addition, it is often important to have data overlap with existing legacy series. If not, does the agency want to begin a new series?

Finally, when statistical agencies use data produced by some other entity, they must ensure that the missions of the two do not conflict in a damaging way. The objectives that underlie the collection or creation of alternative data can be very different from the statistical purposes for which they are sought. Consider the following differences:

- Private firms create and tap data to benefit their bottom line. They may rely on data to make marketing, location, production, procurement, human resources, or investment decisions. They may seek to sell data products, as did the Billion Prices Project.[18] They may, in part, seek corporate visibility, as does ADP with its more timely monthly payroll counts.[19] The resources devoted to curating and storing historical data reflect these motives. No matter their goal, most private firms seek to advance and protect the value of their investment in intellectual property (data and methods) and the privacy of their operations, respondents, and partners. This means, for example, that they may charge high fees or be unwilling to alter operations to accommodate statistical agencies' needs.
- Government agencies that run programs or enforce laws create and store administrative data in service to their missions. They have little incentive to document, store, or curate data beyond the level needed for their operations. Coverage is determined by program parameters. The timeliness and frequency of data collection reflect the pace of operations of the program involved—which could be weekly, monthly, quarterly, or annual. Historical data may not be documented and preserved in a form compatible with current data, if at all. Furthermore, apparently promising data fields that are not in use may not be populated with accurate data.[20]
- Statistical agencies have different goals than private firms and other government agencies. They collect and provide data as a public good. That is, they aim to help the nation's policymakers, businesses, and individuals improve decision-making by supplying statistics that are accurate, objective, relevant, timely, and accessible. To do that, agencies must earn and maintain the trust of respondents and users, emphasizing transparency and confidentiality. And they must get the most from each dollar appropriated for this purpose.

Differences in mission between statistical agencies and data providers mean that nonstandard data may have lower quality, be less representative of the target population, and use different measurement concepts. Furthermore, changes in procedures used to create alternative data are not under the control of the statistical agency. Thus, the statistical agency must be able to audit the data and have problems addressed appropriately. Providers of alternative data can significantly change access conditions, including pricing arrangements. These pricing decisions may be based on corporate citizenship, profit maximization, or monopoly power. An additional risk from incompatible missions concerns financial markets. The ability of a single entity to provide influential data could create the incentive for private-sector employees to manipulate data to influence releases or to front run market-moving data releases.[21] Thus, new legislation may be needed to deter such behavior.

Each nonstandard source poses its own combination of risks on an ongoing basis. That the risks never disappear does not mean that they cannot be successfully managed. However, this risk management is a key reason why nonstandard data rarely, if ever, saves quite as much money or is quite as beneficial as supposed initially. The risks and the need to validate, benchmark, and collect information not found in transactions suggest that, while statistical agencies' overall reliance on survey data is likely to diminish, it is unlikely to disappear.

8.4 Promising Opportunities and Progress

With a framework and the challenges of employing nonstandard data in mind, we now turn to promising opportunities and progress made in leveraging new data to improve productivity measures. In the current economic environment, it is not hyperbole to argue that firms are beginning to realize fully the possible gains from the technical advances of the IT revolution, the internet of things, and improved telecommunications. These advances not only improve the production process of goods, the management of inventory, the provision of services, and thereby the actual productivity of the firms and establishments the economy is composed of, but each could revolutionize the measure of productivity and mechanisms through which data are provided.

The areas in which nonstandard data could augment productivity measurement are as varied as the inputs into the productivity estimation process themselves. For each input, whether hours, output, wages, or other, available data sources might augment or substitute for inputs into measures of labor and MFP. We begin this section by discussing six significant current examples of the promise (at various stages of development) offered by alternative data to improve measures of components of productivity. While hardly exhaustive, these examples demonstrate the richness of opportunities and the challenges involved. We end the section by sketching a future pathway for use of alternative data for measures of productivity. We are intentionally speculative, with the goal of promoting discussion. Many of these ideas require coordination, cooperation, and consensus among the statistical agencies, which is the subject of the next section.

8.4.1 New Motor Vehicles Price Index

The BLS recently improved its methodology for calculating new motor vehicle prices by switching from surveying dealerships to using transactions data. Initially published as a research series in May 2022 with the release of CPI data for April 2022, the BLS released a price index for new cars that uses data purchased from J. D. Power and Associates. This private source of data includes transactions data on new vehicle sales along with detailed characteristics of cars sold. In its construction, BLS utilizes new methods for index calculation that incorporate transaction data with real-time expenditure data. As described and documented extensively by BLS, the index differs vastly in scope, index formula, and levels of aggregation from the prior new vehicle index.[22]

8.4.2 Modeling Interim Estimates of Industrial Production

Many statistical releases are revised or adjusted as more source data become available. One role that nonstandard data could take is to augment inputs into the statistical measurement of productivity to provide more timely estimates.[23] This could be achieved by using more up-to-date indicators of a particular series, employing a proxy, or exploiting a statistical relationship. We now provide an example of how the Federal Reserve's industrial production team uses standard data in a nonstandard way to improve estimates of productivity.[24]

For sectors of the economy where measuring physical output on a quarterly basis is not feasible, the Federal Reserve's industrial production index team estimates output using a relationship between production worker hours—which it can measure monthly—and annual benchmark data on real output (like the real value of engineered wood, for example), typically from Census data. The estimated relationship between growth of hours and growth of real output is called the adjustment factor. For the industrial production indexes based on production worker hours, the adjustment factors are, effectively, measures of labor productivity—that is, they are an estimate of output per unit of labor input.

With the release of the 2018 Annual Revision, the industrial production estimates incorporated the Quarterly Survey of Plant Capacity (QSPC) into monthly estimates for industrial production indexes based on production worker hours.[25] The monthly adjustment factors, or productivity measures, now take signal from QSPC utilization rates.[26] By augmenting the traditional output to labor input relationship with timely data on capacity utilization, estimates of industrial production are more accurate and fold in quarterly data available a month after the quarter ends, as opposed to after several years (when the typical Census benchmarks are released).

8.4.3 Utilization-Adjusted Quarterly MFP

The Federal Reserve Bank of San Francisco publishes a near real-time quarterly series on MFP for the US business sector, adjusted for variations in factor utilization, effort, and the workweek of capital based on Fernald (2014) and Basu, Fernald, and Kimball (2006).[27] The methodology employs a robust growth accounting framework and adjusts for labor effort (proxied by work hours) and the workweek of capital (the amount capital is used in a given week), both important corrections for accurately measuring technology change.[28] Essentially, the estimation procedure takes quarterly NIPA data on output and capital and combines it with information on hours from the BLS productivity and costs release. The productivity estimates are released quarterly, about two months after each quarter ends and, excluding the utilization adjustment, are nearly perfectly correlated with the growth rate of the BLS MFP measure for the private business sector. This example shows that augmenting the standard data inputs into the measurement of productivity is not always necessary, as many of the inputs needed to produce more timely and complete productivity estimates are already in the hands of the national statistical agencies.

8.4.4 Medical Records to Improve Measurement of Medical Prices

The medical services sector poses some of the most important challenges for measuring productivity because of its size, rapid innovation, and unique market features. Health care spending is large and growing—rising steadily from 13.3 percent of GDP in 2000 to 17.6 percent in 2018. However, several studies conclude that medical price indexes are upwardly biased. One reason is that when shifts in treatment occur across different treatment modalities, reduced costs to the consumer and improvements in outcome are not captured by price measures that only account for price inflation for the old treatment. The shift in the treatment of depression from talk therapy to drug therapy is one example. Another is the general replacement of surgical interventions for treating ulcers to the use of a pharmaceutical agent.[29] This bias understates productivity in the sector. In addition, as discussed in chapter 6 of this volume, prices of health care do not adequately adjust for increasing quality, another source of bias.

Presently, there are three principal sources of medical price data: medical bills at providers' locations such as doctors' offices and hospitals (collected in surveys), Medicare reimbursement data collected by the Center for Medicare and Medicaid Research, and health insurance claims records (nonstandard). None of these sources provides outcomes data, such as remission of disease, length of time for healing, and other indicators for patient wellness, thus making quality adjustment difficult.

Despite lack of data on outcomes and comorbidities, BLS and BEA have created experimental disease-based price indexes that correct for a portion of the new goods bias in medical care, specifically the part that arises when less expensive goods and services substitute more expensive treatments that cross medical provider classes.[30] These substitutions often occur as the result of an innovation, such as a new drug that lowers the need to use expensive therapies to treat a disease. Disease-based price indexes report medical inflation by the treatment of disease rather than the good or service that treats the disease. However, they do not at this point account for improved outcomes such as increases in life expectancy coming from an innovation like coronary bypass surgery. Disease-based price indexes are still a work in progress and are not yet ready to replace currently published medical price indexes, which are reported on a goods and services basis.

The BLS PPI program currently uses information on hospital revenues by diagnostic-related grouping (essentially a categorization of medical treatments by disease) to preselect hospital bills for pricing and repricing. A natural question for future consideration is whether electronic medical records will allow BLS to replace in-person data collection with electronic selection and initial pricing of hospital bills. BLS's familiarity with estimating the impact of product characteristics on price may allow use of information available in thousands of medical bills to develop models to reprice any bill in any month with a specific set of initial characteristics.

8.4.5 Wage Records to Improve Timeliness and Granularity and Measures of Wages, Labor Quality, and Hours

Currently, the timeliest official labor market information comes from two monthly BLS surveys: the Current Employment Statistics (CES) Survey of employers and the Current Population Survey (CPS) of households. Labor input data derived from administrative sources—specifically wage and salary data from the Unemployment Insurance (UI) system and from private-sector payroll processors—offer another way to improve productivity measurement. Two promising avenues are being pursued to leverage such data: the use of payroll processor data to improve timely measures of hours, wages, and employment by the Federal Reserve Board and a wage record pilot by the BLS to gain access to UI wage records to construct more accurate and granular measures of jobs, hours, and labor quality.

Researchers at the Federal Reserve Board now leverage information from a payroll processor (ADP) to produce high-quality administrative data on employment, hours worked, and/or wages and total compensation.[31] The advantages of this source are timeliness, new information, and granularity. Information is available within a week of payroll being processed, typically does not entail revisions, and is available at a larger sample size than most statistical surveys.[32] This success could be extended by blending private data with information from the CES and QCEW to improve data timeliness and quality and reduce reliance on surveys. For example, average weekly hours worked are multiplied by employment to arrive at total annual hours worked. Private payroll information on employment could be combined with CES employment to arrive at more robust estimates of private payroll employment and, hence, hours. Indeed, Cajner et al. (2022) take such an approach and find reduced volatility and improved signal from the resultant employment series.

Another opportunity involves the untapped potential of administrative UI wage records. Collecting labor market information via enhanced wage records that include hours of work and job titles to augment current survey programs could help BLS improve productivity measure by making the measure of labor inputs more accurate, timely, and granular. In the longer run, access to wage records would allow BLS to redesign or entirely discontinue two large survey programs: the NCS and the Occupational Employment and Wages Statistics (OEWS) program.

UI wage records cover every US wage and salary job subject to the UI system, so they are far more comprehensive than payroll processor records.[33] However, because employers submit quarterly reports, and states take time to process the data, these records are available with about a six-month lag and so are not as timely as payroll provider records. With access to both payroll processor and UI wage records, BLS could substantially improve timeliness, accuracy, *and* granularity of productivity measures.

Work is underway to address two key challenges to this vision: access and record quality. BLS has no access to UI wage records currently[34] but is running a pilot to provide a model for broad and secure sharing of UI wage records, both across states and with BLS. States individually own their wage records, leading to a set of sensitive issues concerning legal access to their use. There is no overall sharing agreement for these records with the statistical agencies or among states, although there are agreements for various limited data exchanges.[35]

Critically, the effort also aims to add information and resolve inconsistencies among the states. These steps would dramatically improve measurement of labor and MFP. BLS currently models hours and labor quality using the CES Survey, the CPS, and the NCS. Sources of better hours and occupation information to improve estimates have been difficult to obtain. Today's UI wage records are sparse and inconsistent across states; most contain little more than workers' social security numbers, monthly earnings, and employer account numbers. For measuring productivity, the key fields to add are occupation, hours, demographics, and work location.[36] BLS has learned that many states seek to enhance their UI wage records to help understand local skill needs.[37]

Two more developments could change the wage record environment substantially.

- With other philanthropic partners, the US Chamber of Commerce Foundation has launched the Jobs and Employment Data Exchange (JEDx) initiative to bring together a broad set of stakeholders (including BLS) to create open, mutually agreed-upon data standards for employer wage records that would feed into the UI system.[38] To date, they have developed prototype schema for wage records that would improve quality, add key fields (hours, occupation, demographics, start and end dates, and work location), and facilitate statistical agency and researcher access to the data. Stakeholders in seven states now serve on a pilot project to develop implementation plans.[39]

- Congress has allocated funds to address the need for modernization of state UI programs that the COVID-19 pandemic highlighted, including major upgrades to antiquated IT systems, variability in the definition of key concepts across states, and expanding data coverage to contractors and the self-employed.

These developments have promise to provide a means to enhance wage records and BLS access without significantly increasing unfunded burdens on states or employers. A major consequence would be far better measures of labor market inputs to improve accuracy and granularity of productivity statistics.

8.4.6 Credit Card Data to Improve Service Sector Measurement

High frequency statistics on consumer *goods* purchases—derived from the Census Bureau's monthly retail trade surveys—are timely and fairly accurate. *Services*-spending statistics, on the other hand, lag goods-spending data and arrive only at a quarterly frequency. Services spending is roughly two-thirds of total personal consumption expenditures in an economy in which nearly three-quarters of aggregate spending is on personal consumption. As a result, this input into the national income accounts is important to measure in an accurate and timely fashion.[40]

Specifically, the services-spending information used by the BEA to calculate GDP comes from estimates of business revenues from the Census Quarterly Services Survey (QSS).[41] The QSS and Advance QSS (early data for a subset of industries found in the full QSS) are released two-and-a-half and two months after a quarter ends, respectively. The Census Bureau benchmarks the series with the larger Services Annual Survey roughly two years after a given year closes. One way of improving measurement of the service sector would be to leverage information collected by credit card companies or credit card transaction aggregators.[42]

Credit card spending covers a substantial portion of overall spending. Moreover, the use of credit card data would allow for spending to be categorized as e-commerce by leveraging the "card not present" designation for both goods and services. This dichotomy would enable better tracking of e-commerce, an important and growing segment of consumer spending. Indeed, official Census estimates indicate that e-commerce sales have been growing nine times faster than traditional in-store sales since 1998.[43]

Combining card spending data with information on prices,[44] particularly e-commerce prices, should have important implications for productivity, particularly if Census surveys currently miss some e-commerce spending or misallocate e-commerce to traditional brick and mortar spending. Moreover, such data could help address outlet substitution bias from the shift to e-commerce.[45]

The statistical agencies and central banks are already exploring credit and debit card transactions data to improve the timeliness of national accounts estimates and improve estimates of geographic heterogeneity in spending in response to exogenous shocks.[46] For example, at the onset of the pandemic, the BEA leveraged credit card data to supplement the advance estimate of first quarter 2020 GDP.[47] In addition, these data could greatly enhance the measurement of monthly consumer expenditure weights used in the construction of the chained CPI-U. It is important to note that demographic information on these transactions could be used to form the building blocks of developing price indexes by demographic group where underlying data provide information on what and where items are purchased by each demographic group.[48]

8.4.7 Investigating Measurement Issues Using Alternative Data

Not only can nontraditional data augment or replace existing sources, but they can also be used to compare underlying trends and provide points of comparison for validation and the menu of measurement-related issues. Indeed, much of the research underlying the quantification of biases to prices and productivity, such as those associated with outlet substitution bias (discussed above), offshoring (discussed in chapters 2 and 5), lack of quality adjustment (discussed throughout this volume), and substitution bias (the tendency of people to shift their purchases away from items that have increased in price, discussed in chapter 2), is the result of bringing additional and nonstandard data to bear on measurement questions. Examples abound. Houseman et al. (2011) supplement input price indexes with microdata on country-specific prices to measure productivity mismeasurement due to offshoring. Bils (2009) uses scanner data to estimate quality, while Hausman and Leibtag (2010) use scanner data to answer questions about substitution bias. In their investigation of the role of mismeasurement in the productivity slowdown, Byrne, Fernald, and Reinsdorf (2016) use high-quality data for communications equipment and computers to estimate an alternative set of price indexes for the nonfarm business sector.

8.4.8 Employing Microdata to Better Understand Productivity Estimates

While not all are exactly "alternative data," microdata and administrative data can provide insights into productivity and improve its measurement. As noted in Moulton (2018), many studies that helped underpin the examination of measurement problems in BLS price programs resulted from a BLS initiative to open underlying microdata to researchers.[49] The same approach has been applied in a more limited way to productivity. The NBER-CES Manufacturing Industry Database—a joint project between the National Bureau of Economic Research (NBER) and the Center for Economic Studies (CES)—provides researchers a set of industry-level estimates of labor and MFP for the manufacturing sector, creates price deflators, and adjusts for capital stocks and changes in industry definitions. This database allows for the estimation of production functions and facilitates researchers' ability to aggregate estimates under differing assumptions. Moreover, these alternative estimates exhibit differences from the official data despite being built primarily from the same source data.[50] Investigating differences in methodology and productivity estimates has the potential to improve overall productivity measurement.

The joint BLS-Census Dispersion Statistics on Productivity (DiSP) project, an initiative to publicly provide data on the dispersion of official productivity statistics (see Cunningham et al. 2019), provides another example of using underlying microdata to bear on the question of productivity measurement.[51] While the goal of the DiSP project is primarily to convey information on within-industry variation in productivity and productivity dynamics, the project's construction and comparison of Census-based microaggregated productivity and BLS standard-methodology productivity measures is illuminating. The team estimating the productivity numbers compare different measures of inputs and outputs from two methodologies and find that the microaggregated data largely resemble published aggregated data for hours and output. Unfortunately, the correlations between the two series fall when comparing productivity measures. Specifically, the microaggregated labor productivity and BLS labor productivity measures have a correlation of 0.5 when averaging across four-digit NAICS sectors. While the correlations of the aggregate series for total manufacturing are higher, the differences can be attributed to variation in data sources and methodologies. This finding is not necessarily the best of news. The lack of near-perfect correlations when employing much of the same source data for labor productivity reinforces the idea that measuring productivity accurately is a complex task in which near-perfect correlations between different output and labor inputs does not guarantee a high comovement in resultant measures of labor productivity. Importantly, as shown by BLS and Census collaboration in the DiSP program, a nonstandard, bottom-up approach would yield information not contained in the current set of output from BLS productivity programs, such as the dispersion of productivity across establishments.

8.4.9 Looking to the Future: New Directions for Use of Alternative Data

As discussed in the first section, one of the larger challenges in developing estimates of labor and MFP is measuring all the components correctly. As that discussion indicated, the current approach relies heavily on getting data cooperatively from various statistical agencies. The unit of observation for the construction of components is critical. For labor productivity at the industry level, BLS combines measures of industries' output, labor hours, and prices.

Our discussion of using alternative data such as medical records, wage records, and credit card data has been in the context of fitting those data into our current traditional productivity framework. These possibilities are certainly not exhaustive. For example, instead of using a depreciation approach to measure capital inputs (as is now done), think of the benefits of using remote machine monitoring (RMM) to better track capital inputs. RMM entails the addition of a reader to the control box of a piece of capital equipment, ranging from machine tools to medical equipment. The reader provides a feed from the logic control of the machine into a database. Organizations can then employ the high-frequency information on their capital stock to predict maintenance, monitor production, and observe the condition of capital.[52] If statistical agencies could access this information, they would have high-quality data on each piece of capital in a plant and the use of that equipment at a high frequency. A problem in the measurement of MFP is the difficulty of accurately measuring capital, so adding this sort of detailed information about the use of capital inputs would radically transform the measurement of productivity. Moreover, from a data collection perspective, if such a practice were widely adopted, statistical organizations or data aggregators could work with data feeds to almost eliminate respondent burden and collection costs and improve timeliness.

Beyond enhancing data within the existing framework, we can also ask what a perfect system for measuring productivity might look like if developed from scratch. The prime option would be a bottom-up strategy. If we knew output, labor hours, and price changes of output for each establishment, we could test different mathematical approaches to aggregating establishment-level productivity estimates to obtain sectoral-level ones.

Such an approach would require the cooperation of BLS and Census to coordinate samples and data collection efforts to populate measures of output, PPI product repricing, and labor hours for the same establishments. They would then need to share that information to produce the statistics needed by each agency for its individual programs. This approach to sampling, data collection, and estimation would require upgraded interagency cooperation and joint governance, as we discuss in the next section.

And what of the problem of measuring the output of service-providing industries? There is a distinct difference between the challenge of measuring total output in a sector, such as the total value of management consulting services in that industry, versus the problem of measuring such output at an individual establishment. The BLS PPI program has solved this problem for a significant share of service-providing industries by specifying what output it will measure in an initial pricing effort and subsequently repricing those same services. More research would be needed to develop techniques to measure output for the numerator of an establishment productivity estimate; the same information would be used to define prices in the deflator for that same output. Similarly, research would be needed to judge potential conformity of labor hour measures from the same firm.

The possibility of using alternative data in this way is based on the reality that statistical agencies already actively bargain with firms to obtain electronic records for individual establishments and that many types of alternative data (such as medical records and wage records) can be reported at the establishment level. There may be numerous other sources of alternative data, especially from corporate records, that could be utilized in a new framework of measuring productivity at each individual establishment and aggregating up to the sectoral level.

8.5 Agency Reorganization and Data Sharing as Key Steps to Improve Productivity Measurement

As we have seen, the production of productivity statistics and many other measurement concepts in the Federal Statistical system involves the collaboration of various statistical agencies, most notably BLS, BEA, and the Census Bureau. Working together would be greatly facilitated by shared data, resources, facilities, and overall leadership among the agencies.

8.5.1 Issues with the Current Structure of Federal Statistical System

Currently, BEA and Census, while independent of each other, are both within the Department of Commerce. BEA and Census report to the same undersecretary of commerce. BLS is in the Department of Labor. The three agencies remain separate with regard to appropriations, IT infrastructure, resource allocation decisions, governing legislation, data access, professional training, legal staff, and more.

This separation is particularly and inherently problematic for productivity measurement, which uses information from all three agencies. To somewhat oversimplify, to estimate a change in labor productivity, the numerator is derived using price information from BLS and output information from BEA and Census. The denominator is derived from BLS hours information. Over time and by sector, coverage and concepts must align for productivity estimates to be accurate. Yet decisions on survey methods—including decisions on measurement concepts and how they are operationalized, sampling frames and sample selection including geographic coverage, data collection methods, and data dissemination to the public—are made independently by each of the three agencies.

A natural question that arises is whether overcoming challenges to successful and innovative use of administrative and private data for the measurement of productivity and, more generally, for the improvement of the statistical system could be hastened by more focused and unified decision-making across the three agencies.

One approach to changing the governance of the agencies is a formal consolidation of the three agencies, as has been proposed many times, most recently by the Clinton, Obama, and Trump administrations. The two variants of this consolidation are to move BLS from the Department of Labor into the Commerce Department or to move all three agencies into a new, independent statistical agency outside the cabinet, which we will call "StatsUSA." Barriers to consolidation include the expense and effort of reconfiguring administrative structures, loss of size and influence to the losing department(s) and appropriators, possible dilution of contact with data users in the home department and its constituents, and potential risk from putting so much of the statistical system under one roof. Risks of reducing diversification include a set of appropriators targeting the entire StatsUSA when angry with only some of its activities, as happened to Statistics Canada in 2008–2014,[53] and broader dangers from poor or politically influenced top leadership.

Alternatively, could an integrated governance model effectively achieve the same result without needing to formally consolidate the agencies? Since the passage of the Paperwork Reduction Act in 1980, the Office of Statistical and Science Policy (SSP), part of the Office of Information and Regulatory Affairs in the Office of Management and Budget, provides overarching guidance on statistical quality standards and coordinates revisions to the industry, occupation, geographic, and other classification systems used by statistical agencies. However, coordinating decisions on survey methods, operations, and dissemination would require a governance model far more integrated within and across agencies than the SSP provides.

What are the potential benefits to a more unified statistical system, whether accomplished through consolidation or integrated governance?

- Data quality: A unified decision-making process could lead to the development and application of state-of-the-art methods for ensuring a high level of data quality across agencies, opportunities for new statistical products from merging datasets across agencies, pooling of similar data series to provide validation and test for selection biases, and consolidation of efforts to correct issues with acquired data, improving comparability across data series and reducing duplication of effort.
- Access to private sector and tax data: Census, BLS, and BEA must negotiate individually for private sector data, and BLS and BEA lack access to IRS administrative data. For private sector data, purchase prices and/or relationship management costs should be lower when negotiations and contracts are shared across agencies. Regarding administrative data, perhaps the most glaring problem is the inability of BLS and Census to share a common business register caused by Census use of IRS data to construct its register.[54] Business registers provide information and sampling frames that underlie surveys and allow for weighting,

	Percent change from 2012 to 2020			
	Number Establishments		Number of Employees	
Industry	CBP	QCEW	CBP	QCEW
3341	51.9%	17.0%	101.6%	1.1%
3344	−14.5%	5.9%	−3.9%	−2.9%
5415	10.2%	43.5%	37.9%	33.7%

These comparisons show that surveys of activity in three high-tech industries for BLS and Census have quite different coverage and growth. County Business Patterns (CBP) data releases are based on the Census Bureau business register. Quarterly Census of Employment and Wages (QCEW) data releases are based on the Bureau of Labor Statistics business register.

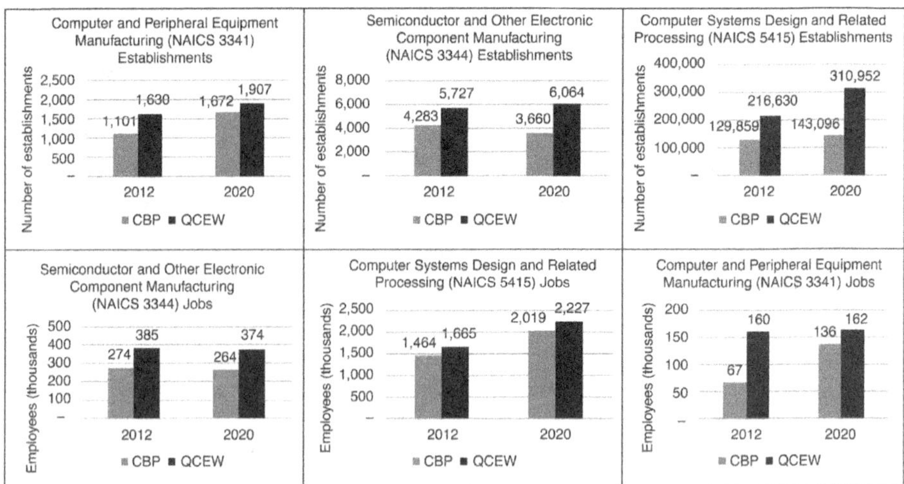

Fig. 8.3 Census Bureau versus BLS Business Register data for three high-tech industries

Source: US Census Bureau County Business Patterns and US Bureau of Labor Statistics Quarterly Census of Employment and Wages.

benchmarking, and validating nonstandard data sources. Discrepancies between the BLS and Census business registers are reflected in industry statistics, confounding users who try to combine business activity measures from Census with labor market information from BLS—as is done in the productivity statistics. Figure 8.3 illustrates recent discrepancies in establishment and employment data for three high-tech industries. For example, the County Business Pattern releases based on the Census Bureau's register show 102 percent growth in jobs in computer and peripheral equipment manufacturing (NAICS 3341) while the QCEW based on the BLS register shows just 1 percent growth. Such discrepancies present a serious barrier to accurate granular productivity statistics.[55]

- Consistency: While shared access to source data is important, so is agreement on assignment to aggregation classifications. Even though all federal government agencies abide by the Office of Management and Budget (OMB)-mandated industry, occupation, and geography classification systems, there is no coordination among statistical agencies on decisions for lower levels of aggregation within those coding structures. As a result, something as simple as defining what Boston is or what detailed industries or products roll up to higher-level aggregates may differ remarkably across (and sometimes within) agencies. Accomplishing consistent and nonoverlapping assignment of industry, occupation, and geographic codes in sample selection and estimation classification systems across agencies would greatly improve the quality and interpretability of data provided to the public and to policy makers.

- Collaboration on innovative research: While Census, BEA, and BLS each do innovative research in their respective program areas, general lack of coordinated and collaborative research limits their ability to address many problems inherent in productivity measurement. Research on disease-based price indexes (by BLS and BEA) and the DiSP project (by BLS and Census) are great examples of the benefits and synergies of collaborative approaches. But they are exceptions. There are many areas in which more proactive collaboration would be beneficial, including credit card research.
- Operations: Costs for skills training, dissemination, file linkage, computer storage and computational capacity, human capital, trusted data facility, and software purchases could be shared across agencies, reducing average burdens.
- Mission compatibility: Integrated governance across agencies could help prevent mission creep, in which independent agencies duplicate the measurement of concepts.

8.5.2 Reorganizing the Statistical Agencies—Opportunities and Prerequisites

Previous administrations have proposed consolidation, and the American Economic Association has expressed its provisional support for such a step.[56] However, to date, reorganization proposals remain vague. They leave open if and how consolidating the agencies would accomplish the important benefits cited above. Without specific elements critical to achieving those benefits, the result may be just a physical and administrative colocation. In our view, the following principles should govern any consolidation:

- *Maintaining the independence and missions of BEA, BLS, and Census:* Federal statistical agencies must have statistical independence from political and policy interference and authority to protect that independence. In addition, each federal statistical agency must be able to serve both its historical mission and the new mission to collaborate to enhance the services provided to the public.
- *Comprehensive data synchronization among BEA, BLS, and Census:* As discussed above, the ability to share administrative data on establishments has the potential to greatly improve classification of establishments by industry and eliminate significant discrepancies that affect estimates of employment, wages, hours, and productivity.

- *Coordinated interagency strategic planning for data collection and dissemination, negotiation with the private sector, joint projects, and common mechanisms for data governance:* A successful reorganization will build on synergies to avoid overlap and improve coordination. This will become more important as agencies move to expand privacy protections for respondents and blend data from multiple sources.
- *Common measurement and statistical methods:* Such coordination within and across agencies for business, household, and worker data will enable internal consistency of aggregate indicators, including productivity, with more disaggregated measures of business activity. This includes using core organizing frameworks to guide economics measurement.
- *Common administrative infrastructure for IT, data access protocols, and other services:* Twenty-first century statistical agencies increasingly rely on advanced computational infrastructure to blend data from disparate sources. To maximize efficient operations, agencies should be able to integrate IT infrastructure, including user portals for access to disparate data sources.[57] However, there is a significant risk that IT decisions viewed as optimal for individual cabinet-level departments may be substantially different from the decisions that would have been made by statistical agencies working collaboratively across departments, and a strong role for departmental leadership could reduce the independence of the statistical agencies. The consolidation of statistical agencies' IT is best undertaken by the agencies themselves.

Note that these elements could be accomplished through coordinated governance without formal consolidation into a StatsUSA. Nevertheless, consolidation is a very feasible path to achieving the innovation and coordination needed to make the substantial and rapid progress that agencies and data users seek. Furthermore, StatsUSA should operate outside of any cabinet department (including Labor or Commerce) to further the independence of official statistics from political influence. We note that every other country with advanced statistical capabilities has chosen a system far more consolidated than the US. We do not take this to be a mere coincidence.

The alternative is a strong coordinated governance mechanism to meet the prerequisites. This entity would need authority to allocate funds, authorize data sharing, and approve sampling, data collection, and estimation methodologies across agencies.

8.6 Conclusions and Recommendations

Nonstandard data holds great promise for improving productivity measurement, yet much of that promise remains unrealized because of very real practical constraints.

Were those constraints relaxed, what could productivity statistics look like 50 years (or less) from now? Simply put, the statistics could be more relevant, reliable, frequent, timely, granular, comparable, and complete. That is, with only a short lag, we could see monthly (perhaps weekly) labor and MFP growth by industry, state, and substate areas. Measures would be comparable across industries and regions and add up to national numbers. Input data series would be available at the same levels of disaggregation as published statistics. Revisions would be less dramatic.

The benefits of such improvements would accrue to users of improved productivity data and to those affected by decisions of the data users. For example, better calibrated monetary policy could smooth economic fluctuations, reducing the incidence of inflation and recession. Better understanding the impact of causes and consequences of productivity growth on a national and local level could improve fiscal policy decisions over infrastructure, disaster relief, and other public investment. Indeed, such data might advance the quality of public discourse and reduce partisan divides. Private investment decisions would also be better guided, to the benefit of communities of stakeholders and national vitality.

To progress toward this panacea, the statistical agencies together must build new processes and statistical products that capitalize on access to streams of high-quality data from both surveys and nonstandard sources. Agencies could discontinue or redesign some existing surveys once they securely tap high-quality administrative and private sector data sources.

Implementing this vision for improved productivity measurement requires upgrading access to those data and capabilities to use them effectively in producing statistics. Those efforts can succeed only with mechanisms to support coordination, research, and agility in BLS, BEA, and Census. Accordingly, we offer the following policy recommendations:

1) Producing productivity and other official statistics should remain a public sector responsibility. Economic theory suggests that public goods (goods for which limiting access to those who pay is impossible and for which one person's use does not reduce availability to others) will be undersupplied by the private sector. Statistics on productivity (and other socioeconomic concerns) are in this category. Those disappointed with productivity measurement today would almost certainly be less satisfied with a private sector solution.

2) The three agencies involved in producing productivity statistics need a coordinated governance model to optimize production processes. Joint governance may not strictly require moving BLS, BEA, and Census into a new StatsUSA outside of a cabinet department. However, such administrative consolidation and independent footing may provide the clearest model and quickest pathway to data sharing, consistent priorities, independence, and efficient sharing of services.

3) Serious underfunding impedes potential progress. Appropriators should fund the statistical agencies better, with more flexibility to move money among programs and multiyear money to facilitate long-term investments. Official statistics are a public good; they are information infrastructure for a decentralized, free market economy. Thus, a dedicated income source may be appropriate. Were a tax on financial transactions imposed to dampen financial market volatility, Congress could dedicate some portion of that revenue to production of official statistics.[58] Alternatively, we could tax the collection and use of private data by tech companies. Many companies depend on official data extensively for weighting, validation, interpolation, extrapolation, and more. Revenues could accrue to the statistical agencies, with tax reductions for data shared with the agencies.

Our final three recommendations cover many of the steps needed to improve input data quality and access.

4) The statistical agencies need more clarity and consistency on privacy and informed consent rules and responsibilities for nonstandard data. Discrepancies and confusion about how to proceed with nonsurvey data collected from third parties, over the internet, or from administrative sources (federal or state) can slow or scuttle promising opportunities. Other laws or rules may be needed to prohibit investors with private access to inputs to official statistics from manipulating or front running releases for their own benefit.

5) Private sector data quality and access needs improvement. We recommend creation of a trusted data center or network/process for the largest firms to provide data for use in federal survey programs—organic data, protected from lawsuits. Furthermore, given the importance of large firms in the US economy, we doubt that the vision outlined above is possible without mandated participation by large firms. In exchange, firms could gain avenues for input into data collection and storage process decisions or even a modest tax reduction. We also recommend that statistical agencies work to encourage development of interoperable records using common schema by industry groups with statistical agency input. Adoption of voluntary standards for data definitions and storage across companies holds great promise for improving the accuracy and coverage of collected data and for significantly reducing respondent burden.

6) Statistical agencies need expanded safe access to government administrative data. Proposals by the Commission on Evidence-Based Policymaking should be enacted to improve federal administrative data and facilitate its use by statistical agencies.[59] This initiative should also be extended in a number of important ways. Statistical agencies need access to each other's data and to IRS records to eliminate inconsistencies across agencies that affect direct and indirect inputs to productivity measurement, including business registers. This philosophy should be extended to grant federal *and* state sta-

tistical agencies access to federally funded, state-owned program data. This would provide BLS with access to state UI wage records to improve measures of labor inputs for productivity statistics. This extension should be the context of needed modernizations to the UI system.

Productivity measurement requires inputs from across the statistical system and could greatly benefit from use of nonstandard data that originates in the private sector or in public entities outside the statistical agencies. Significantly improving productivity statistics calls for statistical agencies to leverage relationships with these entities on both the intensive and extensive margins and to synchronize their activities more fully. Accomplishing this improvement will not be a natural outgrowth of our current federal statistical system but instead will require purposeful and committed efforts within that system along with private sector cooperation and legislative and budgetary support from our elected representatives.

Notes

1. Greenspan (1996).

2. See https://www.nytimes.com/2018/09/08/upshot/economic-parallels-to-the-1990s.html.

3. For information on the labor productivity measures that BLS publishes for the major sectors of the US economy and for major sector multifactor productivity measures, visit https://www.bls.gov/productivity/home.htm. Also see "Technical Information about the BLS Multifactor Productivity Measures" in the *BLS Handbook of Methods*.

4. Examples of papers that analyze productivity over long periods using average productivity growth over subperiods include Stiroh (2001) and Byrne, Oliner, and Sichel (2017).

5. Sectoral output is defined as the gross output of an industry or sector less the amount produced and consumed within that industry or sector. BLS deflators are interpolated using industrial production and intersectoral purchase data from the Census Bureau. See https://www.bls.gov/mfp/outputnote.pdf and https://www.bls.gov/mfp/sectoraloutputrevisions.htm.

6. The BLS excludes nonmarket producers (government and nonprofit sectors) from productivity statistics because the output measures for these sectors are based largely on incomes of input factors. The major two-digit North American Industry Classification System (NAICS) sectors and three-, four-, five-, and six-digit NAICS sectors have varying levels of coverage depending on the sector. For example, at the three-digit subsector level, there are three mining, one utility, 21 manufacturing, three wholesale trade, 12 retail, 11 transportation and warehousing, six information, and two accommodation and food services industries. This structure mirrors the NAICS classification structure.

7. See Eldridge (1999) for more detail on the use of input-based data to extrapolate series of real output. In essence, compared to goods industries, units of output are more idiosyncratic across and within service industries. Thus, adding coverage

of each industry requires an extensive research and development effort into appropriate output measures, deflators, and data collection strategies to generate them.

8. The BLS TFP for Major Industries release started incorporating a new methodology that uses a combination of the Census American Community Survey and BLS Current Population Survey to estimate labor composition in the fall of 2022.

9. For more on KLEMS, see Bureau of Labor Statistics (2007). There is also a set of detailed industry multifactor productivity measures for 86 four-digit NAICS manufacturing industries.

10. Underlying both the numerator and denominator are the different business registers employed by the Census and BLS. See Elvery et al. (2006) and a more recent comparison in figure 8.3.

11. For estimates of the impact of new good and quality biases on productivity measures, see Groshen et al. (2017).

12. For a list of inputs that BEA uses for GDP estimates alone, see Holdren (2014). For a discussion of big data sources and promising opportunities used by the BLS CPI program, see Konny, Williams, and Friedman (2019).

13. See Groshen et al. (2017) for more discussion relevant to this example.

14. Other key classification schemes include the North American Industrial Classification System (for industries), SOC, Standard Metropolitan Areas (for geography), and various demographic classifications (such as race, marital status, and gender). The Office of Management and Budget's Office of Statistical and Science Policy sponsors cross-agency committees that maintain and periodically update classification schemes for use by federal agencies.

15. Another solution would be for statistical agencies and private companies coordinate on particular schema for different types of data. For example, see schema .org, a collaborative community activity that creates, maintains, and promotes schemas for structured data. We note a particular example of schema development in progress in the section on unemployment insurance wage records.

16. One reason for the lack of quarterly benchmarking of the CES to the QCEW is the difference in seasonality. See Robertson (2017).

17. High prices can reflect costs of tailoring the data stream specifically to meet statistical agency requirements (such as curation, sample frame, frequency, or timeliness). They can also reflect high margins sought by the vendor, particularly after an agency becomes dependent on the data source.

18. The Billion Prices Project was an academic initiative at MIT and Harvard that used prices collected from hundreds of online retailers around the world on a daily basis to conduct research in macro and international economics. See http://www.thebillionpricesproject.com/.

19. See https://adpemploymentreport.com/.

20. It is not unusual for data collection instruments to include fields that are not used. This may happen because of a change in laws, regulations, or monitoring strategy or because the field is needed only for a subset of respondents. If fields are not used, agencies are less likely to follow up on missing or incorrect data, so respondents are less likely to rectify issues.

21. The authors are not aware of any example of front running or intentional manipulation by private suppliers of data to statistical agencies. However, expanded use of nonstandard data raises the risks. Employees of statistical agencies are prohibited from such actions by law and by their mission. Were a private company to provide an influential input to a market-moving release such as the Employment Situation, the potential financial gains from manipulating or front running the economic indicators could be very high.

22. In terms of scope, the monthly sample collected approximately 2,000 prices,

but now the administrative data contains information on approximately 250,000 transactions. For more information, see https://www.bls.gov/cpi/factsheets/r-cpi-u-nv.htm and https://www.bls.gov/osmr/research-papers/2019/pdf/ec190040.pdf.

23. See Chen et al. (2019) for a study of the use of nonstandard data to improve the accuracy of initial releases of BEA data.

24. See https://www.federalreserve.gov/releases/g17/About.htm for more information on the Industrial Production and Capacity Utilization release.

25. See https://www.federalreserve.gov/releases/g17/Revisions/20180323/DefaultRev.htm for more detail.

26. The Federal Reserve Board (FRB) designates capacity as the sustainable maximum output and sufficient labor and material inputs. The utilization rate is defined as the ratio of production to capacity for a particular industry.

27. In the Basu, Fernald, and Kimball (2006) methodology, hours per worker is used as a proxy for unobserved input variation, that is, changes in both labor effort and capital utilization. See https://www.frbsf.org/economic-research/indicators-data/total-factor-productivity-tfp/ for more information.

28. The methodology also follows Nalewaik (2011) and combines information on both the income and product sides to better estimate output.

29. See examples in Groshen et al. (2017).

30. Aizcorbe and Nestoriak (2011) and Bradley (2013) discuss this more fully.

31. See Grigsby, Hurst, and Yildirmaz (2021), Cajner et al. (2022), and Kurmann, Lale, and Ta (2020).

32. It is important to note that while information from a payroll provider would entail numerous benefits to the statistical establishment, there would be substantial drawbacks as well. The importance of representativeness and survey design, sample selection, industry affiliation, and, of course, whether businesses sampled are firms or establishments would require substantial investment ensure the usefulness of such data.

33. Employers submit wage records to the state for all covered workers who worked or received pay during the quarter. Covered employees include most corporate officials, all executives, all supervisory personnel, all professionals, all clerical workers, many farmworkers, all wage earners, all piece workers, and all part-time workers. Workers on paid sick leave, holiday, vacation, and the like are also covered. Workers on the payroll of more than one firm receive a record from each employer that is subject to UI. Among the workers excluded are elected officials, proprietors, the unincorporated self-employed, unpaid family members, certain farm, domestic, and railroad workers, and those who earned no wages because of work stoppages, temporary layoffs, illness, or unpaid vacations. For a complete list of exclusions, see https://www.bls.gov/opub/hom/cew/concepts.htm.

34. BLS does have access to UI employer records, which are workplace aggregates that it combines into the QCEW. These are distinct from individual worker wage records.

35. Currently, states provide wage records under mandatory requirements to the Department of Health and Human Services and voluntarily to the Census. By negotiating individually with each state and providing valued aggregated statistics (such as job flows), the Census has gained conditional access to all states' UI wage records for the Longitudinal Employment Household Dynamics (LEHD) program. The state-LEHD agreements have no guarantee of continuity, do not allow sharing among states, do not fund curation, and place a patchwork of restrictions on how data can be used. Various mutual state-sharing agreements allow states to examine issues such as training and job mobility between states and labor sheds or job clusters that spread across state lines.

36. Currently, two states collect occupation job titles: Alaska and Louisiana. Only the state of Washington has hours of work on its wage records. However, other states are in the process of adding more information.

37. States have a keen interest in understanding the skills needs of local employers to assess needs for career and technical education and other training programs. Many states now match wage records to educational administrative data-based courses and training received at community colleges and four-year colleges and universities. For example, see projects conducted by the Administrative Data Research Facility sponsored by the Coleridge Initiative (https://coleridgeinitiative.org/). There are also numerous federal mandates to measure in-demand occupations and industries.

38. The stakeholders include businesses, postsecondary institutions, technical standards organizations, and human resource professionals and their technology vendors. For more information and updates, see https://www.uschamberfoundation.org/JEDx.

39. The seven states are Arkansas, Colorado, Kentucky, Texas, California, Florida, and New Jersey.

40. Triplett and Bosworth's (2004, 2008) work on service-sector productivity provides evidence that much of the productivity gains post-1995 have sourced from the service sector.

41. As revenues, QSS data include final consumption purchases and intrafirm transactions of intermediate inputs.

42. Survey data from financial institutions indicate that total card payments were $6.5 trillion in 2017 (Federal Reserve Board 2018). Third party aggregators provide access to the networks or hardware on which credit card transactions are made, regardless of the credit card company.

43. See Nicholson (2017).

44. See Dolfen et al. (2023).

45. If people are able to pay lower prices online than in brick-and-mortar stores, the shift to e-commerce lowered prices. But official price indexes do not capture the effect of substitution to new outlets on the prices that consumers are paying for an item because these indexes do not compare prices from different outlets. The matched-model procedure these indexes use to link in new outlets and new varieties is discussed in chapter 4.

46. See Aladangady et al. (2019, 2018, 2016), Chen et al. (2019), Scheleur (2016), and Dunn (2016). By contrast, for a comparison of credit card data to point-of-sale data, see Hutchinson (2019).

47. See the technical note: https://www.bea.gov/sites/default/files/2020-05/tech1q20_adv_0.pdf.

48. Similarly, the demographic, geographic, and financial information about account holders in credit card data allows for the reweighting of the card data to be more representative of aggregate national spending.

49. International comparisons are also useful for learning about alternative source data and the possible use of nontraditional data. Importantly, many long-term trends apparent in domestic productivity are evident in other advanced countries, such as the productivity slowdown. See Syverson (2017).

50. For more information, see http://data.nber.org/nberces/.

51. Cunningham et al. (2019) also provide correlations between publicly produced BLS productivity inputs, output, and productivity measures and the NBER-CES database.

52. One organization that provides these services to firms, MachineMetrics, has already started publicly providing real-time utilization measures at the daily fre-

quency. See https://support.machinemetrics.com/hc/en-us/articles/360031436494-Utilization-Report-Reports-.

Relatedly, Siemens push to the Industrial Internet of Things would deploy millions of sensors in factories capturing data on every aspect of the manufacturing process, leading to similar, and possibly more, data on the production process. See Siemens, "Industrial 5G—The Wireless Network of the Future."

53. See Duffy 2014 (https://ottawacitizen.com/news/local-news/the-state-of-statscan-survey).

54. For a description of the problem, see this statement of the American Economic Association's Committee on Economic Statistics: https://www.aeaweb.org/content/file?id=15315.

55. We note, however, that shared access to data is insufficient. For example, the use of IRS data by Census from small businesses as an alternative to direct data collection lowers response burden and collection costs; however, it is not clear how the industry NAICS codes assigned to each unit in IRS data compare to those from the BLS QCEW.

56. See the American Economic Association Committee on Economic Statistics' "Principles and Prerequisites for an Effective Move of the Bureau of Labor Statistics to the Commerce Department," https://www.aeaweb.org/content/file?id=11108.

57. The Federal Information Technology Acquisition Reform Act (FITARA), passed by Congress in December 2014, requires much of the federal government to pursue consolidation of services.

58. See Kasa (1999). The logic is clear because investors rely so heavily on official statistics to inform their trades.

59. See "CEP Final Report: The Promise of Evidence-Based Policymaking" at https://www2.census.gov/adrm/fesac/2017-12-15/Abraham-CEP-final-report.pdf.

References

Aizcorbe, Ana, and Nicole Nestoriak. 2011. "Changing Mix of Medical Care Services: Stylized Facts and Implications for Price Indexes." *Journal of Health Economics* 30 (3): 568–74.

Aladangady, Aditya, Shifrah Aron-Dine, David Cashin, Wendy Dunn, Laura Feiveson, Paul Lengermann, Katherine Richard, and Claudia Sahm. 2018. "High-Frequency Spending Responses to the Earned Income Tax Credit." *FEDS Notes*, June 21. Washington, DC: Board of Governors of the Federal Reserve System.

Aladangady, Aditya, Shifrah Aron-Dine, Wendy Dunn, Laura Feiveson, Paul Lengermann, and Claudia Sahm. 2016. "The Effect of Hurricane Matthew on Consumer Spending." *FEDS Notes*, December 2. Washington, DC: Board of Governors of the Federal Reserve System.

Aladangady, Aditya, Shifrah Aron-Dine, Wendy Dunn, Laura Feiveson, Paul Lengermann, and Claudia Sahm. 2019. "From Transactions Data to Economic Statistics: Constructing Real-Time, High-Frequency, Geographic Measures of Consumer Spending." Finance and Economics Discussion Series 2019–057. Washington, DC: Board of Governors of the Federal Reserve System.

Basu, Susanto, John G. Fernald, and Miles S. Kimball. 2006. "Are Technology Improvements Contractionary?" *American Economic Review* 96 (5): 1418–48.

Bils, Mark. 2009. "Do Higher Prices for New Goods Reflect Quality Growth or Inflation," *Quarterly Journal of Economics* 124 (2): 637–75.
Bradley, Ralph. 2013. "Feasible Methods to Estimate Disease—Based Price Indexes." *Journal of Health Economics* 32 (3): 504–14.
Bureau of Labor Statistics. 2007. "Technical Information about the BLS Multifactor Productivity Measures." September 26. https://www.bls.gov/productivity/technical-notes/multifactor-productivity-method.pdf.
Byrne, David, and Carol Corrado. 2019. "Accounting for Innovations in Consumer Digital Services: IT Still Matters." Finance and Economics Discussion Series 2019–049. Washington, DC: Board of Governors of the Federal Reserve System.
Byrne, David M., John G. Fernald, and Marshall B. Reinsdorf. 2016. "Does the United States Have a Productivity Slowdown or a Measurement Problem?" *Brookings Papers on Economic Activity* 1 (Spring): 109–82.
Byrne, D., Stephen D. Oliner, and Daniel E. Sichel. 2017. "Prices of High-Tech Products, Mismeasurement, and the Pace of Innovation." *Business Economics* 52 (2): 103–13.
Cajner, Tomaz, Leland D. Crane, Ryan A. Decker, John Grigsby, Adrian Hamins-Puertolas, Erik Hurst, Christopher Kurz, and Ahu Yildirmaz. 2020. "The U.S. Labor Market during the Beginning of the Pandemic Recession." Working Paper 27159, May. National Bureau of Economic Research.
Cajner, Tomaz, Leland D. Crane, Ryan A. Decker, Adrian Hamins-Puertolas, and Christopher Kurz. 2022. "Improving the Accuracy of Economic Measurement with Multiple Data Sources: The Case of Payroll Employment Data." In *Big Data for Twenty-First-Century Economic Statistics*, edited by Katharine Abraham, Ron Jarmin, Brian Moyer, and Matthew Shapir, 79:147–70. Studies in Income and Wealth. Chicago: University of Chicago Press.
Chen, Jeffery C., Abe Dunn, Kyle Hood, Alexander Driessen, and Andrea Batch. 2019. "Off to the Races: A Comparison of Machine Learning and Alternative Data for Predicting Economic Indicators." In *Big Data for 21st Century Economic Statistics*, NBER chapters. Chicago: University of Chicago Press.
Cunningham, Cindy, Lucia Foster, Cheryl Grim, John Haltiwanger, Sabrina Wulff Pabilonia, Jay Stewart, and Zoltan Wolf. 2023. "Dispersion in Dispersion: Measuring Establishment-Level Differences in Productivity." *Review of Income and Wealth* 69 (4): 999–1032.
Dolfen, Paul, Liran Einav, Peter J. Klenow, Benjamin Klopack, Jonathan D. Levin, Larry Levin, and Wayne Best. 2023. "Assessing the Gains from E-Commerce." *American Economic Journal: Macroeconomics* 15 (1): 342–70. DOI: 10.1257/mac.20210049.
Duffy, Andrew. 2014. "The State of StatsCan Survey." *Ottawa Citizen*, August 30. https://ottawacitizen.com/news/local-news/the-state-of-statscan-survey.
Dunn, Abe. 2016. "Improving Regional PCE Estimates Using Credit Card Transaction Data." FESAC presentation, Federal Economic Statistics Advisory Committee, June 10. https://www.census.gov/about/adrm/fesac/meetings/2016-06-10-meeting.html.
Eldridge, Lucy P. 1999. "How Price Indexes Affect BLS Productivity Measures." *Monthly Labor Review* 122:35–46.
Elvery, Joel, Lucia Foster, C. J. Krizan, and David Talan. 2006. "Preliminary Micro Data Results from the Business List Comparison Project." Proceedings of the 2006 American Statistical Association Annual Meeting, Alexandria, VA, American Statistical Association.
Federal Reserve Board. 2018. "The Federal Reserve Payments Study: 2018 Annual Sup-

plement." Board of Governors of the Federal Reserve System. https://www.federalreserve.gov/paymentsystems/2018-december-the-federal-reserve-payments-study.htm.

Fernald, John G. 2014. "A Quarterly, Utilization-Adjusted Series on Total Factor Productivity." FRBSF Working Paper 2012–19.

Greenspan, Alan. 1996. "Technological Advances and Productivity." Remarks at the eightieth anniversary awards dinner for the Conference Board, New York, October 16.

Grigsby, John, Erik Hurst, and Ahu Yildirmaz. 2021. "Aggregate Nominal Wage Adjustments: New Evidence from Administrative Payroll Data." *American Economic Review* 111 (2): 428–71.

Groshen, Erica L., Brian C. Moyer, Ana M. Aizcorbe, Ralph Bradley, and David M. Friedman. 2017. "How Government Statistics Adjust for Potential Biases from Quality Change and New Goods in an Age of Digital Technologies: A View from the Trenches." *Journal of Economic Perspectives* 31, no. 2 (spring): 187–210.

Hausman, Jerry, and Ephraim Leibtag, eds. 2010. "CPI Bias from Supercenters: Does the BLS Know That Wal-Mart Exists?" In *Price Index Concepts and Measurement*, edited by W. Diewert, John Greenlees, and Charles R. Hulten. Online edition February 21, 2013. Chicago: Chicago Scholarship Online.

Holdren, Alyssa E. 2014. "Gross Domestic Product and Gross Domestic Income: Revisions and Source Data." *Survey of Current Business* 94 (6): 1–11. https://apps.bea.gov/scb/pdf/2014/06%20June/0614_gross_domestic_product_and_gross_domestic_income.pdf.

Houseman, Susan, Christopher Kurz, Paul Lengermann, and Benjamin Mandel. 2011. "Offshoring Bias in U.S. Manufacturing." *Journal of Economic Perspectives* 25 (2): 111–32.

Hutchinson, Rebecca J. 2019. "Improving Retail Trade Data Products Using Alternative Data Sources." In *Big Data for 21st Century Economic Statistics*, NBER chapters. Chicago: University of Chicago Press.

Kasa, Kenneth. 1999. "Time for a Tobin Tax?" RBSF Economic Letter, Federal Reserve Bank of San Francisco, 1999–12. April 9. https://www.frbsf.org/economic-research/publications/economic-letter/1999/april/time-for-a-tobin-tax/.

Konny, Crystal G., Brendan K. Williams, and David M. Friedman. 2019. "Big Data in the U.S. Consumer Price Index: Experiences & Plans." In *Big Data for 21st Century Economic Statistics*, NBER chapters. Chicago: University of Chicago Press.

Kurmann, Andre, Etienne Lale, and Lien Ta. 2020. "The Impact of COVID-19 on U.S. Employment and Hours: Real-Time Estimates with Homebase Data." Mimeo.

Moulton, Brent R. 2018. *The Measurement of Output, Prices, and Productivity: What's Changed Since the Boskin Commission?* Brookings Institution, Hutchins Center on Fiscal and Monetary Policy. https://www.brookings.edu/wp-content/uploads/2018/07/Moulton-report-v2.pdf.

Nalewaik, Jeremy J. 2011. "The Income- and Expenditure-Side Estimates of U.S. Output Growth: An Update through 2011 Q2." *Brookings Papers on Economic Activity* 2:385–402.

Nicholson, Jessica R. 2017. "New Insights on Retail E-Commerce." ESA Issue Brief #04–17, July 26. https://www.commerce.gov/sites/default/files/migrated/reports/new-insights-retail-e-commerce.pdf.

Robertson, Kenneth W. 2017. "Benchmarking the Current Employment Statistics Survey: Perspectives on Current Research." *Monthly Labor Review* (November). US Bureau of Labor Statistics. https://doi.org/10.21916/mlr.2017.27.

Scheleur, Scott. 2016. "Economic Directorate's Retail Big Data Overview." FESAC presentation, Federal Economic Statistics Advisory Committee, June 10. https://www.census.gov/about/adrm/fesac/meetings/2016-06-10-meeting.html.

Stiroh, Kevin J. 2001. "What Drives Productivity Growth?" *Economic Policy Review* 7, no. 1 (March). Federal Reserve Bank of New York.

Syverson, Chad. 2017. "Challenges to Mismeasurement Explanations for the US Productivity Slowdown." *Journal of Economic Perspectives* 31, no. 2 (Spring): 165–86.

Triplett, Jack E., and Barry P. Bosworth. 2004. *Services Productivity in the United States: New Sources of Economic Growth.* Washington, DC: Brookings Institution Press.

Triplett, Jack E., and Barry P. Bosworth. 2008. "The State of Data for Services Productivity Measurement in the United States." *International Productivity Monitor* 16 (Spring): 53–71.

Index

The letter *f* or *t* following a page number denotes a figure or table respectively.